FODOR'S

NEW EDITION

BED & BREAKFASTS AND COUNTRY INNS

MID-ATLANTIC REGION

DELIGHTFUL
PLACES TO
STAY AND GREAT
THINGS TO DO
WHEN YOU
GET THERE

ISBN 0–679–02562–6

Fodor's Bed & Breakfasts and Country Inns:
Mid-Atlantic Region

Editor: Craig Seligman
Art Director: Fabrizio La Rocca
Cartographer: David Lindroth
Illustrators: Alida Beck
Cover Photograph: Geoffrey Clifford/Woodfin Camp
Design: Fabrizio La Rocca and Tigist Getachew

Special Sales

Fodor's Travel Publications are available at special discounts for bulk purchases for sales promotions or premiums. Special editions, including personalized covers, excerpts of existing guides, and corporate imprints, can be created in large quantities for special needs. For more information, contact your local bookseller or write to Special Markets, Fodor's Travel Publications, 201 East 50th Street, New York, NY 10022. Inquiries from Canada should be directed to your local Canadian bookseller or sent to Random House of Canada, Ltd., Marketing Department, 1265 Aerowood Drive, Mississauga, Ontario L4W 1B9. Inquiries from the United Kingdom should be sent to Fodor's Travel Publications, 20 Vauxhall Bridge Road, London, England SW1V 2SA.

MANUFACTURED IN THE UNITED STATES OF AMERICA
10 9 8 7 6 5 4 3 2 1

Contributors

Mary Ann Hemphill, *a travel writer who lives in Williamsburg, revised the Virginia chapter. She has published in* Food and Wine *and* The Los Angeles Times *and contributes to* Fodor's Alaska *and* Fodor's Cruises and Ports of Call.

Alan Hines, *who wrote the chapter on Pennsylvania, is a novelist and screenwriter living in Bucks County, Pennsylvania.*

Bill Kent, *a novelist in Philadelphia, wrote the chapter on New Jersey. He is also the author of* Fodor's Vacations on the Jersey Shore.

Dale Leatherman *lives in Falling Water, West Virginia, and revised the West Virginia chapter. She is a freelance writer and a senior editor at* Spur, *the magazine of Thoroughbred and country life.*

Rathe Miller, *who updated the chapters on New York and New Jersey, is also a contributor to* Fodor's Philadelphia. *He lives in Philadelphia and writes frequently for the* Philadelphia Inquirer.

Carolyn Price, *a former editor at* Fodor's, *now lives and writes in southeastern Pennsylvania. She revised the Pennsylvania, Delaware, and Maryland chapters.*

Deborah K. Shepherd, *author of the New York chapter, is a social worker and freelance journalist.*

Susan Spano, *who lives in New York City's West Village, contributed the original chapters on Delaware, Maryland, Virginia, and West Virginia. She has written about travel for the* New York Times, New Woman, *and* British Heritage.

Contents

Foreword

While every care has been taken to ensure the accuracy of the information in this guide, the passage of time will always bring change, and, consequently, the publisher cannot accept responsibility for errors that may occur.

All prices and listings are based on information supplied to us at press time. Details may change, however, and the prudent traveler will avoid inconvenience by calling ahead.

Fodor's wants to hear about your travel experiences, both pleasant and unpleasant. When an inn or B&B fails to live up to its billing, let us know and we will investigate the complaint and revise our entries where the facts warrant it.

Send your letters to the editors of Fodor's Travel Publications, 201 E. 50th Street, New York, NY 10022.

Introduction

Fodor's Bed & Breakfasts, Country Inns, and Other Weekend Pleasures *is a complete weekend planner that tells you not just where to stay but how to enjoy yourself when you get there. We describe the B&Bs and country inns, of course, but we also help you organize trips around them, with information on everything from parks to beaches to antiques stores—as well as nightlife and memorable places to dine. We also include names and addresses of B&B reservation services, should properties we recommend be full or should you be inspired to go in search of additional places on your own. Reviews are divided by state and, within each state, by region.*

All inns are not created equal, and age in itself is no guarantee of good taste, quality, or charm. We therefore avoid the directory approach, preferring instead to discriminate—recommending the very best for travelers with different interests, budgets, and sensibilities.

It's a sad commentary on other B&B guides today that we feel obliged to tell you our reviewers visited every property in person, and that it is they, not the innkeepers, who wrote the reviews. No one paid a fee or promised to sell or promote the book in order to be included in it. Fodor's has no stake in anything but the truth: A dark room with peeling wallpaper is not called quaint or atmospheric, it's called run-down; a gutted 18th-century barn with motel units at either end is called a gutted 18th-century barn with motel units at either end, not a historic inn.

Is there a difference between a B&B and a country inn? Not really, not any more; the public has blurred the distinction—hence our decision to include both in the title. There was a time when the B&B experience meant an extra room in someone's home, often with paper-thin walls and a shared bathroom full of bobby pins and used cotton balls. But no longer; Laura Ashley has come to town with her matching prints, and some B&Bs are as elegant as the country's most venerable inns. The only distinction that seems to hold is that a B&B was built as a private home and an inn was built for paying guests. Most B&Bs, but not all, serve breakfast, and some serve dinner, too; most inns have full-service restaurants. B&Bs tend to be run by their owners, creating a homey, family feeling (which can be anathema to those who relish privacy), while inns are often run by managers; but the reverse is true, too. B&Bs can cost more than inns, or less. B&Bs tend to be smaller, with fewer rooms, but not always. The truth is that many B&Bs are called so only to circumvent local zoning laws.

What all places in this guide—B&Bs or country inns—offer is the promise of a unique experience. Each is one of a kind, and each exudes a sense of time and place. All are destinations in themselves—not just places to put your head at night, but an integral part of a weekend escape.

So trust us, the way you'd trust a knowledgeable, well-traveled friend. And have a wonderful weekend!

***

A word about the service material in this guide:

A second address in parentheses is a mailing address that differs from the actual address of the property. A double room is for two people, regardless of the size or type of beds; if you're looking for twin beds or a king- or queen-size bed, be sure to ask.

Rates are for two in the high season, and include breakfast; ask about special packages and off-season discounts. Mandatory state taxes are extra. Most places leave tipping to the discretion of the visitor, but some add a service charge to the bill; if the issue concerns you, inquire when you make your reservation, not when you check out.

What we call a restaurant serves meals other than breakfast and is usually open to the general public. Inns listed as MAP (Modified American Plan) require guests to pay for two meals, usually breakfast and dinner. The requirement is usually enforced during the high season, but an inn may waive it if it is otherwise unable to fill all its rooms.

Regarding bathrooms: Travelers accustomed to staying in motels may blanch at the notion of anything other than a private bath, but if you reject a lodging solely for this reason, you'll be missing out on some stunning homes— farmhouses and mansions alike—that furnish generous facilities but simply can't promise a private bathroom for each individual. If it matters to you, however, be sure to ask before you make your reservation.

Some inns don't welcome children below a certain age, so if you're traveling with kids, you should check when making your reservation.

B&Bs don't have phones or TVs in rooms unless otherwise noted. Pools and bicycles are free; "bike rentals" are not. Properties are open year-round, unless otherwise noted.

Michael Spring
Editorial Director

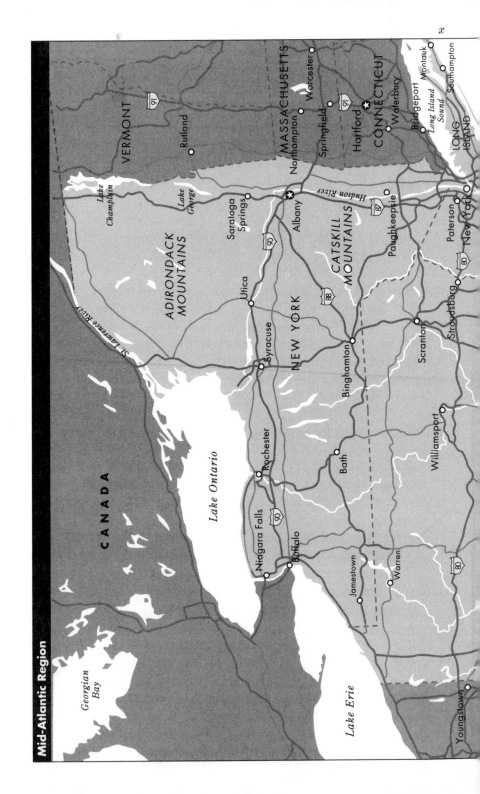

Mid-Atlantic Region

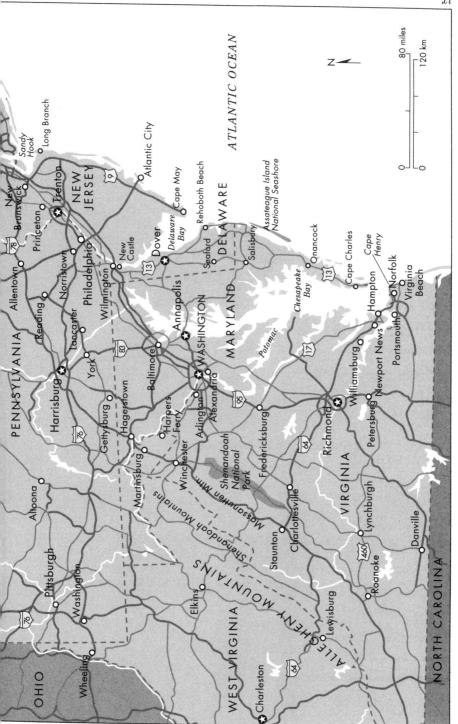

Special Features at a Glance

Name of Property	Accessible for Disabled	Antiques	On the Water	Good Value	Car Not Necessary	Full Meal Service	Historic Building	
DELAWARE								
The Addy Sea			✓				✓	
The Boulevard Bed & Breakfast				✓	✓			
Cantwell House		✓		✓			✓	
Guest Quarters Suite Hotel Wilmington	✓				✓	✓		
The Inn at Canal Square	✓		✓					
The Janvier-Black House			✓				✓	
The New Devon Inn	✓	✓						
The Pleasant Inn								
Spring Garden Bed & Breakfast Inn		✓		✓			✓	
The Towers		✓					✓	
William Penn Guest House		✓		✓			✓	
MARYLAND								
The Admiral Fell Inn	✓		✓		✓	✓	✓	
Ashby 1663		✓	✓				✓	
The Atlantic Hotel		✓				✓	✓	
Back Creek Inn	✓		✓					
Brampton		✓					✓	
Chanceford Hall	✓	✓					✓	
Gibson's Lodgings	✓	✓					✓	
Glasgow Inn		✓	✓				✓	
Gross' Coate 1658		✓	✓				✓	
The Inn at Antietam		✓						
The Inn at Buckeystown		✓					✓	

Romantic Hideaway	Luxurious	Pets Allowed	No Smoking Indoors	Good Place for Families	Near Arts Festivals	Beach Nearby	Cross-Country Ski Trail	Golf Within 5 Miles	Fitness Facilities	Good Biking Terrain	Skiing	Horseback Riding	Tennis	Swimming on Premises	Conference Facilities
				✓		✓									
			✓	✓						✓					
	✓								✓						✓
✓	✓					✓									✓
✓	✓		✓												
✓	✓					✓									✓
						✓				✓					
✓			✓							✓					
✓			✓											✓	
										✓					
✓	✓														✓
✓	✓		✓						✓	✓			✓	✓	
✓							✓	✓		✓					
✓				✓											
✓	✓							✓		✓					
✓	✓									✓				✓	
										✓					✓
✓			✓			✓		✓		✓			✓		
✓	✓	✓	✓							✓				✓	
✓	✓		✓				✓			✓					
✓										✓					

Name of Property	Accessible for Disabled	Antiques	On the Water	Good Value	Car Not Necessary	Full Meal Service	Historic Building	
The Inn at Mitchell House		✓					✓	
The Inn at Perry Cabin	✓	✓	✓			✓	✓	
John S. McDaniel House				✓			✓	
The National Pike		✓					✓	
The Robert Morris Inn		✓	✓			✓	✓	
St. Michael's Manor		✓	✓	✓			✓	
Shaw's Fancy		✓						
Spring Bank		✓					✓	
State House Inn						✓	✓	
The Strawberry Inn	✓	✓					✓	
The Tavern House		✓	✓	✓			✓	
The Turning Point		✓				✓		
Vandiver Inn		✓					✓	
Wades Point Inn	✓			✓			✓	
The White Swan Tavern		✓					✓	
Widow's Walk Inn		✓					✓	
The William Page Inn	✓	✓						
NEW JERSEY								
The Abbey		✓			✓		✓	
Ashling Cottage		✓			✓		✓	
BarnaGate Bed and Breakfast		✓		✓	✓		✓	
Barnard Good House		✓			✓		✓	
Bayberry Barque		✓					✓	
Cabbage Rose Inn		✓		✓			✓	

Romantic Hideaway	Luxurious	Pets Allowed	No Smoking Indoors	Good Place for Families	Near Arts Festivals	Beach Nearby	Cross-Country Ski Trail	Golf Within 5 Miles	Fitness Facilities	Good Biking Terrain	Skiing	Horseback Riding	Tennis	Swimming on Premises	Conference Facilities
✓				✓						✓					
✓	✓								✓	✓			✓	✓	✓
✓			✓					✓		✓					
										✓			✓		
✓	✓		✓			✓				✓			✓		
✓			✓			✓				✓					
✓		✓													
			✓							✓					
✓	✓														✓
										✓			✓		
✓										✓					
✓										✓					
✓														✓	
✓			✓					✓		✓					
✓	✓							✓		✓					
			✓							✓					
	✓														
✓	✓		✓		✓	✓		✓		✓					
✓			✓		✓	✓		✓		✓					
			✓		✓	✓		✓		✓			✓		
✓	✓		✓		✓	✓		✓		✓					
✓			✓		✓	✓				✓					
✓			✓		✓		✓	✓							

Name of Property	Accessible for Disabled	Antiques	On the Water	Good Value	Car Not Necessary	Full Meal Service	Historic Building	
Candlelight Inn		✓					✓	
Captain Mey's Inn		✓			✓		✓	
The Carriage House				✓	✓			
The Carroll Villa					✓	✓	✓	
Cashelmara Inn		✓	✓		✓		✓	
The Chalfonte		✓		✓	✓	✓	✓	
Charlesworth Hotel			✓					
The Chateau	✓				✓			
Chestnut Hill		✓			✓		✓	
Chimney Hill Farm		✓					✓	
Colligan's Stockton Inn		✓				✓	✓	
Colvmns by the Sea		✓	✓		✓		✓	
Conover's Bay Head Inn		✓			✓			
Henry Ludlam Inn		✓	✓				✓	
Hollycroft		✓					✓	
Holly House				✓			✓	
Inn at Millrace Pond		✓				✓	✓	
Jeremiah H. Yereance House		✓			✓		✓	
Jerica Hill		✓					✓	
The Mainstay Inn and Cottage		✓			✓		✓	
The Manor House		✓			✓		✓	
Normandy Inn		✓					✓	
Old Hunterdon House		✓			✓		✓	
Peacock Inn		✓				✓	✓	
Pierrot by the Sea		✓					✓	

Romantic Hideaway	Luxurious	Pets Allowed	No Smoking Indoors	Good Place for Families	Near Arts Festivals	Beach Nearby	Cross-Country Ski Trail	Golf Within 5 Miles	Fitness Facilities	Good Biking Terrain	Skiing	Horseback Riding	Tennis	Swimming on Premises	Conference Facilities
✓			✓		✓	✓		✓		✓					
✓	✓		✓		✓	✓		✓		✓					
			✓	✓	✓	✓		✓		✓					
			✓		✓	✓		✓		✓					
✓			✓	✓	✓	✓		✓		✓					
			✓	✓	✓	✓		✓		✓					✓
			✓												
					✓	✓	✓	✓		✓			✓		
✓			✓		✓		✓	✓							
✓	✓		✓		✓		✓	✓							
		✓			✓		✓	✓							✓
✓	✓		✓		✓	✓		✓		✓					
			✓		✓	✓		✓		✓					
			✓		✓			✓		✓				✓	
✓					✓	✓		✓		✓					
			✓		✓			✓		✓					
✓	✓			✓	✓		✓	✓		✓			✓		✓
			✓		✓			✓		✓					
✓			✓		✓		✓	✓		✓					
✓	✓		✓		✓	✓		✓		✓					
			✓		✓	✓		✓		✓					
					✓	✓		✓		✓					✓
✓	✓		✓	✓	✓		✓	✓		✓					
		✓			✓			✓		✓					✓
			✓		✓	✓		✓		✓					

Name of Property	Accessible for Disabled	Antiques	On the Water	Good Value	Car Not Necessary	Full Meal Service	Historic Building	
The Queen Victoria	✓	✓			✓		✓	
Sea Crest by the Sea		✓					✓	
The Seaflower		✓			✓		✓	
Springside				✓	✓		✓	
Stewart Inn		✓		✓			✓	
The Studio		✓					✓	
Victoria Guest House		✓					✓	
The Victorian Rose		✓			✓		✓	
The Virginia Hotel					✓	✓	✓	
The Whistling Swan Inn		✓					✓	
Wilbraham Mansion and Inn		✓			✓		✓	
The Wooden Rabbit		✓			✓		✓	
NEW YORK								
The Adelphi Hotel		✓					✓	
Albergo Allegria				✓				
Anthony Dobbins Stagecoach Inn		✓		✓			✓	
The Balsam House			✓			✓		
Bassett House Inn		✓						
Beaverkill Valley Inn	✓		✓			✓		
The Bent Finial Manor		✓		✓			✓	
The Bird and Bottle Inn						✓	✓	
Captain Schoonmaker's Bed-and-Breakfast		✓	✓	✓			✓	
The Chester Inn		✓		✓			✓	
Chestnut Tree Inn		✓						

Romantic Hideaway	Luxurious	Pets Allowed	No Smoking Indoors	Good Place for Families	Near Arts Festivals	Beach Nearby	Cross-Country Ski Trail	Golf Within 5 Miles	Fitness Facilities	Good Biking Terrain	Skiing	Horseback Riding	Tennis	Swimming on Premises	Conference Facilities
	✓		✓		✓	✓		✓		✓					✓
✓			✓		✓	✓		✓		✓					
			✓		✓	✓		✓		✓					
			✓		✓	✓		✓		✓					
			✓		✓		✓	✓		✓				✓	
✓				✓	✓			✓		✓					
			✓		✓	✓				✓				✓	
✓			✓		✓	✓		✓		✓					
	✓				✓	✓		✓		✓					✓
			✓		✓		✓	✓		✓					
			✓		✓	✓		✓		✓				✓	
			✓	✓	✓	✓		✓		✓					
✓	✓				✓									✓	
				✓	✓		✓	✓			✓			✓	
✓	✓							✓					✓		
✓					✓	✓	✓			✓	✓			✓	
		✓			✓	✓				✓					
✓	✓			✓		✓	✓	✓	✓	✓			✓	✓	✓
✓	✓	✓													
✓	✓														
✓							✓			✓				✓	
			✓				✓				✓				
✓	✓		✓		✓			✓							

Name of Property	Accessible for Disabled	Antiques	On the Water	Good Value	Car Not Necessary	Full Meal Service	Historic Building
Country Road Lodge		✓	✓	✓			
Crislip's Bed and Breakfast	✓	✓		✓			✓
Deer Mountain Inn						✓	
Donegal Manor Bed and Breakfast		✓		✓			✓
The Eggery				✓			
The Friends Lake Inn			✓	✓		✓	
Greenville Arms		✓		✓		✓	✓
The Gregory House				✓		✓	
Hedges' Inn					✓	✓	
The Hill Guest House				✓			
Hilltop Cottage Bed and Breakfast				✓			
Hudson House, A Country Inn			✓		✓	✓	✓
The Huntting Inn		✓			✓	✓	✓
Inn at Lake Joseph			✓			✓	✓
The Inn at Saratoga	✓	✓				✓	
The Inn at Shaker Mill				✓		✓	✓
The Inn on Bacon Hill				✓			
The Lamplight Inn							
Lanza's				✓		✓	
Le Chambord		✓				✓	✓
The Maidstone Arms					✓	✓	✓
The Mansion		✓					✓
Mansion Hill Inn						✓	✓
Maple Ridge Inn		✓					✓
The Martindale Bed and Breakfast Inn		✓		✓			

Romantic Hideaway	Luxurious	Pets Allowed	No Smoking Indoors	Good Place for Families	Near Arts Festivals	Beach Nearby	Cross-Country Ski Trail	Golf Within 5 Miles	Fitness Facilities	Good Biking Terrain	Skiing	Horseback Riding	Tennis	Swimming on Premises	Conference Facilities
							✓				✓				
		✓	✓	✓											
✓	✓					✓									
				✓											
				✓	✓		✓				✓	✓			
✓				✓		✓	✓			✓	✓			✓	✓
				✓	✓		✓	✓		✓	✓			✓	✓
				✓										✓	
✓						✓		✓		✓					
						✓		✓		✓					
			✓			✓									
				✓											
	✓					✓		✓		✓			✓		✓
				✓		✓	✓			✓				✓	✓
				✓	✓			✓	✓						✓
✓		✓		✓	✓		✓			✓	✓			✓	✓
			✓		✓		✓			✓					
✓	✓					✓	✓			✓	✓	✓			
							✓			✓					
✓	✓							✓							✓
✓					✓	✓		✓		✓					
✓	✓					✓				✓				✓	
		✓													
✓	✓	✓	✓				✓			✓					
✓			✓								✓	✓			

Name of Property	Accessible for Disabled	Antiques	On the Water	Good Value	Car Not Necessary	Full Meal Service	Historic Building	
The Merrill Magee House	✓	✓		✓		✓	✓	
Mill House Inn (East Hampton)		✓			✓		✓	
Mill House Inn (Stephentown)				✓				
The Old Post House Inn		✓			✓	✓	✓	
Pig Hill Inn		✓			✓			
Plumbush Inn		✓				✓	✓	
Point Lookout Mountain Inn				✓		✓		
Ram's Head Inn			✓			✓		
The Redcoat's Return				✓		✓		
Sanford's Ridge Bed & Breakfast		✓		✓			✓	
Saratoga Bed and Breakfast		✓						
Saratoga Rose				✓		✓	✓	
Scribner Hollow Motor Lodge						✓		
The Sedgwick Inn		✓		✓		✓	✓	
The 1770 House		✓			✓	✓	✓	
Simmons Way Village Inn		✓				✓	✓	
The Six Sisters		✓						
The Swiss Hutte						✓		
Troutbeck		✓				✓	✓	
The Village Latch Inn		✓					✓	
The Village Victorian Inn		✓						
The Westchester House		✓					✓	
PENNSYLVANIA								
Adamstown Inn		✓		✓				

	Romantic Hideaway	Luxurious	Pets Allowed	No Smoking Indoors	Good Place for Families	Near Arts Festivals	Beach Nearby	Cross-Country Ski Trail	Golf Within 5 Miles	Fitness Facilities	Good Biking Terrain	Skiing	Horseback Riding	Tennis	Swimming on Premises	Conference Facilities
					✓										✓	✓
						✓	✓		✓		✓					
				✓	✓			✓			✓	✓			✓	
							✓		✓		✓					
	✓	✓	✓								✓					
	✓	✓									✓					
			✓		✓	✓		✓			✓	✓				✓
	✓	✓	✓		✓		✓				✓			✓	✓	✓
	✓				✓	✓		✓			✓	✓				
			✓						✓						✓	
					✓	✓			✓		✓					
	✓							✓			✓					
					✓			✓	✓		✓	✓		✓	✓	✓
	✓		✓		✓			✓			✓	✓				✓
	✓	✓				✓	✓	✓			✓					
	✓	✓						✓			✓					✓
				✓		✓		✓	✓		✓					
			✓		✓	✓		✓	✓		✓		✓	✓	✓	✓
	✓	✓						✓	✓		✓			✓	✓	✓
	✓	✓	✓		✓		✓		✓		✓			✓	✓	✓
	✓	✓		✓							✓					
	✓	✓		✓		✓		✓	✓		✓					
						✓						✓				

Name of Property	Accessible for Disabled	Antiques	On the Water	Good Value	Car Not Necessary	Full Meal Service	Historic Building	
Ash Mill Farm		✓		✓			✓	
The Bankhouse Bed and Breakfast				✓			✓	
Barley Sheaf Farm		✓					✓	
The Beach Lake Hotel		✓		✓		✓	✓	
The Bechtel Mansion Inn		✓		✓			✓	
Bed and Breakfast at Walnut Hill		✓		✓			✓	
Beechmont Inn		✓		✓				
The Brafferton Inn		✓		✓			✓	
Bridgeton House		✓	✓				✓	
Brookview Manor				✓			✓	
Bucksville House	✓	✓		✓			✓	
The Cameron Estate Inn	✓	✓				✓	✓	
Century Inn		✓		✓		✓	✓	
Churchtown Inn		✓		✓		✓	✓	
Clearview Farm Bed and Breakfast		✓		✓			✓	
Cliff Park Inn		✓				✓	✓	
Doneckers	✓	✓		✓		✓	✓	
The Doubleday Inn		✓		✓				
Duling-Kurtz House & Country Inn				✓		✓	✓	
Emig Mansion		✓					✓	
Evermay-on-the-Delaware		✓	✓	✓		✓	✓	
Fairfield Inn		✓				✓	✓	
Fairville Inn		✓		✓			✓	
The French Manor						✓		
General Sutter Inn		✓		✓		✓	✓	

Romantic Hideaway	Luxurious	Pets Allowed	No Smoking Indoors	Good Place for Families	Near Arts Festivals	Beach Nearby	Cross-Country Ski Trail	Golf Within 5 Miles	Fitness Facilities	Good Biking Terrain	Skiing	Horseback Riding	Tennis	Swimming on Premises	Conference Facilities
✓			✓	✓	✓										
			✓	✓	✓										
✓	✓				✓									✓	✓
✓															
✓	✓		✓												
✓					✓			✓		✓					
✓				✓	✓					✓					
✓				✓	✓		✓	✓		✓					
✓	✓		✓		✓					✓					
			✓							✓					
✓			✓	✓	✓					✓		✓			
✓	✓						✓	✓		✓	✓	✓	✓		✓
✓	✓		✓										✓		
✓	✓			✓	✓		✓			✓					
✓			✓	✓	✓		✓	✓		✓					
				✓			✓	✓		✓	✓				✓
				✓	✓					✓					
✓	✓		✓	✓	✓		✓			✓					
	✓			✓	✓			✓		✓					✓
✓	✓		✓												✓
✓	✓				✓					✓					
✓				✓	✓		✓			✓	✓				
✓	✓			✓	✓					✓					
✓	✓									✓					
		✓		✓	✓										✓

Name of Property	Accessible for Disabled	Antiques	On the Water	Good Value	Car Not Necessary	Full Meal Service	Historic Building	
Glasbern						✓		
Hamanassett		✓					✓	
Highland Farms		✓		✓			✓	
Highpoint Victoriana		✓		✓				
The Historic Farnsworth House Inn		✓		✓		✓	✓	
The Inn at Fordhook Farm		✓					✓	
The Inn at Meadowbrook		✓		✓		✓	✓	
Inn at Phillips Mill		✓	✓	✓		✓	✓	
The Inn at Starlight Lake			✓	✓		✓	✓	
Isaac Stover House		✓	✓				✓	
The King's Cottage		✓						
Limestone Inn		✓		✓			✓	
The Logan Inn			✓	✓	✓	✓	✓	
Longswamp Bed and Breakfast		✓		✓			✓	
Meadow Spring Farm		✓		✓				
The Mercersburg Inn		✓				✓	✓	
The Old Appleford Inn		✓		✓			✓	
The Overlook Inn						✓	✓	
Pace One						✓	✓	
Patchwork Inn		✓		✓				
Pinetree Farm		✓					✓	
The Priory	✓						✓	
Scarlett House		✓					✓	
The Settlers Inn						✓	✓	
Smithton Country Inn		✓		✓			✓	

Romantic Hideaway	Luxurious	Pets Allowed	No Smoking Indoors	Good Place for Families	Near Arts Festivals	Beach Nearby	Cross-Country Ski Trail	Golf Within 5 Miles	Fitness Facilities	Good Biking Terrain	Skiing	Horseback Riding	Tennis	Swimming on Premises	Conference Facilities
✓	✓			✓			✓			✓				✓	✓
✓				✓	✓			✓		✓			✓	✓	
✓				✓			✓			✓					
✓				✓	✓										
✓	✓		✓		✓			✓		✓					✓
✓				✓	✓		✓			✓	✓	✓	✓	✓	
✓	✓			✓			✓			✓					
✓				✓		✓	✓			✓	✓		✓	✓	✓
✓	✓			✓			✓			✓					
			✓		✓										
✓				✓	✓					✓					
				✓	✓										✓
✓	✓			✓			✓			✓					
				✓						✓				✓	
✓	✓		✓	✓	✓		✓	✓		✓	✓				✓
✓			✓	✓	✓			✓		✓					
✓				✓	✓		✓	✓		✓	✓			✓	✓
		✓					✓			✓	✓	✓	✓	✓	✓
			✓	✓	✓					✓					
✓	✓		✓				✓	✓		✓			✓	✓	
				✓											✓
✓			✓					✓							
		✓		✓		✓	✓	✓		✓	✓				✓
✓	✓	✓	✓		✓										

Name of Property	Accessible for Disabled	Antiques	On the Water	Good Value	Car Not Necessary	Full Meal Service	Historic Building	
The Sterling Inn		✓				✓	✓	
Sweetwater Farm		✓				✓	✓	
Swiss Woods	✓			✓				
The Tannery Bed and Breakfast				✓	✓			
The Wedgwood Inn	✓	✓						
The Whitehall Inn	✓	✓		✓			✓	
VIRGINIA								
Applewood		✓		✓				
The Ashby Inn and Restaurant		✓					✓	
Ashton Country House		✓		✓				
The Bailiwick Inn	✓	✓				✓	✓	
Belle Grae Inn	✓	✓				✓	✓	
Bleu Rock Inn						✓		
Brookside		✓					✓	
The Burton House and Hart's Harbor House				✓				
Caledonia Farm	✓	✓					✓	
The Channel Bass Inn		✓						
Chester		✓					✓	
Clifton	✓	✓	✓			✓	✓	
Colonial Capital		✓						
Colonial Manor Inn				✓				
The Conyers House		✓					✓	
Edgewood		✓					✓	
Fassifern		✓					✓	

Romantic Hideaway	Luxurious	Pets Allowed	No Smoking Indoors	Good Place for Families	Near Arts Festivals	Beach Nearby	Cross-Country Ski Trail	Golf Within 5 Miles	Fitness Facilities	Good Biking Terrain	Skiing	Horseback Riding	Tennis	Swimming on Premises	Conference Facilities
✓	✓			✓			✓	✓		✓	✓			✓	
✓	✓	✓			✓		✓	✓		✓				✓	✓
			✓	✓		✓	✓			✓	✓				
			✓	✓	✓										
✓	✓		✓		✓										
✓	✓		✓		✓		✓			✓					
			✓	✓	✓			✓		✓					
✓	✓				✓					✓		✓			✓
			✓					✓		✓					
✓	✓		✓		✓			✓		✓					✓
					✓			✓							✓
✓			✓							✓					✓
✓			✓		✓					✓					
			✓							✓					
			✓				✓			✓	✓				✓
✓						✓				✓					
		✓			✓					✓					
✓	✓		✓		✓			✓		✓			✓	✓	✓
			✓	✓				✓		✓					
			✓							✓					
✓		✓	✓		✓					✓		✓			✓
✓										✓				✓	✓
			✓							✓					

Name of Property	Accessible for Disabled	Antiques	On the Water	Good Value	Car Not Necessary	Full Meal Service	Historic Building	
Fort Lewis Lodge			✓			✓		
Fountain Hall	✓	✓		✓				
The Garden and the Sea Inn		✓					✓	
High Meadows and Mountain Sunset	✓	✓					✓	
The Holladay House		✓					✓	
Hotel Strasburg		✓				✓	✓	
The Inn at Gristmill Square		✓					✓	
The Inn at Little Washington		✓				✓		
The Inn at Monticello		✓						
The Inn at Narrow Passage		✓	✓	✓			✓	
Jordan Hollow Farm		✓				✓	✓	
Joshua Wilton House		✓					✓	
L'Auberge Provençale		✓					✓	
Lavender Hill Farm			✓	✓				
Liberty Rose		✓						
Miss Molly's		✓	✓				✓	
The Morrison House	✓	✓			✓	✓		
Newport House		✓						
The Norris House Inn		✓					✓	
North Bend Plantation		✓	✓	✓			✓	
Nottingham Ridge		✓	✓	✓				
Oak Spring Farm and Vineyard		✓		✓			✓	
Pickett's Harbor		✓	✓					
The Pink House		✓		✓			✓	
Prospect Hill	✓	✓				✓	✓	

Romantic Hideaway	Luxurious	Pets Allowed	No Smoking Indoors	Good Place for Families	Near Arts Festivals	Beach Nearby	Cross-Country Ski Trail	Golf Within 5 Miles	Fitness Facilities	Good Biking Terrain	Skiing	Horseback Riding	Tennis	Swimming on Premises	Conference Facilities
				✓						✓				✓	✓
			✓							✓					
✓	✓				✓	✓				✓					
✓	✓	✓	✓							✓					✓
										✓					
										✓					✓
				✓	✓			✓			✓		✓	✓	✓
✓	✓									✓					✓
			✓		✓					✓				✓	
✓				✓			✓			✓	✓				
✓				✓				✓		✓	✓	✓			✓
				✓			✓	✓		✓	✓				✓
✓	✓						✓					✓			
			✓							✓	✓				
✓			✓		✓			✓		✓					
			✓			✓				✓					
✓	✓				✓			✓		✓					✓
			✓	✓	✓			✓		✓					
			✓		✓			✓		✓					✓
			✓	✓						✓				✓	
			✓	✓		✓				✓					
✓			✓							✓					
			✓			✓				✓				✓	
✓					✓			✓		✓					
✓	✓								✓	✓				✓	✓

Name of Property	Accessible for Disabled	Antiques	On the Water	Good Value	Car Not Necessary	Full Meal Service	Historic Building	
The Red Fox Inn	✓	✓				✓	✓	
The Richard Johnston Inn		✓		✓	✓		✓	
Rocklands								
Sea Gate				✓				
Seven Hills Inn								
The Shadows		✓					✓	
The Silver Thatch Inn		✓					✓	
Sleepy Hollow Farm				✓				
Sycamore Hill								
Thornrose House		✓		✓				
Trillium House	✓							
200 South Street	✓	✓						
War Hill Inn		✓		✓				
The Watson House				✓				
Welbourne	✓	✓		✓			✓	
Willow Grove Plantation		✓					✓	
Woodstock Hall		✓					✓	
The Year of the Horse			✓					
WEST VIRGINIA								
Aspen Hall		✓					✓	
Bavarian Inn and Restaurant	✓	✓	✓			✓		
Boydville		✓					✓	
The Cardinal Inn				✓			✓	
The Carriage Inn		✓					✓	

Romantic Hideaway	Luxurious	Pets Allowed	No Smoking Indoors	Good Place for Families	Near Arts Festivals	Beach Nearby	Cross-Country Ski Trail	Golf Within 5 Miles	Fitness Facilities	Good Biking Terrain	Skiing	Horseback Riding	Tennis	Swimming on Premises	Conference Facilities
										✓					✓
			✓		✓			✓							
			✓		✓									✓	✓
					✓	✓				✓					
				✓						✓					✓
✓			✓	✓	✓					✓					✓
✓			✓		✓			✓					✓		
				✓						✓					
			✓		✓										
			✓		✓			✓		✓			✓		
							✓	✓	✓		✓	✓	✓		✓
					✓			✓		✓					✓
			✓	✓	✓			✓		✓					
✓			✓		✓	✓				✓					
		✓								✓					
										✓					
			✓							✓					
				✓		✓									
✓			✓		✓			✓							
✓	✓		✓	✓	✓		✓	✓		✓			✓	✓	✓
✓			✓		✓			✓		✓				✓	
			✓				✓			✓	✓	✓			✓
✓								✓		✓		✓			

Name of Property	Accessible for Disabled	Antiques	On the Water	Good Value	Car Not Necessary	Full Meal Service	Historic Building
Cheat Mountain Club			✓	✓		✓	✓
The Cottonwood Inn		✓					✓
The Country Inn	✓	✓		✓		✓	✓
The Current		✓	✓	✓			✓
Dunn Country Inn		✓					✓
The General Lewis Inn	✓	✓				✓	✓
Hampshire House 1884		✓					
Highlawn		✓					✓
Hillbrook		✓					✓
Hilltop House Hotel and Restaurant	✓		✓	✓		✓	✓
The Inn at Elk River			✓	✓		✓	
James Wylie House		✓					✓
Lynn's Inn		✓		✓			
Prospect Hill		✓					✓
The Thomas Shepherd Inn		✓					✓
The Wayside Inn		✓		✓			✓

Romantic Hideaway	Luxurious	Pets Allowed	No Smoking Indoors	Good Place for Families	Near Arts Festivals	Beach Nearby	Cross-Country Ski Trail	Golf Within 5 Miles	Fitness Facilities	Good Biking Terrain	Skiing	Horseback Riding	Tennis	Swimming on Premises	Conference Facilities
				✓			✓			✓	✓	✓			
				✓	✓			✓		✓					
✓					✓		✓	✓			✓	✓			✓
		✓	✓	✓			✓			✓	✓	✓			
✓			✓				✓			✓		✓			
✓		✓		✓	✓		✓			✓		✓	✓		
			✓		✓										
✓	✓				✓		✓	✓		✓	✓	✓			
✓	✓									✓					
				✓	✓		✓			✓		✓			✓
				✓			✓	✓		✓	✓	✓			
✓			✓	✓			✓								
✓			✓		✓		✓	✓				✓			✓
✓				✓			✓			✓					
✓			✓				✓	✓		✓					✓
			✓		✓		✓						✓		

New York

The Adelphi Hotel, **14**
Albergo Allegria, **29**
Anthony Dobbins Stagecoach Inn, **47**
The Balsam House, **1**
Bassett House Inn, **50**
Beaverkill Valley Inn, **36**
The Bent Finial Manor, **5**
The Bird and Bottle Inn, **46**
Captain Schoonmaker's Bed-and-Breakfast, **38**
The Chester Inn, **2**
Chestnut Tree Inn, **15**
Country Road Lodge, **6**
Crislip's Bed and Breakfast, **9**
Deer Mountain Inn, **31**
Donegal Manor Bed and Breakfast, **7**
The Eggery, **32**
The Friends Lake Inn, **3**
Greenville Arms, **27**
The Gregory House, **24**
Hedges' Inn, **51**
The Hill Guest House, **58**
Hilltop Cottage Bed and Breakfast, **4**
Hudson House, A Country Inn, **43**
The Huntting Inn, **52**
Inn at Lake Joseph, **48**
The Inn at Saratoga, **16**
The Inn at Shaker Mill, **26**
The Inn on Bacon Hill, **20**
The Lamplight Inn, **11**
Lanza's, **37**
Le Chambord, **42**
The Maidstone Arms, **53**
The Mansion, **13**
Mansion Hill Inn, **22**
Maple Ridge Inn, **21**
The Martindale Bed and Breakfast Inn, **35**
The Merrill Magee House, **8**
Mill House Inn (East Hampton), **54**
Mill House Inn (Stephentown), **25**
The Old Post House Inn, **56**
Pig Hill Inn, **44**

New York

Ogdensburg
Potsdam
Canton
Kingston
Watertown
Carthage
Newton Falls
Tupper Lake
Adirondack
Adams
Lowville
Old Forge
Lake Ontario
Oswego
Fulton
Cleveland
Remsen
Camden
Ohio
Rome
Northville
Utica
Syracuse
Clyde
Oneida
Mohawk River
Rock
Cazenovia
Auburn
Geneva
Hamilton
Sche
Finger Lakes
Penn Yan
Interlaken
Cobleskill
Cooperstown
Dryden
Oneonta
Watkins Glen
Ithaca
Whitney Point
Windham
Tannersville
Walton
Corning
Binghamton
Elmira
Lewbeach
Catskill Pa
Livingston Manor
Monticello
Forestburg
Middletown
Goshen
Scranton
Wilkes-Barre
NEW JERSEY
0
60 miles
90 km
Allentown

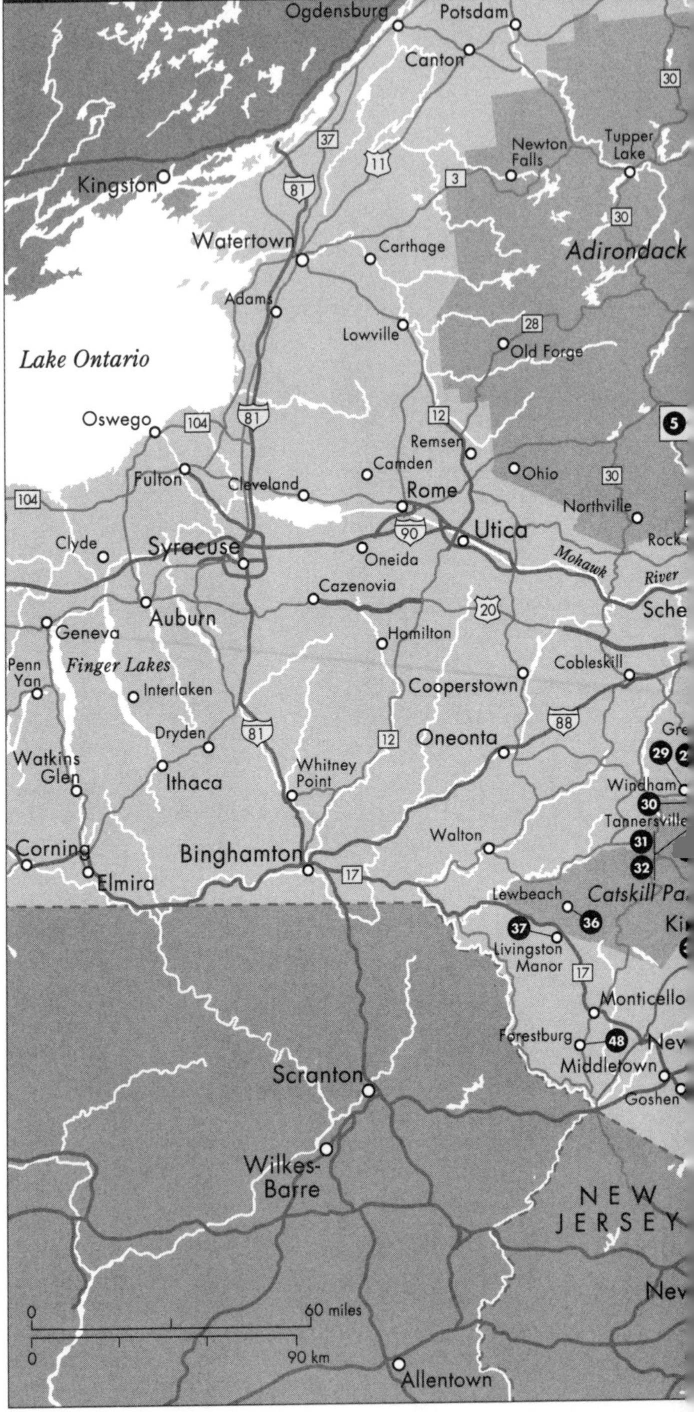

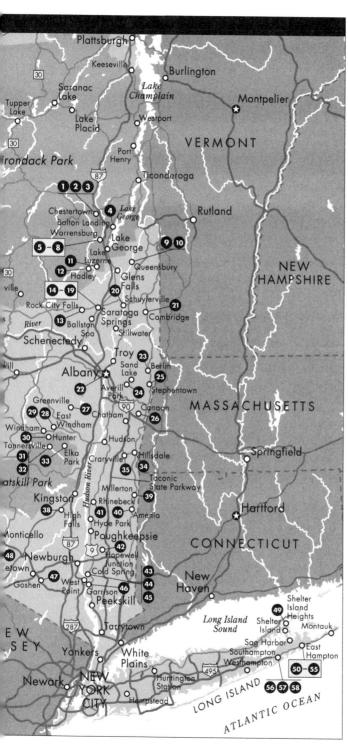

3

Plumbush Inn, **45**

Point Lookout
Mountain Inn, **28**

Ram's Head Inn, **49**

The Redcoat's
Return, **33**

Sanford's Ridge
Bed & Breakfast, **10**

Saratoga Bed and
Breakfast, **17**

Saratoga Rose, **12**

Scribner Hollow
Motor Lodge, **30**

The Sedgwick Inn, **23**

The 1770 House, **55**

Simmons Way
Village Inn, **39**

The Six Sisters, **18**

The Swiss Hutte, **34**

Troutbeck, **40**

The Village
Latch Inn, **57**

The Village
Victorian Inn, **41**

The Westchester
House, **19**

The Lake George Region

*At the gateway to a 6-million-acre forest preserve known as
Adirondack Park lies 32-mile-long Lake George,
a four-season nirvana for those who like to vacation
outdoors amid pine groves and pristine lakes. To be honest,
not all of this "Queen of American Lakes" is pristine.
There are plenty of ersatz Indian tepees, neon motel signs,
and cheap-souvenir emporiums—in Lake George Village
and at other lakeside outposts. Yet the lake itself, although
not immune to 20th-century evils of acid rain and other
pollutants, is probably as lovely as it was when it was
discovered, in 1646. Other beautiful waterways in the area,
most notably Lake Luzerne, Friends Lake, the Sacandaga
River, and the northernmost reaches of the Hudson River,
are worth visiting.*

*All this water naturally encourages water sports, including
fishing for record-breaking bass and white-water rafting.
Visitors also enjoy canoeing, swimming, and sunning on
the lakeside beaches. At times other than the peak summer
season, travelers come to the region for hiking, mountain
climbing, and bird-watching; in winter they're drawn to the
many cross-country ski trails and the excellent downhill
slopes of Gore Mountain and Hickory Ski Center, where
skiers at all levels will find reasonable lift rates and no
long lines.*

*The area near Lake Luzerne is, surprisingly, dude-ranch
country and the home of the oldest rodeo in the United
States. Horses are available for trail rides. Warrensburg,
an old lumber-mill town with more than 40 antiques shops,
is a mecca for those seeking the perfect Adirondack chair,
twig settee, or Victorian washstand. The region also has
a variety of restaurants from which to choose. You'll find
everything from exceptional hamburgers (at a roadside
shack in Lake Luzerne called the Brass Bucket, where*

there's sometimes a two-hour wait) to haute cuisine, in places where you might expect more modest fare.

Places to Go, Sights to See

Fort William Henry (Lake George Village, tel. 518/668–5471). If you're a fan of James Fenimore Cooper, you'll want to stop at this site, which figured so prominently in *The Last of the Mohicans*. The British constructed the fort in 1755; it was burned by the French in 1757. The restored complex presents visitors with a picture of life during the French and Indian War, and history tours, with demonstrations of military skills, are given in July and August.

Great Escape Fun Park (Lake George, tel. 518/792–6568). New York State's largest theme park, Great Escape has 100 rides and attractions with names like Steamin' Demon Loop Corkscrew Rollercoaster and Raging River Ride.

Hyde House (Glens Falls, tel. 518/792–1761). A 1912 Italian Renaissance-style mansion, Hyde House is filled with French 18th-century and Italian Renaissance antiques. It also houses **The Hyde Collection** of Old Masters and American art, from the late-Gothic to the 20th century.

Lake George Steamboat Cruises (tel. 518/668–5777) and **Lake George Shoreline Cruises** (tel. 518/668–4644) offer many lake tours, including brunch, lunch, dinner, and moonlight cruises, some with entertainment and some on an authentic Mississippi paddle wheeler, the *Minne-Ha-Ha*.

World's Largest Garage Sale. Each fall in Warrensburg more than 500 dealers and private sellers gather to purvey a mixed bag that might contain anything from priceless antiques to tomorrow's collectibles (Batman lunchboxes, anyone?). More than 150,000 visitors attend. For exact dates, call the Warrensburg Chamber of Commerce (tel. 518/623–2161).

Restaurants

Rene's (tel. 518/494–2904), near Chestertown, serves Continental cuisine and scrumptious French desserts in a mountain setting. In Lake George, the **Shoreline Restaurant and Marina** (tel. 518/668–2875) specializes in prime rib, veal, and fresh seafood dishes. Moderately priced American cuisine, including steaks and seafood, is on hand at the **Garden in the Park** (tel. 518/792–1121) at the Queensbury Hotel in Glens Falls. Some of the best Italian food in the Lake George area can be found at **Mario's** (tel. 518/668–2665).

Tourist Information

Chestertown Chamber of Commerce (Box 490, Chestertown 12817, tel. 518/494-2722). **Lake George Chamber of Commerce** (Box 272, Lake George 12845, tel. 518/668-5755). **Lake Luzerne Chamber of Commerce** (Bridge St., Box 222, Lake Luzerne 12846, tel. 518/696-3500). **Warren County Department of Tourism** (Municipal Center, Lake George 12845, tel. 800/365-1050).

Reservation Services

American Country Collection (4 Greenwood La., Delmar 12054, tel. 518/439-7001). **Bed and Breakfast Association of Saratoga, Lake George and Gore Mountain Region** (Box 99, Lake Luzerne 12846, for a brochure on member establishments).

The Balsam House

A forest preserve, mountain views, a private beach on Friends Lake, comfortable rooms, and sophisticated fare—you'll find all these at Balsam House. Built in 1845 as a farmhouse, the building became a vacation lodge in 1891; in 1982 owner Frank Ellis turned it into a year-round, full-service inn. Innkeepers Bruce and Helena Robbins, assisted by an able and knowledgeable staff, make sure guests lack nothing during their stay.

Guests have access to all the offerings of the Adirondacks, but they're certainly not roughing it in the wilderness. The bold Victorian decor (with a parlor painted a deep plum color and a forest-green living room enhanced by mauve rattan chairs and an Oriental rug) and the Perrier Jouet in the inn's French restaurant come as a surprise in this off-the-beaten-track location, but, delightfully, it all works.

A few Victorian antiques furnish the guest rooms, and chenille spreads cover several of the beds. There's a bilevel suite with a narrow spiral staircase, and a downstairs suite offers a wet bar and a pull-out sofa. Upstairs is a chamber with a king-size canopy bed. Room 30 features a skylight and a view of nearby Gore Mountain.

The inn's beach on Friends Lake has its own dock, canoes, paddleboat, and screened bungalow. Bikes are available for rental, and hiking trails abound. Winter sports fans will find nearby cross-country ski trails, and they can also go ice fishing on Friends Lake. The inn's two restaurants offer cosmopolitan cuisine. Escargots, ceviche, and duck *framboise* may be accompanied by a selection from Le Papillon's extensive wine list. Open-grill specialties are served in the pine-panel Atateka Hearth and Grill.

The actress Mary Frann, from TV's *Newhart*, stayed at the inn to soak up atmosphere and pick up pointers before assuming the role of innkeeper on that long-running show. Rumor has it that the three backwoods brothers on the show—Larry, Darryl, and Darryl—were inspired by a couple of colorful locals who stop in here from time to time. Larry, Darryl, and Darryl—and vintage champagne? Somehow nothing seems incongruous here. It all adds up to a delightful stay.

Address: *Friends Lake, Chestertown, NY 12817, tel. 518/494-2828, fax 518/494-4431.*
Accommodations: *19 double rooms with baths, 1 suite.*
Amenities: *Restaurants, air-conditioning in some rooms, TV in parlor.*
Rates: *$75–$110; full breakfast; MAP available. AE, DC, MC, V.*
Restrictions: *No pets, closed 3 weeks in Nov. and 3 weeks in spring.*

The Bent Finial Manor

The Bent Finial, definitely among the most elegant bed-and-breakfasts in the area, is certainly one of the most opulent. The stunning 1904 Queen Anne Victorian mansion opened in 1989. Owner Patricia Scully, a former vice-president for an oil-and-gas company, searched for three years from Maine to South Carolina before she found her dream house, which had been built by cattle baron Lewis Thomson.

During the Civil War, Thomson made his fortune supplying beef to Union troops. Like many of the other *nouveaux riches* of his era, he wanted his home to duplicate the opulent excesses of the European nobility—and he succeeded. Twenty-three kinds of wood—including oak, birch, hemlock, pine, and several varieties of cherry—make up the floors, moldings, wainscoting, and the impressive staircase. You enter the front parlor between Corinthian columns; all the rooms have their original beveled, etched, or stained-glass windows.

It's to Pat's credit that the furnishings do justice to this magnificent house. The parlor contains a Victorian game table (for chess, cards, or backgammon). Breakfast is served on a Victorian dining table set with antique linens and fine china. The color scheme in the upstairs Master Chamber complements the plum hues of its stained-glass windows. The Eastlake Chamber, furnished in eponymous style, has an antique dressmaker's dummy clothed in a Victorian frock—"My first guest," jokes Pat.

Pat's sense of whimsy is reflected in the antique Teddy bear (dressed like Theodore Roosevelt, complete with wire-rim glasses) perched on the stairway landing—and Teddy also reflects her sense of history. The original blueprints for the house hang on the wall of a landing. Each guest leaves a pin in one of the wall maps to mark the state or country from which he or she hails.

Before you leave, make sure Pat tells you the peculiar story of how the house got its name.

Address: *194 Main St., Warrensburg, NY 12885, tel. 518/623-3308.*
Accommodations: *4 double rooms with baths.*
Amenities: *1 room with fireplace and private porch.*
Rates: *$85–$95; full breakfast. No credit cards.*
Restrictions: *No smoking in bedrooms, pets by special arrangement.*

The Lamplight Inn

I n 1890 the Lamplight Inn, a grand Victorian Gothic in the village of Lake Luzerne, was built by a wealthy bachelor lumberman as his summer playhouse. One can only guess at the romantic trysts of this 19th-century playboy, but adjoining doors (no longer used) to two other bedrooms from the master bedroom hint at the possibilities.

Today, the Lamplight is a romantic bed-and-breakfast for 20th-century guests, thanks to innkeepers Gene and Linda Merlino. In 1984 they were still dating when they bought this mansion on a whim. Within a year they were husband and wife; they spent their honeymoon painting the front porch. Honeymooning guests and couples who may or may not be considering a wedding in the future love the Lamplight, as room-diary accolades attest: "Our privacy was respected and our newness as a couple treated with gentleness and humor," one newlywed wrote, and there have been quite a few proposals uttered on bended knee under this romantic roof.

The decor helps considerably. The downstairs sitting room has its original chestnut molding, wainscoting, and unusual keyhole staircase. On cool evenings the room is lit by two fireplaces. Wicker chairs beckon visitors to the comfortable front porch, and the airy dining room provides the perfect backdrop for Linda's granola and muffins and Gene's peach crepes and three-egg omelets.

Guest rooms are Victorian in the romantic sense of the word—they are flowery and lacy. One of the nicest places to stay is the Canopy Room, with an original carved-oak mantel, hearth tiles, and a gas fireplace. In a newly constructed wing is a unique room that perfectly matches the rest of the house: The Skylight Room has a carved-oak, high-back Victorian bed covered in an antique patchwork quilt, with a skylight overhead. It's hard to choose a room here, because so much love and attention to detail have gone into each one.

A guest entry in the Canopy Room diary probably sums up the Lamplight experience best: "Your rocking chairs, soft quilts, and warm hospitality have transformed us back into human beings."

And isn't that the purpose of getting away from it all?

Address: *2129 Lake Ave., Box 70, Lake Luzerne, NY 12846, tel. 518/696–5294.*
Accommodations: *10 double rooms with baths.*
Amenities: *Air-conditioning, 5 rooms with fireplaces; beach across street.*
Rates: *$75–$140; full breakfast. AE.*
Restrictions: *No smoking in bedrooms, no pipes or cigars, no pets, 2-night minimum on weekends.*

The Chester Inn

Since it was built, in 1837, only three families have occupied the Greek Revival mansion that now houses The Chester Inn Bed and Breakfast. Originally it was the home of Charles Fowler, a wealthy merchant. Today the inn sits right on Chestertown's Main Street, but it has 13 acres of meadows out back.

A love of history and fond memories of European B&B stays persuaded Bruce and Suzanne Robbins to open an inn. Bruce, who had worked in construction, and Sue, who was in retail sales, carefully researched the house's past and attended to every detail in its restoration (they even had an original shade of paint reproduced by computer). Guests are pampered with candlelit breakfasts served on Syracuse Federal-style china with sterling and crystal. Three guest rooms are furnished with Victorian antiques; a fourth, the Library Suite, is decorated in a spare, Shaker-like maner. While in Chestertown, don't miss the Robbinses' restored, turn-of-the-century ice-cream parlor and museum, one block from the inn.

Address: *Box 163, Main St., Chestertown, NY 12817, tel. 518/494-4148.*
Accommodations: *2 double rooms with baths, 2 suites.*
Amenities: *Dinner available.*
Rates: *$75–$100; full breakfast. MC, V.*
Restrictions: *No smoking, no pets, 2-night minimum on holiday weekends.*

Country Road Lodge

You'll find nothing fancy at the Country Road Lodge: This was once a small, rustic camp cottage at the end of a long, winding dirt road, and, with some additions and improvements, it still is. "What we have is *setting*," brag the owners, Steve and Sandi Parisi. Perched close enough to the churning Hudson River to practically fall in, and surrounded by mountain vistas, the lodge is totally secluded. The hiking and cross-country ski trails go on for miles through the forests.

The Parisis keep the small guest rooms clean and comfortable; the unpretentious decor is "early garage sale," with some nice patchwork quilts. Steve worked on Madison Avenue before opening the lodge to skiers in 1974 (the Hickory Ski Center—Mogul Madness—is just down the way). Hearty breakfasts are provided for hikers, skiers, and those who wish to just sit on the riverbank and commune with nature. Good conversation abounds: The meal sometimes lasts for hours.

Address: *HCR 1, No. 227 Hickory Hill Rd., Warrensburg, NY 12885, tel. 518/623-2207.*
Accommodations: *2 double rooms with baths, 2 doubles share a bath.*
Amenities: *Lunch and dinner served on winter weekends.*
Rates: *$52; full breakfast. No credit cards.*
Restrictions: *No pets.*

Crislip's Bed and Breakfast

You can see the Green Mountains of Vermont from the Italianate veranda of the Crislip's Bed and Breakfast. The Federal house, built in 1805 and remodeled in 1848 in the popular Greek Revival style, was owned by Queensbury's first doctor, who later became town supervisor. Queensbury is about halfway between Saratoga Springs and Lake George—near but just far enough off the beaten track.

Joyce Crislip is a former teacher, and her husband, Ned, teaches music. The hosts' musical interests are in evidence throughout the house: A Steinway grand piano is the focal point of the living room; the framed, 15th-century score of a Gregorian chant hangs on the wall of the studio. The Blue Room, with its canopied, carved mahogany bed and mahogany highboy, is favored by honeymooners; and the first-floor studio (with a kitchenette) is often the choice of older couples. The Green Room has a king-size four-poster bed. Ned will gladly give you the tour and tell you the details of the period antiques that fill the house.

Address: *R.D. 1, Box 57, Ridge Rd., Queensbury, NY 12804, tel. 518/793–6869.*
Accommodations: *3 double rooms with baths.*
Amenities: *TV in two rooms and in common room.*
Rates: *$45–$75; full breakfast. MC, V.*
Restrictions: *No smoking, small pets permitted by arrangement.*

Donegal Manor Bed and Breakfast

Irish hospitality characterizes Donegal Manor, a bed-and-breakfast housed in an 1820 building with Italianate Victorian additions in the middle of Warrensburg. Owner Dorothy Dill Wright hails from Donegal, Ireland. She worked downstate as a nurse before opening this B&B and its accompanying antiques shop, run by her husband, John. An Irish-pine dresser in the dining room displays her collection of Blue Willow and Flow Blue china, and an old Irish churn stands nearby. A 1776 cradle and a Victorian marble-top washstand are among the many family heirlooms in the house.

The previous owner informed the Wrights that James Fenimore Cooper had been a guest here while doing research for *The Last of the Mohicans.* So you'll find they have a Cooper Room, with a double spindle bed covered with a velvet patchwork quilt, and views of two nearby church steeples. The Cooper Suite, where the author would have slept, has the original 1820 floors and beams, a fireplace, a 6-foot tub, and a view of Hackensack Mountain.

Address: *117 Main St., Warrensburg, NY 12885, tel. 518/623–3549.*
Accommodations: *1 double room with bath, 2 doubles share a bath, 1 suite.*
Amenities: *Air-conditioning, cable TV in suite and parlor.*
Rates: *$55–$95; full breakfast. MC, V.*
Restrictions: *Smoking in parlor and on porch only, no pets.*

The Friends Lake Inn

The New York State record small-mouth bass was caught in Friends Lake, but you don't have to be an angler to enjoy the Friends Lake Inn and all it has to offer. This traditional Adirondack lodge was built in stages. The original building was a farmhouse constructed around 1850; a later addition served as a boardinghouse for workers in local tanneries. Innkeepers Greg and Sharon Taylor are avid skiers, and at the inn they have established a cross-country ski touring center with trails; they also offer special packages for alpine skiing.

After a day spent skiing (or fishing, rafting, canoeing, or hiking), guests gather at the inn's restaurant, which has received culinary accolades. With its pressed-tin ceiling and original chestnut woodwork, it is a romantic spot for lingering. Guest rooms are small, simple, and cozy and are furnished with antique beds and oak dressers. The most popular rooms are the ones with a view of the lake and those with Jacuzzis.

Address: *Friends Lake Rd., Chestertown, NY 12817, tel. 518/494-4751.*
Accommodations: *16 double rooms with baths.*
Amenities: *4 rooms with Jacuzzis, 6 rooms with queen-size pull-out couches, restaurant, wine bar; beach.*
Rates: *$65–$165; full breakfast; MAP available. MC, V.*
Restrictions: *Smoking in common rooms only, no pets, 2-night minimum on weekends, 3-night minimum on holiday weekends.*

Hilltop Cottage Bed and Breakfast

Once the caretaker's house on a Lake George estate, Hilltop Cottage is now an easygoing, reasonably priced alternative to the ersatz log cabins and tacky motels that proliferate in this popular resort area. Running a bed-and-breakfast comes naturally to retired educators Anita and Charlie Richards. Anita's parents lived in the 11-room house, and her mother rented rooms to tourists. During the 1920s and early '30s the building housed students of the legendary Metropolitan Opera diva Marcella Sembrich, who had a summer home nearby.

The moldings, floors, and banister in this vine-covered house are made of Adirondack fir, and all the antique beds are covered with printed quilts from the 1940s and '50s. A former toolshed on the estate has been converted into a cottage for two and is paneled in knotty pine.

Address: *Box 186, Rte. 9N, Bolton Landing, NY 12814, tel. 518/644-2492.*
Accommodations: *1 double room with bath, 2 doubles share a bath, 1 cottage.*
Amenities: *Cable TV and refrigerator in cottage.*
Rates: *$45–$65; full breakfast. No credit cards.*
Restrictions: *No smoking indoors, no pets, 2-night minimum on holiday weekends.*

The Merrill Magee House

In a grove of trees adjacent to a 19th-century bandstand sits the Merrill McGee House, a Greek Revival mansion built around 1840. The great-grandfather of Grace Merrill Magee, for whom the inn is named, fought in the American Revolution. Innkeepers Florence and Ken Carrington owned housekeeping cottages on Lake George for 30 years. A brief, unhappy retirement led to a new career as proprietors of this irresistible country inn.

The house overlooks gardens where weddings are often held, and a field of wildflowers lies in back. Most of the guest rooms are located in a new (but architecturally compatible) building behind the inn. All the new rooms have fireplaces and are decorated country style, with antique beds, patchwork quilts, and folk art. The inn features what may be the oldest (circa 1928) private swimming pool in New York State—it's a beauty. In summer guests can also enjoy evening concerts performed at the bandstand.

Address: *2 Hudson St., Warrensburg, NY 12885, tel. 518/623-2449.*
Accommodations: *10 double rooms with baths, 2 doubles share a bath.*
Amenities: *Restaurant, tavern, air-conditioning, pool, whirlpool.*
Rates: *$85–$100; full breakfast. AE, D, DC, MC, V.*
Restrictions: *No smoking in dining room or bedrooms, no pets, 2-night minimum on summer and holiday weekends, closed mid-Mar.–mid-Apr.*

Sanford's Ridge Bed & Breakfast

Sanford's Ridge is just a five-minute drive from the commercial stretch of Route 9, and yet it has a removed, bucolic feeling. In 1990 owners Carolyn and Bob Rudolph (she's a synagogue administrator, and he's controller at a garnet mine) restored the 1797 Federal-style house, with its 14-foot ceilings, wide-plank pine floors, and fireplaces.

The three guest rooms are furnished with an eclectic collection of antiques. The spacious Webster Room has a queen-size canopied four-poster, a fireplace, a bath with a claw-foot tub, and a view of the Adirondacks. The Sanford Room has a fireplace and a four-poster double bed decked with a patchwork quilt handmade by Carolyn.

The carriage house, attached to the main house, serves as a common room; it's one big, open room with exposed wooden beams and lots of windows. You can shoot a game of pool on the regulation slate table here or sit by the fire and look out at the mountains.

Address: *Ridge Road (RR 1, Box 70), Queensbury, NY 12804, tel. 518/793-4923.*
Accommodations: *3 double rooms with baths.*
Amenities: *TV in common room; swimming pool.*
Rates: *$60–$85; full breakfast. MC, V.*
Restrictions: *No smoking, no pets, 2-night minimum on holiday weekends.*

Saratoga Rose

The Victorian mansion now housing this bed-and-breakfast inn was built in 1885 as a wedding gift for the daughter of one of the founding fathers of Hadley, a tiny Adirondack village between the Sacandaga and Hudson rivers. "I guess that's why it works so well for us," says innkeeper Nancy Merlino. "We're on an extended honeymoon here."

Nancy and her husband and co-owner, Anthony (he's also the chef for the inn's restaurant), married and in 1988 found the inn. The couple are proud of the acclaimed restaurant, which serves American regional and Italian cuisine. Candlelit dinners are served in the romantic, Victorian dining room with burgundy curtains and a fireplace, or on what is probably the only bright-pink veranda in the Adirondacks. The guest rooms have Victorian furnishings and decor; two rooms have oak high-back beds, and one has a fireplace. The Victorian Room even has a pink fainting couch, and the Garden Room has a private deck with a 20th-century conceit: a whirlpool bath.

Address: *4174 Rockwell St. (Box 238), Hadley, NY 12835, tel. 518/696–2861.*
Accommodations: *3 double rooms with baths, 1 suite.*
Amenities: *Restaurant, bar.*
Rates: *$60–$125; full breakfast. D, MC, V.*
Restrictions: *Smoking downstairs only, no pets, 2-night minimum Aug. and on holiday weekends.*

The Capital and Saratoga Region

Reminders of America's past—political, commercial, and social—abound in New York's Capital and Saratoga region. A favorite of visitors seeking both history and 20th-century diversions, the area encompasses the city of Albany, the nation's sixth largest port, at the northernmost point of the navigable Hudson. Once on the decline—as described in Ironweed *and other works of William Kennedy, a local favorite son—Albany is currently enjoying the revitalization of its downtown area. The additions to the city of the Nelson A. Rockefeller Empire State Plaza (completed in 1978) and the Knickerbocker Arena have inspired the restoration of surrounding neighborhoods. A tour of the city often includes the governor's mansion and the State Capitol—one of the few such buildings without a dome. You won't want to miss the Performing Arts Center, nicknamed "The Egg" for obvious reasons. It makes the Albany skyline unlike any other in the world.*

Landlocked though Saratoga is, it boasts a natural asset: a prehistoric sea, trapped under limestone and capped with a layer of shale. The mineral waters that bubble through the cracks in the shale have made Saratoga Springs and the neighboring Ballston Spa a noted resort for two centuries. Here visitors still "take the cure," sampling mineral waters from various fountains strategically located around town. Bring a drinking cup, and don't expect the water to taste like Evian or Perrier. Each spring reputedly possesses different elements conducive to health. The cure may include a trip to one of the area's mineral baths (several of which are located in Saratoga Spa State Park) and a massage.

"The August Place to Be," as Saratoga Springs advertises itself, attracts crowds each August, when the five-week thoroughbred-racing season is the centerpiece of a series of festive events. Lodging and seats at the city's excellent

restaurants are hard to come by during this time; and hotel, inn, and bed-and-breakfast rates often shoot up to nearly twice the normal prices. To really enjoy this lovely city we recommend a visit at other times of the year.

Saratoga is a great place for strolling, with its superb Victorian architecture, especially along Union Avenue, North Broadway, Lake Avenue, and Circular Street. And don't miss the scene of the 1777 Battle of Saratoga, the "turning point of the Revolution," now a national historic park (tel. 518/664–9821) between the nearby towns of Stillwater and Schuylerville.

Places to Go, Sights to See

Historic Cherry Hill (Albany, tel. 518/434–4791). This Georgian home, built in 1787 by Philip Van Rensselaer, was inhabited by five generations of his family, until 1963. The furnishings range from 18th-century artifacts and 19th-century Chinese exports to early-20th-century kitchen appliances. The first floor is wheelchair accessible.

New York State Capitol (Albany, tel. 518/474–2418). Built between 1867 and 1899 at a cost of $25 million, the seat of New York State government incorporates several styles of architecture. The interior features elaborate carvings and an impressive staircase. It's wheelchair accessible.

New York State Museum (Albany, tel. 518/474–5843). Lifelike dioramas of New York State's past (including some depicting immigrant life in New York City in the late 19th and early 20th centuries) and a reproduction of an Iroquois village, including a full-size "long house," make this museum one of Albany's most popular attractions. Also featured are changing art exhibits, films, lectures, demonstrations, and hands-on displays. The museum is an absorbing adventure for children. It's wheelchair accessible as well.

Saratoga Race Course (Saratoga Springs, tel. 518/584–6200). The nation's oldest thoroughbred track, in operation since 1863, is the focus of Saratoga's August social scene. Post time is 1 PM. Early risers may breakfast at the trackside café (tel. 518/584–6200) and watch morning workouts. The National Museum of Racing and Thoroughbred Hall of Fame (tel. 518/584–0400), right by the track, touches on every aspect of the sport and includes a reconstructed training barn and portraits of such champions as Man o' War and Secretariat.

Saratoga Spa State Park (between Rtes. 9 and 50, tel. 518/584–2535). The land that now makes up this 2,000-acre park was reserved in 1909 to protect the area's unique mineral springs. Mineral baths (some of which still operate) were opened in the 1920s, and in the '30s the Works Progress Administration completed the spa buildings. The park has an Olympic-size swimming pool, golf courses, tennis courts, and ice-skating rinks. It is also the home of the Saratoga Performing Arts Center (tel. 518/584-9330), summer host of the New York City Opera, the New York City Ballet, the Philadelphia Orchestra, and the Newport Jazz Festival–Saratoga.

Yaddo (Saratoga Springs, tel. 518/584-0746). This 19th-century estate was the summer home of Katrina and Spencer Trask, wealthy patrons of the arts. Yaddo is their permanent legacy to creative work, an enclave where artists, writers, and musicians may work without disruption. Since 1926 more than 3,000 artists have resided here, including John Cheever, Langston Hughes, Katherine Anne Porter, Aaron Copland, and Milton Avery. Yaddo's gardens, modeled on turn-of-the-century Italian designs, complete with statuary, are open to the public.

Restaurants

In the capital, you can get generous servings of seafood at **Jack's Oyster House** (tel. 518/465-8854) or join the locals, who for more than 70 years have been eating Italian at **Lombardo's** (tel. 518/462-9180). **Eartha's Kitchen** (Saratoga Springs, tel. 518/583-0602) has an eclectic chalkboard menu including mesquite-grilled seafood dishes. Adirondack fare—venison, trout, and rabbit in Hunter's sauce—is featured at the **Springwater Inn** (Saratoga Springs, tel. 518/584-6440).

Tourist Information

Albany County Convention and Visitors Bureau (52 S. Pearl St., Albany 12207, tel. 518/434-1217 or 800/258-3582). **Rensselaer County Regional Chamber of Commerce** (31 2nd St., Troy 12180, tel. 518/274-7020). **Saratoga County Chamber of Commerce** (494 Broadway, Saratoga Springs 12866, tel. 518/584-3255).

Reservation Services

The American Country Collection (4 Greenwood La., Delmar 12054, tel. 518/439-7001). **Bed and Breakfast Association of Saratoga, Lake George and Gore Mountain Region** (Box 99, Lake Luzerne 12846, for brochure on member establishments). **Bed and Breakfast USA, Ltd.** (Box 606, Croton-on-Hudson 10520).

The Adelphi Hotel

If Kublai Khan had decreed that his stately pleasure dome be built in late-19th-century Saratoga instead of in Xanadu, he might have come up with the Adelphi Hotel. This lodging is nothing like home, unless home is an Italian palazzo, with the requisite piazza and ornamented by a maze of Victorian fretwork. The opulent lobby is done in a style so reminiscent of La Belle Epoque that one could picture the Divine Sarah Bernhardt holding court amid its splendor. It's hard to believe that not too long ago the Adelphi stood empty, evidence of fortune gone sour. Saratogans shook their heads and laughed at what they took to be the foolhardiness of Gregg Siefker and Sheila Parkert when they bought the place in 1988, but no one's laughing anymore: The hotel is one of Saratoga's showpieces, its lobby bar and café a gathering place for natives and visitors alike (in July it's a favorite hangout of members of the New York City Ballet).

No two rooms are the same: All the furnishings are eclectic—and recherché. If you seek accommodations that hark back to the Adirondack camps enjoyed by some of America's wealthiest families, ask for Room 16, the Adirondack Suite, with Mission-style furniture manufactured in upstate New York, a twig settee, Papago Indian baskets on the wall, and a wood-paneled bathroom. If you yearn for the south of France but can't afford to go there, the Riviera

Suite (Room 12) may lessen the pangs somewhat. Its sitting area, furnished with rattan, is graced with a Mediterranean mural; an amusing Casbah painting hangs on the bedroom wall; and the bathroom is decorated in apricot tones. Other rooms are furnished with Tiffany lampshades, brass-and-iron beds with crocheted bedspreads, wicker settees, and Victoriana.

The Adelphi was built when Saratoga was known as the Queen of the Spas. Today the city is still the center of a lively and elegant social scene, especially in August, when the raceway is open—but keep in mind that Saratoga has a lot to offer during the other 11 months of the year, when hotel reservations are easier to come by.

Address: *365 Broadway, Saratoga Springs, NY 12866, tel. 518/587–4688.*
Accommodations: *17 double rooms with baths, 18 suites.*
Amenities: *Restaurant (open July and Aug.), bar, air-conditioning, cable TV, and phones in bedrooms, room service; swimming pool.*
Rates: *$70–$290; Continental breakfast. AE, MC, V.*
Restrictions: *No pets, 3-day minimum on weekends in Aug., closed Nov.–Apr.*

The Mansion

Rock City Falls, a 19th-century mill town 7 miles west of Saratoga Springs, seems an unlikely destination for travelers. The Kayaderosseras Creek still flows, but the mills and factories are quiet. Aside from a few antiques shops, there doesn't seem to be much that would draw visitors to this sleepy village . . . not much, that is, until one spots the Mansion, one of the most elegant and romantic bed-and-breakfasts you'll encounter anywhere. The Venetian villa–style residence, soon to be listed on the National Register of Historic Places, was built in 1866 as a summer home for George West, a prominent industrialist and inventor of the folding paper bag. No expense was spared in the construction of the 23-room mansion; it has 12-foot etched-glass doors, marble fireplaces with inlaid mantels, copper and brass lighting fixtures, and Tiffany chandeliers.

It is a credit to proprietor Tom Clark and innkeeper Alan Churchill, who restored the mansion, that this bed-and-breakfast is both sumptuous and friendly. The art books stacked invitingly in the library are for browsing, perhaps while sipping iced tea or Saratoga water on the side porch on a lazy summer afternoon. Classical music—anything from Bach to Berlioz—wafts through the house. The art, which Tom collects on his travels, invites close inspection. The antique parlor organ is there for playing. All the guest rooms are en-

ticing, but the Four-poster Room, with its queen-size carved bed, and the Queen Room, with garden views, are particularly handsome.

And there are the flowers. Baskets of fuchsia hang from the porches; roses, peonies, and delphiniums fill the gardens; and bouquets of fragrant Casablanca lilies and foxglove may greet you in the front hall or parlors. Throughout the year floral arrangements brighten every guest room. Alan of the green thumb even grows orchids: In one guest room the mauve of an orchid plant picks up the colors of the bedspread.

Alan nurtures his guests the way he nurtures his flowers—you are made to feel like a treasured friend in this hospitable house. Everything here—from the Victorian furnishings to the homemade fruit breads served with breakfast—is in excellent taste. As Alan says, "The house demands it. It's so special."

Address: *Rte. 29, Box 77, Rock City Falls, NY 12863, tel. 518/885–1607.*
Accommodations: *4 double rooms with baths, 1 suite.*
Amenities: *Air-conditioning; swimming pool.*
Rates: *$85–$150; full breakfast. No credit cards.*
Restrictions: *No smoking in dining room, no pets, 2-night minimum in Aug. and on holiday weekends, closed Thanksgiving and Christmas.*

Maple Ridge Inn

I n Cambridge, right in the middle of "Grandma Moses Country" near the New York–Vermont border, is a distinctive Victorian mansion with a Texas accent. The Dallas connection is owner Ken Riney, a purveyor of fine antique jewelry and silver, who by his own admission spent "a fortune" restoring and furnishing the 1869 estate and turned it into a bed-and-breakfast both opulent and relaxed. The antique silver coffee service, the 1840s silver urn, and the silver fruit baskets are not just for display—they're used every morning for breakfast in the main dining room. The same goes for the Tiffany china.

Guest rooms show off gems from Ken's collection: a Victorian carved-walnut bed in a downstairs bedroom, a European carved settee and a leather wing chair in one upstairs room, and a dresser from Saratoga's old Grand Union Hotel in another. Most bedrooms have Tiffany lamps, Persian carpets, and silver dresser sets.

Because his guests' ease is paramount, Ken favors comfortable, contemporary, white-leather couches rather than Victorian chairs in the parlor, where in the afternoons visitors often gather for tea or brandy. It doesn't matter that the couches are not antiques: They blend in perfectly because Ken's taste is impeccable.

He is no less knowledgeable when it comes to food. Only the freshest ingredients, mostly homegrown, go into the breakfasts he serves: The eggs come from Maple Ridge hens, and preserves are made from fruit nurtured on the property. On summer afternoons guests relishing the view from the porch might be treated to homemade cakes or pies along with their iced tea.

The Cambridge area offers abundant antiques shops and auctions. In the fall, tours to view the foliage are popular; summer draws guests to the attractions of nearby Saratoga. But most visitors to Maple Ridge like to "set and stay awhile." It's that kind of place, run by that kind of host (and it may be the only country inn to have been featured on *Life Styles of the Rich and Famous*).

Address: *Rte. 372 (RD 1, Box 391 C), Cambridge, NY 12816, tel. 518/677-3674.*
Accommodations: *4 double rooms with baths, 1 suite.*
Amenities: *Air-conditioning, cable TV and phones in rooms; antiques shop in Carriage House, airport and New York City limousine service arranged.*
Rates: *$175–$250; Continental breakfast. No credit cards.*
Restrictions: *No smoking indoors, pets permitted with prior arrangement, 2-night minimum in Aug. and Oct.*

The Sedgwick Inn

The Sedgwick Inn, a rambling New England farmhouse with Victorian additions, was built in 1791 as a stagecoach stop. It sits on 12 verdant acres at the foot of the Berkshires, in Berlin; it was once a favorite getaway of New York politicos and their cronies and later became a popular tavern. It is said that Cole Porter once performed here. Today the inn combines all three of its earlier incarnations: It's a way station, where vacationers and second-home owners stop to refresh themselves on their journeys to points north; New York City residents come to get away from it all; and the inn's renowned restaurant (with live piano music on Friday and Saturday nights) draws visitors and locals alike.

Another major draw is innkeeper Edie Evans. Twelve years ago she bought the then-defunct inn—she had been a psychiatric social worker—and spent a year restoring it. You can sense her presence throughout the establishment, from her original sculptures in the living room to her blueberry muffins at breakfast.

If the bedrooms could talk they might say, "Lincoln could have slept here." Of course, there's no record that the 16th president ever did pass through Berlin, but if he had he might have felt right at home in Room 9, with its four-poster bed and Oriental rug; and he probably would have been delighted with the king-size bed in Room 7 and the book-lined shelves in Room 11.

Edie is particularly proud of her restaurant. It's not just the food and drink that soothe the soul here but also the innkeeper's attitude: "We only have one sitting a night for each table," she notes. "We don't want our guests to feel rushed."

Behind the inn there's a six-unit motel annex. The rooms there, decorated with Cushman Colonial furnishings, are less expensive than those in the main house. Edie has transformed an old carriage house behind the inn into a gift shop; there you can find antiques, crafts, and one-of-a-kind items.

Address: *Rte. 22, Berlin, NY 12022, tel. 518/658-2334.*
Accommodations: *10 double rooms with baths, 1 suite.*
Amenities: *Restaurant, TV with VCR in some rooms, room service; gift and gourmet shops.*
Rates: *$65–$100; full breakfast. AE, D, DC, MC, V.*
Restrictions: *Smoking in motel only, pets in motel with advance arrangements, 2-night minimum on holiday weekends.*

Chestnut Tree Inn

This 1860 Empire-style bed-and-breakfast on a side street near the center of Saratoga Springs, in easy walking distance of Broadway, Congress Park, and the track, has a somewhat colorful history: It was a notorious flophouse. Bruce DeLuke, a retired firefighter, and his wife, Cathleen, both antiques dealers, have turned the place into an alluring, romantic retreat. Wicker furnishings, cabbage roses, and old-lace decor prevail, and the exterior color scheme of pink, mauve, and gray is repeated in the bedrooms and common areas.

The inn offers a first-floor double room, with an antique brass-and-iron bed and pink Victorian lamp (which imparts an appropriate rosy glow). There is a tiny but charming bunga-low in the back yard, which has a loft bed for children. The atmosphere here is easy and undemanding. Guests are free to mingle or not, and breakfast is laid out on a leisurely basis; you can serve yourself anytime of the morning.

Address: *9 Whitney Pl., Saratoga Springs, NY 12866, tel. 518/587–8681.*
Accommodations: *8 double rooms with baths, 2 doubles share 1 bath.*
Amenities: *Cable TV in parlor; off-street parking.*
Rates: *$55–$200; Continental breakfast. MC, V.*
Restrictions: *No smoking, no pets, 3-night minimum in Aug. and on special-event weekends, closed Nov.–mid-Apr.*

The Gregory House

Guests at this inn set in the center of the small village of Averill Park in Rensselaer County have been known to come down to breakfast in their bath-robes—it's that kind of place. The "old Gregory house" is a local landmark, dating back to the 1830s. The Miller family bought it in 1991. Chris, a graduate of the Culinary Institute of America, applies his New York- and European-honed talents in the kitchen, and Melissa does the baking and acts as the concierge.

The inn's common room, with a beamed cathedral ceiling and fireplace, is furnished with Victorian originals and reproductions. Bedroom decor tends to four-posters, rocking chairs, and Oriental rugs.

Averill Park, a once-bustling resort area, is today a quiet Albany suburb. Seasonal pleasures include sports afforded by the nearby lakes and two major ski areas, Brodie Mountain and Jiminy Peak.

Address: *Rte. 43, Box 401, Averill Park, NY 12018, tel. 518/674–3774 or in NY 800/303–3774, fax 518/674–2977.*
Accommodations: *12 double rooms with baths.*
Amenities: *Restaurant, air-conditioning, phones in rooms, cable TV in common room; swimming pool.*
Rates: *$60–$75; Continental breakfast. AE, DC, MC, V.*
Restrictions: *No pets.*

The Inn at Saratoga

Although the Inn at Saratoga, built about 1880, lacks Victorian charm (in a city that is chock-full of Victoriana), its midtown location is convenient. It also offers amenities not found in the city's small inns and bed-and-breakfasts. Guests who are reluctant to give up such creature comforts as room service and whirlpool baths can be quite comfortable in the inn's ersatz Victorian bedrooms. And they can have their whirlpool baths courtesy of the inn's arrangement with the local YMCA.

All the bedrooms are similarly furnished; the differences lie only in size or color scheme. They feature Victorian-style antiques, stuffed chairs, four-poster beds, and brass lamps. The two honeymoon suites and two minisuites have comfortable seating areas. The inn's most attractive features are its Earl Grey dining room and the English garden in the rear of the building, where guests may have breakfast or afternoon tea.

Address: *231 Broadway, Saratoga Springs, NY 12866, tel. 518/583-1890.*
Accommodations: *23 double rooms with baths, 9 single rooms with baths, 6 suites.*
Amenities: *Restaurant, banquet facilities, air-conditioning, cable TV in rooms; use of nearby YMCA pool and whirlpool.*
Rates: *$65-$320; Continental breakfast. AE, D, DC, MC, V.*
Restrictions: *No pets, 2-night minimum in Aug., 3-night minimum on the Traver's Stakes weekend.*

The Inn on Bacon Hill

The Inn on Bacon Hill is on Wall Street, just a few minutes' drive from downtown Saratoga Springs. But the street bears no resemblance whatsoever to the *other* Wall Street—this one runs through some of the state's lushest farmland. The Italianate Victorian farmhouse, built in 1862, retains its original garden, carefully restored (along with the house) by Andrea Collins-Breslin and her mother, Millie.

Andrea, a former specialist in employee relations and education, left the corporate world to spend more time with Millie and to get involved in a more "people-oriented" job. She's an ideal hostess—sensitive to her guests' needs without infringing on their privacy. A golden retriever, Vicki, serves as greeter.

The congenial and homey inn has rooms furnished with antique cannonball, four-poster, or Jenny Lind beds. The downstairs suite features a Victorian parlor with a baby grand piano. Outside you'll find a flower garden, a gazebo, and a view of the Green Mountains of Vermont. The setting, the house, the hostess—all combine to make the Inn on Bacon Hill a lovely getaway.

Address: *200 Wall St., Schuylerville, NY 12871, tel. 518/695-3693.*
Accommodations: *2 double rooms with baths, 2 doubles share 1 bath.*
Amenities: *Air-conditioning.*
Rates: *$65-$135; full breakfast. MC, V.*
Restrictions: *No smoking, no pets, 2-night minimum on Aug. weekends.*

Mansion Hill Inn

Albany's only downtown inn, Mansion Hill, stands around the corner from the governor's mansion and occupies several adjacent restored Victorian-era buildings, one of which was once the neighborhood saloon. Owners Maryellen and Steve Stofelano (she's a bank vice-president and he once taught high school) bought the buildings in 1984 and finished their first renovation project the following year. Steve calls their place "an oasis in a downtown residential neighborhood." The inn's attractive restaurant soon became the neighborhood's hub—and Steve its unofficial mayor.

Accommodations range from double rooms with queen-size beds to two huge suites—each with a living room, den, full kitchen, bedroom, bath, and balcony. Furnishings are undistinguished but comfortable, and the carpeted halls and stairways are cozy underfoot. Those who wish to explore Albany will find the State Capitol, the Empire State Plaza, and numerous historic sights easily accessible.

Address: *115 Philip St., Albany, NY 12202, tel. 518/465-2038.*
Accommodations: *14 double rooms with baths, 5 suites.*
Amenities: *Restaurant, air-conditioning, cable TV in rooms, 1 room disabled-accessible.*
Rates: *$95-$145; full breakfast. AE, D, DC, MC, V.*

Mill House Inn

On 1972 Frank and Romana Tallet bought an "old, falling-down" sawmill in Stephentown that was considered so hazardous it was about to be demolished. After a year of extensive renovation it was reincarnated as Mill House Inn, a place as warm and inviting as a mug of hot cider on a brisk fall day. The Tallets, who moved to the country for a simpler life, pride themselves on the number of guests who return year after year to enjoy the inn's hospitality.

Rough-hewn paneling and heavy beams are found throughout the inn. The piano and crackling fire in the common room are comforting during ski season, the time when the inn is probably at its best (Jiminy Peak and Brodie Mountain ski areas are just 2 and 3 miles away), and two of the suites have fireplaces. In summer, the swimming pool becomes a gathering place. The Red Suite was named after its onetime occupant Lucille Ball. And the windows in the bilevel Stargazing Suite are positioned so that you can lie in bed at night and . . . need we say more?

Address: *Rte. 43, Stephentown, NY 12168, tel. 518/733-5606.*
Accommodations: *7 double rooms with baths, 5 suites.*
Amenities: *Air-conditioning; swimming pool.*
Rates: *$80-$145; Continental breakfast, afternoon tea. AE, MC, V.*
Restrictions: *No smoking, no pets, 2-night minimum July and Aug. weekends.*

Saratoga Bed and Breakfast

Amid the new wave of bed-and-breakfasts in the town, Saratoga Bed and Breakfast is a pioneer—it's been eight years since Kathleen and Noel Smith opened their 1860 Victorian home to guests. The operation is a family affair—even Bates Motel, the dog, gets into the act: He's the official welcoming committee. The rooms are charming, more farmhouse-country than high Victorian, as befits a house on the outskirts of the city that boasts "the very last address" in Saratoga proper. They are named for the city's gracious old hotels. Handmade, signed quilts adorn the antique beds. The largest room, Union Hall, offers a carved-oak bed, wicker furnishings, and a view of pine trees from every window.

Noel is a former restaurateur, and his full Irish breakfasts are the high point of a stay here. If you can move after breakfast, Kathleen, an amiable ambassador for her native city, will set up an itinerary.

Address: *Church St., Saratoga Springs, NY 12866, tel. 518/584–0920.*
Accommodations: *8 double rooms with baths.*
Amenities: *Air-conditioning, cable TV in common room.*
Rates: *$65–$195; full breakfast. AE, MC, V.*
Restrictions: *Smoking only in sitting room, no pets, 2-night minimum on Aug. weekends.*

The Six Sisters

On busy Union Avenue, just across the street from Saratoga's thoroughbred racetrack, stands this unique Victorian home with a scallop-edge roof and basket-weave porches. Owned by Kate Benton and Steve Ramirez, the inn is named in honor of Kate and her five sisters. Kate is a former high school guidance counselor from a native Saratoga family of 12, but the name Six Sisters and Six Brothers was a bit unwieldy. She attended college in Hawaii ("If you had 11 siblings, wouldn't you want to get as far away as possible?"), where she met Steve.

One of the most inviting of the guest rooms is furnished in tropical style, with wicker chairs, a king-size brass-and-iron bed, and some of

Steve's evocative photos of Hawaii on the wall. Steve is a terrific cook, so breakfast—which includes what may be the best corn bread north of the Mason-Dixon Line and delightful conversation with the hosts—is a real drawing card.

Address: *149 Union Ave., Saratoga Springs, NY 12866, tel. 518/583–1173.*
Accommodations: *3 double rooms with baths, 1 suite.*
Amenities: *Air-conditioning, refrigerators in rooms, TV in parlor.*
Rates: *$60–$215; full breakfast. No credit cards.*
Restrictions: *No smoking, no pets, 2-night minimum on weekends Apr.–Nov., 5-night minimum in Aug.*

The Westchester House

This Queen Anne Victorian structure was built in 1885 by a master carpenter in Saratoga to house his own family. The elaborately carved fireplaces, fluted columns, handcrafted chestnut moldings, and other details make this bed-and-breakfast especially impressive. Innkeepers Stephanie and Bob Melvin furnished the house with antiques and works of art, but there is no air of the museum here. The Melvins—he worked in government and she sang opera in Washington, DC (you may be able to convince her to sing an aria)—are outgoing and are happy to converse on subjects ranging from the Eastlake influence on their house to the culture and history of their adopted city.

The guest rooms are tastefully furnished with such antique treasures as Louis XVI bedroom sets, oak washstands, Empire chests, and an art-nouveau cheval mirror. The hosts point out that the Victorians were the most eclectic of collectors and believe that they and the Westchester House "embody the true Victorian spirit."

Address: *102 Lincoln Ave. (Box 944), Saratoga Springs, NY 12866, tel. 518/587-7613.*
Accommodations: *7 double rooms with baths.*
Amenities: *Air-conditioning.*
Rates: *$70–$200; Continental-plus breakfast. AE, MC, V.*
Restrictions: *Smoking on porch only, no pets, 4-night minimum in Aug., closed Jan.*

The Catskills

*The Catskills are the stuff of legends both old and new.
Several hundred years ago, Washington Irving's Rip Van
Winkle took a 20-year nap in these mountains. In more
modern times, such popular performers as Milton Berle,
Eddie Fisher, Sid Caesar, and Jackie Mason got their starts
at Catskills resorts.*

*The region's tradition of hospitality and fine dining dates
back about 100 years. Originally the area attracted
a number of wealthy New Yorkers who built their summer
residences here, but it wasn't until such resorts as
Grossinger's and the Nevele arrived on the scene, during
the 1920s, that the Catskills became known across the
country. Famous for the prodigious amounts of food they
served, these establishments once catered to a primarily
Jewish clientele, but today the major resorts attract a more
diverse group of vacationers.*

*The Catskills still have their ethnic enclaves—East Durham
and Leeds draw a great number of Irish-Americans, Round
Top and Purling reflect a German influence, Haines Falls
and Tannersville promote a number of Italian attractions,
and a Ukrainian festival is held each year near Lexington
and Jewett. The mountains everywhere, however, are the
main lure for those who want a country vacation just
a few hours' drive from Manhattan.*

*The area offers a variety of outdoor and seasonal
pleasures, not the least of which is the region's natural
beauty, which can be enjoyed whether you're fishing from
one of the many Catskills lakes or streams or sitting on
a front porch with a mountain view. Golfers have a choice
of more than 40 courses. Alpine skiers can schuss down
various slopes, including Belleayre Mountain, Big Vanilla
at Davos, Bobcat, Cortina Valley, Deer Run, Holiday
Mountain, Hunter Mountain, and Ski Windham. Miles of*

pristine cross-country ski trails are also accessible, both at a number of the larger resorts and at Eldred Preserve, Frost Valley, Hyer Meadows, and White Birches.

The Catskills attract a good number of anglers because the waters here teem with fish. One of the most famous trout-fishing streams in the United States—the Beaverkill—lies in the southern part of the area. Mountain-climbing enthusiasts find some of the East Coast's most challenging treks among the Catskill speaks. In addition, biking and hiking trails are plentiful.

Antiques, art, and craft's aficionados continue to find treasures in small towns and along back roads. The Woodstock Art Colony is noted for its galleries, boutiques, and restaurants. It was not, however, the location of the major celebration of the 1960s peace-and-love generation—that landmark cultural event occurred in a field on Max Yasgur's farm, in Bethel, about 45 minutes from Woodstock.

Places to Go, Sights to See

Bronck Museum (Coxsackie, tel. 518/731–8862). Listed on the National Register of Historic Places, this complex of Dutch Colonial houses (one dating to 1663) and 19th-century barns has been a working farm for eight generations of the Bronck family. Exhibits include 18th- and 19th-century furnishings and art.

Catskill Game Farm (Catskill, tel. 518/678–9595). Rare and exotic animals from around the world can be seen here, and children will be well entertained at the petting zoo. Kids (the two-legged kind) bottle-feeding kids (the four-legged kind) makes for interesting photos.

Hunter Mountain Festivals (Hunter Mountain, tel. 518/263–3800). Each summer this ski area hosts major ethnic and music festivals, attracting visitors from all over the country. Events include the Game Fair and World Sporting Exposition; the German Alps Festival, with oompah bands and a Hummel-figurine look-alike contest; two country music festivals; the Celtic Festival; and the Mountain Eagle Indian Festival, which draws 400 tribes from throughout North America.

Opus 40 and **Quarryman's Museum** (Saugerties, tel. 914/246–3400). Professor Harvey Fite spent 37 years creating this 6½-acre sculpture garden—ramps, terraces, fountains, and a monolith—in an abandoned quarry. Sunset concerts are given in the summer.

Tubing the Esopus (Phoenicia). A 5-mile stretch of theEsopus Creek, between Shandaken and Mt. Pleasant, is the place to be on hot summer days in the Catskills. Visitors enjoy taking an inner tube to drift with the current and ride the rapids. The **Town Tinker** (Bridge St., tel. 914/688–5553) rents tubes and will show you how and where to tube; it offers beginner and advanced courses.

Restaurants

Rudi's Big Indian (Big Indian, tel. 914/254–4005) started in the '60s as a vegetarian-sandwich shop and has evolved into a hip, moderately priced Continental-cuisine restaurant. Fine northern Italian and Yugoslavian dishes are featured at **La Griglia** (Windham, tel. 518/734–4499). **La Grillade** (Glenford, tel. 914/657–8630) is a charming French country restaurant.

Tourist Information

Delaware County Chamber of Commerce (97 Main St., Delhi 13753, tel. 607/746–2281). **Greene County Promotion Department** (Box 527, Catskill 12414, tel. 518/943–3223; outside NY, 800/542–2414). **Sullivan County Office of Public Information** (100 North St., Box 5012, Monticello 12701, tel. 914/794–3000, ext. 5010; outside NY, 800/343–INFO; in NY, 800/882–2287). **Ulster County Public Information Office** (Box 1800, Kingston 12401, tel. 914/331–9300; outside NY, 800/342–5826).

Beaverkill Valley Inn

have laid aside business, and gone a-fishing," wrote Izaak Walton in *The Compleat Angler;* Walton would probably have loved the Beaverkill, America's most famous fly-fishing stream. Although the Beaverkill Valley Inn, built in 1893 as a boardinghouse at Lew Beach, never played host to Walton, Jimmy Carter, Robert Redford, Sigourney Weaver, Gary Trudeau, Jane Pauley, and assorted Kennedys have all been guests here. Owned and developed by Laurance Rockefeller and managed by able innkeeper Christine Dennis, the inn caters to those who cherish privacy. Its surrounding forests and nearby fields, preserved as "forever wild," are protected from development.

This is not to say that accommodations are rustic—not by a long shot. A comfortable, old-money look enhances the place. White-painted rocking chairs line the wide porch, a welcoming fire warms the living room on frosty days, and the dining-room windows offer a panoramic view of the grounds. The card and billiard rooms, with their green-shade lamps, have a clubby, masculine atmosphere; they call to mind an era when men took leave of their female companions to enjoy their after dinner brandy and cigars.

The fare that precedes that postprandial brandy is sumptuous, with such offerings as poached Norwegian salmon with watercress sauce, and fillet of beef with blue-cheese sauce. All baked goods are made on the premises, and the inn uses homegrown herbs and salad greens.

Guest rooms are simply furnished with brass-and-iron beds, comfortable chairs, handmade quilts, and good reading lamps. Many of the rooms have twin beds.

Although fishing is the main draw here (the inn has a package arrangement with the Wulff Fly Fishing School nearby), it's certainly not the only attraction. A converted barn with a cathedral ceiling houses a heated swimming pool, a help-yourself ice-cream parlor, a theater, and a children's playroom. Sports enthusiasts also have access to tennis courts, hiking, and cross-country ski trails, and skating in winter.

Address: *Lew Beach, NY 12753, tel. 914/439-4844.*
Accommodations: *11 double rooms with baths, 9 doubles share 5 baths.*
Amenities: *Restaurant, bar, conference facilities, games rooms, 1 room disabled-accessible; stocked pond; Beaverkill fishing.*
Rates: *$280–$330; breakfast, lunch, afternoon tea, dinner. AE, MC, V.*
Restrictions: *Smoking in card room and on porch only, no pets, 2-night minimum stay on weekends, 3-night minimum on holiday weekends.*

Captain Schoonmaker's Bed-and-Breakfast

Y ou'll find it easy to lose yourself in the past at this meticulously restored 1760 Hudson Valley stone house. Americana is everywhere. The place at High Falls even claims its own Early American ghost, Captain Fred. The hosts, Sam and Julia Krieg, also very friendly, are quite knowledgeable about local history. Julia teaches third grade, and Sam is a biology professor at the State University of New York (the stuffed golden eagle on the landing once presided over his classroom).

Captain Schoonmaker's is, actually, four different places: the stone house, with four bedrooms (one with a fireplace), a living room, dining room, library, solarium, and canopied decks; the 1840 Towpath House, a half mile from the main house; Krum House, an 1876 Victorian in town; and the 1820 Carriage House, in front of the main house.

In the days when mules towed barges through New York State's canals, the Towpath House was the home of the lock tender for the Delaware and Hudson Canal. Guest rooms here (one with a fireplace) have four-poster, cannonball, or Victorian beds; pine cupboards; blanket chests; and wing chairs.

The Krum House has two large rooms with private baths. The Carriage House rooms, the most sought-after and romantic, overlook a trout stream with a private waterfall. The two upstairs were once a hayloft, and the original beams have been left exposed. One downstairs room has a brass bed and a tree growing through the middle of a private deck. A Lone Star quilt covers the canopy bed in the other.

Probably only the Kriegs' famous breakfasts could tear guests away from their waterfall rooms—it's hard to ignore seven courses of such culinary delights as lemon poppy-seed cake, cheese soufflé, and blueberry strudel. Guests breakfast at an antique black-walnut table by the dining-room fireplace. Against the wall stands an antique printer's cabinet. The livingroom has another fireplace and an Early American cupboard used to display quilts and coverlets. Nearby is the De Puy Canal House, a highly touted restaurant with an international menu.

Address: *Rte. 213 W, (RD 2, Box 37), High Falls, NY 12440, tel. 914/687-7946.*
Accommodations: *2 double rooms with baths, 10 doubles share 5 baths.*
Amenities: *Cable TV in library-den; swimming and trout fishing in stream.*
Rates: *$75–$85; full breakfast. No credit cards.*
Restrictions: *No pets, 2-night minimum on weekends mid-Sept.–Thanksgiving, closed Christmas week.*

The Redcoat's Return

Up a twisting mountain road in the Catskill Game Preserve, you'll encounter a little bit of the spirit of England at the Redcoat's Return. Once the center of a potato-and-dairy farm, the 1860 home at Elka Park was later a summer boardinghouse. Now this lodging is known in the area for its Saturday-night prime rib and Yorkshire pudding and for its English country hospitality.

Tom (the Redcoat) and Peg Wright have owned the inn since 1973; he was once a chef on the *Queen Mary* and she was an actress. The inn features extensive art and antiques collections that bring together mementos of trips abroad—and there's a moose head, named Basil, over the fireplace. Tom, who has a quirky sense of humor, says that he plays golf in his spare time and that "Peg is interested in metaphysics." Both are practiced conversationalists. Tom is full of stories about his objets d'art, which include a cricket bat and a framed antique scarf commemorating the first boxing match between an Englishman and an American, in 1860. Winston and Zoe, the Wrights' Bernese mountain dogs, can also be charming hosts.

The Wrights have chosen to preserve the atmosphere of the old boarding house, so rooms are small but pleasantly cozy. All the mattresses are new, but the antique iron beds and oak dressers are part of the original decor. Third-floor bedrooms have eaved ceilings, and one large room offers two double beds. The eight guest rooms that share four baths are all supplied with bathrobes for guests.

Hikers should enjoy the numerous trails that lead from the inn onto nearby Overlook, Indian Head, Twin, and Hunter mountains. There are cross-country trails and three alpine ski areas close by. Spring anglers have access to a trout stream on the property, and golfers will find several fine courses a short drive away.

Antiques shops and galleries are available for the less athletic, and for those who really want to sit and do nothing it's hard to beat the view from the inn's porch. It's also hard not to gain weight after sampling Tom's chocolate mousse, English-sherry trifle, and apple pie à la mode.

Address: *Platte Cove (Dale La.), Elka Park, NY 12427, tel. 518/589–6379 or 518/589–9895.*
Accommodations: *6 double rooms with baths, 8 doubles share 4 baths.*
Amenities: *Restaurant.*
Rates: *$70–$95; full breakfast. AE, MC, V.*
Restrictions: *No pets, 2-night minimum on Feb. and Oct. weekends; 3-night minimum on holiday weekends, closed Apr. 1–Memorial Day.*

Albergo Allegria

his gingerbread Victorian mansion in the northern Catskills—midway between Ski Windham and the White Birches cross-country trails—was originally two cottages that were part of a 19th-century summer boardinghouse colony. Owners Lenore and Vito Radelich had the two structures joined in 1985: The new middle section is indistinguishable from those sections built in 1867.

The bed-and-breakfast is noted for its stunning oak floors, original chestnut moldings, and keyhole windows. Guest rooms take their names from the seasons and months of the year: June has a stained-glass window, a cathedral ceiling, and a terrific view of Ski Windham; and Summer, the honeymoon suite, of-fers a king-size bed, a skylight, and a double whirlpool bath. The high quality of the food reflects the Radeliches' 25 years in the restaurant business. And if you're wondering whether the swimming hole by the waterfall out back is deep enough for diving—it was back when Johnny Weissmuller filmed his first *Tarzan* movie there.

Address: *Rte. 296, Windham, NY 12496, tel. 518/734-5560.*
Accommodations: *15 double rooms with baths, 1 suite.*
Amenities: *TV in rooms; swimming hole.*
Rates: *$45–$175; full breakfast. MC, V.*
Restrictions: *No smoking in public areas, no pets, 2-night minimum on weekends.*

Deer Mountain Inn

f Deer Mountain Inn in Tannersville resembles a lodge designed for European nobility, it's no accident. Owner Danielle Gortel and her husband come from the mountains of Poland: It was only natural that these two avid skiers settle in Catskills ski country and that they keep an inn that resembles Spala, the ancient hunting seat of Polish kings.

Built as a private residence, the circa-1900 mansion stands in a 15-acre wooded enclave. This place is lushly packed with mountain ambience—moose heads, boar heads, bearskin rugs, paintings of European mountain villages, and heavy, overstuffed furniture. It is said that the house was once owned by the notorious gangster Legs Diamond.

Today the focus of the gracious cherry-paneled living room is a huge stone fireplace. In winter an après-ski snack of cheese, sausages, and wine is served by a bone-warming fire. The inn has a bright, airy breakfast room, and glass doors lead to the deck, a romantic spot for a summer evening. Some guest rooms have fireplaces, pine wainscoting, and diamond-pane windows.

Address: *Rte. 25 (Box 443), Tannersville, NY 12485, tel. 518/589-6268.*
Accommodations: *7 double rooms with baths or showers.*
Amenities: *Restaurant.*
Rates: *$95–$135; full breakfast. AE, MC, V.*
Restrictions: *Smoking in public areas only, no pets.*

The Eggery

I n this 1901 farmhouse a chess set sits on an antique game table standing by a picture window that overlooks a leafy bower. A player piano waits nearby, and in winter a cheery fire welcomes guests to the relaxed bed-and-breakfast, at a 2,200-foot elevation near the small town of Tannersville. The Dutch Colonial farmstead became a tourist house in 1935 and continued as such until the late 1970s. In 1979 Abe and Julie Abramczyk—a former hospital administrator and a registered nurse, both avid skiers—opened the Eggery, so named because of the property's earlier incarnation. Julie is a friendly host who loves to chat with her guests.

Oak predominates in the common areas—there are Mission Oak chairs in the living room, a handcrafted bar in the dining room, and a stunning balustrade leading upstairs. Guest rooms are simply furnished, with antique beds, many of them made of brass. The wrap-around porch is a peaceful spot for contemplating the seasonal pleasures of the Catskills rising 4,100 feet nearby.

Address: *County Rd. 16, Tannersville, NY 12485, tel. 518/589–5363.*
Accommodations: *13 double rooms with baths, 1 suite.*
Amenities: *Cable TV in rooms.*
Rates: *$75–$95, suite price on request; full breakfast. AE, MC, V.*
Restrictions: *No pets, 3-night minimum on holiday weekends, 2-night minimum on other weekends.*

Greenville Arms

S tart with a turreted 1889 Queen Anne Victorian (built by William Vanderbilt as a private residence) on a tree-lined street in the center of the small town of Greenville. Add columned porches with the obligatory wicker rockers and gliders, croquet on the lawn, a brook, a carriage house, an intimate restaurant, and admirable antiques, and you have the Greenville Arms.

This delightful property features a swimming pool, a lit shuffleboard court, two playgrounds on 6 acres, and nearby golf and tennis. It's an activity-filled retreat for families and groups. The inn also offers 14 yearly painting workshops, with distinguished artist-instructors, in the heart of Thomas Cole and Frederick Church country.

Eliot and Tish Dalton are the inn's newest owners. Eliot may be the only innkeeper in the state who was once a tugboat captain. Tish's background in the graphic arts has stood her in good stead in decorating the inn.

Address: *RD 1 (Box 2), Greenville, NY 12083, tel. 518/966–5219.*
Accommodations: *14 double rooms with baths.*
Amenities: *Restaurant, 1 room with air-conditioning; swimming pool.*
Rates: *$75–$125; full breakfast. D, MC, V.*
Restrictions: *Smoking in bedrooms only, no pets, 2-night minimum on holiday weekends.*

Inn at Lake Joseph

This circa-1870 Victorian mansion, once the vacation estate of Cardinals Hayes, Spellman, and Cook, sits on 20 acres of lawn and woods. Surrounded by a 2,000-acre wildlife preserve, it's an ideal countryplace in which to relax, which is exactly why innkeeper Ivan Weinger bought the property.

Ivan, an artist and communications consultant, is in his element presiding over elegant dinners (such as pheasant stuffed with pheasant mousse) either on the screen porch or in the Victorian dining room. After dinner, guests may play a game of billiards or choose from a collection of 80 videotapes.

Guest rooms have Victorian-style wallpaper and antique furnishings; three rooms have fireplaces, and four have Jacuzzis. The carriage house, with a beamed ceiling, kitchen, and two bedrooms, is suitable for a family. The private lake here is said to have the best bass fishing in the state. Miles of cross-country ski trails span the property, and equipment is available for rent.

Address: *400 Saint Joseph's Rd., Forestburg, NY 12777, tel. 914/791–9506.*
Accommodations: *8 double rooms with baths.*
Amenities: *Restaurant; swimming pool, lake.*
Rates: *$118–$218; breakfast, afternoon tea, dinner. AE, MC, V.*
Restrictions: *No smoking in dining room, no pets, 2-night minimum on weekends.*

Lanza's

When asked what a retired Navy man is doing running an inn in the landlocked southern Catskills, Dick Lanza counters with the story of the boatswain who carried an anchor on his shoulders. When asked why, he dropped the anchor and stated: "This is where I'll stay." The 1905 farmhouse in Livingston Manor has been a boardinghouse, a hotel, and even a bowling alley.

Lanza's sits in the heart of Sullivan County's trout haven, and anglers fly-fish on the nearby Beaverkill and Willowmec rivers. The property consists of 7 acres, complete with a beaver pond and herb and flower gardens. Guests may breakfast in the greenhouse dining room, surrounded by native pine and a variety of plants. A downstairs tap room has a fireplace, TV, and game machines, and pizza is served there. Guest rooms have recently been refurbished with antiques from various periods. One room features an art deco–style bedroom set, and another has a high-back Victorian oak bed and an oak dresser (the same one advertised for $5.95 from the 1905 Sears Roebuck catalog).

Address: *RD 2 (Box 446), Livingston Manor, NY 12758, tel. 914/439–5070.*
Accommodations: *8 double rooms with baths.*
Amenities: *Restaurant, tap room.*
Rates: *$72–$84; full breakfast. AE, D, DC, MC, V.*
Restrictions: *No pets, 2-night minimum on holiday weekends.*

Point Lookout Mountain Inn

On a clear day, you can see the mountain ranges of five states from Point Lookout Mountain Inn. The Victorian-style bed-and-breakfast lies on the Mohican Trail at a stagecoach stop. The first Point Lookout tower, built as a tourist attraction, was used during World War II for spotting enemy aircraft. It was destroyed by fire in 1965, when the present structure was built.

In 1980 schoolteachers Rosemary Jensen, Mariana Di Toro, and her brother Lucio Di Toro bought what was then an abandoned discothèque, and the inn is once again a travelers' haven. The quiet rooms are tastefully decorated in low-key mountain style in desert tones. The best colors, however, are provided by spectacular sunrises, sunsets, fall foliage, and rainbows, which come free at Point Lookout. The inn's health-oriented restaurant combines a variety of cuisines, including Italian and Mexican. Guests can raid the refrigerator and choose from breakfast goodies left on the table.

Address: *Rte. 23, (Box 33), East Windham, NY 12439, tel. 518/734–3381.*
Accommodations: *13 double rooms with baths.*
Amenities: *Restaurant, TV in rooms.*
Rates: *$65–$125; Continental breakfast. AE, DC, MC, V.*
Restrictions: *Pets permitted with deposit, 2-night minimum on winter weekends.*

Scribner Hollow Motor Lodge

If your idea of the perfect inn involves flocked Victorian wallpaper and museum-quality antiques, then you'll hate Scribner Hollow. This Catskills ski lodge at the edge of Hunter Mountain is very much a product of the 1960s, when it was built, and the '70s, when it expanded. The decor is haute Jetsons, with wall-to-wall carpeting that sometimes continues up the wall, world-of-tomorrow furniture, and, here and there, mirrored paneling or even mirrored canopy beds. The basement holds a campy "grotto" done up to look like a cave pool, replete with a hot tub, sauna, and bar.

The staff is winningly warm, standard rooms are roomy (although the bathrooms aren't), and suites can sleep an entire family if privacy isn't an issue. The pricey tab includes a big breakfast and dinner.

Address: *Rte. 23–A, Hunter, NY 12442, tel. 518/263–4211 or 800/395–4683, fax 518/263–5266.*
Accommodations: *28 double rooms with baths, 10 suites, 26 condos.*
Amenities: *Restaurant, fireplaces in 22 rooms, air-conditioning, conference facilities; indoor and outdoor pools, tennis.*
Rates: *$160–$350; full breakfast, dinner. Condos (without meals) $200–$350. AE, D, MC, V.*
Restrictions: *No pets, 2-night minimum on weekends during winter and summer high season, 3-night minimum on holiday weekends.*

The Hudson River Valley

Few of America's waterways can compete with the Hudson River's combination of majestic grace and history. From the earliest explorations of the continent, in the 17th century, through the Revolutionary War, this 315-mile-long river has played an important part in the development of the nation.

Long a major thoroughfare of commerce, the Hudson was home to the first commercial steam-power boat, Fulton's Clermont; *several years later the opening of the Erie Canal clinched the river's claim as the nation's most important waterway; and in the mid-1800s the river port of Hudson even became a center of the whaling industry.*

The natural beauty of the river has attracted many prominent artists and writers. In the 19th century the Hudson River School of painters was formed, inspired by the noble river and by the works of Washington Irving, one of the first American writers to be recognized abroad. As we retreat up the Hudson from where it empties into the Atlantic Ocean at Manhattan, we behold the same beautiful vistas—the majestic hills and splendid palisades—that inspired those 19th-century artists. Many old river towns, such as Tarrytown, Cold Spring, and Hudson, retain the atmosphere of the distant past, and some have even been restored to their 19th-century glory.

The valley merits careful exploration by the traveler. The largely unspoiled countryside includes prosperous farms and splendid estates once inhabited by some of America's most distinguished families: the Roosevelts, Vanderbilts, Harrimans, and Rockefellers. In addition to visiting those palatial estates, visitors can explore numerous historical sites, such as Philipsburg Manor (the residence of a 17th-century Dutch shipping magnate), Sunnyside (home of Washington Irving), Stony Point Battlefield, and

Washington's Headquarters in Newburgh. Also, the valley is home to some of the nation's most prestigious institutes of higher learning: the U.S. Military Academy at West Point, Vassar College, Sarah Lawrence College, and Bard College. The Culinary Institute of America, which has schooled many prominent chefs, is in the area.

Travelers can reach the Hudson and its valley both on Hudson River cruises and on Amtrak. Driving through the valley, however, gives explorers more freedom to visit historic places and pursue antiquing, hiking, fishing, sailing, and hot-air ballooning as the mood strikes.

The valley's seasonal pleasures include cross-country skiing in state parks in winter, strolls through historic gardens in spring, summer picnics on river bluffs, and leaf watching and apple picking in fall. The many valley orchards make the region one of the country's chief apple producers: A perfect excursion could include a picnic in one of the area's pick-your-own orchards—with dessert right off the tree, of course. The Hudson Valley's vineyards are also starting to build a worldwide reputation, and many can be visited.

Places to Go, Sights to See

The Culinary Institute of America (Hyde Park, tel. 914/471–6608). Many of this country's leading chefs received their training at CIA, which was founded in New Haven in 1946. In 1972 the school moved to its present site, a former Jesuit seminary at Hyde Park, overlooking the Hudson River. More than 4,000 meals are prepared here every day, and visitors may dine at any of the institute's four restaurants: the award-winning American Bounty, the Escoffier, St. Andrew's Café, and the Caterina de Medici Dining Room. Reservations are required, and jackets are suggested for men.

Franklin Delano Roosevelt National Historic Site (Hyde Park, tel. 914/229–9115 for tour information). The Roosevelt family estate, retreat of our 32nd president, is in Hyde Park. Here visitors will find the setting of some of Roosevelt's "fireside chats," as well as many of his personal effects, including his wheelchair and books. The graves of the president and his wife, Eleanor, are in the Rose Garden, next to the house. The FDR Library and Museum are also on the grounds.

Hudson Valley Wineries. There are a number of notable wineries on both sides of the river. Most are open to the public—some by appointment—and offer tours, tastings, and restaurants. Among them are *Cascade Mountain Vineyards*, on Flinthill Road in Amenia (tel. 914/373–9021); *Millbrook Vineyards*, on Wing and Shunpike roads in Millbrook (tel. 914/677–8383); *Brotherhood* (America's oldest winery), in Washingtonville (tel. 914/496–9101); and *Clinton Vineyards*, in Clinton Corners (tel. 914/266–5372).

Olana State Historic Site (Hudson, tel. 518/828–0135, reservations advised). The home of Hudson River School artist Frederick Edwin Church commands a stunning view of the river. The Persian-style mansion is surrounded by gardens and carriage trails. The house, designed by the artist and built between 1870 and 1891, is shown by guided tour only, April 15 through October 31, but the grounds are open year-round for outdoor pursuits such as walking, running, and cross-country skiing. Olana is outside the city of Hudson, near the Rip Van Winkle Bridge.

The Shaker Museum (Old Chatham, tel. 518/794–9100). This off-the-beaten-track museum houses the largest collection of Shaker artifacts in the United States. More than 40,000 items, from baskets to wagons, are on display in the eight buildings that make up the exhibition. A museum shop featuring reproductions of Shaker furniture and a small restaurant are on the grounds.

The United States Military Academy (tel. 914/938–2638 for tour information). Known simply as West Point, the academy has been the training ground for U.S. Army officers since 1802. The site is also the country's oldest military base in continuous operation. Athletic events (especially the yearly contest between the Army and Navy football teams) draw many visitors to the post. There's also an outstanding military museum.

Restaurants

Painter's Tavern (Cornwall-on-the-Hudson, tel. 914/534–2109) offers an ecletic blackboard menu, with dishes flavored from its own herb garden. In season you can eat your seafood or steak outside and admire the Hudson at **Dockside Harbor** (Cold Spring, tel. 914/265–3503). Fresh breast of duck in cognac sauce is one of the French specialties at **Chez Marcel** (Rhinebeck, tel. 914/876–8189).

Tourist Information

Hudson River Valley Association (42 Catherine St., Poughkeepsie 12601, tel. 914/452–4910 or 800/232–4782).

Reservation Service

American Country Collection (4 Greenwood La., Delmar 12054, tel. 518/439–7001).

Anthony Dobbins Stagecoach Inn

Since 1740, only three families have owned the Anthony Dobbins Stagecoach Inn. The present proprietor, Margo Hickock, takes pleasure in imagining what the original inn—complete with common room and bundling boards—must have been like. In its present incarnation as a bed-and-breakfast, the inn is no doubt a great deal more comfortable than its 18th-century predecessor. It even has an elevator.

The house is charmingly furnished with English antiques, some of which are family heirlooms."Nothing matches, but everything fits," says Margo, a former fashion model who once ran a spa for the Gabor sisters and now guides aspiring young models.

Even the furnishings are steeped in history. Margo's family is descended from both Wild Bill Hickok and William Penn, and the room named for Mr. Penn boasts a bed that belonged to the founder of the Crown Colony of Pennsylvania. (The shaded area on the headboard may very well be where he rested his head.) The Hickok Room has twin canopy beds and an antique love seat, and, with the neighboring Green Room, which has a fireplace, can be made into a double suite. The Blue Room, with flowered wallpaper and Williamsburg-blue trim, features an antique brass bed, fireplace, sun deck, and private bath.

Among the many artful touches are all-cotton sheets; antique lace-trimmed, linen hand towels; and homegrown flowers placed in each room throughout spring and summer. You can breakfast on the terrace by the reflecting pool or in the sunroom by the fountain, with a pink flamingo. A collection of Currier and Ives prints and paintings of horses adorns the inn's spacious entry hall, but for the real thing, visitors need only walk half a block to the race track. Goshen is known as the Cradle of the Trotters, and the harness track here is the nation's oldest. Tennis courts are also a short walk away, and hot-air-balloon rides can be arranged at a nearby airport.

Address: *268 Main St., Goshen, NY 10924, tel. 914/294-5526.*
Accommodations: *2 double rooms with baths, 1 double suite.*
Amenities: *Air-conditioning in 2 rooms, TV in common rooms, fruit and candy in each room.*
Rates: *$85–$130; Continental breakfast, afternoon tea. No credit cards.*
Restrictions: *Smoking in sunroom only, no pets, 2-night minimum on weekends.*

The Inn at Shaker Mill

The Inn at Shaker Mill is an unusual establishment for two reasons: its Shaker decor and its gregarious host, Ingram Paperny.

As befits a converted 1823 Shaker mill, the rooms are simply furnished in a comfortable but utilitarian style. Pegboards hang from the plaster walls, and in the Shaker tradition the common room has a barrel roof—though it also boasts a glass wall that looks out on the mill's picturesque brook and waterfalls.

After 25 years in the business, Mr. Paperny has been called the doyen of New England innkeepers. A stay at the inn is like spending time in the home of a fascinating new friend. As might be expected of a former consultant to the United Nations, Ingram is an internationalist; he speaks four languages and relishes playing host to an eclectic bunch of visitors. During summer he brings European hiking and cultural groups to the United States, acts as their tour leader and host, and encourages them to mix with the American guests at the inn. He is also a woodworker and is responsible for all the carpentry done in the building.

The inn is unique in another way: It charges per person, so singles who want to get away from the city can retreat to a place that doesn't put the emphasis on couples (which isn't to say that a room overlooking the waterfalls wouldn't serve as a romantic retreat for two). Also, several of the rooms are large enough to accommodate families: The stone-wall, wood-beam suites on the third floor can sleep six.

The inn's hospitality extends to meals as well. Breakfasts include juice, fresh fruit, cereals, yogurt, cheese, bagels, muffins, breads, and eggs. Dinners vary with the whim of the chef—one night it might be a West Indian spread, another night, Chinese—and include wine. On Saturday nights in summer there are outdoor barbecues.

Address: *Cherry La., off Rte. 22, Canaan, NY 12029, tel. 518/794–9345, fax 518/794–9344.*
Accommodations: *20 double rooms with baths.*
Amenities: *Restaurant, air-conditioning in some rooms; swimming pond, sauna.*
Rates: *$80–$300; full breakfast. MC, V.*
Restrictions: *No smoking in dining room.*

Le Chambord

Although it is housed in an 1863 Georgian mansion one minute from the Taconic Parkway, Le Chambord could easily be the focal point of an antebellum southern plantation. In fact Scarlett O'Hara would feel right at home on its pillared veranda. The mansion's involvement with things southern is more than skin-deep, however: The trap door under the inn's bar leads to a former stop on the Underground Railroad.

Miss O'Hara was not far from the mind of innkeeper Roy Benich when he named the latest additions to Le Chambord: Tara Hall, containing 16 rooms; and Butler Hall, which has corporate and banquet facilities. Both structures are in keeping with the genteel traditions of the opulent dining and banquet rooms and the nine handsome bedrooms in the main building.

Roy, a former art-and-antiques dealer, has designed Le Chambord for aesthetic appeal and treats it as his home. "It's my wife and children," he says. He lives on the premises and laments that he works up to 19 hours a day on the inn and the restaurant. (You'll know that he's a bachelor as soon as you see him in one of the outrageous neckties for which he is renowned.) He chooses all the art and antiques for the inn, and his taste is impeccable (and nothing like his taste in neckties). Not many dining rooms can boast

a $20,000 antique Chinese breakfront, and not many bedrooms and sitting rooms have sofas and wing chairs covered in imported floral tapestries. For the cost of each of these chairs, "you can furnish two Holiday Inn rooms and have $200 left over," Roy laughs. No expense has been spared in selecting furniture and accessories—or food and wine, for that matter.

The owner's focus on visual delights is shared by his Parisian chef, Henry Benveniste. The two have collaborated on an elegant menu that satisfies both the palate and the eye.

Despite such luxuries, the inn is quite affordable. True, the wine list offers a 1929 Château Lafite Rothschild for $1,500—but there are also good wines in the $15 range.

Address: *2075 Rte. 52, Hopewell Junction, NY 12533, tel. and fax 914/221-1941.*
Accommodations: *25 double rooms with baths.*
Amenities: *Restaurant, air-conditioning, cable TV in rooms; facilities (including fax) for corporate meetings, health club.*
Rates: *$105; Continental breakfast. AE, DC, MC, V.*
Restrictions: *No pets, closed Christmas Day.*

Simmons Way Village Inn

Simmons Way Village Inn, set on a wide expanse of lawn in the middle of Millerton, was built by the village's first merchant in 1854 and was transformed into a handsome country inn in 1983.

Current owners Richard and Nancy Carter (he is a management consultant and educator, she is a bank vice-president) bought Simmons Way in 1987 with the idea of running an inn that combined "European civility and American comfort" and served the best in international cuisine.

There are two common rooms on the first floor, one of which opens onto the inviting front porch, where guests may eat breakfast in the warmer months. The main dining room was added in 1986 but is hard to distinguish from the original structure.

The bedrooms (six on the second floor and three on the third) are furnished with English and European country antiques. Each has its own charm; but Room 5, with its rose-floral wallpaper, queen-size antique iron bed, embroidered bedspread, wicker love seat, and 6-foot French bathtub with hand-held shower, is perhaps the most romantic. Room 2, the Bridal Suite, offers a private covered porch, marble fireplace, and queen-size crown-canopy bed; and Room 4 has peach walls, an English brass canopy bed, swag curtains, and a stripped-pine armoire.

If one can bear to leave these lovely rooms (where breakfast may be taken, if desired) and venture beyond the inviting front porch, the surrounding area is well worth exploring. A swimming pool is 3 miles away, golf courses are close by, and the inn offers special weekday packages that include tickets to the nearby Lime Rock (auto) Race Track—where you might just catch a glimpse of Paul Newman, who frequently races there.

"We strive for a full country-inn ambience," says Richard, "—rooms, spirit, and cuisine." Pink swordfish is a specialty of the highly rated restaurant, and the extensive wine list goes all the way up to a $350 Lafite Rothschild.

Address: *33 Main St., Millerton, NY 12546, tel. 518/789-6235.*
Accommodations: *9 double rooms with baths, 1 suite.*
Amenities: *Restaurant, air-conditioning, banquet facilities, cable TV and phone in common room, complimentary sherry.*
Rates: *$125-$150; full breakfast, afternoon tea or wine. AE, MC, V.*
Restrictions: *Smoking in designated areas only, no pets, 2-night minimum on weekends May 1–Nov. 1, 3-night minimum on holiday weekends.*

Troutbeck

This Tudor-style manor house set amid 442 gracious acres outside the hamlet of Amenia figured prominently in American literary and political history. It was once home to Myron B. Benton, whose circle of friends included Emerson, Thoreau, and John Burroughs. The estate served as a gathering place for the likes of Sinclair Lewis, Teddy Roosevelt, and Lewis Mumford in the early 20th century, and black leaders formed the NAACP under its roof.

Today Troutbeck also serves the movers and shakers of the corporate world as a conference center during the week. On weekends, however, it is transformed into one of the area's most romantic country inns, the vision of genial innkeeper Jim Flaherty and his partner, Bob Skibsted.

Guests lack nothing here. The Troutbeck package includes three gourmet meals a day, an open bar, and access to all sorts of recreational activities, ranging from tennis, swimming (indoor and outdoor), fishing, and cross-country skiing to strolling through walled gardens and watching video movies or major sports events on satellite TV.

Most guest rooms are suitably romantic, although the rooms in the main house seem more so. For the premium prices charged by Troutbeck, guests might prefer a canopied, fireplaced, sun-porched room in the manor house (with its leaded-glass windows, 12,000-book oak-panel library, and comfortable English country appointments) or the Garden House (overlooking the walled gardens) to the Americana offered in the neighboring Century Farmhouse rooms. Of course, guests in any of the buildings have access to all the inn's amenities.

If you can tear yourself away from the estate, the surrounding area is prime antiquing territory, and guests can take elegant prepared picnics with them on excursions. The inn will also transport guests to concerts at Tanglewood, dance performances at Jacob's Pillow, and Shakespeare at the Mount.

Address: *Leedsville Rd. (Box 26), Amenia, NY 12501, tel. 914/373–9681, fax 914/373–7080.*
Accommodations: *29 double rooms with baths, 5 doubles share 3 baths.*
Amenities: *Restaurant, air-conditioning, banquet facilities.*
Rates: *$375–$475; three meals, wines, and spirits. AE.*
Restrictions: *Pipes and cigars not permitted in dining rooms, no pets, closed weekdays for conferences.*

The Bird and Bottle Inn

The Bird and Bottle Inn in Garrison predates the Revolutionary War and was once a way station on the old Albany–New York post road. Today it is a homey but sophisticated country inn and restaurant with a well-deserved international reputation—and it's only an hour from Manhattan. The inn's owner, Ira Boyar, has been in the hospitality industry for more than 25 years, and he applies his expertise to all aspects of the inn, from marketing to menu choices.

All the elegantly Colonial rooms have fireplaces. The Emily Warren Room offers a queen-size canopy bed draped in rose-colored fabric. The John Warren Room boasts the original wainscoting and fireplace, and the suite has a private terrace. The cottage suite, 50 yards from the inn, appeals to couples seeking a secluded getaway. The wooded setting includes Indian Creek, babbling along the back of the inn, and hiking along miles of historic roads.

Address: *Old Albany Post Rd., Rte. 9 (R 2, Box 64), Garrison, NY 10524, tel. 914/424-3000, fax 914/424-3283.*
Accommodations: *2 double rooms with baths, 1 suite, 1 cottage.*
Amenities: *Restaurant, air-conditioning.*
Rates: *$195–$215; breakfast and dinner. AE, DC, MC, V.*
Restrictions: *No pets, 2-night minimum on weekends with Sat. reservation, closed first 2 weeks in Jan.*

Hudson House, A Country Inn

From the foot of Main Street in the charming 19th-century village of Cold Spring, this 1832 inn (the second oldest inn in continuous operation in the state) takes in spectacular views of the Hudson River, West Point, and Storm King Mountain. Visitors here should request a room facing the river.

The entire inn, from the wood-paneled bar and sitting area downstairs to the 15 guest rooms, was renovated in 1981. Many rooms are furnished with old-fashioned painted-iron beds (quite a few have twin beds), and all feature country decor and accessories. River-view rooms on the second floor open onto a wraparound porch. One of the two suites, with twin beds in one room and a double in the other, has just one bathroom and is best suited for a family.

Guests without cars will find the Hudson House an ideal spot for a weekend of antiquing and exploring on foot—the railroad station is just 500 feet from the inn's door.

Address: *2 Main St., Cold Spring, NY 10516, tel. 914/265-9355.*
Accommodations: *11 double rooms with baths, 2 suites.*
Amenities: *Restaurant, air-conditioning.*
Rates: *$70–$200; Continental breakfast midweek, full on weekends. AE, MC, V.*
Restrictions: *No pets, 2-day minimum on weekends.*

The Martindale Bed and Breakfast Inn

The Martindale Bed and Breakfast Inn is located in rural Columbia County. The 1852 building is a Hudson Valley "bracket house," a hybrid of southern, Victorian, and Federal architecture. It was in the same family for 134 years before it began its new life as a bed-and-breakfast. It is now supervised by innkeepers Terry and Soll Berl—a retired teacher and a physician, respectively.

The Berls opened up a warren of small, dark spaces and turned it into a comfortable, airy, and elegant B&B. The wide-board floors found throughout are originals, and the chestnut molding was fashioned from trees growing on the property when the house was built.

Guest rooms have antique brass or four-poster oak beds and are graced with 19th-century prints and dried-flower wreaths. The antiques-furnished sitting room has a TV, VCR, and CD player, but guests often prefer to pass the time in the homey kitchen munching on Terry's muffins and scones.

Address: *Rte. 23, Craryville, NY 12521, tel. 518/851–5405.*
Accommodations: *2 double rooms with baths, 2 doubles share a bath.*
Amenities: *TV with VCR in parlor, dinner available with 24 hour's notice.*
Rates: *$60–$65; full breakfast. No credit cards.*
Restrictions: *Smoking on veranda only, 2-day minimum on weekends June–Labor Day and Oct.*

Pig Hill Inn

There aren't any real pigs in residence, and the Federal-style building wasn't built on a hill named for swine, but owner Wendy O'Brien's affection for porkers is evident throughout Pig Hill Inn: There's a painted-piggy floor cloth in the entryway, and folk-art pig carvings are set amid antiques throughout the inn's three floors. Guests enter the inn by way of an antiques store on the first floor.

Each guest room is unique. Room 1 imparts a rustic feeling, with Indian rugs, antlers hung above the fireplace, and a settee made from birch logs. Room 6 contains a full four-poster bed and inviting burgundy wing chairs, and Room 7 has its own wood-burning stove and a stunning antique pine armoire.

The downstairs sitting room has rag rugs, comfortable chairs, and a collection of classic children's books, including *Charlotte's Web*, whose main character is a pig named Wilbur. The fictional Wilbur had to settle for slops in the barn, but guests at Pig Hill are pampered with breakfast in bed of shirred eggs and freshly baked breads or maybe a spinach-filled soufflé roll.

Address: *73 Main St., Cold Spring, NY 10516, tel. 914/265–9247.*
Accommodations: *4 double rooms with baths, 4 doubles share 2 baths.*
Amenities: *Air-conditioning, fireplaces in some rooms.*
Rates: *$90–$155; full breakfast: AE, D, DC, MC, V.*
Restrictions: *No smoking, no pets.*

Plumbush Inn

Plumbush, once the estate of American-born marquise Agnes Rizzo dei Ritii, was transformed into an elegant Hudson Valley restaurant in 1976. Several years later, Swiss-born owners Giere Albin and Ans Benderer, who grew up in the hotel-and-restaurant business, decided to convert the Victorian mansion's unused second floor to overnight accommodations.

The grounds are fenced in and nicely landscaped; the buildings are painted—well, plum. Inside, the walls of the Marchesa Suite are covered with flowered paper; the room is furnished with a large iron-and-brass bed and Victorian settee and has a full bath. Two smaller rooms have similar Victorian appointments and private baths.

Breakfast includes homemade croissants, pastries, jams, juices, coffee, and tea and may be served in the guest rooms or on the small downstairs porch. Local attractions include lush golf courses, state parks for hiking and cycling, and the antiques shops in Cold Spring, five minutes away.

Address: *Rte. 9D, Cold Springs, NY 10516, tel. 914/265-3904.*
Accommodations: *2 double rooms with baths, 1 suite.*
Amenities: *Restaurant, air-conditioning, cable TV in sitting room.*
Rates: *$95–$125; Continental breakfast. AE, MC, V.*
Restrictions: *Smoking in restaurant area only, closed Mon. and Tues.*

The Swiss Hutte

At the foot of the Catamount Ski Area, in a picture-perfect setting, is the Swiss Hutte, a chalet that's more reminiscent of the Alps than of the Berkshires.

Gert and Cindy Alper are the energetic couple who have owned the inn since 1986. Swiss-born Gert, who started his training at 15 as a chef's apprentice, runs the kitchen while Cindy oversees the dining room and lodgings.

There are three bedrooms in the inn itself, with 12 more in the nearby motel. Although the motel rooms were refurbished in 1992 and are large and bright, with private terraces, their ambience is typical of motels. The charm of the Swiss Hutte has more to do with its set-

ting, service, and food than with its bedrooms. Gert's Continental specialties are irresistible, and guests can always work off the calories on the inn's tennis courts or in its pool during summer. In winter a day on the slopes could easily justify a second helping of the inn's famous raspberry-cream pie.

Address: *Rte. 23, Hillsdale, NY 12529, tel. 518/325-3333.*
Accommodations: *15 double rooms with baths, 1 double suite.*
Amenities: *Restaurant, air-conditioning, phones and TV in rooms; swimming pool, tennis.*
Rates: *$150–$160, MAP. MC, V.*
Restrictions: *2- or 3-night minimum on holiday weekends, depending on season, closed mid-Mar.– mid-Apr.*

The Village Victorian Inn

With a chandelier right out of *Gone with the Wind* in the spacious front entry hall, flowered wallpaper and an Oriental rug in the parlor, and fish net-canopy beds heaped with heartshaped lacy throw pillows, "romantic" seems to be the only word to describe Rhinebeck's circa-1860 Village Victorian Inn. The inn is on the National Register of Historic Places, and it reflects the dream of owners Judy and Richard Kohler to restore the house to its original elegance.

All the guest rooms are lovely. The Blue Room, with its king-size bed and working fireplace, is often chosen by honeymooners. The Green Room has an intricately carved queen-size Victorian bed and a mirrored armoire. The focal point of the Red Room is an extraordinarily elaborate antique brass bed.

Guests who can be lured from the wicker chairs on the front porch enjoy local antiquing or watching vintage aircraft in action at the Old Rhinebeck Aerodrome, 4 miles away.

Address: *31 Center St., Rhinebeck, NY 12572, tel. 914/876-8345.*
Accommodations: *5 double rooms with baths.*
Amenities: *Air-conditioning.*
Rates: *$175–$225; full breakfast. AE, MC, V.*
Restrictions: *No smoking, no pets, 2-night minimum on weekends.*

Eastern Long Island

The eastern end of Long Island first attracted English colonists in the 1640s. They fled the harsh New England winters for the ocean-tempered island and founded the towns of East Hampton and Southampton. The East Hampton area (called Maidstone by these settlers) was purchased from the Shinnecock tribe for 20 coats, 24 hatchets, 24 hoes, 24 looking glasses, and 100 tools the tribe would use for making wampum. The vacationtime invasion of the farming communities on the island's bucolic eastern end began in the late 19th century and mushroomed when the Long Island Railroad started service to the region from Manhattan's Pennsylvania Station.

Today the ocean is the area's big draw. Those not lucky enough to own beachfront property "south of the highway" (the Montauk Highway) have access to miles of white, sandy public beaches. Although the beaches are free, passes are required for parking. A number of bed-and-breakfasts and inns offer free passes to guests. One pleasant way to avoid parking charges is to bike to the beach.

In summer the South Fork, from Southampton to Montauk, is one big—and somewhat crowded—playground for the tan, chic, and well heeled. Summer housing is expensive, though there are a few notable bargains. The main thoroughfare to the eastern end of the island is Route 27, a two-lane nightmare on summer weekends. For those who don't want to drive, there's the Hampton Jitney bus and limousine service from Manhattan (tel. 212/936–0440) and a local airport, as well as numerous marinas for docking the family yacht.

Summer in the area brings warm ocean breezes, boutiques, chic night spots, and roadside stands brimming with the bounty of Long Island's farms. It's a wonderful time here, but the beach is still there the rest of the year, when

*nothing is as crowded—something to consider when
planning your trip. The ocean sometimes remains warm
enough for swimming into October, and restaurant
reservations are certainly easier to come by out of season.*

*Not all of Eastern Long Island is trendy and developed.
The North Fork is an agricultural area, with some of the
state's most productive farms. Thanks to conservationists,
more than 6,800 acres on the South Fork have been turned
into nature preserves. Eastern Long Island's salt marshes,
dunes, pine barrens, woodlands, and grasslands are home
to many endangered species of flora and fauna, and
preservationists are determined that at least part of the
island will stay as it was in the 1600s, when the first big
real-estate deal was completed.*

Places to Go, Sights to See

Home Sweet Home Museum (East Hampton, tel. 516/324–0713). The
childhood home of poet John Howard Payne, who wrote the song "Home
Sweet Home" in the early 1800s, is now a museum in a simple 1660 rough-
shingle house, which features a three-century collection of furnishings and
a 19th-century windmill. It's open all year.

Long Island Wineries. The area claims a dozen wineries. Climate and the
makeup of the soil here provide unique growing conditions, and the area is
fast becoming a source of award-winning wines. The town of Cutchogue is
home to four wineries, including *Bedell Cellars* (tel. 516/734–7537), *Bidwell
Vineyards* (tel. 516/734–5200), *Hargrave Vineyard* (tel. 516/734–5158), and
Peconic Bay Vineyards (tel. 516/734–7361). Peconic offers *Lenz Winery* (tel.
516/734–6010) and *Pindar Vineyards* (tel. 516/734–6200). Other North Fork
vineyards include *Jamesport Vineyards* (Jamesport, tel. 516/722–5256),
Mattituck Hills Winery (Mattituck, tel. 516/298–5964), and *Pallmer Winery*
(Aquebogue, tel. 516/722–4080). The South Fork vineyards are
Bridgehampton Winery (Bridgehampton, tel. 516/537–3155) and
Southampton Winery (Southampton, tel. 516/726–7555). Many vineyards
offer tours and tastings.

Mashomack Preserve (Shelter Island, tel. 516/749–1001). The Nature
Conservancy, a nonprofit organization that manages the world's largest
privately held nature preserve, protects and maintains a pristine 2,039-acre
habitat on Shelter Island. The salt marsh and wooded areas are home for
a number of endangered species, including the osprey and the oystercatcher.
Osprey nesting areas may be observed (and should be left undisturbed) all

over the island. The preserve is open for hiking every day but Tuesday, and guided walks are offered.

Summer Festival, John Drew Theater of Guild Hall (East Hampton, tel. 516/324–4050). The festival—which is actually year-round—features theater; concerts; a film series; children's events; and lectures on the arts, the environment, and politics. Memberships, subscriptions, and single-event tickets are available.

Whale Watch Cruises (Montauk, tel. 516/728–4522). The Okeanos Ocean Research Foundation, a nonprofit marine-science organization, runs daily trips from May through September on its 90-foot cabin cruiser, *Finback II,* which is staffed by trained volunteers. Usually several whales are spotted on each voyage (about 20 miles out to sea from Montauk Point). Sighting a mother whale showing off her calf could be the high point of an Eastern Long Island vacation.

Restaurants

Grilled seafood is the specialty at **The Laundry** (East Hampton, tel. 516/324–3199). The **American Hotel Restaurant** (Sag Harbor, tel. 516/725–3535) is a fine (but pricey) French country restaurant, with more than 1,200 wines on the wine list. If you're looking for basic American cuisine at moderate prices, the **Driver's Seat** (Southampton, tel. 516/283–6606) is the place.

Tourist Information

East Hampton Chamber of Commerce (4 Main St., East Hampton 11937, tel. 516/324–0362, for information on Wainscott, East Hampton Village, Springs, Amagansett, and Montauk). **Sag Harbor Chamber of Commerce** (Box 116, Sag Harbor 11936, tel. 516/725–0011). **Shelter Island Chamber of Commerce** (Box 598, Shelter Island 11964, tel. 516/749–0399). **Southampton Chamber of Commerce** (76 Main St., Southampton 11968, tel. 516/283–0402). **Greater Westhampton Chamber of Commerce** (Box 1228, Westhampton Beach, 11978, tel. 516/288–3337).

The Huntting Inn

Huge elms and maples surround the Huntting Inn, a pre-Revolutionary landmark set on 2½ acres in the midst of East Hampton Village. The 1699 house, originally a saltbox, was built by the Church of England for the Reverend Nathaniel Huntting. In 1751 Huntting's widow, probably short of cash, turned her home into a public house, and it's been an inn ever since. During the American Revolution it became the only neutral meeting ground in the area.

Innkeeper Linda Calder (who also manages Hedges' Inn, owned by the same corporation) has been here since 1980. Her degree from the Fashion Institute of Technology in New York City comes in handy in matters of inn decor. Her warmth, boundless energy, and good humor are evident as she tends to the needs of guests in the two inns.

The inn's dining room will look familiar to Manhattan's restaurant cognoscenti—it's run by the Palm Restaurant and has similar decor, including a pressed-tin ceiling, oak wainscoting, wide-board floors, bentwood chairs, a brass-rail bar, and drawings of celebrities lining the walls. As at the Palm, steaks and lobsters come in colossal proportions.

Guest rooms have cotton-chintz floral-print wall coverings. A number of antique beds are brass, iron, or a combination of both. One of the most charming rooms here is also the smallest, with a single brass-and-iron bed, a hand-crocheted bed cover, and lace curtains. The suite, done in a blue-and-white scheme, has wicker furnishings with flowered cushions, and balloon shades on the windows. It also offers a king-size bed and a queen-size pull-out couch to accommodate families.

Across the street you'll find public tennis courts, and there's a golf course nearby. The inn provides guests with town stickers for parking in beach areas. The main village beach features a pavilion with lifeguards and refreshments. Other beaches in the area are more secluded but have few or no amenities. The inn lies within walking distance of all of East Hampton's shops, theaters, and museums.

Address: *94 Main St., East Hampton, NY 11937, tel. 516/324–0410, fax 516/324–8751.*
Accommodations: *17 double rooms with baths, 3 single rooms with baths, 1 suite.*
Amenities: *Restaurant, air-conditioning.*
Rates: *$95–$250; cold buffet breakfast. AE, MC, V.*
Restrictions: *No pets, 2-night minimum on weekends May–June and Sept.–Oct., 3-night minimum on weekends July–Aug., 5-night minimum July 4 and Labor Day weekends, closed Jan. 1–mid-Mar.*

Ram's Head Inn

Ospreys nest atop the telephone poles by this inn on Shelter Island. A yellow and white awning shelters the patio, and a beached rowboat sits in a children's play area on the wide front lawn. The voice of Billie Holiday is often heard in the dining room. The 1929 center-hall Colonial-style building is all weathered shakes, white trim, and green shutters. Guests can walk to a gazebo by the tennis courts, and a grassy path leads down to 800 feet of beachfront on Coecles Harbor. Summer guests are cooled by bay breezes.

In June 1947, the nuclear physicists Enrico Fermi, J. Robert Oppenheimer, and Edward Teller attended a conference here on the foundations of quantum mechanics. The event is remembered with a framed document hanging in the entrance hall. Today guests will find the Ram's Head a serene setting for a meeting, an executive getaway, a family retreat, or a romantic weekend à deux.

Owners James and Linda Ecklund and innkeeper Brian Moorehead collaborate in running the place, and each fills in wherever necessary to make sure guests are taken care of. In 1980 the Ecklunds bought the inn in a rather "decayed state," as they put it, and have spent the intervening years restoring it.

The common rooms are often flooded with natural light. The lounge, decorated in a nautical theme, features ships' lanterns and a model sloop on the mantel. Green wicker couches have flowered cushions, and the library is the perfect spot for a rainy-day read. Here framed sheet music lines the walls, and a piano occupies an honored place. Every Sunday from 7 to 11 PM, a local jazz group livens up the atmosphere. The dining-room menu stresses fresh seafood creatively prepared and presented. Specialties include shellfish bisque garnished with caviar and lobster, and braised red snapper accompanied by oyster mushrooms and artichokes.

Guest rooms are simple, bright, and airy; some have porches. Those with a water view are often requested, but in summer the harbor can be glimpsed only through the leaves of majestic oak trees.

Address: *108 Ram Island Dr., Shelter Island Heights, NY 11965, tel. 516/749-0811.*
Accommodations: *5 double rooms with baths, 4 doubles share 2 baths, 4 suites.*
Amenities: *Restaurant, free use of boats and tennis court.*
Rates: *$65–$195; Continental buffet breakfast. AE, MC, V.*
Restrictions: *Smoking in lounge only, no pets, 3-night minimum on holiday weekends, 2-night minimum other weekends.*

The 1770 House

At various times in its history the 1770 House, actually a 1740 Colonial built for one of East Hampton's earliest families, has been a general store; a dining hall for students at the Clinton Academy next door; and, finally, an inn that had its heyday in the 1940s and '50s. When Sidney and Miriam Perle bought it, in 1977, it had been in a state of decline for several years. The Perles—he was in the retail business, and she ran a cooking school—were undaunted by the formidable restoration needed to return the building to its former glory.

Guest rooms have been furnished with fine antiques of various periods and origins. One room has a fireplace and an English-style carved canopy bed. Another has an Early American highboy. The inn's elegant library features English-pine paneling and a fireplace. The dining room has raspberry walls, which hold the owners' extensive collection of clocks and apothecary jars. "The kitchen," jokes Miriam, "is painted smoked salmon."

The Perles' well-kept secret, the nearby Philip Taylor House, is the family's private residence, but it contains three opulent bedrooms that are available to guests. Miriam's description of the place is forthright: "This is a drop-dead house." The core of the house was built in 1650; at the turn of this century its owners transformed it into a beige-stucco Elizabethan minipalace. Were she alive today, Marie Antoinette would most likely lose her head over the French antiques in the Boxwood Room—so named because it overlooks the magnificent English boxwood and Italianate columned garden. The Pear Tree Room, in the 1650 wing of the house, has massive ship's beams of English pine and a queen-size canopy bed. The Wisteria Room boasts an English-pine canopy bed and pine armoire. All the rooms have fireplaces, and several have balconies. The house is filled with intricately crafted wood, architectural embellishments, and museum-quality antiques from seven historic periods. (You would need a guided tour and a handbook to appreciate the collection fully.)

Address: *143 Main St., East Hampton, NY 11937, tel. 516/324–1770.*
Accommodations: *10 double rooms with baths, 2 suites.*
Amenities: *Restaurant, air-conditioning.*
Rates: *1770 house, $105–$225 (call ahead for Philip Taylor house rates); full breakfast. AE, MC, V.*
Restrictions: *Smoking discouraged, no pipes or cigars, no pets, 4-night minimum on summer weekends, 2-night minimum other weekends.*

The Village Latch Inn

The theatrical air to the 5-acre compound that makes up the Village Latch Inn is no accident. Owner Marta White spent her life in the theater, and she revels in setting a stage. Her husband and fellow innkeeper, Martin, is a photographer who used to work in commercial films. The main house is "old Southampton, turn-of-the-century, Gatsby-style," says Marta. The circa-1900 building, once the annex to Southampton's most opulent hotel, may have been a Sanford White design. Near the main house are what Marta refers to as the "outbuildings," which were part of the old Merrill Lynch estate. These include the Terry Cottage, which features a comfortable living room, with flowered wallpaper, and Victorian dining room; the Potting Shed, where the first American locomotive was built and which is now used for corporate meetings; six modern duplexes with private decks; and two other large houses connected by a Victorian greenhouse. One of these houses has a distinguished collection of Mexican folk art.

The living room in the main house could be the set of a movie—perhaps *Around the World in 80 Days with Auntie Mame*. Plush leopard-print cushions and gold- and silver-threaded pillows are tossed artfully on the couches. Balinese marionettes hang from the walls. It's all eccentric, eclectic, and artsy—and it works.

No guest room resembles another, and Marta is always changing things. "If I'm not creating space, then it's boring," she comments. The rooms are decorated with a collection of antiques from different periods. Despite its lavishness, the inn is cozy—the sort of place where guests can help themselves to coffee or a cold drink any time of the day, even if the sign says KITCHEN CLOSED.

A number of the buildings can be rented to groups, and the facilities have been used for everything from fashion shoots to family reunions. The greenhouse is the perfect setting for an intimate wedding. The inn is a five-minute walk from town and a mile from the beach.

Address: *101 Hill St. (Box 3000), Southampton, NY 11968, tel. 516/283-2160 or 800/54-LATCH.* **Accommodations:** *27 double rooms with baths, 6 suites, 6 duplexes.* **Amenities:** *Lunch catering on request, air-conditioning, cable TV and phones in rooms on request; swimming pool, tennis courts.* **Rates:** *$85-$350; Continental breakfast. AE, D, DC, MC, V.* **Restrictions:** *Pets only by prior arrangement, 3-night minimum July and Aug. weekends, 2-night minimum other weekends.*

Basset House Inn

A portrait of humorist Will Rogers, who believed that "friends are merely strangers who haven't met," occupies a prominent spot in Bassett House Inn, an 1830 Colonial-style building on the outskirts of East Hampton. Rogers is innkeeper Michael Bassett's hero. Michael, a former photographer, has created a relaxed place. His taste in decorating runs to the eclectic. World War I Red Cross posters deck the halls, and in the living room an old cookstove stands next to a doctor's scale. Guest rooms, too, contain furniture from a variety of periods. Room 5 has an oak spindle bed and a fireplace; the suite is furnished with a painted oak Victorian bed and matching dresser. Don't expect the decor to be exactly the same when you get there—

rooms change according to Bassett's whim. It may be a little rough around the edges, but from the rusty basset hound outside to the slightly risqué Ms. Gimble hanging over the piano, the place offers loads of character and lots of fun.

Address: *128 Montauk Hwy., East Hampton, NY 11937, tel. 516/324–6127.*
Accommodations: *7 double rooms with baths, 1 double and 2 singles share 2 baths, 2 suites.*
Amenities: *Air-conditioning, cable TV in some rooms. Well-behaved pets allowed by arrangement.*
Rates: *$65–$175; full breakfast. AE, MC, V.*
Restrictions: *2-night minimum on summer weekends, 4-night minimum some holidays.*

Hedges' Inn

If you're up early enough, you might see pheasants searching out breakfast in the front yard of Hedges' Inn. The property sits across from a greensward and pond where cattle grazed in the mid-1600s, when the area was first settled. In winter, when skaters glide over the frozen pond, the vista is a Currier and Ives print brought to life.

The inn, now owned by the Palm Management Corporation, was built as a private residence in 1774. A varied selection of flowers in brilliant hues lines the brick path to the columned front porch, where visitors can ease themselves into green-cushioned wicker chairs and enjoy the passing scene. Guest rooms are attractively furnished with patch-

work quilts, frilly shams, and throw pillows. You sit down to breakfast at English-pine tables adorned with baskets of blooms, in a small, sunny dining room. A buffet is set on a carved-pine hutch. In warm weather, guests dine on the canopied flagstone patio.

Address: *74 James La., East Hampton, NY 11937, tel. 516/324–7100.*
Accommodations: *11 double rooms with baths.*
Amenities: *Restaurant, air-conditioning.*
Rates: *$100–$195; cold buffet breakfast. AE, MC, V.*
Restrictions: *No pets, 3-night minimum on July and Aug. weekends, 5-night minimum July 4 and Labor Day weekends.*

The Hill Guest House

Built around 1890, the Hill Guest House is the Hamptons without frills. Located a mile from the village of Southampton and a two-minute drive from the beach, the house offers clean and pleasant accommodations at low rates. Owners Mauro and Ronnie Salerno have been here since 1964, when they came for a two-week vacation at the guest house and ended up buying it. Mauro was in the meat business ("Selling rooms is the same as selling sausages," he says with a laugh) and today spends his spare time swimming and serving as a hospital volunteer. Ronnie is a gourmet cook who "does *The New York Times* crossword puzzle in ink," boasts Mauro.

The rooms have twin beds (which can be pushed together); most beds are made of antique iron painted to match the decor. The front porch has painted wicker chairs, and on cool evenings the living-room fireplace is the cheery focal point of the inn.

Address: *535 Hill St., Southampton, NY 11968, tel. 516/283–9889 or 718/461–0014 (Nov.–Apr.).*
Accommodations: *1 double room with bath, 2 doubles share 1 bath; 3 doubles share 2 hall baths.*
Rates: *$60–$75; breakfast extra. No credit cards.*
Restrictions: *No pets, 2-night minimum on weekends June and Sept., 3-night minimum on weekends July and Aug., closed Nov.–Apr.*

The Maidstone Arms

The original settlers of East Hampton called the village Maidstone, after their native village in England, so it's not surprising that the Maidstone Arms has the air of a British seaside resort. The Victorian inn, built in the 1830s, features porches with white-wicker furniture, blue-and-white–striped awnings, and an English perennial garden—the perfect spot for tea on a balmy afternoon. In 1992, Gordon Campbell-Gray, a Scottish hotelier, took over the inn. There is a professional, well-run air about the place.

Rooms are brightly decorated: Some walls are stenciled, and others have wallpaper with a flower motif. White dotted-swiss curtains and lots of wicker complete the furnishings.

One suite has its own sun porch. One of the three cottages (which are rented by the week during the summer) has a queen-size sleigh bed, and each has a fireplace.

Address: *207 Main St., East Hampton, NY 11937, tel. 516/324–5006.*
Accommodations: *12 double rooms with baths, 4 suites, 3 cottages.*
Amenities: *Restaurant, air-conditioning, cable TV in rooms; limo service from jitney, train, and East Hampton airport.*
Rates: *$160–$275; Continental breakfast. AE, MC, V.*
Restrictions: *No pets, 4-night minimum on holiday weekends, 3-night minimum other weekends.*

Mill House Inn

On the shadow of East Hampton's landmark Hook Windmill, across from the village green, is the appropriately named Mill House Inn. This 1790 saltbox reminiscent of New England architecture was converted to a Dutch Colonial in 1890. In 1987, Barbara and Kevin Flynn left California—she was a software engineer, he was a manager of a steamship company—to buy a bed-and-breakfast "back east." Now they preside over this charming place, where clematis climbs the screen porch and geraniums sprout from the window boxes.

Barbara stenciled the walls and is also responsible for the guest-room curtains, some made of Laura Ashley fabrics. Rooms have Colonial-period antiques, including a queen-size canopy bed and a four-poster. Guests breakfast on walnut waffles or French toast with cream cheese and apricot preserves. To work off breakfast they borrow the inn's bikes and pedal to the beach a mile away.

Address: *33 N. Main St., East Hampton, NY 11937, tel. 516/324–9766.*
Accommodations: *6 double rooms, with baths.*
Amenities: *Beach passes.*
Rates: *$85–$165; full breakfast, afternoon beverages. AE, MC, V.*
Restrictions: *No smoking in bedrooms, no pets, 3-night minimum on weekends, 4-night minimum on holiday weekends May–Aug.*

The Old Post House Inn

The Old Post House is New York State's oldest privately owned and occupied English wood frame house. Innkeepers Ed and Cecille Courville (he's a retired executive) share wonderful stories with their guests about the building's history (ask about the archaeological dig in the basement). The hand-hewn beams, which still have their bark on them, date from the early 1700s, and a chimney brick found during the inn's restoration is thought to date from 1684.

Furnished with American antiques, the guest rooms are named for local historical figures. The charming Lizbeth White Room displays a Dresden Plate quilt (many of the inn's quilts are for sale). The Lion Gardiner Room has flowered wallpaper, a four-poster bed, and an afghan-covered blanket chest. Guests breakfast in the common room or take trays out to the porch. The nearby Methodist church sounds its carillon each day at noon—a perfect old-fashioned accompaniment to this old-fashioned village inn.

Address: *136 Main St., Southampton Village, NY 11968, tel. 516/283–1717.*
Accommodations: *7 double rooms with baths.*
Amenities: *Air-conditioning.*
Rates: *$80–$160; Continental breakfast. AE, D, DC, MC, V.*
Restrictions: *No pets, 2-night minimum on weekends June–Sept., 3-night minimum on holiday weekends.*

Pennsylvania

Pennsylvania

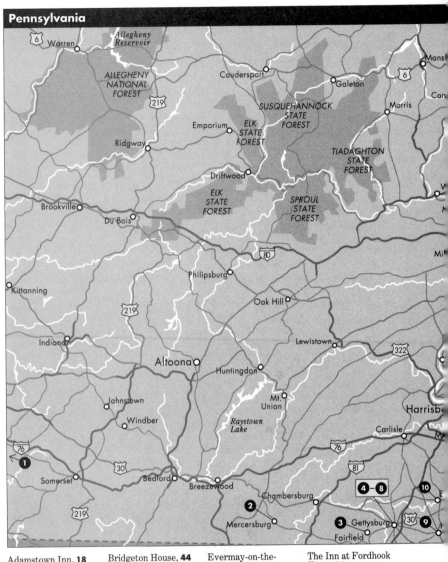

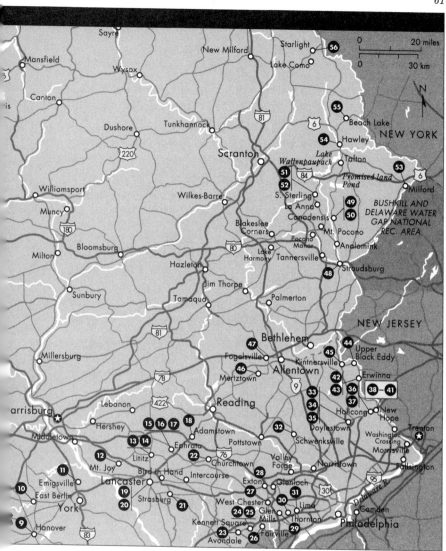

The Poconos

*Though the Poconos are best known as the Honeymoon
Capital of the World, the land of the glitzy motel, with
heart-shape beds, hot tubs, and bottomless champagne
glasses, the "other" Poconos may be Pennsylvania's best-
kept secret. The northeast corner of the state, bordering the
Delaware River, encompasses 2,400 square miles of
mountainous wilderness, with lakes, streams, waterfalls,
woods, and enchanting country inns.*

*The region consists of four counties: Carbon, Monroe, Pike,
and Wayne. The discovery of anthracite coal in Carbon
County led to its development as a mining region,
a railroad center, and a land of opportunity for European
immigrants. The town of Mauch Chunk, founded in 1815
(now called Jim Thorpe, after the great Native American
athlete), became home to a dozen coal and railroad
millionaires. Monroe County, along the Delaware River,
was first inhabited by the Delaware and Shawnee tribes,
then settled by the Dutch in 1659, and by the English and
Germans a century later. In the 1820s people began visiting
the Poconos in summer for the crisp mountain air.
Boardinghouses were built along the Delaware Water Gap,
Monroe County developed a small resort industry, and by
1900 thousands were coming each summer from
Philadelphia and New York City.*

*A back-roads drive through the woodlands and rolling hills
will turn up dairy farms and quaint villages, country
stores, and lots of antiques and crafts shops. In winter
there are downhill and cross-country skiing, ice skating,
snowmobiling, and sledding. In summer there are theater,
golf and tennis, boating, swimming, horseback riding, and
hiking. And any time after a full day, you'll find a good
night's sleep in a country inn.*

Places to Go, Sights to See

Bushkill Falls (Bushkill, tel. 717/588–6682). The Niagara of Pennsylvania, on 300 acres, has trails leading to eight waterfalls. There's an exhibit of Pennsylvania wildlife, and there are picnic grounds, fishing, paddleboats, and a silversmith shop.

Grey Towers (Milford, tel. 717/296–6401). You can tour the house and gardens of the stone ancestral home of Gifford Pinchot, first chief of the U.S. Forest Service and twice governor of Pennsylvania.

Jim Thorpe (Rte. 209). This late-Victorian mountain-resort town, once called Mauch Chunk (from the Native American *Machktschunk*, Mountain of the Sleeping Bear), has first-rate antiques shops and galleries, the Asa Packer Museum, St. Mark's Church, Flagstaff Park, the Overlook, and a restored railroad station.

Lake Wallenpaupack (between Greentown and Hawley). Year-round activities along the 52-mile shoreline of the largest recreational lake in the state include waterskiing, swimming, boating, fishing, snowmobiling, ice skating, cross-country skiing, and ice fishing. Hiking trails lead to scenic overlooks.

Pocono Indian Museum (Bushkill, tel. 717/588–9164). Exhibits of artifacts and crafts and a replica of a longhouse trace the history of the Delaware Indians.

Promised Land State Park (10 mi north of Canadensis, tel. 717/676–3428). This natural forest and recreational area of 11,010 acres, filled with deer, bear, and smaller game, has seasonal sports, picnic grounds, and 25 miles of marked hiking trails.

Quiet Valley Living Historical Farm (Stroudsburg, tel. 717/992–6161). Authentically costumed "family members" reenact farm life in a 1765 log house. Demonstrations include spinning, baking, gardening, and tending the animals.

Ski Areas and Resorts

You'll find beginner, intermediate, and expert trails in the region. All have ski schools, rentals, cross-country ski trails, ice skating, and night skiing. Many offer indoor swimming, tennis, racquetball, and entertainment. Inquire about midweek packages.

Alpine Mountain, Analomink, tel. in PA, 717/595–2150; outside PA, 800/233–8240. **Blue Mountain Ski Area,** Palmerton, tel. 215/826–7700. **Camelback,** Tannersville, tel. 717/629–1661. **Fernwood,** Bushkill, tel. 717/588–9500. **Jack Frost Mountain,** Blakeslee, tel. 717/443–8425. **Mount Airy Lodge,** Mt. Pocono, tel. in PA, 717/839–8811; outside PA, 800/441–4410. **Mount Tone,** Lake Como, tel. 717/798–2707. **Pocono Manor Inn and Gold Resort,** Pocono

Manor, tel. in PA, 717/839–7111; outside PA, 800/233–8150. **Shawnee Mountain,** Shawnee-on-Delaware, tel. 717/421–7231. **Split Rock Resort,** Lake Harmony, tel. in PA, 717/722–9111; outside PA, 800/255–7625. **Tanglwood,** Tafton, tel. in PA, 717/226–9500; outside PA, 800/341–5700.

Restaurants

Every single bed-and-breakfast or country inn that we mention in this section, with the exception of Brookview Manor, houses its own restaurant (you'll find MAP meal plans much more common here than in other areas of the state). You should reconsider an otherwise justifiable bias against in-hotel eating when you travel here, and sample the victuals at any one of our recommendations—the caliber of cuisine and service is outstanding and categorically outranks local dining options in presentation and performance. But if you still resist the notion or are looking for more variety, here's a handful of creditable restaurants within easy driving distance of our entries.

A young couple runs the small (maximum seating 30–35) but celebrated **Le Gorille** (tel. 717/296–8094) in Shahola, near Milford; contemporary American recipes predominate here. In Cresco, the **Golden Goose** (tel. 717/595–3788) has a Continental menu with an all-inclusive bargain at around $15 a pop. **Peppe's** (tel. 717/421–4460), in East Stroudsburg, does manicotti and bay scallops in the Italian tradition. Mount Pocono's **B.J.'s Gathering** (tel. 717/839–8305) also offers moderately priced fare in a casual atmosphere, but American-style.

Tourist Information

Pocono Mountains Vacation Bureau, Inc. (Box CIB, Stroudsburg 18360, tel. 717/424–6050 or 717/421–5791; 24-hour ski hotline, 717/421–5565).

The French Manor

The 43-acre setting is aristocratic and the views exquisite. Rolling hills and mountain ranges reveal themselves periodically as you drive up the winding, wooded road toward the crest of Huckleberry Mountain to the fieldstone manor house with a slate roof, coopermullioned windows, and arched oak door.

It was built between 1932 and 1937 as a summer residence for mining tycoon and art collector Albert Hirschorn, who modeled it after his château in southern France. After changing hands several times, the house became an inn in 1985 and in 1990 was bought by Ron and Mary Kay Logan, who own and manage the nearby Sterling Inn.

The 27-foot-high Great Room, with a vaulted cherry-wood ceiling and a mammoth plastered-stone fireplace at each end, makes a spectacular restaurant. French doors with leaded glass open onto a slate terrace that has a sweeping view of the countryside. The guest rooms, named after European cities, have cypress-panel walls and ceilings and are decorated in a mix of contemporary style and French antique reproductions. "Venice" has an ornate headboard on its king-size bed. Baths have old-fashioned tile with pedestal sinks. The carriage-house suite, recently renovated, is furnished like the manor house but has smaller rooms. Though it is secluded, its feeling of

newness makes it not nearly as nice as the larger house.

A full-service, no-smoking dining room with a full liquor license treats guests to an à la carte menu that changes about every two months and features highly touted French cuisine. A recent selection included grilled beef tenderloin nestled on a roasted garlic and tomato concassée cream; and fresh salmon baked in a sauce of champagne, white peppercorn, and asparagus.

With grandiose views as a backdrop, you can take peaceful walks or go cross-country skiing. Golf, horseback riding, and other recreations are nearby. The medieval atmosphere of the house—and the thoughtful service of the Logans and their staff—create the timeless feeling that you have really gotten away from it all.

Address: *Huckleberry Rd. (Box 39), South Sterling, PA 18460, tel. 717/676-3244 or 800/523-8200, fax 717/676-9786.*
Accommodations: *4 double rooms with baths, 2 doubles share 1 bath, 2 suites.*
Amenities: *Restaurant open daily for lunch and dinner, air-conditioning in bedrooms, TV in lounge; croquet.*
Rates: *$180–$240 (full breakfast and dinner); $120–$180 (breakfast only). AE, D, MC, V.*
Restrictions: *Smoking in designated areas only, no pets.*

The Inn at Meadowbrook

Guests who arrive at The Inn at Meadowbrook after dark are often relieved to find they aren't lost. On the long and winding 4½ wooded miles from Tannersville you may begin to think you've missed it, but suddenly, around a corner, there it is, blanketed by soft light and trees and chirping night sounds: a white clapboard manor house with green trim. And just across the road is a white mill house that's part of the inn. If you're going to get pleasantly lost anywhere in the Poconos, this is the place to do it.

For many years the 1867 house and its 43 acres were a horse farm, and in 1985 Kathy and Bob Overman bought the estate and turned it into a bed-and-breakfast. Kathy, an artist who loves to garden, has given each of the guest rooms a distinctive decor. Bob, the resident gourmet chef, has mastered the celebrated raspberry-cinnamon-raisin pudding recipe you may be lucky enough to sample for breakfast.

You can curl up with a book on the leather sofa in the light-flooded parlor or in wing chairs that face the fireplace, or you can simply gaze out the windows at the pond, gazebo, and mill house. The spacious hunter-green dining room, added in the '20s, is a setting out of *The Great Gatsby*, with 15-foot ceilings, arched columns, and tall Palladian windows on three sides framing the gardens, the

rushing brook with footbridge, and a pond. French doors open onto the terrace for dining in warm months.

The guest rooms are furnished with English and American antiques and country pieces. There are patchwork quilts, lots of books, wicker chairs, and convenient reading lamps. Room 9, a favorite of guests, has rich burgundy paisley draperies, hunter-green walls, an antique brass bed, and a view of the stables. The Overmans haven't raised their rates here for three years.

On the inn's own grounds you can swim, fish, play tennis, ice-skate, and take leisurely walks with a picnic lunch. Bob and Kathy can arrange horseback riding and carriage and sleigh rides. The area also has its share of antiques shops and flea markets.

Address: *Cherry Lane Rd. East (RD 7, Box 7651), Stroudsburg, PA 18301, tel. 717/629–0296.*
Accommodations: *10 double rooms with baths, 6 doubles share 2 baths.*
Amenities: *Restaurant (dinner Wed.–Sat. in winter, Wed.–Sun. in summer), TV with VCR in recreation room; swimming pool, 2 tennis courts, shuffleboard, pond.*
Rates: *$50–$85; full breakfast. AE, MC, V.*
Restrictions: *Smoking in common rooms only, no pets, 2-day minimum on weekends.*

The Inn at Starlight Lake

The hamlet of Starlight, nestled in the foothills of the Moosic range, was once a railroad stop, and in 1909 this Adirondack-style lodge was built on the lake nearby to serve passengers. Today the sprawling white-and-green clapboard inn looks much as it did around the turn of the century, and it's just as peaceful. Jack and Judy McMahon have been innkeepers here since 1974. Before that they lived in New York City and worked in the theater, where they met while performing.

The rambling parlor, with its wood-burning stove, stone fireplace, and baby-grand piano, sets the homey, lodgelike mood. There's a comfortable mixture of antiques, Mission oak furniture, and well-lived-in pieces, with numerous Tiffany-style lamps for reading. In winter you might expect Bing Crosby to step out and warble "White Christmas."

Guest rooms on the second and third floors are simple and unpretentious, with framed prints on floral-papered walls, crocheted doilies, and lots of magazines. You'll find iron beds and marble-top dressers, but mostly a hodge-podge of old and not-so-old furniture. A row of recently renovated cottages is furnished with wicker and antique reproductions. The suite has a king-size bed and a whirlpool bath for two; above it is another charming room with an iron bed and a fieldstone fireplace.

Chef David Giles presides in the dining room. He offers such choices as duck with two sauces and a seafood sausage made of scallops, shrimp, and fillet of sole. Everything served is made on the premises, including breads, pastas, ice cream, and pastries.

No motors are allowed on the 45-acre lake, so it's quiet and crystal clean for swimming and fishing. On occasional murder-mystery weekends, whodunits are performed by the Starlight Players. In winter there's ice skating, and the McMahons' son, a certified ski instructor, can take you down the property's slopes or show you the best trails for cross-country skiing. On crisp autumn mornings you are likely to see deer or flocks of wild turkeys through the early mist.

Address: *Starlight, PA 18461, tel. 717/798–2519 or 800/248–2519.*
Accommodations: *20 double rooms with baths, 2 doubles share bath, 1 suite, 3-bedroom Family House.*
Amenities: *Restaurant, bar, TV with VCR in sunroom, baby-sitting arranged; tennis court, canoes, bicycles.*
Rates: *$115–$200; full breakfast, dinner. MC, V.*
Restrictions: *No smoking in dining room, no pets, 2-day minimum in season, 3-day minimum on holidays, closed first 2 weeks in Apr.*

The Settlers Inn

This rambling Tudor-style grand hotel built in 1927 has been restored as a country inn. It's on a well-traveled bend of Route 6, five minutes from Lake Wallenpaupack, but once you enter the high-ceilinged living room, with its chestnut beams and massive stone fireplace, you'll forget about the location. Antique marble-top tables, Victorian chairs and sofas evoke the atmosphere of an English country hotel. The rooms, furnished with "early attic" antiques, also have Early American memorabilia.

The popular dining room is the domain of Grant Genzlinger, who's not only chef-innkeeper but also a student of ancient Chinese languages. He and his wife, Jeanne, share innkeeping duties with their partner, Marcia Dunsmore, and distinguish themselves mightily in the kitchen arts. The flavorful, amply portioned dinners testify to the proprietors' assiduous search for locally grown ingredients as well as to their loyalty to regional specialties. Dishes reflect the joy of a year-round pursuit of the best and brightest in the Pennsylvania agricultural community. Witness the cheddar pasta supper dish, composed of fettuccine, leeks, and spinach tossed in a sauce of Up Country Pennsylvania sharp cheddar and Forest Home Dairy fresh cream; or the chicken schnitzel, a scallop of chicken dipped in a light lemon and thyme batter, scented with nutmeg, sautéed, and served with fettuccine and roasted zucchini, peppers, yellow squash, onions, and tomatoes.

If you detect a sometimes whimsical, sometimes earnest voice in the menu descriptions, trust it for its very contradictions. The trio in charge does it all with a winning combination of dead seriousness and an insouciant aptitude for gustatory lucky strikes. Where else would you find garlic additions to an entrée honored on the menu as the "errant lily"?

The location is ideal for getting to winter or summer sports, and the town has enough antiques shops to keep you browsing for days.

Address: *4 Main Ave., Hawley, PA 18428, tel. 717/226–2993 or 800/833–8527.*
Accommodations: *15 double rooms with baths, 3 double suites.*
Amenities: *Restaurant, air-conditioning, TV in sitting room, 2 meeting rooms, 1 large banquet room.*
Rates: *$75–$140; full breakfast. AE, MC, V.*
Restrictions: *Ask about pets.*

The Sterling Inn

R on Logan, owner of the Sterling Inn, has put together a 10-page document tracing the site's history, from its occupation by the Nini subtribe (a branch of the Lanni Lenape) all the way up to his and his wife's proprietorship. "There is little wonder why the Indians would choose this particular site for their village," he observes. "Mountains on either side, the Wallenpaupack Creek with an abundance of trout, level fertile land, bubbling springs, and plenty of deer, bear, and other game."

It's still lovely here today, and this in itself is testimony to Ron and Mary Kay Logan's talent, energy, and restraint. The inn consists of an inviting white clapboard main house with hunter-green rooftop, built in 1857, and a cluster of cottages. It all sits nestled in a forested valley traversed by nature trails and winding waterways. The couple provides once-a-week lectures and guided nature walks, conducted by local author John Serrao, so that guests can absorb more than a glimpse of the 105 surrounding acres of birch, hemlock, and American beech, not to mention the wildflowers and bird life.

A fresh, countrified air prevails inside the inn, notwithstanding a few modern embellishments—a heated indoor pool, a poolside bar, and a spa. The dining room, open to guests and nonguests alike, is dominated by an enormous stone fireplace and decorated with a delicate floral-patterned wallpaper, pink tablecloths and woodwork, and bright blue cotton curtains over broad window valances. Resident chef George Pelepko Filak, a graduate of the Culinary Institute in Hyde Park, is happy to accommodate special diets, but each standard menu is lavished with entrées like medallions of veal lombardi; scampi with scallops, garlic, and wine; and steamed red snapper.

The rooms, accented by playful ruffles and flounces, echo the clean, bright-eyed ingenuousness of the downstairs dining room. They all have private baths; fireplace suites and cottages are available. The Logans offer several discount package rates. Romance and privacy give visitors here a true escape. Winter delights include horse-drawn sleigh rides and cross-country skiing; in the summer diversions such as swimming, hiking, horseback riding, and fishing abound.

Address: *South Sterling, PA 18460, tel. 717/676–3311, 717/676–3338, or 800/523–8200.*
Accommodations: *38 double rooms with baths, 16 suites.*
Amenities: *Indoor swimming pool, spa, restaurant; 9-hole putting course, cross-country ski trails, nature trails.*
Rates: *$130–$220; full breakfast, dinner. AE, D, MC, V.*
Restrictions: *No smoking in dining room, no pets.*

The Beach Lake Hotel

In 1986 Roy and Erika Miller, lovers of antiques, restoration, and cooking, left their careers in health administration to become keepers of this Victorian country inn. The eggplant-colored two-story clapboard building in the sleepy village of Beach Lake began as a hotel and tavern around 1859. The antiques-filled lobby, with wainscoted walls and ceilings, was once a general store. The inn is furnished throughout with Victorian oak and walnut, and everything is for sale. The parlor has a 15-foot ceiling, a velvet sofa, and a grandfather clock. In the formal dining room lace tablecloths and crystal-globe lamps on each table enhance the dinners prepared by Erika on Thursday through Monday. The guest rooms, each unique, have carved head-boards, lace-canopy beds, rocking chairs, armoires, and imported lace curtains. There are pedestal sinks in the bathrooms. Though the lake is only a short walk away, and ski areas are nearby, you might want to spend your time on the upstairs porch just rocking or reading.

Address: *Main and Church Sts. (Box 144), Beach Lake, PA 18405, tel. 717/729–8239.*
Accommodations: *6 double rooms with baths.*
Amenities: *Restaurant, air-conditioning in bedrooms, pub with TV.*
Rates: *$95; full breakfast. MC, V.*
Restrictions: *Smoking in public areas only, no pets, 2-day minimum on holiday weekends.*

Brookview Manor

Ever wonder what you did with your old Monopoly game? Well, Lee and Nancie Cabana, the proprietors at Brookview Manor, have an international stockpile. Informality, idleness, and comfort are the bywords here. The Cabanas and their young daughter, Erin, were taken by this cream-colored summer residence, built in 1911 for a wealthy family from Scranton. They promptly signed up for a seminar for innkeepers in New Hope, transported themselves from Erie, and plunged into the business.

The main structure and adjacent carriage house support four working fireplaces, original stained-glass windows, comfortable country furnishings, and occasional views of Broadhead Creek (Room 2 overlooks it). The property itself covers only 4 acres but is strategically surrounded by 400 acres of privately owned forest. Guests are free to roam the long, wooded trail, which leads to a 50-foot waterfall. For dinner the Cabanas recommend the nearby Pine Knob Inn or the Golden Goose restaurant in Cresco.

Address: *Route 447 (RR 1, Box 365), Canadensis, PA 18325, tel. 717/595–2451.*
Accommodations: *6 double rooms with baths.*
Amenities: *TV in den, pool table, Ping-Pong, games room.*
Rates: *$65–$145; full breakfast. AE, MC, V.*
Restrictions: *No smoking indoors, no pets, 2-night minimum on holiday weekends.*

Cliff Park Inn

This historic country inn, built as a homestead in 1820, has been in innkeeper Harry W. Buchanan's family for four generations. The three-story white-clapboard Colonial building with green trim is a mile west of Milford, and its 600 acres overlook one of the country's first golf courses. In the main parlor you'll find a wealth of Victorian family heirlooms, Buchanan ancestral portraits, and a stone fireplace. Guest rooms are decorated with family antiques and reproductions; some have porches that overlook the golf course. Three nearby cottages, ideal for families or groups, have exposed beams, large fieldstone fireplaces, and eclectic furnishings. The chef is a member of the renowned *Chaîne des Rôtisseurs*, a society of chefs. In the winter season, guests can make full use of the 7 miles of marked cross-country ski trails. During summer months, the inn's maple-shaded veranda is a favorite gathering place. There you can watch the golfers and the deer that come at dusk.

Address: *Cliff Park Rd. (RD 4, Box 7200), Milford, PA 18337, tel. 717/296-6491 or 800/225-6535, fax 717/296-3982.*
Accommodations: *19 double rooms with baths.*
Amenities: *Restaurant, air-conditioning, conference facilities, TV with VCR in meeting rooms; 9-hole golf course, pro shop, stable.*
Rates: *$140–$150 (full breakfast and dinner); $100–$115 (breakfast only). AE, D, DC, MC, V.*
Restrictions: *No pets, closed Dec. 24–25.*

The Overlook Inn

Just outside Canadensis is a yellow three-story inn with a porch around it so high that when you're on it you feel as though you're up in the pines. Arthur and Debbie Bolger, innkeepers who grew up in the business, have furnished the guest rooms in this 1870 Victorian farmhouse in a mix of Early American reproductions and Victorian antiques. The rooms downstairs are cozy. On cool evenings, a fire crackles in the stone fireplace in the living room, and from the window seat in the library you might see deer grazing on the lawn. Nothing's fussy here, yet gourmet dinners in the dining room do attract a well-dressed following. The Bolgers will glady point you to the trails for cross-country skiing on the inn's 15 wooded acres or help you plan a drive down scenic back roads. Promised Land State Park, where cross-country ski trails traverse county-size grounds, is only 10 minutes away; it's a bountiful prospect for the nature lover.

Address: *Dutch Hill Rd., Canadensis, PA 18325-9755, tel. 717/595-7519 or 800/441-0177, fax 717/223-7304.*
Accommodations: *18 double rooms with baths, 2 suites.*
Amenities: *Restaurant, air conditioners available, telephones in rooms, TV in library; swimming pool, conference facilities.*
Rates: *$75–$95; breakfast, high tea, dinner. AE, MC, V.*
Restrictions: *No pets, 2-day minimum on weekends.*

New Hope/Bucks County

Since the 1930s, when Bucks County was discovered by Broadway's smart set, the area has been a popular retreat from the hectic urban pace. The rolling hills, stone barns, and quaint covered bridges that once attracted George S. Kaufman, Dorothy Parker, and Oscar Hammerstein II can still be found here in abundance. But easy access from Philadelphia (one hour) and New York (two hours) has brought crowds and traffic jams on summer weekends.

Despite its rapid growth, much of Bucks County's 625 square miles remains bucolic. The sleepy, sylvan beauty of the 18th- and 19th-century villages and the lush banks of the Delaware River make it an enchanting place to explore. You'll see many of Pennsylvania's famous "bank barns" (built against a bank or hill, so wagons could roll right into the loft). Stray off the beaten path and you will discover ageless scenic roads that centuries ago were the forest trails of the Leni-Lenape Indians. George Washington's Continental Army later used these roads to reach the Delaware River, which it crossed on an icy Christmas Eve in 1776.

New Hope, settled in the early 1700s, is the heart of Bucks County. This idyllic village on the Delaware River is a tapestry of stone houses, narrow streets and alleys, hidden courtyards, and charming restaurants. Doylestown, the county seat, an important coach stop in the 18th century, is today a showcase of American architecture and fine museums of Americana.

Places to Go, Sights to See

Bucks County Carriages (tel. 215/862–3582) offers 30-minute tours of New Hope in horse-drawn carriages, daily in summer and weekends only in spring and fall.

Bucks County Playhouse (New Hope, tel. 215/862–2041), housed in a mid-18th-century mill, presents Broadway drama and musical hits. The season runs from May through Christmas.

Bucks County Vineyards and Winery (3 mi south of New Hope, tel. 800/362–0309; in PA, 800/523–2510) is open for tours and wine tastings.

Farley's Bookshop (New Hope, tel. 215/862–2452) is a booklover's boon, an independent operation that houses well-stocked, gloriously disheveled, and eminently perusable stacks.

Fonthill (Doylestown, tel. 215/348–9461) was designed and constructed by Henry Chapman Mercer, a leader in the Arts and Crafts movement, a noted antiquarian and archaeologist, and a pioneer ceramicist. Built with all the grandeur of a medieval castle, the house contains collections of decorative tiles, prints, prehistoric pottery, and memorabilia.

Ghost Tours of New Hope (tel. 215/357–4558) consist of one-hour walks by lantern lights to explore the haunted spots of the area.

Historic Fallsington (Fallsington, tel. 215/295–6567) is the 300-year-old village where William Penn attended Quaker meetings. The restored buildings span three centuries.

The James A. Michener Art Museum of Bucks County (Doylestown, tel. 215/340–9800) opened in 1988. The renowned author grew up in Doylestown. Twentieth-century American art is the focus; rotating exhibits showcase everything from quilt making to photography to the performing arts.

Mercer Museum (Doylestown, tel. 215/345–0210) contains a collection of early Americana, tools, and implements of trades and crafts before mass production. There are antique vehicles, a log house, and a 14,000-volume library.

Moravian Pottery and Tile Works (Doylestown, tel. 215/345–6722) is now restored as a living-history museum; here you can watch tiles being made.

New Hope Mule Barge Co. (tel. 215/862–2842) offers one-hour excursions on the Delaware Canal, through the countryside, and past 18th-century cottages and artists' workshops.

Parry Mansion (New Hope, tel. 215/862–5652), a restored stone house built in 1784 by Benjamin Parry, a prosperous merchant and mill owner, is furnished in period antiques that date from the late-18th to the early 20th century.

Pearl S. Buck House (Hilltown, tel. 215/249–0100), the home of the Pulitzer- and Nobel Prize–winning author has its original furnishings, including many Chinese artifacts.

Peddler's Village (Lahaska, tel. 215/794–4000) is a re-created 18th-century village of 62 old-fashioned country shops and "Early American" restaurants.

Pennsbury Manor (Morrisville, tel. 215/946–0400) is William Penn's reconstructed 17th-century country estate. The estate's 43 acres contain the manor house (with period furnishings), outbuildings, livestock, and gardens.

Quarry Valley Farm (Lahaska, tel. 215/794–5882) is a working farm with many animals to pet.

Rice's Sale and Country Market (Solebury, tel. 215/297–5993) offers bargains in clothing, antiques, linens, shoes, and plants Tuesday from dawn to 1 PM.

Washington Crossing Historic Park (tel. 215/493–4076) has the old McConkey's Ferry Inn, replicas of Durham boats (the type George Washington used), a restored gristmill, a wildflower preserve with displays, lectures, and trails.

Restaurants

In Doylestown, you can walk from the Mercer Museum to **B. Maxwell's Restaurant and Victorian Pub** (tel. 215/348–1027). Entrées run $12–$20. **Russell's 96 West** (tel. 215/345–8746) is a little pricier (entrées $17–$21), but there's a $14.95 early-bird special.

For a *very* casual evening (burgers, darts, pool, and music), try the Australian-run **Wookey Hole Pub** (tel. 215/794–7784), in Buckingham, between Doylestown and New Hope. New Hope proprietors recommend the cuisine at the **Inn at Phillips Mill** (*see below*) and at **Martine's** (tel. 215/862–2966), which offers Continental nouvelle dinners for $8–$20 in its downstairs pub and second-story dining room. **Odette's Restaurant** (tel. 215/862–2432) is famous for the cabaret performers it attracts from all over the world.

From New Hope, it's a quick jaunt across the bridge to New Jersey and **Meils Bakery and Restaurant** (tel. 609/397–8033) in Stockton. Everything's homemade, with large portions at moderate prices; you can pick up a bottle of wine across the street before dinner. Farther north, the **Harrowe Inne** (tel. 215/847–2464) in Ottsville specializes in Continental dining and fine wines. Or take Route 32 upriver from New Hope to the small town of Kintnersville and check out the down-home **Great American Grill and Food Store** (tel. 215/847–2023) for ribs, chicken, and onion rings.

Tourist Information

Bucks County Tourist Commission (152 Swamp Rd., Doylestown 18901, tel. 215/345–4552). **New Hope Borough Information Center** (Box 141, 1 W. Mechanic St., New Hope 18938, tel. 215/862–5880).

Barley Sheaf Farm

Turn off well-traveled Route 202 10 minutes from New Hope, and you'll see sheep grazing in the pastures on either side of a sycamore-flanked lane. At the end is Barley Sheaf Farm, the 1740 mansard-roofed fieldstone house that in the '30s was the hideaway of playwright George S. Kaufman. Today this charming 30-acre farm, though just around the bend from the bustling antiques shops of Peddler's Village, manages to retain the quiet gentility that prevailed when Lillian Hellman, Alexander Woollcott, and Moss Hart visited here.

The swimming pool, a duck pond, and the bank barn add texture and a relaxed appeal to the house and grounds, which have been designated a National Historic Site. Until 1979 this was the home of innkeepers Don and Ann Mills, who then decided to open their farm to travelers. Barley Sheaf Farm was Bucks County's first B&B, and with good reason it has become one of the most noted.

The house and adjacent cottage are furnished in a mixture of English and American antiques, with rich Oriental rugs scattered over the wide-plank floors. Guests gather in the common room, by the fire, for chess, checkers, and conversation.

The bedrooms on the second and third floors have elegant views. The rooms are decorated with floral prints and brass-and-iron beds. Personal touches complement the antique furnishings: doll collections, family photographs, and paintings by Ann. Don was president of a fragrance company before retiring to Barley Sheaf, and perfume bottles decorate the antique bureaus.

The cottage is cozy, and in winter months there's always a crackling fire. The three bedrooms here are decorated with American folk art, both antique and reproduction. Each room has sloping eaves, hooked rugs, and antique pine furniture. Though the rooms are small, the cottage is perfect for families.

You should expect to hear noises in this rural setting—the noises of a working farm: the baaing of sheep, the buzzing of bees (which manufacture 300 pounds of honey annually), and the occasional rumble of a tractor. But that means you can count on the abundant breakfasts (which include eggs, bread, jams, and honey) to be farm fresh.

Address: *Rte. 202 (Box 10), Holicong, PA 18928, tel. 215/794–5104.*
Accommodations: *8 double rooms with baths, 2 suites.*
Amenities: *Air-conditioning in bedrooms, TV in study; swimming pool, badminton, croquet, meeting room in barn.*
Rates: *$95–$175; full breakfast. V.*
Restrictions: *No pets, 2-day minimum on weekends, 3-day minimum on holidays, closed Christmas week.*

Evermay-on-the-Delaware

Thirteen miles north of New Hope is Evermay-on-the-Delaware, a romantic country hotel with a carriage house and cottage set on 25 parklike acres between the river and the canal. Here Victorian elegance is still very much in fashion.

The mansion, which is on the National Register of Historic Places, was built in 1720 and had a third floor added in 1870. From 1871 through the early 1930s, it was a popular country hotel. It was abandoned for many years and then bought by veteran innkeepers Fred Cresson and Ron Strouse. After meticulous restoration, they reopened it in March 1982. You will find Fred and Ron to be unobtrusive, genteel hosts; their style is in keeping with the hotel's tradition of understated elegance.

In the stately wainscoted double parlor you can meet for afternoon tea or for an aperitif in the evening. The fireplace is inset with Mercer tiles, and there are crystal chandeliers, tapestry rugs, a Victorian grandfather clock, and brocade camelback settees. Breakfast is served in a conservatory off the back parlor. The bedrooms, carefully decorated with Victorian antiques and named after Bucks County notables, have wide-plank squeaky floors; some retain their original fireplaces. Carved walnut beds, massive headboards, marble-top dressers, Victorian wallpaper, and fresh fruit and flowers

are everywhere. Ask for one of the six bedrooms in the main house that face the river. The carriage house may be preferable for groups traveling together. It has a two-bedroom suite with sitting room and bath on the second floor and two double rooms on the ground floor.

A weekend stay at the Evermay is incomplete without the seven-course prix fixe dinner, which is mandatory one night. Ron, a gourmet chef who trained with James Beard, serves unforgettable contemporary American cuisine.

The Evermay is ideally located for enjoying the countryside in any season. If you venture out into the meadows or into the old barn you will run across sheep and peacocks.

Address: *River Rd., Erwinna, PA 18920, tel. 215/294-9100, fax 215/294-8249.*
Accommodations: *14 double rooms with baths, 1 suite.*
Amenities: *Restaurant, air-conditioning and phones in bedrooms; hookups for modem.*
Rates: *$80–$155; full breakfast, afternoon tea. MC, V.*
Restrictions: *No pets, 2-day minimum with Sat. reservation, 3-day minimum on holidays, closed Christmas Eve.*

The Inn at Fordhook Farm

he Inn at Fordhook Farm, set
on 62 acres a mile and a half
from the center of Doylestown,
is the Burpee family estate. There's
a bank barn and a carriage house,
surrounded by the fields and meadows where W. Atlee Burpee first
tested seeds for his company before
the turn of the century. The oldest
part of the fieldstone-and-plaster
house with a mansard roof dates
from 1740. Through the years, additions were carefully made to blend
architecturally with the original
structure. Burpee's grandchildren,
Blanche Burpee Dohan and her
brother Jonathan Burpee, grew up
here. Thinking that a bed-and-
breakfast would be a good way to
preserve the family home, they
opened it to guests in 1985.

The house, furnished throughout
with a mixture of English and American antiques, is a living legacy of
photographs, china, furniture, grandfather clocks, and other Americana.
In the dining room, the mantel is inlaid with Mercer tiles, and the long
mahogany table is set with heirloom
china each morning for breakfast.
French doors open to a large terrace
shaded by 200-year-old linden trees,
with a view of the broad, sweeping
lawn. In the bedrooms, you will find
floral prints, quilts, 19th-century
four-poster beds, window seats, and
family photographs and portraits.

The carriage house is a spacious
two-bedroom suite not quite as carefully decorated as the main house,
but ideal for a family or for two couples. The chestnut-paneled Great
Room there, once a study, has
a vaulted ceiling and Palladian windows, and children's books, photographs, and other Burpee
memorabilia everywhere. Seeds are
still tested on 2 acres beside the carriage house.

The style at Fordhook Farm is
a quiet, casual elegance. When
Blanche and Jonathan are away, it is
in the capable hands of Elizabeth
Romanella, who previously worked
for the New York Historical Society
and the Pennsylvania Academy of
Fine Arts. Elizabeth serves an elaborate Saturday tea—by the fire during the winter, outdoors on the
generous terrace in warm months.
And to the delight of gardening
wonks, she arranges welcome baskets for each room, complete with
a sample packet of Burpee seeds.

Address: *105 New Britain Rd.,
Doylestown, PA 18901, tel. 215/345–
1766.*
Accommodations: *3 double rooms
with baths, 4 doubles share 2 baths.*
Amenities: *Air-conditioning in bed-
rooms, conference room.*
Rates: *$93–$175; full breakfast. AE,
MC, V.*
Restrictions: *No smoking, no pets,
2-day minimum on weekends, 3-day
minimum on holidays.*

Inn at Phillips Mill

Perched at a bend in the road, in a tiny hamlet on the Delaware Canal near New Hope, is a 1750 stone inn that looks like an illustration from Grimm's Fairy Tales. There may be no country inn with a setting more romantic than the Inn at Phillips Mill. Built as a barn and a gristmill, it once stood next to the village piggery—a copper pig with a wreath around its neck now welcomes you from just above the deep-blue door.

Around the turn of the century, landscape painter William Lathrop bought the gristmill and started Bucks County's first artists' colony. In the early 1970s, the building and its walled garden caught the imagination of Brooks and Joyce Kaufman. Thinking it had the look of a European village, they bought it; Brooks, an architect, started the renovation, and Joyce began doing the interior. They opened in 1977.

The guest rooms are small, but they will enchant you. Some are tucked imaginatively into nooks and under eaves, and each is whimsically furnished. There are brass and iron and late-19th-century four-poster beds, and an eclectic mix of antiques, wicker, quilts, dried bouquets, hand-painted trays, embroidered cloths on night tables, Provençal fabrics, floral wallpapers, and oil paintings. The cottage, also decorated in a mix of French country and American antiques, has a bedroom, a bath, and a living room with a stone fireplace. If you wish, breakfast will be delivered to your bedroom door in a big basket. When you lift the blue-and-white checkered cloth, you will find muffins and a pot of coffee or tea.

Phillips Mill is famous for its restaurant, and rightly so. The candlelit tables in the three dining rooms are intimately nestled into nooks and crannies under low, rough-beamed ceilings. The menu is French and may feature confit of duck with rosemary sauce, medallions of veal and sweetbreads in a caper cream demi-glacé, or roulade of sole and salmon mousse with citrus sauce. Two pastry chefs on the premises, Roz Schwartz and Thomas Millburn, prepare "les délices de la maison" (house delights).

The winding back roads are perfect for hiking, bicycling, or driving to see the fall foliage.

Address: *N. River Rd., New Hope, PA 18938, tel. 215/862–2984.*
Accommodations: *5 double rooms with baths, 1 suite.*
Amenities: *Restaurant, air-conditioning in bedrooms; swimming pool.*
Rates: *$75–$85; Continental breakfast extra. No credit cards.*
Restrictions: *No pets, BYOB, 3-night minimum on holiday weekends, closed early Jan.–early Feb.*

The Wedgwood Inn

You can't miss the Wedgwood Inn. This hip-gabled 1870 Victorian clapboard house on a tree-lined street is only two blocks from the center of New Hope, and it's painted bright Wedgwood blue. It has a large veranda loaded with pots of flowers and hanging ferns, a porte-cochère, and garden walks that wind around to a gazebo. The companion property next door, called Umplebe House, was built of plaster and stone about 1830 in the Classic Revival tradition. It has walls that are 26 inches thick, brick walkways through flowering gardens, and a carriage house in back. Down the street a block or two is another companion property, the Aaron Burr House, a six-bedroom Victorian with a maximum capacity of 18 guests, popular for business conferences. It has two suites, one with a stone fireplace and one with gas.

Innkeeping seemed a logical profession for owners Nadine Silnutzer and Carl Glassman, 10-year veterans of the B&B game. They like gardening, and they delight in finding antiques at auctions and flea markets. Carl and his colleague Ripley Hotch have just published a new book, *How to Start and Run Your Own Bed & Breakfast Inn* (Stackpole Books)— testimony to the hosts' knowledge of the business.

Wedgwood pottery, oil paintings, handmade quilts, and fresh flowers are everywhere in the sunny interior.

The parlors in both houses have coal-fed fireplaces and plush Victorian sofas and chairs. The windows are covered with lace swag curtains. Persian rugs lie on hardwood floors. Both houses have quirky odd-size bedrooms with bay windows and Victorian antiques, brass beds, and four-posters. The circa-1890 carriage house has a small sitting room and a glass-enclosed porch, a kitchenette, and a four-poster in the loft that overlooks a small deck. It's a private retreat that's ideal for reading a novel, or maybe writing one.

Days begin casually with a "Continental-plus" breakfast, served in the sun porch, the gazebo, or if you prefer, in bed. If you ask, Carl and Dinie will get you theater tickets, make dinner reservations, and arrange picnics, dinner in the gazebo, or a moonlight carriage ride.

Address: *111 W. Bridge St., New Hope, PA 18998, tel. 215/862–2570.*
Accommodations: *10 double rooms with baths, 2 doubles share a bath, 2 suites.*
Amenities: *Air-conditioning in bedrooms, TV in parlors, concierge services; swimming and tennis privileges for nominal fee at nearby club, complimentary carriage rides, disabled-accessible unit.*
Rates: *$75–$180; Continental breakfast, afternoon tea. AE, MC, V.*
Restrictions: *No smoking indoors, 2-day minimum on weekends, 3-day minimum on holiday weekends.*

The Whitehall Inn

en minutes southwest of New Hope and five minutes from Peddler's Village is the Whitehall Inn, a white plaster-over-stone manor house, circa 1794, set on 12 rolling acres, with a huge white barn and stables at the side. It is one of the most peaceful and secluded inns in Bucks County.

Two transplanted Oklahomans, Mike and Suella Wass, are responsible for elevating the business of innkeeping to a fine art. No guest will feel neglected here; from the moment you cross the threshold, the Wasses convince you with seeming effortlessness (or perhaps it's hard work) that your visit is important to them. Some establishments have lost this gift—the host greets you with a "you're on your own" dispatch—but this couple encourages your interest in the area, engages you in conversation, and ultimately earns your compliments. After years in their niche, the Wasses continue to stand above the rest.

Inside the house, past the sunroom, are high ceilings, Oriental rugs on wide-plank floors, and windows with deep sills. The parlor has a fireplace, a late-19th-century pedal organ, comfortable contemporary sofas with lots of Victorian lamps, and the soothing sounds of antique clocks ticking everywhere. The bedrooms (four with fireplaces) are furnished in a mixture of late Victorian and American country antiques. You will find a basket of apples, a bottle of Bucks County wine, and Crabtree and Evelyn soaps, colognes, and shampoos. The linens are imported, and in winter you sleep between flannel sheets.

Heirloom china and ornate Victorian sterling flatware are used for breakfast, a sybaritic and beautifully orchestrated four-course feast, with lighted tapers on the table and sideboards. The Wasses keep your menu on file, so you'll never get a repeat unless you make a special request.

High tea is served at 4 each afternoon with crystal, china, and silver. In summer, you can relax by the pool, play tennis, or go horseback riding. In October, you can walk in the gardens or fields, enjoy the foliage, and spend evenings by the fire in the candlelit parlor. Lovers of chocolate and/or chamber music should inquire about special-event weekends here.

Address: *1370 Pineville Rd., New Hope, PA 18938, tel. 215/598-7945.*
Accommodations: *4 double rooms with baths, 2 doubles share bath.*
Amenities: *Air-conditioning in bedrooms; swimming pool, tennis.*
Rates: *$130–$170; full breakfast, high tea. AE, DC, MC, V.*
Restrictions: *No smoking, no pets.*

Ash Mill Farm

A sh Mill Farm, on 11 pastoral acres, is 10 minutes by car from both New Hope and Doylestown. As you turn up the long drive off Route 202, you will pass sheep grazing in the meadows and then come to the charming buff plaster-over-stone 1790 Federal manor house with the large veranda. When Jim and Patricia Auslander moved from New York City and became innkeepers in 1989, Jim traded in legal briefs for cookbooks and Patricia called upon her corporate managerial skills. They refurbished Ash Mill with eclectic treasures collected from Ireland and England, American antiques, and Shaker reproductions. The downstairs rooms have high ceilings, random-width floors, and deep-set windows; the bedrooms have tranquil views, rag rugs, canopy beds, and antique Irish armoires. Several magazines and sales catalogs have organized fashion shoots here because of Ash Mill's exterior and interior charms. If an outing is in order, antiques shops and Peddler's Village are only minutes away.

Address: *Rte. 202 (Box 202), Holicong, PA 18928, tel. 215/794-5373.*
Accommodations: *3 double rooms with baths, 2 doubles share 1 bath, 1 suite.*
Amenities: *Air-conditioning in bedrooms, breakfast in bed on request.*
Rates: *$75-$125; full breakfast, afternoon tea, complimentary brandy. No credit cards.*
Restrictions: *Smoking on veranda only, no pets, 2-day minimum with Sat. reservation, 3-day minimum on holiday weekends.*

Bridgeton House

A t the foot of the bridge to Milford, New Jersey, is a three-story 1836 Federal brick building that has been a residence and a general store. In 1982, with a dozen years of inn experience behind them, Beatrice and Charles Briggs completely transformed it into a terra-cotta-colored bed-and-breakfast. You will find American country antiques, reproductions, and contemporary furnishings. Five rooms on the riverside have four-posters, country quilts, and screened-in private porches with breathtaking views of the morning mist. A spiral staircase leads to a huge third-floor penthouse suite so ultra-high-tech you might think you were in Manhattan. But the view—as though you're suspended over the Delaware—tells you otherwise. In winter, the cozy sitting room is a perfect place to gaze out at the snow falling on the river. In summer, you can watch people paddle canoes and float lazily along in inner tubes—or you might indulge.

Address: *River Rd. (Box 167), Upper Black Eddy, PA 18972, tel. 215/982-5856.*
Accommodations: *6 double rooms with baths, 2 suites, garret, penthouse.*
Amenities: *Air-conditioning in bedrooms, fireplaces in dining room and in suites.*
Rates: *$65-$180; full breakfast. No credit cards.*
Restrictions: *No smoking indoors, no pets, 2-day minimum on weekends, 3-day minimum on holiday weekends, closed Dec. 24-25.*

Bucksville House

This gem of a bed-and-breakfast on 5½ acres in northern Bucks County was once a stagecoach stop. Innkeepers Barbara and Joe Szallosi restored the 1795 Colonial fieldstone-and-stucco house while she wasn't teaching and he wasn't doing carpentry. The living room is decorated in English and American antiques, and in the den (once the tavern), you will find a coal stove to curl up in front of. The dining room, once the old wheelwright shop, has a walk-in fireplace, a Mercer tile floor, and a long country table. Dried herbs and antique baskets hang from the beams of the low ceiling. In the bedrooms, antiques blend nicely with reproductions handcrafted by Joe—cupboards and pencil-post beds. In 1992, Joe bought 12,000 bricks and built a courtyard terrace and herb garden. And a new, spacious unit equipped for disabled visitors was christened the same year. Grapes grow on an arbor near the gazebo, and Joe makes his own wine. Chances are, he will bring a bottle up from the cellar for you to sample.

Address: *4501 Durham Rd. and Buck Dr., Kintnersville, PA 18930, tel. 215/847-8948.*
Accommodations: *4 double rooms with baths, 1 suite.*
Amenities: *Air-conditioning in bedrooms, cable TV in den, fireplaces in 3 bedrooms; fish pond, outdoor deck and gazebo.*
Rates: *$85–$125; full breakfast. AE, D, MC, V.*
Restrictions: *No smoking, no pets.*

Highland Farms

Bordering the Doylestown Country Club golf course is the 1740 fieldstone country manor that was once home to lyricist Oscar Hammerstein II. Innkeepers John and Mary Schnitzer bought the estate and opened it as a bed-and-breakfast on Valentine's Day, 1988. The elegant, high-ceilinged rooms are furnished in American and English antiques. Flanking a foyer with a grandfather clock and a Victorian pierglass are a spacious parlor and a formal dining room. Wicker and ferns fill a sunroom that overlooks a white carriage house, bank barn, and a 60-foot pool. The library is richly decorated with green velvet sofas and chairs and a collection of Hammerstein memorabilia. You can spend cozy evenings by the fire here watching a musical from the video collection. The bedrooms have flowered curtains and canopy beds, and each has a magnificent view. You will wake to the aroma of fresh hazelnut coffee and, in late summer, the sight of corn growing "as high as an elephant's eye."

Address: *70 East Rd., Doylestown, PA 18901, tel. 215/340-1354.*
Accommodations: *2 double rooms with baths, 2 doubles share bath.*
Amenities: *Air-conditioning in bedrooms, cable TV with VCR, and phone in library; swimming pool, tennis court.*
Rates: *$125–$175; full breakfast. AE, MC, V.*
Restrictions: *Smoking in library only, 2-day minimum on weekends, 3-day minimum on holidays.*

Isaac Stover House

Thirteen miles north of New Hope, the Isaac Stover House, on 13 tranquil acres, overlooks the Delaware River. The stately exterior of this Victorian Federal mansion hardly prepares you for the highly theatrical decor inside. When radio and TV personality Sally Jessy Raphael opened her bed-and-breakfast in 1988, she decorated it with a mishmash of antiques, treasures from her travels, and a rich, ever-expanding clutter of Victoriana. It works. Jokingly, Sally calls it "Nouveau Bordello." Faux marble arches in the foyer, real black marble fireplaces, red velvet settees, and lush moiré draperies in the parlor transform the house into a whimsical stage setting. Bedrooms have their own fanciful themes, such as Emerald City and Loyalty Royalty. Each bed has a thick down comforter and mountains of pillows (where chocolate truffles await you). After your sumptuous three-course breakfast, innkeeper Susan Tettemer, a veteran of other Bucks County inns, will gladly help plan your daily outings.

Address: *River Rd. (Box 68), Erwinna, PA 18920, tel. 215/294–8044.*
Accommodations: *4 double rooms with baths, 2 doubles share bath, 1 suite.*
Amenities: *Air-conditioning in bedrooms, phone and TV in 2nd-floor alcove, picnics provided.*
Rates: *$100–$250; full breakfast and afternoon tea. AE, MC, V.*
Restrictions: *No smoking in bedrooms, no pets, 2-day minimum on weekends.*

The Logan Inn

This Colonial tavern and inn in the heart of New Hope was established in 1727. Legend has it that George Washington stayed here five times. Restaurateur Steve Katz recently bought the shuttered fieldstone inn and, with innkeeper Gwen Davis, embarked on a major renovation. Wide hallways lead into spacious bedrooms with four-posters and Victorian and Colonial reproductions. Lace curtains and baskets of flowers fill the deep-set window embrasures that overlook the river and the village's main thoroughfare. The tavern has a Colonial fireplace, a dartboard, and restored 18th-century murals of hunting scenes. A wall of stained glass gives a Victorian elegance to the Garden Dining Room. A huge canopied patio encourages a booming summer business. The Logan is within easy walking distance of all area sights. Gwen, a longtime resident who has worked with the historical preservation society, will fill you in on local lore, arrange tours, and get tickets to nearby attractions.

Address: *10 W. Ferry St., New Hope, PA 18938, tel. 215/862–2300.*
Accommodations: *15 double rooms with baths, 1 suite.*
Amenities: *Restaurant, tavern, air-conditioning in bedrooms, cable TV and phones in bedrooms, 1 meeting room with kitchen in annex.*
Rates: *$95–$150; full breakfast. AE, MC, V.*
Restrictions: *No pets, 2-day minimum on weekends Memorial Day–Labor Day, 3-day minimum on holiday weekends.*

Pinetree Farm

Two miles outside Doylestown is a white stucco-and-fieldstone 1730 Quaker farmhouse that has been carefully restored by innkeepers Joy and Ron Feigles. Joy jokes that she majored in hotel administration "and then 29 years later we bought an inn." The interior is white, light, and airy, and it's decorated with American Colonial antiques and reproductions. A solarium overlooks the swimming pool and 16 acres of pine trees. The bedrooms have stenciling, Oriental rugs, marble fireplaces, writing desks, four-poster beds, iron beds, and in the Pink Room, a canopied white twig bed that's a masterpiece. Stuffed toy lambs are perched on each bed; the deep window seats have mounds of pillows to curl up into, and the view makes you want to reread Jane Austen. The Feigles, lifelong residents of Doylestown, have plenty of suggestions if you should want to explore nearby villages or shop for antiques.

Address: *2155 Lower State Rd., Doylestown, PA 18901, tel. 215/348-0632.*
Accommodations: *2 double rooms with baths, 2 doubles share 1 bath.*
Amenities: *Air-conditioning in bedrooms, cable TV in study; swimming pool, tennis court.*
Rates: *$125–$150; full breakfast. No credit cards.*
Restrictions: *No smoking, no pets, 2-day minimum on weekends, 3-day minimum on holiday weekends.*

The Brandywine River Valley

About an hour from Philadelphia, where southeastern Pennsylvania meets northern Delaware, the Brandywine River flows lazily from West Chester to Wilmington, amid rolling hills where streams wind through dense woodlands. The pastoral valley has sheltered artists and millionaires, Revolutionary War soldiers, and slaves on the Underground Railroad. Today it looks much as it did 250 years ago.

Beginning in 1623 the Dutch, the Swedes, and the English moved in successively, coexisting with the Leni-Lenape Indians, the region's earliest residents. But it was not until 1682 that William Penn and the English finally stabilized the region. Quaker millers and farmers began to settle here in the early 1700s. Powder mills supplied munitions for George Washington's army, and in the fall of 1777 more than 30,000 soldiers fought the Battle of Brandywine. After a resounding defeat Washington's army camped over the winter at nearby Valley Forge until that famous Christmas crossing over the Delaware River.

Early in this century the illustrator Howard Pyle and other artists began building the reputation of the Brandywine School, dominated today by three generations of Wyeths—N. C., Andrew, and James. A century before the Wyeths began capturing the local landscape on canvas, the du Pont family was ornamenting it with grand mansions and gardens. Pierre-Samuel du Pont, the patriarch, escaped with his family from post-Revolutionary France and settled in northern Delaware. His son Eleuthère Irénée (E. I.) founded the Du Pont Company in 1802 and made the family fortune, first in gunpowder and iron, later in chemicals and textiles (see Delaware, The Wilmington area).

*Log cabins, 18th-century stone farmhouses, and the ornate
estates of the du Ponts are all reminders of the past. Today
you can visit world-famous formal gardens and museums
of the decorative arts. You can explore backcountry roads
and antiques shops (without the crowds that you find in
Bucks County), then check into a restful country inn.*

Places to Go, Sights to See

Brandywine Battlefield State Park (Chadds Ford, tel. 215/459–3342). British
troops defeated the Continental Army here in the fall of 1777. On the site
are two restored farmhouses that once sheltered Washington and Lafayette.

Brandywine River Museum (Chadds Ford, tel. 215/388–7601). This restored
Civil War–era gristmill, on the banks of the Brandywine River, now houses
a collection of landscape paintings, American illustrations, and works by
three generations of Wyeths. Outside are gardens and nature trails.

Franklin Mint Museum (Franklin Center, tel. 215/459–6168). The world's
largest private mint creates collectibles—books, records, jewelry, furniture,
porcelain, bronzes, and crystal.

Longwood Gardens (Kennett Square, tel. 215/388–6741). The grounds boast
some 350 acres of magnolias and azaleas in spring; roses and water lilies in
summer; fall foliage; and winter camellias, orchids, and palms in
a 19th-century arboretum.

Valley Forge National Historical Park (Valley Forge, tel. 215/783–7700). On
these 3,500 serene acres, George Washington's army endured the winter of
1777–1778. There are picnic areas and 6 miles of paved trails.

Restaurants

In Dilworthtown, just south of West Chester on Route 202, you'll find the
Dilworthtown Inn (tel. 215/399–1390), a French Continental dining room in
a 1785 Colonial edifice. Entrées average $18–$20, and the lobster is
renowned. **La Cocotte** (tel. 215/436–6722), in the heart of West Chester on
West Gay Street, specializes in French country cuisine: light lunches and
elegant dinners.

In the Kennett Square area: **Pasta Garden** (tel. 215/444–4040) may not look
particularly comely in its shopping-center setting, but it's pleasant for
cocktails and dependable for moderately priced and very tasty pastas, veal,
and seafood. An 18th-century barn set on 20 landscaped acres houses **The
Stone Barn** (tel. 215/347–2414), an all-American establishment serving up
beef and shrimp dishes until Sunday afternoon, when it goes Scandinavian
with a smorgasbord. **The Terrace Restaurant** (tel. 215/388–6771), on Route

1, occupies a wonderful site overlooking the landscaped grounds of Longwood Gardens. The presentation and service are graceful, and the clientele is international. For light fare downtown, head over to the **Kennett Square Inn** (tel. 215/444–5688) for burgers.

One mile north of the Brandywine River Museum you'll find **Chadds Ford Cafe** (tel. 215/558–3960), a casual, moderately priced spot for sandwiches and soups or unpretentious dinner fare. For rich country cooking and a creditable wine list, try **Pace One** (tel. 215/459–9784) in Thornton. Prices for the lamb, seafood, and pasta dishes are medium to medium-high.

Tourist Information

Tourist Information Center for the Brandywine Valley (Rte. 1, Kennett Square 19348, tel. 215/388–2900 or 800/228–9933). **Valley Forge Convention & Visitors Bureau** (Box 311, Norristown 19404, tel. 215/278–3558).

Reservation Services

B&B of Chester County (Box 825, Kennett Square 19348, tel. 215/444–1367). **B&B Connections** (Box 21, Devon 19333, tel. 215/687–3565 or 800/448–3619). **B&B of Valley Forge/Philadelphia** (Box 562, Valley Forge 19481–0562, tel. 215/783–7838).

Duling-Kurtz House & Country Inn

On a country road midway between Valley Forge and the Brandywine Battlefields is the Duling-Kurtz House & Country Inn. Down a driveway lined with converted gas street lamps are formal gardens, a Victorian-style gazebo, and a footbridge that crosses a stone-lined brook. The 1830s farmhouse and the adjacent barn, both white plaster over fieldstone, were elegantly restored and opened in 1983. Raymond Carr and David Knauer, who did the restoration, named the property after their mothers. The new owner, Michael Person—who hails from Vienna, Austria, and has a background in hotel management—has orchestrated a massive upgrading since taking over in 1992, and he is a decidedly hands-on operator. He staunchly defends the concept of fine dining and lodging at affordable prices, and he runs an intimate, service-oriented inn.

The guest rooms (in the barn) have been restored and furnished in Williamsburg period reproductions. You will find marble-top sinks; Oriental rugs; writing desks; and canopied, brass, and four-poster beds. One suite has its own courtyard; two have working fireplaces. Rooms are named for historic figures: Honeymooners often request the George Washington Room, with its king-size, cherry-wood canopy bed and a step-down bathroom with a claw-foot tub. A Continental breakfast is served on china in the parlor.

A sheltered brick walkway connects the barn and the farmhouse restaurant, which is also furnished with Colonial reproductions. Near the entrance you'll discover an unusual 18th-century beehive bread oven. Four of the dining rooms have stone fireplaces, and richly mullioned windows detail the dining areas. *The Philadelphia Inquirer* has praised French chef Gilles Morte. Michael insists that fine cuisine needn't mean breaking the bank; dinner entrées run as low as $13.

You can stroll through peaceful wooded areas adjoining the inn, and when it's warm you can enjoy tea in the gazebo. Museums and battlefields are not far away, and Michael and his staff will point you to the best antiquing and skiing.

Address: *146 S. Whitford Rd., Exton, PA 19341, tel. 215/524–1830, fax 215/524–6258.*
Accommodations: *15 double rooms with baths, 3 suites.*
Amenities: *Restaurant open Mon.–Sat., air-conditioning in bedrooms, cable TV and phones in bedrooms, room service; 3 conference rooms with catering.*
Rates: *$50–$120; Continental breakfast. AE, D, DC, MC, V.*
Restrictions: *No pets, closed Christmas and New Year's Day.*

Fairville Inn

In the heart of Andrew Wyeth country, on the road between Winterthur Museum and Longwood Gardens, this country-house inn set on 5½ acres behind a split-rail fence is surrounded by estates, beautiful gardens, and miles of country back roads. The hub of the inn is a cream-colored 1826 Federal plaster-over-double-brick house with black shutters. A Victorian-style veranda across the front makes an open porch on the second floor. In back are the barn and carriage house, smaller clapboard and fieldstone buildings that were recently constructed by an Amish family who live nearby.

Swedish-born Ole Retlev and his wife, Patricia, both former ski instructors, owned two different inns in Mt. Snow, Vermont. But, as Ole explains, "There's more to draw travelers here on a year-round basis." So, in 1986, they moved to the Brandywine River valley and opened the Fairville Inn.

The rooms are bright and airy, appealingly furnished with Queen Anne and Hepplewhite reproductions. Before the fireplace in the living room are two blue settees, with a large copper-top coffee table between them. An antique Swedish linen cupboard, flowered draperies, and potted plants give the room an understated "relaxed formal feel," as Ole calls it. The bedrooms in the main house, all of quirky size and shape, are done in light, elegant country colors and are carpeted. You will also find four-poster beds, canopy beds, settees, writing desks, floral wallpapers—and fresh roses. The four rooms in the barn are somewhat smaller, but all have working fireplaces. Siding from the old barn has been used for mantels and paneling, and some of the sinks have copper drainboards.

Two suites in the carriage house have private terraces and balconies that overlook a pond and rolling farmland; three units have fireplaces. They are at the back of the property and away from traffic noise. With cathedral ceilings and old barn timbers for beams and mantels, they are also the most architecturally interesting.

Canoeing, hiking, antiquing, and museum-browsing are only some of the area's pastimes. Or why not attend a polo match during one of the warmer months?

Address: *Rte. 52 (Box 219), Fairville, PA 19357, tel. 215/388–5900, fax 215/388–5902.*
Accommodations: *13 double rooms with baths, 2 suites.*
Amenities: *Air-conditioning, cable TV, and phones in bedrooms.*
Rates: *$100–$165; Continental breakfast, afternoon tea. AE, D, MC, V.*
Restrictions: *No pets.*

Hamanassett

Meet Evelene Dohan, the proprietor of Hamanassett: She has taught, run a catering business, and gone home a multiple champion from the Philadelphia Flower Show. Her gifts are evident both on the grounds and in the interior buildings of this secluded estate.

The hilltop residence overlooks 36 acres of woods and meadow, shaded garden pathways, and stone-walled ponds. In April and May, approaching guests pass through a fragrant lane of rhododendrons and azaleas, blossoming in profusion along the ellipse that fronts the main house. Inside, the innkeeper's cut-flower arrangements grace each room; potted plants and hanging ferns flood the light-filled solarium. Mrs. Dohen, who came as a bride in 1950 and raised her children here, has appointed her rooms with four-poster canopied beds, Oriental rugs, and handsome dark wood antiques. And she single-handedly serves up delectable country breakfasts with homemade jams, compotes, and freshly baked confections.

Hamanassett was built in 1856 for Dr. Charles Meigs, a Philadelphia pioneer in obstetrics, but what you see today bears little resemblance to the doctor's summer retreat. As Mrs. Dohen will tell you, the little farmhouse then consisted of just "three rooms down, and three rooms up." But in 1870 her late husband's grandfather purchased the estate.

His son—her father-in-law—didn't like the sensation of enclosure, and so he added onto and redefined the original structure (including the pumpkin pine flooring). He installed arched passageways instead of doors between rooms on the first floor, so the main body of the house feels united, allowing fluid movement from room to room and a less obstructed flow of light. Before ascending the main staircase, note the blue-and-white delft tile depiction of human history encased in the broad white arch to your right: The story begins with the expulsion from the Garden of Eden.

You may find yourself so seduced by the beauty this proficient innkeeper has created that you won't want to venture outside it. But if you do, all the most popular points of interest are only minutes away. Hamanassett sits just off well-traveled Route 1, but its acreage makes an ample buffer between the estate and the roadway.

Address: *Rte. 1 (Box 129), Lima, PA 19037, tel. 215/459-3000.*
Accommodations: *6 double rooms with baths, 2 doubles share a bath.*
Amenities: *Solarium, air-conditioning.*
Rates: *$85–$120; full breakfast. No credit cards.*
Restrictions: *Smoking in solarium only, no pets, 2-night minimum on weekends May–June and Oct.–Nov. and on holiday weekends.*

Scarlett House

It's been around only since October 1990, but Scarlett House has risen quickly to the top with its comfort, beauty, and professionalism. The house sits right in the heart of Kennett Square's historic district. While the rough granite exterior may not seduce you, the minute you walk into the front door (flanked by leaded glass panes and twin inglenooks) you'll pledge allegiance to this residence. It was built in 1910 by a prominent Quaker businessman for his son, Robert Scarlett, who lived here until the 1960s.

Much of this inn's allure has to do with the innkeeper, Susan Lalli Ascosi, a soft-spoken but savvy host who is the former director of marketing at the University of Pennsylvania. She and her engineer husband, who live with their young son on the third floor, are admirers of Victoriana—with a few reservations. Susan explains that most of the furnishings were part of a collection they'd acquired at house sales and auctions well before they started the business, but she also acquired enough knowledge and decorative sense to take some license with Victorian tradition by manipulating color schemes. Where Victorians would have stayed with darker tones, Susan has splashed pastels on the wooden walls of her bedchambers and strictly limited the figurine-filled shelves. Her entire interior is striking for its ambience of polished order and marked lack of "stuff."

The second-floor master suite will give you an idea of her taste. Its walls are pink, trimmed at the top with a light floral border. But the Victorian walnut bed is the room's decided cynosure. It's a stunner, with a huge Renaissance headboard looking down on all-cotton, hand-ironed sheets. Walnut reappears in a more ornately carved dresser with a framed full-length mirror; an exquisite plain-faced corner cupboard of the same wood, crafted by an Amish man in 1820, sits directly opposite.

Business travelers have closed deals in this place; women have completed theses; amorous young couples have basked in its charms. All guests eventually gravitate to the sitting room on the second floor: It faces south, so it's engulfed by light. This is a perfect place to leaf through all the local literature (including restaurant listings, with current menus) that Susan keeps.

Address: *503 W. State St., Kennett Square, PA 19348, tel. 215/444-9592.*
Accommodations: *1 double room with bath, 2 doubles share a bath, 1 suite.*
Amenities: *Cable TV, fireplace, and newspapers in downstairs parlor.*
Rates: *$65–$95; Continental breakfast. D.*
Restrictions: *No smoking indoors, no pets, 2-night minimum on holiday weekends, closed Christmas Eve–New Year's Day.*

Sweetwater Farm

Fifteen minutes east of Chadds Ford, at the end of a circular driveway, is a stately 1758 Georgian fieldstone manor house with shutters the color of lemon custard. Sweetwater Farm once sheltered weary Revolutionary War soldiers and the Marquis de Lafayette and was a refuge for slaves on the Underground Railroad.

In the fields around the 16-room house, thoroughbreds, sheep, and goats graze amid wildflowers. From each window there are views of majestic maples on the 15 lush acres, and of the 50 undeveloped acres beyond. Though Jonathan Propper and Mike Gretz are both from the area and accustomed to its charm, they couldn't help but be drawn to this gentleman's farm; they bought Sweetwater in 1989. Innkeeper Barbara Pietsch arrived in 1992.

Inside you will find tall, deep-set windows and a sweeping center-hall staircase. Almost every room has a wood-burning fireplace, random-width floors of oak and pine, and original paintings. Rustic Pennsylvania primitive pieces are mixed with authentic 18th- and 19th-century antique furnishings. The nine guest rooms have handmade quilts on canopy beds and four-posters, embroidered spreads, dried-flower wreaths, and hidden nooks containing odd collectibles.

There are a library, with a fireplace and wall of books, a living room, and a sunroom with TV, which becomes a "boardroom" for small business meetings and luncheons. In warm weather, the broad back veranda overlooking the fields and the swimming pool is a favorite spot.

Breakfast, served in the dining room in front of the fireplace, features everything from sweet-potato waffles or puff pancakes with brown-sugar syrup to home-fried potatoes with sausage and bacon. Five cottages, also furnished in American antiques, are the ultimate romantic hideaways, with fireplaces, kitchens, and four-poster canopied beds. Museums, historic houses, and antiques shops are all nearby.

Address: *50 Sweetwater Rd., Glen Mills, PA 19342, tel. 215/459-4711, fax 215/358-4945.*
Accommodations: *3 double rooms with baths, 2 doubles share a bath, 5 cottages.*
Amenities: *Air-conditioning; swimming pool, 9 boarding stalls, conference room.*
Rates: *$145-$225; full breakfast. AE, MC, V.*
Restrictions: *No smoking in bedrooms, 2-night minimum with Sat. reservation in high season.*

The Bankhouse Bed and Breakfast

Just outside West Chester is an 18th-century stucco-over-stone house built into the bank of a hill. It once housed the servants of a large estate. Innkeepers Diana and Michael Bové, who both worked in media services at a nearby university, opened their home to travelers in 1988, and Diana now manages the bed-and-breakfast full-time.

You enter the second-floor guest rooms by an outside staircase. (The two double rooms can be rented as a single suite, with private bath, on request.) The homey upstairs sitting room has an extensive collection of books, games, and brochures; and bedrooms are decorated with 19th-century oak antiques, stenciling, and fresh roses from Diana's English gardens. Guests often linger in the narrow dining room over a hearty country breakfast—Diana specializes in apple soufflé pancakes and custard French toast with hot orange syrup—and they can look down through one deeply recessed window out to the pond and the split-rail fence that borders a meadow across the road. You can gaze at the scenery; or you can explore the shops in West Chester, canoe the Brandywine, or bike down country lanes.

Address: *875 Hillsdale Rd., West Chester, PA 19382, tel. 215/344–7388.*
Accommodations: *2 double rooms share a bath.*
Amenities: *Air-conditioning.*
Rates: *$65–$85; full breakfast. No credit cards.*
Restrictions: *No smoking, no pets.*

Bed and Breakfast at Walnut Hill

This white clapboard-and-fieldstone Pennsylvania mill house just outside Kennett Square was built before 1840. Proprietors Tom and Sandy Mills, who have lived here for three decades, opened it as a bed-and-breakfast in 1985. Across the crooked little road, beyond horses grazing in the meadow, is a creek, where it's so quiet you can hear every trickle as you watch for Canada geese, deer, or the occasional red fox to meander across the meadow. The house is warmly decorated with early-19th-century country antiques and reproductions; you'll find bunches of dried herbs and flowers, pie safes, and a New England whaler's lamp over the table. The bedrooms are furnished with writing desks, Victorian wicker, and pencil-post beds. The paneling throughout is made from old barn siding. Sandy—a trained social worker, gourmet cook, and morning person par excellence—and Tom are glad to offer tips on the best routes for biking, or hiking, or touring. This amiable couple like to think that their guests arrive as strangers but leave as friends.

Address: *214 Chandlers Mill Rd., Avondale, PA 19311, tel. 215/444–3703.*
Accommodations: *2 double rooms and 1 single share 1 bath.*
Amenities: *Air-conditioning, cable TV in family room, indoor hot tub.*
Rates: *$60–$75; full breakfast. No credit cards.*
Restrictions: *Smoking in common room only, no pets.*

Highpoint Victoriana

About 5 winding miles outside Skippack is Highpoint Victoriana, a hip-roofed, redbrick three-story house that has been restored to its 1901 elegance by innkeepers Debbi and Albert Slotter. The sitting room has a wood stove, marble-top tables, and plush 1860 rococo chairs and settees; sliding doors open to a formal dining room, and there's a pump organ in the alcove that you are welcome to play. But one nonpaying guest, a bodiless friendly spirit, has a fondness for Big Band music, and you may be greeted with faint strains of it at breakfast. All the rooms have rich reproduction Victorian wallpapers with natural wood trim. In the bedrooms, you will find oak headboards, washstands, and writing desks. From the swing on the wraparound porch there is a magnificent view of farmland. You can hike, browse through the many antiques shops in Skippack, visit nearby Valley Forge, or ski at Spring Mountain.

Address: *723 Haldeman Rd., Schwenksville, PA 19473, tel. 215/287-6619.*
Accommodations: *3 double rooms and 1 single share 3 baths.*
Amenities: *Air-conditioning in bedrooms.*
Rates: *$55-$70; full breakfast. MC, V.*
Restrictions: *Smoking in public areas only, no pets.*

Meadow Spring Farm

Just minutes north of Kennett Square and Longwood Gardens, up a country lane past grazing cows, is the brick Colonial 1836 house of this 50-acre working farm. Anne Hicks arrived here as a bride more than 40 years ago, raised five children, and in 1984 opened it as a bed-and-breakfast. She's an accomplished cook, craftswoman, and collector of dolls and family antiques. You'll find big, sunny farmhouse bedrooms, with fireplaces, Amish quilts, family photographs, a Chippendale bed with a crocheted canopy, and a carved sleigh bed with a headboard 7 feet tall. There are also two spacious, warmly appointed rooms over the garage. Anne serves breakfast on the long mahogany table in the dining room, or in the solarium, a glassed-in porch overlooking the flower gardens. You may want to take a hayride or, in winter, enjoy the solarium's hot tub. With Temba, the farm dog, you can stroll with your children through the meadows or visit the pigs and lambs in the barns.

Address: *201 E. Street Rd. (Rte. 926), Kennett Square, PA 19348, tel. 215/444-3903.*
Accommodations: *5 double rooms with baths, 2 doubles shares a bath.*
Amenities: *Air-conditioning in bedrooms, TV in bedrooms, games room with pool table and table tennis, hot tub, kitchen and laundry privileges; swimming pool.*
Rates: *$55-$75; full breakfast. No credit cards.*
Restrictions: *No pets.*

Pace One

Set in a secluded hamlet, Pace One makes a charming base from which to explore the nearby museums and countryside. Innkeeper Ted Pace, who comes from a family of restaurateurs, bought the four-story 1740 fieldstone barn 13 years ago and transformed it into a country inn. You'll find the original hand-hewn popular beams and walls that are 2 feet thick, hung with the work of local artists. Dormer windows make the six guest rooms cozy; they're furnished with Shaker-style oak beds, dressers, and small writing tables, handmade by a local craftsman. Downstairs, the heart of Pace One, is an excellent restaurant and a taproom that has the feel of an authentic Colonial tavern. In a labyrinth of intimate dining areas Ted serves what he calls "country imaginative" cooking. Pace One maintains the highest standards of service and cuisine, yet Ted and his staff are not stuffy—the atmosphere is warm and casual.

Address: *Thornton and Glen Mills Rds. (Box 108), Thornton, PA 19373, tel. 215/459-3702, fax 215/558-0825.*
Accommodations: *7 double rooms with baths.*
Amenities: *Restaurant, air-conditioning and phones in bedrooms, free use of nearby tennis and racquetball courts, 3 conference rooms with catering.*
Rates: *$65–$85; Continental breakfast. AE, DC, MC, V.*
Restrictions: *No pets, closed Christmas Day.*

Lancaster County/Amish Country

*Lancaster County, the Pennsylvania Dutch country, lies 65
miles west of Philadelphia. In the wilderness of the early
18th century, this vast, rolling farmland became home to
the so-called Plain People—the Amish, Mennonites,
Dunkards, and Brethren—German and Swiss immigrants
escaping religious persecution. The Pennsylvania Dutch
population consists of about 20 sects, and they aren't
Dutch at all; the name comes from "Deutsch," or German.
They came to Pennsylvania to live, work, and worship in
harmony. Today, in clinging to traditional dress and
a centuries-old way of life, their descendants have turned
their backs on the modern world—and have attracted the
world's attention. In this patchwork quilt of cultures many
small farms are still worked with horses and mules, and
buggies are a frequently seen mode of transportation. Few
power lines disturb the tranquil countryside.*

*The Amish are a prime attraction of, though not the only
lure to, the area. Lancaster (which the English named after
the city in Lancashire) is an intriguing town of restored
Colonial homes, taverns, shops, and churches. It is the
nation's oldest inland city, dating from 1710, and it was
the nation's capital for one day during the Revolution,
when Congress fled Philadelphia after the Battle of
Brandywine.*

*The region can be hectic, especially on summer weekends.
Busloads of tourists on their way to souvenir and crafts
shops and outlet stores often jam Routes 30 and 340, the
main thoroughfares. But there is still charm here if you
take the back roads, getting off the well-trodden path. Here
on country lanes you will find the general stores, one-room
schoolhouses, and hand-painted signs advertising quilts or
produce and eggs outside Amish farms.*

Places to Go, Sights to See

Abe's Buggy Rides (Bird-in-Hand, no tel.). Abe will give you background information on the Amish during a 2-mile spin down country roads in an Amish family carriage.

Amish Country Tours (between Bird-in-Hand and Intercourse, tel. 717/392–8622). Of the variety of tours conducted in large buses or minivans, the most popular are the two- and four-hour Amish farmland trips.

The Amish Homestead (Lancaster, tel. 717/392–0832). A house-and-farm tour that provides an introduction to Amish life. (It is a simulated enterprise and is not Amish-run.) You'll learn about Amish origins, worship, courtship, marriage, and honeymoon rituals.

Central Market (Lancaster, tel. 717/291–4740). One of the oldest covered markets in the country is located in Lancaster. This is where the locals shop for fresh produce, meats, and baked goods.

Ephrata Cloister (Ephrata, tel. 717/733–6600). Here you can get a look at a religious communal society of the 1700s best known for its publishing center, a cappella singing, Fraktur (ornate decorative calligraphy), and medieval-style German architecture.

Green Dragon Farmers Market and Auction (Ephrata, tel. 717/738–1117). In this traditional agricultural market, Amish and Mennonite farmers sell meats, fruits, vegetables, fresh-baked pies, and dry goods at 450 indoor and outdoor stalls.

Lititz. This town was founded by Moravians who settled in Pennsylvania to do missionary work. Along a tree-shaded main street are 18th-century cottages and shops selling antiques, crafts, and clothing. Nearby are the *Julius Sturgis Pretzel House* (tel. 717/626–4354), the nation's oldest pretzel bakery, and the Wilbur Chocolate Company's *Candy Americana Museum outlet* (tel. 717/626–0967).

Pennsylvania Farm Museum of Landis Valley (Lancaster, tel. 717/569–0401). Displays on Pennsylvania rural life and folk culture before 1900.

People's Place (Intercourse, tel. 717/768–7171). This excellent introduction to the Amish, Mennonites, and Hutterites includes hands-on exhibits on transportation, dress, and schools and on the effects of growing old and mutual aid in these communities.

Strasburg Rail Road (Strasburg, tel. 717/687–7522). Wooden coaches are pulled by a steam locomotive on this scenic 9-mile excursion.

Wheatland (1½ mi west of Lancaster, tel. 717/392–8721). The restored 1828 Federal mansion of James Buchanan, the only U.S. president from Pennsylvania.

Wilbur Chocolate Museum and Outlet (Lititz, tel. 717/626–0967). One of the suppliers for Godiva chocolates offers a candy-making demonstration (with free samples) and a small museum of candy-related memorabilia.

Restaurants

Family-style is big in Lancaster County, and so is reasonably priced food—which is not to say you can't find sophisticated cuisine here. Less expensive options in Lancaster include the casual **D & S Brasserie** (tel. 717/299–1694); **The Family Style Restaurant** (tel. 717/393–2323); and **Plain 'N Fancy** (tel. 717/768–8281), which heaps huge portions on your plate and is part of a complex of gift shops, museums, and outlet stores. **Isaac's Deli, Inc.** (tel. 717/393–6067), is good for sandwiches, soups, and desserts.

For more refinement, Lancaster's **Windows on Steinman Park** (tel. 717/295–1316) specializes in French food. **The Restaurant at Doneckers** (tel. 717/738–2421), in Ephrata, is a gem of a place with both low-cost, low-cholesterol selections and sophisticated French cuisine—for which you pay a few dollars more. The honest-to-goodness Pennsylvania Dutch cooking at **Groff's Farm Restaurant** (tel. 717/653–2048) in Mount Joy, a small town west of Lancaster, has become world-renowned. **Log Cabin** (tel. 717/626–1181) in Leola and **Market Fare Restaurant** (tel. 717/299–7090) in Lancaster are dependable and moderately priced. The casual **Historic Revere Tavern** (tel. 717/687–8602), on Route 30 outside of Lancaster in Paradise, is a bit pricier, but the 18th-century building is warm and inviting.

Last but not least, consider an option many inns offer their guests: Make dinner reservations at the home of a local Amish couple via your innkeeper and sample authentic Pennsylvania Dutch cuisine in a traditional Amish setting.

Tourist Information

Mennonite Information Center (2209 Millstream Rd., Lancaster 17602, tel. 717/299–0954). **Pennsylvania Dutch Convention & Visitors Bureau** (Dept. 2064, 501 Greenfield Rd., exit off Rte. 30, Lancaster 17601, tel. 717/299–8901).

Reservation Services

Bed & Breakfast of Lancaster County (Box 19, Mountville 17554, tel. 717/285–5956). **Hershey Bed & Breakfast Reservation Service** (Box 208, Hershey 17033, tel. 717/533–2928).

Churchtown Inn

Across from the historic church in this tiny Pennsylvania Dutch village is the Churchtown Inn, a circa-1735 Georgian fieldstone inn and carriage house that are listed on the National Register of Historic Places. From 1804 to 1853 the inn was the home of Edward Davies, a member of the 25th Congress and a state legislator. Once you enter the restored mansion you will know it was built for the gentry.

To the right of the entryway are two parlors with Victorian antiques and original ornate mantels. Here each evening, innkeepers Jim Kent and Stuart and Hermine Smith entertain guests with music and conversation. Before opening their bed-and-breakfast in April 1987, the three stayed at 150 B&Bs in six states to pick up ideas. Back in New Jersey Hermine was a health-food retailer, Stuart was a choral director whose choirs appeared at Lincoln Center and Carnegie Hall, and Jim was an accountant and ballroom-dancing teacher. (He'll gladly give you a quick lesson.) Stuart is known to delight guests with a concert on the grand piano, or he might wind up an antique music box from the inn's fine collection.

The 15-room center-hall mansion is decorated throughout with European and American antiques. The glassed-in garden room, where breakfast is served, overlooks farmland and a distant mountain range. A onetime summer kitchen with a walk-in fireplace has been converted into a den with a TV with VCR. Guest rooms have antique marble sinks, and brass or iron, sleigh or carved, or four-poster canopy beds. You'll find wardrobes, washstands, and TV cabinets handmade by an Amish craftsman. Each room has a sitting area. The dormer rooms on the third floor are cozy but have low ceilings.

On many weekends special packages are offered that include scheduled events. These vary from Victorian balls, carriage rides, and murder mysteries to authentic Amish wedding feasts, barbecues with music, cabaret, classical string quartets, and festive holiday dinners. The inn is close to antiques and crafts markets, the Reading outlets, and Amish farms. You can bike, hike, fish, or cross-country ski in nearby French Creek State Park.

Address: *Rte. 23, Churchtown (2100 Main St., Narvon, PA 17555), tel. 215/445–7794.*
Accommodations: *6 double rooms with baths, 2 doubles share a bath, 1 suite in carriage house.*
Amenities: *Air-conditioning and TV in 6 rooms; TV in den.*
Rates: *$49–$125; full, 5-course breakfast. MC, V.*
Restrictions: *Smoking in reception room only, no pets, 2-night minimum on weekends, 3-night minimum on holiday weekends.*

Clearview Farm Bed and Breakfast

U p a winding road along the base of a mountain ridge in northern Lancaster County is a beautifully restored three-story limestone farmhouse built in 1814. It sits on 200 acres of peaceful Pennsylvania farmland, and there's a huge bank barn nearby. There's also a pond out front that's the domain of two swans. The setting of Clearview Farm is elegantly pastoral; it's the kind of place you want to keep secret. Mildred and Glenn Wissler bought the house when they married more than 30 years ago. Glenn is a farmer who also has a good eye for color, and Mildred is a talented decorator who grew up learning about her father's antiques business. After working together to choose the right furnishings and decorations, they opened the bed-and-breakfast in 1989.

Country antiques and collectibles are mixed with exquisite Victorian furnishings throughout. You'll find a fireplace in the den, and there are hooked rugs on the original random-width floors. Exposed beams and limestone walls give the kitchen a homey feel. Guest rooms are lushly textured with lots of colors and patterns. The Royal Room has an ornately carved walnut Victorian bed, a Victorian étagère displaying turn-of-the-century knickknacks, Victorian chairs, and marble-top tables. The Princess Room is lavished with lace and fitted with a canopy bed, a Victorian marble-top dresser, and

a washstand. The Garden Room has an antique iron and brass bed in an alcove of flowered draperies, a French marble-top dresser, and a wicker chaise and chair. In the rooms on the third floor, hand-pegged rafters and limestone walls are exposed. Here you'll find homemade quilts, country antiques, and a doll collection.

Breakfast is served by candlelight in the formal dining room or in the screen porch that overlooks the fields. The dining room has elegant draperies and Victorian-print wallpaper. Six days a week, Mildred prepares a full country breakfast, and on Sunday, Continental breakfast.

The mountain ridge behind the house is great for hiking or quiet walks. In autumn, you can enjoy the fall foliage by car or by bike—just follow Clearview Road; it's one of those scenic back roads you always hear about. Nearby are Wahtney's Inn (an excellent restaurant), farmers' markets, and five antiques malls.

Address: *355 Clearview Rd., Ephrata, PA 17522, tel. 717/733-6333.*
Accommodations: *3 double rooms with baths, 2 doubles share bath.*
Amenities: *Air-conditioning in rooms, TV in family room.*
Rates: *$69–$89; full breakfast. MC, V.*
Restrictions: *No smoking indoors, no pets.*

Limestone Inn

I
n the very heart of the Amish country, in Strasburg's historic district, is the Limestone Inn. This elegant bed-and-breakfast, listed on the National Register of Historic Places, was built about 1786 as a merchant's residence. From 1839 to 1860 the principal of the noted Strasburg Academy boarded about 50 boys here. After the Civil War, the house served as an orphanage.

The 14-room house, based on a symmetrical five-bay Georgian plan, has a central hallway. The building also has some Germanic overtones, and details like the pent roof and the decorative stonework called "tumbling" between the second-floor windows give the inn a distinctive architectural sense.

Innkeepers Jan and Dick Kennell are both natives of New Hampshire. Friends who ran a B&B gave them the idea of establishing their own, and they opened the Limestone in May 1985. Dick was with the Department of Agriculture and Forestry in Washington, DC, for 30 years; and Jan, who is versed in Colonial history, was a tour guide in Annapolis.

Though antique clocks in the elegant rooms tick away, time stands still. The inn is furnished with Colonial and primitive family antiques and reproductions, and you'll find whitewashed walls, wide-planked wavy floors, and Williamsburg colors in every room. In the keeping room there are woven woolen rugs, lots of books and folk art, and settees in front of the fireplace. A spinning wheel stands in the corner. There are old family photographs and a player piano in the living room. Up the steep, narrow stairs you'll find the guest rooms, with old pegged doors, quilts, trunks, and Wilbur chocolates under your pillow. On the third floor, the original numbers on the doors show where boys from the academy once slept.

For the multicourse breakfast, served in the dining room at a long table set with a lace cloth, Dick, an excellent chef, may whip up his French toast or sourdough pancakes. He and Jan often serve their guests in period costumes.

The Limestone Inn is quiet and homey, and it's close to antiquing facilities. The Kennells have Amish friends nearby who have quilts for sale for less than you'd pay in commercial centers. With advance notice, they will set you up for dinner at an Amish home.

Address: *33 E. Main St., Strasburg, PA 17579, tel. 717/687-8392.*
Accommodations: *6 double rooms with baths.*
Amenities: *Air-conditioning.*
Rates: *$75–$95; full breakfast. AE.*
Restrictions: *No smoking in bedrooms, no pets, 2-night minimum on holiday weekends.*

Smithton Country Inn

Twelve miles north of Lancaster is the best inn in all of Pennsylvania Dutch country: the Smithton Country Inn, which began taking in lodgers in 1763. It was built by Henry and Susana Miller, who were householders of the Ephrata Community, an 18th-century Protestant monastic sect. Stone walls and flower gardens surround the fieldstone building on a hill overlooking the Ephrata Cloister. Innkeeper Dorothy Graybill is Pennsylvania Dutch. She bought Smithton in 1979, attentively restored it down to the most minute detail, and reopened it in 1982.

At dusk, lamps are lit in each window. The first floor has a Great Room and library to the right, and a dining room, where breakfast is served, to the left. Upstairs, guest rooms are individually decorated, but in each you'll find a working fireplace, antique or handmade reproduction furniture, handmade quilts, reading lamps, stenciling, minirefrigerators, and chamber music. Feather beds are kept in trunks for guests who request them. Flannel nightshirts, coordinated to the color scheme of the room, hang on wooden pegs behind the doors. Many rooms have canopy beds; some have whirlpool baths.

The attached duplex suite has its own entrance. Inside there are a living room, a snack area, a queen-size bed, a twin cupboard bed, and a whirlpool bath. In 1992,

Dorothy added a new unit, the Purple Room, on the second floor facing the back gardens. It includes hand-planed cherry woodwork and floors, an exposed-stone wall, a fireplace, a king-size canopied bed, an all-ceramic bathroom, and a whirlpool.

Numerous decorative influences come from the nearby Ephrata Cloister. The hand-hewn doors are pegged and have wooden hardware. Dorothy's partner, Allan Smith, hand-planed the old floorboards and made the clay tiles for the bathrooms and a Cloister-inspired buffet for the dining room.

Guest's enjoy Smithton's breakfast, served by candlelight—usually a plate of fresh fruit, juice, Pennsylvania Dutch waffles, and pastry. Afterward, Dorothy gives tips on the proper etiquette when meeting the Plain People of Lancaster County. This is the place to find out how to avoid the tourist traps and spend your time at authentic preserves of the area's heritage.

Address: *900 W. Main St., Ephrata, PA 17522, tel. 717/733–6094.*
Accommodations: *7 double rooms with baths, 1 suite.*
Amenities: *Air-conditioning in bedrooms.*
Rates: *$65–$170; full breakfast. AE, MC, V.*
Restrictions: *No smoking, inquire about pets, 2-night minimum with Sat. reservation and on holidays.*

Adamstown Inn

Adamstown, the antiques capital of Pennsylvania, is 20 minutes northeast of Lancaster. This three-story yellow-brick Victorian house is on a residential street in the heart of the antiques district. It was built in 1838 and rebuilt in 1925. Tom and Wanda Berman, both avid antiques collectors, left Baltimore and their banking careers to open a bed-and-breakfast in April 1989. You'll find leaded-glass windows and doors, magnificently refinished chestnut woodwork, and wallpaper in Victorian motifs. Each guest room is decorated with family heirlooms, handmade quilts, lace curtains, Oriental rugs, and fresh flowers. Baskets of towels and soaps sit on Victorian beds. Two rooms have a two-person whirlpool bath. On summer weekends more than 2,000 antiques dealers exhibit their wares in Adamstown. You can browse through stalls, or, if you're looking for something specific, the Bermans can direct you. They'll also point you to nature trails and biking paths.

Address: *62 W. Main St., Adamstown, PA 19501, tel. 215/484-0800 or 800/594-4808.*
Accommodations: *4 double rooms with baths.*
Amenities: *Air-conditioning in rooms, cable TV in 3 bedrooms, morning coffee, tea, or hot chocolate; off-street parking.*
Rates: *$60–$95; Continental breakfast. MC, V.*
Restrictions: *Smoking in mudroom only, no pets, 2-night minimum on weekends Apr.–Dec.*

The Cameron Estate Inn

On 15 wooded acres 15 miles west of Lancaster stands a redbrick Federal mansion built in 1805, listed on the National Register of Historic Places. A trout-stocked stream flows beneath an arched stone bridge nearby, and the veranda overlooks a sweeping lawn. Between towering oaks you can see an 18th-century church and Amish farms. Abe and Betty Groff, longtime area residents, opened their country inn in 1981 after Betty had started a restaurant in her home 5 miles away. Wide hallways and a central staircase lead to guest rooms furnished with Williamsburg reproductions. Seven of the bedrooms have working fireplaces; in all of them you'll find quilts, four-posters, sitting areas, and writing desks. The restaurant here serves exquisite Continental fare, and Groff's Farm Restaurant is famous for its Pennsylvania Dutch cuisine.

Address: *1895 Donegal Springs Rd., Mount Joy, PA 17552, tel. 717/653-1773.*
Accommodations: *16 double rooms with baths, 2 doubles share bath.*
Amenities: *Restaurant, air-conditioning in rooms, TV with VCR in sitting area, conference facilities in restaurant; bicycles, access to swimming pool and tennis courts.*
Rates: *$65–$110; Continental breakfast. AE, D, DC, MC, V.*
Restrictions: *No pets.*

Doneckers

The Guest House at Doneckers is a trio of joined turn-of-the-century brick Victorian houses across from the Restaurant at Doneckers. It's part of the "town within a town" developed by Bill Donecker that has a department store, a noted French restaurant, two bed-and-breakfasts (the recently opened 1777 House is a few blocks away), and a warehouse mall of artists, craftspeople, antiques, and art galleries called Artworks. The inn is furnished with French and American antiques, and antique hooked rugs hang on the stenciled walls. In the bedrooms you will find sinks in reproduction Victorian vanities, upholstered headboards, and fresh fruit. Some suites have fireplaces and/or whirlpool baths. Doneckers is neatly packaged; you never have to get in your car. But if you should venture forth, the authentic Amish countryside is only minutes away.

Address: *318 N. State St., Ephrata, PA 17522, tel. 717/738–9502, fax 717/738–9554.*
Accommodations: *13 double rooms with baths, 2 doubles share bath, 4 suites.*
Amenities: *Restaurant open Thurs.–Tues., air-conditioning in rooms, cable TV in common room.*
Rates: *$59–$149; Continental breakfast. AE, D, DC, MC, V.*
Restrictions: *No pets, 2-night minimum on holiday weekends, closed Dec. 24–25.*

General Sutter Inn

This three-story, redbrick inn, built in 1764 in Georgian style, overlooks the village square. It's said to be the oldest Pennsylvania inn in continuous operation. Originally known as Zum Anker, the name was changed in 1930 to honor John Augustus Sutter, the gold-rush pioneer who retired to Lititz. Richard Vetter was an Episcopal priest and then an assistant headmaster before becoming innkeeper here with his wife, Joan, in 1980. Inside, the decor is decidedly Victorian. In the parlor, there are medallion-backed sofas before the fireplace, marble-top tables, a pump organ, and crystal parlor lamps. Lovebirds and finches twitter in Victorian wire cages. Guest rooms are decorated with antique country and Victorian furnishings. The General Sutter is frayed around the edges just enough to add to its authenticity. There's a spacious tree-shaded terrace out front, where you can relax and watch the passing parade of villagers, and it's only a short walk to the Wilbur Chocolate Factory (the maker of Godiva chocolates) and the town's lovely Moravian Square.

Address: *14 Main St., Lititz, PA 17543, tel. 717/626–2115.*
Accommodations: *8 double rooms with baths, 2 suites.*
Amenities: *Restaurant, coffee shop, air-conditioning in rooms, TV and phones in rooms, library, 2 conference rooms can be combined.*
Rates: *$70–$90. AE, MC, V.*
Restrictions: *No pets.*

The King's Cottage

Tucked away in a quiet residential corner of Lancaster is a Spanish Mission Revival house, built in 1913, that's listed on the National Register of Historic Places. Hosts Jim and Karen Owens opened their bed-and-breakfast in 1987. He's an engineering consultant and she's a former educator. The interior is a successful blend of many different architectural styles: The living room has an Art Deco fireplace, the elegant library is Georgian-influenced, the bright and cheerful Florida Room has rattan furniture and ceiling fans, and the dining room has a crystal chandelier and fine Chippendale reproductions. The guest rooms are furnished in 18th-century reproductions with some antiques. Inside antique wardrobes, you'll find fluffy terry-cloth robes. The Princess Room has three walls of windows and a private balcony that overlooks the water garden. Karen and Jim will be glad to make arrangements for you to have dinner with an Amish family. They also handle small business conferences with great aplomb.

Address: *1049 E. King St., Lancaster, PA 17602, tel. 717/397–1017.*
Accommodations: *8 double rooms with baths.*
Amenities: *Air-conditioning in rooms, cable TV in library; off-street parking.*
Rates: *$75–$120; full breakfast, afternoon tea. D, MC, V.*
Restrictions: *No smoking, no pets, 2-night minimum on weekends, 3-night minimum on holiday weekends.*

Patchwork Inn

Three miles east of Lancaster is Patchwork Inn, a pre–Civil War Victorian clapboard farmhouse with deep blue shutters. When Lee Martin retired from the Marine Corps, he and his late wife, Joanne, wanted to turn their love for country antiques and quilt collecting into practical use. They opened their bed-and-breakfast in 1987. Today Lee continues innkeeping and quilt collecting with a new wife and partner, Anne, whose background is in food and nutrition. They enjoy giving guests tips about bidding at auctions and showing them how to tell the quality of a good quilt. In the living room, you'll find contemporary sofas and rocking chairs before the stone fireplace. There are extensive collections—including one of old phones—and quilts everywhere. Lee has more than 60 he displays and puts on beds. Guest rooms have ceiling fans and are furnished with antique oak. The suite, with kitchenette, has its own entrance. The Martins have storage facilities for bikes and detailed maps of the best and most scenic routes for pedal-pushers.

Address: *2319 Old Philadelphia Pike, Lancaster, PA 17602, tel. 717/293–9078 or 800/584–5776.*
Accommodations: *1 double room with bath, 2 doubles share bath, 1 suite.*
Amenities: *Air-conditioning; bike storage; off-street parking.*
Rates: *$60–$80; Continental breakfast, afternoon tea. MC, V.*
Restrictions: *No smoking, no pets, 2-night minimum on holiday weekends.*

Swiss Woods

In northern Lancaster County, nestled in rolling, wooded hills that overlook a lake, is Swiss Woods. When you enter the white brick modified Swiss chalet, Debrah Mosimann will greet you with a glass of chilled Swiss-made sparkling cider. She's a Lancaster County native who met her husband, Werner, in Austria while working with an interdenominational mission. They built their bed-and-breakfast on 30 acres of family-owned land and opened it in 1986. Swiss Woods is bright and airy, with natural woodwork, and it's decorated in country contemporary style. In the common room, there's a large sandstone fireplace to curl up in front of; in the bedrooms, you'll find handmade Swiss rugs, goose-down covers, and Swiss chocolates. Two rooms have whirlpool baths, and every room has either a balcony or a patio from which you can enjoy a spectacular view. The Mosimanns keep a canoe for guests, and they'll direct you to the best trails for hiking or biking.

Address: *500 Blantz Rd., Lititz, PA 17543, tel. 717/627–3358 or 800/594–8018, fax 717/627–3483.*
Accommodations: *6 double rooms with baths, 1 suite.*
Amenities: *Air-conditioning in bedrooms, TV in suite and in common room, Jacuzzis, kitchenette for guest use, dinner prepared on request.*
Rates: *$66–$105; full breakfast. D, MC, V.*
Restrictions: *No smoking, no pets, 2-night minimum on weekends, 3-night minimum on holidays.*

Gettysburg/York

Gettysburg and York are in the middle of Pennsylvania's east-west axis, near the Maryland state line. The Susquehanna River is the region's eastern border, and to the west is the Allegheny National Forest. Thousands of visitors are drawn each year to these two relatively small places that have been the sites of significant events in U.S. history.

Gettysburg dates from the early 1700s, when Samuel Gettys acquired 381 acres from the descendants of William Penn. Gettys' son James eventually had town lots drawn up and gave the area his family name. Every schoolchild knows that Gettysburg was the site of the bloodiest Civil War battle. The three-day encounter, in July 1863, claimed 51,000 lives and was a turning point in the war. Five months later President Abraham Lincoln dedicated the cemetery at Gettysburg and gave his famous address.

Thirty miles from Gettysburg is York, first settled in 1736 and named after the city of York, England. In Colonial days, its fields were so fertile that it was known as the Breadbasket of America. Between September 30, 1777, and June 28, 1778, York was the site of the nation's capital. During that period the Continental Congress met at the York Courthouse and adopted the Articles of Confederation, the first document to describe the Colonies as the United States of America.

A visit to Gettysburg and York today gives a unique insight into 18th- and 19th-century life. Gettysburg remains a small town of about 7,000 people, in the midst of apple orchards and rolling hills. Visitors can tour the historic battlefield and see the battle reenacted through various media. York, with a population of about 42,000, has preserved and restored much of its Federal and Victorian architecture. In both towns you will discover brick walkways, carved doors, stained-glass windows, and houses with cast-iron trim. You will find relatively unspoiled the surrounding gently sloping farmlands, where cannon once roared, rifles cracked, and drums rolled. Passing through villages you will see taverns, quaint shops, and inns with candle-lit windows, one of which may be your lodging for the night.

Places to Go, Sights to See

Battlefield Bus Tours (Gettysburg, tel. 717/334–6296). This two-hour, 23-mile tour with taped commentary narrated by Hollywood personalities creates a "you are there" experience.

Eisenhower National Historic Site (tel. 717/334–1124). At the Gettysburg Visitor Center you can purchase tickets and board shuttle buses to visit the farm home of President and Mrs. Dwight D. Eisenhower. The 495-acre estate includes a 15-room Georgian-style home, an 1887 bank barn, and lots of memorabilia.

General Lee's Headquarters (Gettysburg, tel. 717/334–3141). Lee and his staff made their battle plans in this fieldstone house in Gettysburg, which now contains a fine collection of Civil War uniforms and relics.

Gettysburg National Military Park (tel. 717/334–1124) consists of the historic 3,500 acres where the Battle of Gettysburg was fought. The best way to see it is from your car, following a step-by-step narrated tour. Licensed battlefield guides can be engaged at the visitor center, which is a good place to begin your tour.

Golden Plough Tavern (York, tel. 717/845–2951). This Germanic half-timber building dating from 1741 contains a fine collection of furnishings from the early 18th century.

Jennie Wade House & Olde Town (Gettysburg, tel. 717/334–4100; outside PA, 800/447–8788). The home of Gettysburg's heroine, the battle's only civilian casualty, has been carefully restored. Behind the house is a re-created village courtyard with shops of the era.

Lincoln Room Museum (Gettysburg, tel. 717/334–8188). The house and bedroom where Lincoln finished the final draft of his Gettysburg Address have been preserved, with many original furnishings.

York County Colonial Courthouse (York, tel. 717/845–2951 for the gift shop). Artifacts and memorabilia are displayed in this reconstruction of the building where the Continental Congress adopted the Articles of Confederation in 1777.

Restaurants

East of Gettysburg, look for **Altland House** (Abbotstown, tel. 717/259–9535), whose dining room and pub both boast a creative menu with entrées under $20, and **Hofbrauhaus** (Abbotstown, tel. 717/259–9641), which features German specialties. **Patty and John's** (Hanover, tel. 717/637–2200) sits right on the edge of a golf course; American-cuisine entrées run $12–$19.

In Gettysburg, service at the casual **Blue Parrot Bistro** (tel. 717/337–3739) is exemplary; the menu lists an array of $7–$12 entrées such as pasta, stew, ribs, and tenderloin. At **The Historic Farnsworth House Inn** (tel. 717/334–8838) patrons have a choice of $12–$18 entrées ranging from scallops to Yankee pot roast, and young guests may order from their own children's menu. **Herr Tavern** (tel. 717/334–4332), featuring classical American and European cuisine, is pricier but offers a freebie wildly popular with out-of-town clientele: chauffeured limousine service to and from the restaurant. Go to **Dobbin House Tavern** (tel. 717/334–2100) for "general amusements and merrymaking," or to the attached **Alexander Dobbin Dining Room** for something more elegant and sedate (and more expensive: entrées run $15–$19).

For family dining, try the nearby **Foot of the Mountain Restaurant** (Cove Gap, tel. 717/328–2960); its two dining areas make both formally and informally dressed visitors completely at home.

Tourist Information

Gettysburg Travel Council (35 Carlisle St., Gettysburg 17325, tel. 717/334–6274). **York County Convention and Visitors Bureau** (1 Market Way E., Box 1229, York 17405, tel. 717/848–4000). **York County Visitor Information Center at Meadowbrook** (Whiteford Rd., York 17402, tel. 717/755–9638).

The Bechtel Mansion Inn

In 1897 the leading local businessman built this 28-room Queen Anne mansion in the center of town as a residence for his family. It's such a fanciful, through-the-looking-glass place that you'll know it at once. The yellow-brick-and-white-trim building has a high pointed turret, a long curved porch, and lush Victorian gardens.

Owners Charles and Mariam Bechtel live in Fairfax, Virginia, where he is a manager for Bell Atlantic; but every weekend they are resident hosts. Charles grew up on a nearby farm and will give you inside tips on touring the countryside. Innkeeper Ruth Spangler, who is always on hand, is knowledgeable about local history and customs.

The Bechtel, which became an inn in 1983, has been carefully furnished with American and European 19th-century antiques. It's on the National Register of Historic Places. Guests with a love of art and architecture will appreciate the intricate artisanship that went into the building and restoration of the house. Many rooms have original brass chandeliers. The Victorian parlor has vertical shutters, sliding pocket doors, and a handsome mantel—all in elegant cherry wood. The dining room has etched-glass windows and a large window seat. The breakfast room was the original kitchen, and you'll find French windows in the chimney corner, and handmade furniture, pottery, and paintings by local artists throughout the house.

Each bedroom is furnished in antiques, with handmade Pennsylvania quilts, lace curtains, and a brass chandelier. In many you will find built-in wardrobes with full-length mirrors, and two have private balconies. Bathrooms retain their original ornate Victorian decor (though the plumbing is new). One of the most popular is the Sara Leas Room, with its turret-shaped bay window and view of East Berlin's National Historic District.

You can easily spend a weekend exploring the Bechtel's nooks and crannies. Its location—almost equidistant from York, Gettysburg, and Hershey—makes it an ideal base for touring the area.

Address: *400 W. King St., East Berlin, PA 17316, tel. 717/259-7760.*
Accommodations: *4 double rooms with baths, 4 doubles share 2 baths, 2 suites.*
Amenities: *Air-conditioning in bedrooms, TV with VCR in common areas, gift shop in carriage house.*
Rates: *$78–$130; Continental breakfast, afternoon tea. AE, D, MC, V.*
Restrictions: *No smoking indoors, no pets, 2-night minimum on holiday weekends.*

The Brafferton Inn

A stay at the Brafferton Inn may be the most pleasant way to get a full sense of Gettysburg's historical richness. The 14-room stone house built in 1786, the first residence in town, faces a mid-19th-century street and has an adjacent seven-room pre–Civil War clapboard addition. On the first day of the battle, a bullet shattered an upstairs window. It lodged in the mantel and is still there today. During the war, services were held here while the church was being used as a hospital. And just down the street is the house where Lincoln completed his Gettysburg Address.

Mimi and Jim Agard purchased the property in the early 1980s, completely restored it, and in April 1985 opened the historic bed-and-breakfast inn. It is now listed on the National Register of Historic Places. Jim, who is chairman of the art department at Gettysburg College, had previously restored five houses in Vermont. And prior to becoming an innkeeper, Mimi was in public relations in New York City.

The inn has high ceilings, oversize doors, and odd nooks, turns, steps up and steps down that will constantly surprise you. It glows with Colonial colors. Above the original fireplace in the living room is an 1860 portrait of Robert E. Curtis, Jim's forefather. Here you'll also find wing chairs, a chimney cupboard, a player piano, and a primitive mural on four walls that depicts the area's historic buildings.

An atrium connects the stone house to the addition. This area, with brick floors and walls, is decorated with primitive pieces, pottery, and Oriental and hooked rugs. Farm implements are displayed on the walls, and opened antique cupboards are filled with old books. Down a wooden walkway is a deck where dahlias, zinnias, petunias, and marigolds grow.

The guest rooms, with 18th-century stenciling on whitewashed walls, are furnished with country antiques and family pieces. You'll also find oil paintings, prints, and drawings—many by Jim's father, an artist. A local potter made the basins for washstands and dressers that have been transformed into sinks.

After a candlelight breakfast set to classical music, you can relax in the atrium while you plan the day. The inn is an easy walk from the battlefield, shops, and restaurants.

Address: *44 York St., Gettysburg, PA 17325, tel. 717/337–3423.*
Accommodations: *6 double rooms with baths, 5 doubles share 2 baths.*
Amenities: *Air-conditioning in bedrooms; off-street parking.*
Rates: *$80–$125; full breakfast. MC, V.*
Restrictions: *Smoking in atrium only, no pets.*

The Doubleday Inn

The Doubleday Inn is set amid the breastworks of the Gettysburg Battlefield and offers Civil War enthusiasts a bird's-eye view of where it all began. The white-clapboard Colonial-style house, built in 1929, sits on the Oak Ridge section of the Gettysburg Battlefield.

Sal Chandon, a recording engineer, and his wife, Joan, who worked for Jim Henson of Muppets fame, had been looking for a business to work in together. Sal's passion for the Civil War brought them to Gettysburg, where Joan's brother is a licensed battlefield guide. In spring 1987, they bought the property, which is within the national park, renovated the house completely, and became innkeepers. They named the inn after Abner Doubleday, who fought that first day of the battle.

The main parlor, whose windows overlook the sloping battlefield, has authentic period furnishings—an 1880s Victorian couch, a turn-of-the-century pump organ, and a claw-foot coffee table. Civil War–related memorabilia can be found throughout the house, along with amusing period treasures, such as a stereoscope and a magic lantern that Joan and Sal like to demonstrate for their guests. The bedrooms are decorated in a mix of antique Victorian and country French, and you will find four-posters, brass beds, iron beds, and an oak pineapple bed.

You can browse through the 600-book library devoted to the battle and on Saturday evenings (and occasional Wednesdays) join in a discussion led by a Civil War historian. Often Joan's brother drops by to meet guests and answer questions.

An elaborate home-cooked breakfast is served by waitresses in period dress in the formal dining room, complete with candlelight, crystal, and odd pieces of turn-of-the-century china. From 4 to 6 each afternoon, tea, drinks, and hors d'oeuvres are served in the main parlor. There are three outdoor patios and a screened-in porch where the Chandons entertain guests with barbecues on special occasions.

Sal and Joan are the kind of enthusiastic hosts who will make dinner reservations, arrange tours, and share tips on local antiquing.

Address: *104 Doubleday Ave., Gettysburg, PA 17325, tel. 717/334-9119.*
Accommodations: *5 double rooms with baths, 4 doubles share 2 baths.*
Amenities: *Air-conditioning, turndown service; picnics available.*
Rates: *$75–$100; full breakfast, afternoon tea. MC, V.*
Restrictions: *No smoking, no pets, 2-night minimum on holiday weekends.*

The Mercersburg Inn

Mercersburg, at the foot of the Blue Ridge Mountains, is a historic village off I–81, an hour and a half from Washington, DC. This country inn, on the outskirts of town, is an impressive Classic Revival redbrick structure with white trim, adorned with numerous porticoes, porches, and terraces.

Owner Fran Wolfe grew up in Delaware, where her mother operated a guest house. Fran later completed a series of restoration projects, including a 150-year-old log cabin in North Carolina; then, in 1986, she tackled this estate, transforming it into an elegant inn.

It's the kind of place where you expect something romantic has either happened or will. In the entrance hall, twin staircases wind dramatically to the second floor, and rose and green Scaglioli columns accent the chestnut wainscoting. The classic Arts and Crafts sunroom has a tiled floor and fireplace, high beamed ceilings, and a wall of broad windows. It's done in peach and blue, with white wicker furniture and flowered upholstery and curtains. You can sit back on the deep window-seat cushions and admire the stately grounds.

Restored antiques and locally handmade pieces fill the spacious guest rooms. You will find four-poster, canopy, brass, and king-size beds. Some rooms have fireplaces; others have private balconies with views of the mountains. In the tiled, high-ceilinged bathrooms there are antique needle showers, pedestal sinks, and free-standing tubs. Each bathroom has been meticulously restored to its turn-of-the-century grandeur.

In the formal mahogany-paneled dining room, there are a deep green marble fireplace, leaded-glass built-in cabinets, Tiffany stained-glass light fixtures, and parquet floors. Here the award-winning restaurant known as the Morel serves six-course dinners and an à la carte menu of regional new American cuisine.

A bit farther north is a pocket of Amish country that most tourists never hear about. Fran can tell you how to get to the Gettysburg Battlefield or the nearby Whitetail ski slopes.

Address: *405 S. Main St., Mercersburg, PA 17236, tel. 717/328–5231, fax 717/328–3403.*
Accommodations: *15 double rooms with baths.*
Amenities: *Restaurant open Wed.–Sun., downstairs tavern, air-conditioning and phones in bedrooms, TV with VCR in games room, conference room.*
Rates: *$110–$180; Continental breakfast. AE, MC, V.*
Restrictions: *No smoking indoors, no pets, 2-night minimum on fall-foliage and ski-season weekends and holidays.*

Beechmont Inn

This 1834 Federal redbrick town house, with black shutters and window boxes overflowing with flowers, is on a tree-lined street in Hanover, about 13 miles south of Gettysburg and York. In 1986 Monna Hormel, a veteran bed-and-breakfast guest, left a career in retailing to open the inn. She has furnished it with elegant Federal-period antiques and replicas. In the library are 18th-century books and a collection of Civil War memorabilia. One suite has a marble fireplace, and one has a whirlpool. Up the winding staircase, guest rooms have four-poster beds, writing desks, and lace curtains. During warmer months you can relax in the old-fashioned glider in the landscaped courtyard; and some morning, should you decide not to join the other guests in the dining room, you can enjoy breakfast in bed. This area is a gold mine of antiques shops, and hiking and swimming are nearby.

Address: *315 Broadway, Hanover, PA 17331, tel. 717/632–3013.*
Accommodations: *4 double rooms with baths, 3 suites.*
Amenities: *Air-conditioning and phones in bedrooms; off-street parking.*
Rates: *$70–$125; full breakfast, afternoon tea. AE, MC, V.*
Restrictions: *Smoking in guest rooms only, no pets, 2-night minimum on weekends.*

Emig Mansion

This elegant Victorian Greek Revival mansion, 10 minutes north of York, is a treat to the senses. It has gorgeous leaded and stained-glass windows, intricate inlaid flooring, ornate molding, and Victorian antiques throughout. Breakfast is served in a noval bay with curved-glass windows at one end of the formal dining room or at the walnut dining table that's long enough to seat 30. In guest rooms you will find brass, iron, and massively carved beds. Three rooms have fireplaces. This house was built in 1850 by John Emig, Jr., who made his fortune producing the commercial wagons that hauled goods along 19th-century roads. Innkeeper Jane Llewellyn, who also sells real estate, bought and extensively restored the mansion several years ago. She opened it as a bed-and-breakfast in June 1984. There are antiques shops and factory outlets nearby. Or you can just relax on the expansive porch and gaze across the road at the old wagonworks, just as the Emig family did 100 years ago.

Address: *3342 N. George St. (Box 486), Emigsville, PA 17318, tel. 717/764–2226.*
Accommodations: *3 double rooms with baths, 4 doubles share 2 baths.*
Amenities: *Air-conditioning in rooms; off-street parking, conference room.*
Rates: *$85–$110; full breakfast. MC, V.*
Restrictions: *Smoking on balconies only, no pets.*

Fairfield Inn

This fieldstone structure with its two-story open gallery is in a sleepy little village 8 miles west of Gettysburg. Built as a plantation home in 1757, it became a hotel and stagecoach stop in 1823. David Thomas managed a hotel in Washington, DC, before he bought the inn in 1976. Throughout you will find random-width floors, low ceilings, original brass hardware, crystal chandeliers, lace curtains, and a Williamsburg-influenced mix of antiques and reproductions.

The inn is well known for its classic country fare. (In fact, Mrs. Dwight Eisenhower frequently chose to entertain here.) Fall-foliage spectators should ease their way up to Arendtsville from here for the National Apple Harvest Festival in October—

it's as close to a state fair as some city folk will ever get, and children will glory in it. The Gettysburg battle sites are nearby, but you may be content just to relax in this carefully restored inn that is steeped in so much history.

Address: *Main St., Fairfield, PA 17320, tel. 717/642-5410.*
Accommodations: *2 double rooms share 1 bath.*
Amenities: *Restaurant, air-conditioning in common areas and bedrooms; meeting room.*
Rates: *$50–$65; Continental breakfast. AE, MC, V.*
Restrictions: *No smoking in dining room, no pets, closed Sun., Mon., 1st week Feb., and 1st week Sept.*

The Historic Farnsworth House Inn

Confederate sharpshooters once occupied this 1810 redbrick Federal house near the National Cemetery, and you can still see lots of bullet holes. Loring H. Shultz sells Civil War prints and books in a shop next door, and he and his family opened the bed-and-breakfast in 1989. The lushly Victorian guest rooms have antique marbletop dressers, beds with fishnet canopies, and Oriental rugs scattered before the fireplaces. A wicker-filled sunroom is the perfect place to relax; it looks out on gardens where, in summer, you can dine in the open air, alongside a stone-lined stream that provided water for both armies. The restaurant specializes in mid-19th-century food, and an excellent house specialty is a game pie of pheasant, duck, and turkey. In the attic and

basement, the Shultzes display their collection of artifacts from daily life in the Civil War period. During high season Mr. Shultz's daughter, Patty O'Day, dresses up in period costume and tells some pretty spooky ghost stories by candlelight down in the cellar—a treat that children love.

Address: *401 Baltimore St., Gettysburg, PA 17325, tel. 717/334-8838.*
Accommodations: *5 double rooms with baths.*
Amenities: *Restaurant, air-conditioning in bedrooms, TV in sunroom.*
Rates: *$75–$85; full breakfast, afternoon tea. AE, D, MC, V.*
Restrictions: *Smoking in sunroom only, no pets, 2-night minimum on some weekends.*

The Old Appleford Inn

This bed-and-breakfast, a few blocks from Lincoln Square, is a gray brick Italianate Victorian house built in 1867, with a carriage house in back. The house has a gabled roof and arched windows framed by black shutters. Frank and Maribeth Skradski, hosts since 1987, stayed here first as guests and fell in love with the place. Before starting a life of innkeeping, he was a research engineer in Illinois and she owned an antique-clothing shop. There's a gracious Victorian parlor with a baby-grand piano; a library with lots of books, Civil War memorabilia, and a wonderful collection of old Kodak cameras; and a plant-filled sunroom with a well-stocked fridge. Two of the guest rooms have ornamental fireplaces, and all are decorated with Victorian antiques and brass beds, sleigh beds, and iron beds—some so high you have to climb up into them. Throughout, Maribeth has found ingenious ways to display antique clothing. The Skradskis offer gift certificates for one- to five-night stays.

Address: *218 Carlisle St., Gettysburg, PA 17325, tel. 717/337–1711, fax 717/334–6228.*
Accommodations: *11 double rooms with baths, 1 suite.*
Amenities: *Air-conditioning in bedrooms; off-street parking.*
Rates: *$78–$98; full breakfast, afternoon tea. AE, D, MC, V.*
Restrictions: *No smoking, no pets, 2-night minimum on weekends May–Nov.*

The Tannery Bed and Breakfast

Two blocks from the National Cemetery and the visitor center is a tan, Gothic-structured house with chocolate-brown trim and a gabled roof. In 1868, when a Mr. Rupp built the clapboard house, his tannery business was right next door. Charlotte Swope's grandfather bought the house in 1920, and she was born and raised here. After retiring from running a tire dealership, Charlotte and her husband, Jule, opened their bed-and-breakfast in May 1989 and named it after the tannery, which is no longer standing. In the early '20s, the interior of the house was completely renovated. The result was an interesting blend of periods: Light, clean-lined modernism met lofty Victoriana, and the charm still manages to shine through. Guest rooms are decorated with soothing Williamsburg colors and new carpeting. You will find traditional reproductions and a handful of family antiques. There's a wide, airy porch where you can sit and rock and watch a world of Civil War buffs go by. The Tannery is a low-key kind of place that will appeal to mature travelers.

Address: *449 Baltimore St., Gettysburg, PA 17325, tel. 717/334–2454.*
Accommodations: *5 double rooms with baths.*
Amenities: *Air-conditioning in bedrooms, TV in sitting room; off-street parking.*
Rates: *$65–$95; Continental breakfast. MC, V.*
Restrictions: *No smoking, no pets.*

Off the Beaten Track

Century Inn

This hand-hewn stone building with a long porch and two large stone chimneys on either end is listed on the National Register of Historic Places. Since 1794, Century Inn has offered hospitality to travelers passing through this village 35 miles south of Pittsburgh. In 1945, Dr. and Mrs. Gordon Harrington restored the inn and furnished it with heirlooms and rare American antiques. Today, their daughter-in-law, Megin Harrington, continues the tradition. In the parlors are two identical fireplaces, a display of antique paperweights and glassware, and an original flag from the Whisky Rebellion that hangs above one mantel. The guest rooms are as carefully furnished with antiques as the public areas. Superb meals are served in the five dining rooms. In the Keeping Room (the original kitchen), the massive fireplace has a hand-forged crane and curious cooking utensils. Megin will gladly direct you to the best places for antiquing, boating, and skiing—which are all within a short distance.

Address: *Main St., Scenery Hill, PA 15360, tel. 412/945-6600 or 412/945-5180.*
Accommodations: *9 double rooms with baths, 3 suites.*
Amenities: *Restaurant with conference facilities, air-conditioning in bedrooms; tennis court, croquet.*
Rates: *$78–$130; full breakfast. No credit cards.*
Restrictions: *No pets, closed Dec. 23–Feb. 13.*

Glasbern

You will understand why Al and Beth Granger chose this name (which means "glass barn" in Old English) when you see their country inn. Glasbern is a 19th-century German bank barn, tucked into a quiet valley 10 miles west of Allentown, and the Grangers have reconstructed it of stone, wood—and lots of glass. The Great Room resembles a lofty stone sanctuary, with a fireplace and hand-hewn beams that crisscross through the high, open spaces. Guest rooms are decorated traditionally, with standard antique reproductions, and in contemporary style with glass tables and wicker. Brick walkways lead to a farmhouse and a carriage house, both renovated and similarly decorated—there's a certain sameness about the decor. Some suites have whirlpool baths, kitchenettes, and private entrances. Nine rooms have fireplaces. Skiing, hiking, and antiquing are close by, but you may find you're content with just being on these 113 peaceful acres in the middle of nowhere.

Address: *Pack House Rd. (RD 1, Box 250), Fogelsville, PA 18051-9743, tel. 215/285-4723 or 800/654-9296, fax 215/285-2862.*
Accommodations: *14 double rooms with baths, 7 suites.*
Amenities: *Restaurant with conference facilities open Tues.–Sat., air-conditioning in bedrooms, TV with VCR and phones in bedrooms; swimming pool, bicycles.*
Rates: *$95–$225; full breakfast. MC, V.*
Restrictions: *No pets, 2-night minimum on fall weekends in suites.*

Longswamp Bed and Breakfast

This white clapboard Federal manor house is in a rural village about 15 minutes southwest of Allentown. Elsa and Dean Dimick restored the house, which was built in 1789, and opened it as a bed-and-breakfast in 1983. When they're not innkeeping, he's chief of medicine at the Lehigh Valley Hospital, and she's a professional chef. In the parlor, with its wood-pegged floors, deeply set windows, and settees before the fireplace, you can sit and enjoy the Dimicks' vast collection of books and music. The large, sunny guest rooms are decorated in a mix of Pennsylvania and Victorian antiques, with Amish quilts and one-of-a-kind antique iron beds. The cottage at the side, used by the Underground Railroad, is much more haphazardly decorated, with antiques and family hand-me-downs. Golf, tennis, and horseback riding are nearby, and the Dimicks can help you map out drives down scenic back roads through farmland or to antiques shops for browsing.

Address: *Main St. (RD 2, Box 26), Mertztown, PA 19539, tel. 215/682-6197.*
Accommodations: *6 double rooms with baths, 4 doubles share 2 baths, 2 suites.*
Amenities: *Air-conditioning in bedrooms, TV in summer kitchen; hiking trails on 40 adjoining acres.*
Rates: *$60–$75; full breakfast, afternoon tea. MC, V.*
Restrictions: *No smoking in guest rooms, no pets.*

The Priory

It's appropriate that innkeeper Mary Ann Graf should purchase the flour and wheat berries for the breakfast bread she serves her guests from the Benedictines at St. Vincent's College; after all, the Priory was once a monastery. Mary Ann and Edward, her husband, purchased the building in 1984. They promptly embarked on a million-dollar renovation, transforming the brick, tin-ceilinged monks' residence into a 24-room inn complete with private baths and handsome public rooms for business and social events. What was monastic more than a century ago is now warmed by Victorian lace, oil lamps, wrought-iron beds, and armoires. As testimony that Mary Ann has done something right, the YWCA named her Pittsburgh's Entrepreneur of the Year in 1988.

Notwithstanding the modern amenities, you may still be affected by the structure's meditative past and have to pull yourself away from private contemplation for shopping or sightseeing in downtown Pittsburgh, just across the river.

Address: *614 Pressley St., Pittsburgh 15212, tel. 412/231-3338, fax 412/231-4838.*
Accommodations: *24 double rooms with baths.*
Amenities: *Air-conditioning, TV, and phone in rooms; weekday-morning transportation downtown.*
Rates: *$65–$135; Continental breakfast. AE, D, DC, MC, V.*
Restrictions: *No pets.*

New Jersey

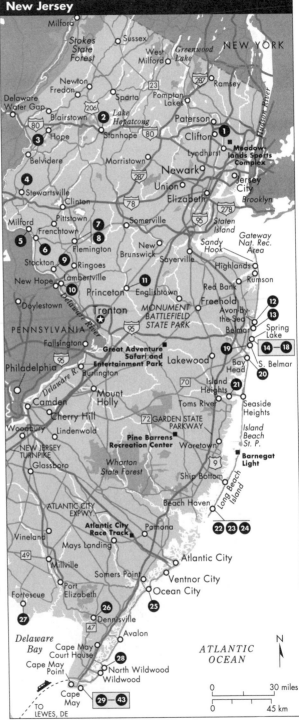

The Jersey Shore

Nowadays the 127-mile stretch of sandy beaches, bays, marshes, and inlets along the Jersey shore is one of the busiest vacation destinations in the country. It has been discovered, colonized, divided, subdivided, developed, renovated, and restored so many times that the few natural get-away-from-it-all places remaining are now exceptions.

Swimming and water sports predominate. Fishing, on the ocean or in the back bays, is convenient by party or charter boat. Murky visibility limits, but does not preclude, the joys of scuba. You're at most a short car trip away from golf, horseback riding, and tennis; and bicycling on most boardwalks is permitted during early-morning hours.

Proximity to the beaches or bays (for boaters) is desirable, although beach areas tend to be noisy and busy at the height of the season. Admission to all New Jersey beaches, with the exception of those in Atlantic City, Wildwood, and Cape May Point, requires a beach tag, which most bed-and-breakfasts provide free or for a small fee. Island Beach State Park in Ocean County, a 12-mile stretch of virtually pristine beaches and overgrown dunes, charges $4 to $5 per carload, with free admission on Tuesday.

If you'd like to sidestep the crowds, visit during the off-season: September is the best month. The days then are shorter, the breezes cooler, the ocean warm and tranquil, and most restaurants and attractions are still open. May is also pleasant. The cold, quiet months of November and December are becoming popular for business retreats.

One component of a Jersey shore vacation is an evening in Atlantic City, where casino gambling has created a new style of adult-oriented entertainment and extravagance. Unfortunately, the benefits from this "new" industry (backroom gambling has existed in Atlantic City for more than 150 years) have yet to change the city's overall run-down condition.

Places to Go, Sights to See

Albert Hall (Waretown; information, tel. 609/971–1593). Though the hall burned down in 1992, the concerts—of folk music, bluegrass, and old-time pinelands ballads—are still held every Saturday night at 8 at various locations around town.

Allaire State Park (between Farmingdale and Lakewood, tel. 908/938–2371). This 18th-century ironworks village is surrounded by 3,000 acres.

Amusement parks. Boardwalk amusement rides are best in *Wildwood* and *Seaside Heights*. The *Great Adventure* (tel. 908/928–1821) theme park, southwest of Freehold, has the best roller coasters and an enclosed safari park.

Cape May County Historical Museum (Cape May Court House, tel. 609/465–3535). Period Victorian clothing and furniture, early whaling instruments, and the lens from the Cape May lighthouse are among the variety of items in this 1755 house.

Cape May County Park (Cape May Court House, tel. 609/465–5271). The pleasantly landscaped park area contains a picnic ground, playground, bike trail, gazebo, tennis courts, and a 25-acre zoo with more than 300 species. It has facilities for the disabled.

Flea markets. Monmouth County flea markets and auctions include *Collingwood Auction & Flea Market* (tel. 908/938–7941), in Howell; *The Englishtown Auction* (tel. 908/446–9644), in Englishtown; and *The Great American Flea Market* (tel. 908/308–1105), on Rte. 9, just north of Rte. 195.

Garden State Arts Center (Holmdel, tel. 908/442–9200). Many of the entertainers who perform in Atlantic City's casinos also appear here.

Leamings Run Botanical Gardens (Swainton, tel. 609/465–5871). These are 27 spectacular theme gardens in Cape May County.

Lenox China factory (tel. 609/641–3700). China and giftware may be purchased at retail prices at the site on Tilton Road in Pomona in Galloway Township. Bargain hunters should consider calling in October, when the store has an annual week-long sale.

Lighthouses. At the northern end of the shore is the *Sandy Hook Light* (tel. 908/872–0092), the oldest continuously operating lighthouse in the country. *Navesink Twin Lights* (tel. 908/872–1814) is about 8 miles south, in Highlands. *Barnegat Light* (tel. 609/494–2016), the famous red-and-white tower built in 1858 and known as Old Barney, is at the northernmost end of

Long Beach Island, in Barnegat Light State Park, which reopened in 1991 after extensive renovations. The *Hereford Inlet Light* in North Wildwood (1st and Central Aves., tel. 609/729–1714) is the top floor of a small Victorian frame building.

Monmouth Battlefield State Park (Freehold, tel. 908/462–9616). Here Molly Pitcher earned her place in American history books.

Monmouth County Parks (tel. 908/842–4000). Free and low-price events, including country fairs, musicals, and Broadway shows, in various parks within the County Park system are presented June through August.

Noyes Museum (Oceanville, tel. 609/652–8848). This unusual museum has displays on New Jersey folklore and fine art.

Racetracks. Horse-racing fans can visit *Monmouth Park* (Oceanport, tel. 908/222–5100) and *Atlantic City Race Course* (McKee City, tel. 609/641–2190).

Sandy Hook (tel. 908/872–0092). Part of the Gateway National Recreation Area, Sandy Hook includes America's oldest operating lighthouse (built in 1764), public beaches, gun emplacements, an old Army weapon range and military encampment, a nature center, changing rooms and showers, and a fabulous view of New York Harbor.

South Jersey Regional Theater (Somers Point, tel. 609/653–0553). The company presents revivals, classics, and new American drama in Atlantic County.

Surflight Theater (Beach Haven, tel. 609/492–9477). Summer-stock plays and Broadway revivals on Long Beach Island.

War games. *Outdoor Adventures* (near Chatsworth, tel. 609/762–1500) offers weekly war games involving safe, nonprojectile-firing weapons.

Wineries. Worth visiting are *Renault Vineyard* (Egg Harbor City, tel. 609/965–2111) and *Balic Winery* (Mays Landing, tel. 609/625–2166).

Restaurants

In Monmouth County consider **Doris and Ed's** (Highlands, tel. 908/872–1565) for seafood, **Farmingdale House** (Farmingdale, tel. 908/938–7951) for genuine northern Italian cuisine, and the **Fromagerie** (Rumson, tel. 908/842–8088) for French cuisine. **Harry's Lobster House** (Sea Bright, tel. 908/842–0205) serves excellent, sophisticated Continental fare, and **Harrigan's Pub** (Sea Girt, tel. 908/449–8228) is an unpretentious tavern with inexpensive grilled seafood, chops, and chicken.

On Long Beach Island, **Harvey Cedars Shellfish Company** (tel. 609/494–7112) serves steamed shrimp, clams, and simple flatfish in a casual atmosphere. **Romeo's** (tel. 609/492–0025) is a good Italian seafood restaurant, and **Terrace Tavern** (tel. 609/494–7051) serves inexpensive, generally well prepared grilled seafood and tavern fare.

In Atlantic County, beyond Atlantic City, **Marriott's Seaview Resort** (tel. 609/652–1800), in Galloway Township, has a delicious seafood buffet and Sunday brunch. **Tre Figlia** (tel. 609/965–3303), in Pomona, is one of the region's best northern Italian restaurants. **Little Rock Cafe** (tel. 609/823–4411) is a charming bistro in Ventnor. **The Clam Bar** (tel. 609/927–8783) in Somers Point (a short drive from Longport and Ocean City) has inexpensive steamed and fried seafood.

In Cape May County, north of Cape May City, the **Deauville Inn** (Strathmere, tel. 609/263–2080), a former speakeasy, does dockside surf-and-turf well. An inexpensive choice in Wildwood is the **Ravioli House** (tel. 609/522–7894). For dress-up hotel-style dining, Ocean City's **Flanders Hotel** (tel. 609/399–1000) serves American cuisine in dignified turn-of-the-century dining rooms. **The Whitebrier Inn** (Avalon, tel. 609/967–5225) offers surf-and-turf in a formal atmosphere, with some Continental and nouvelle items, and a good Sunday brunch.

Tourist Information

Atlantic City Visitors Bureau (Dept. of Public Relations, 2311 Pacific Ave., Atlantic City 08401, tel. 609/348–7100). **Cape May County Chamber of Commerce** (Box 74, Cape May Court House 08210, tel. 609/465–7181). **Long Beach Island-Southern Ocean County Chamber of Commerce** (265 W. 9th St., Ship Bottom 08753, tel. 609/494–7211). **Monmouth County Dept. of Public Information/Tourism** (27 E. Main St., Freehold 07728, tel. 908/431–7476). **New Jersey Division of Travel and Tourism** (CN 826, Trenton 08625, tel. 609/292–2470). **Ocean County Tourism Advisory Council** (CN 2191, Administration Bldg., Toms River 08753, tel. 908/929–2163).

Reservation Services

Bed & Breakfast of New Jersey (103 Godwin Ave., Suite 132, Midland Park, 07432, tel. 201/444–7409). **Northern New Jersey Bed & Breakfast/ Temporary Lodgings** (11 Sunset Trail, Denville, NJ 07834, tel. 201/625–5129).

Normandy Inn

T his huge Italianate villa with Queen Anne touches was built for the Audenried family of Philadelphia around 1889 and became a guest house in 1909. In 1982 the inn was bought by Michael and Susan Inginio, who have slowly transformed it into a textbook of high-Victorian furnishings.

There are no reproductions or modern pieces of furniture in the Normandy. Everything is genuine American Victorian, from the formerly gaslit chandeliers, and the magnificent dark rococo bedroom sets to the Renaissance Revival parlor set carved with women's faces. The Inginios will happily show you their favorite pieces, including the 1875 "Darth Vader" bed.

"We didn't think we'd get into anything like this, and we certainly didn't think we'd get so involved in period furnishings," Mike says. "Before we bought the inn, we had an ice-cream business in Toms River. We sold that, took a year off, thought about what we wanted, found this place, and, you know what they say, if you're going to do anything, you'd better do it right the first time." The Inginios also host B&B seminars and innkeeper workshops.

The Normandy, a two-minute walk from the beach, has become the standard against which the other bed-and-breakfasts in Spring Lake are measured. The inn's museum-quality furnishings create a formal atmosphere that the Inginios deliberately undercut, urging guests to relax. "To see a guest curl up on a sofa with a book is just what I want," Mike explains.

The five-to six-course hot breakfasts make it easy to skip lunch. All rooms have private baths; the tower room is built into the cupola, so its bathroom is down a flight of stairs. Guests staying in the tower room are provided with bathrobes. In the 1930s a garage was added, above which is a one-bedroom apartment, in contemporary style, with a two-person, green marble Jacuzzi.

Address: *21 Tuttle Ave., Spring Lake, NJ 07762, tel. 908/449-7172.*
Accommodations: *15 double rooms and 2 singles with baths, 1 suite.*
Amenities: *Air-conditioning in bedrooms, cable TV in parlor and in rooms; bicycles, beach towels, onsite parking for 9 rooms, transportation to and from train and bus.*
Rates: *$98–$146; full breakfast. AE, MC, V.*
Restrictions: *No smoking in dining room; no pets, 2-night minimum July–Aug. and on weekends Mar.–Nov.; 3-night minimum on holiday weekends, 4-night minimum on weekends July–Aug.*

Pierrot by the Sea

This 1865 inn is a showplace of the skills of its owners, Richard and Catherine Burdo. Richard does professional Victorian restoration of buildings, furniture, and lighting, and Catherine is a fashion coordinator.

The restoration of Pierrot by the Sea is accurate to the high-Victorian era (1876–1890), including its color scheme, furnishings, chandeliers, woodwork, and stained glass. The one exception is a single 12-foot-tall mahogany reproduction of a bedroom set that Richard made to see how closely he could match the style. (He matched it perfectly.) "An architect who stayed with us begged us to sell it to him," Catherine says. "We told him it wasn't for sale."

The light wicker in the inn's first-floor parlor contrasts with the heavy woods and somber bedroom sets in the floors above. The bedrooms are light and airy, despite being furnished with Oriental rugs, flowered chintz draperies, and that highly carved walnut Victorian furniture. You can see the ocean from the majority of the rooms, and the inn is within walking distance of restaurants, the movies, outdoor amusements, and theater.

Before opening the Pierrot in 1984, the Burdos owned the Pierrot restaurant in Philadelphia. In the formal dining room of Pierrot by the Sea they serve multicourse northern Italian dinners on weekends ($35 per person, bring your own Chianti), and their five-course hot breakfasts are the most elaborate served at any inn on Long Beach Island. Quiches and eggs Benedict compete with unusual cheese, herb, and sausage breads.

The modern beach-block motels across the street clash jarringly with the Pierrot, and their proximity generates a degree of street noise on Saturday nights in summer, but the air conditioners, when turned on, mask the sound.

Address: *101 Centre St., Beach Haven, NJ 08008, tel. 609/492–4424.*
Accommodations: *6 double rooms with baths, 3 doubles share 2 baths, 1 suite.*
Amenities: *Air-conditioning in 3 bedrooms, cable TV in common room, fireplace in parlor; beach towels, beach tags, chairs.*
Rates: *$85–$150; full breakfast, afternoon tea. No credit cards.*
Restrictions: *No smoking indoors, no pets, 2-night minimum on weekends, 3-night minimum on holiday weekends, closed Nov.–Mar.*

Ashling Cottage

Goodi Stewart calls the style of her 1880 cottage Carpenter Gothic "because, as far as we can tell, the carpenter made it up as he went along." The intimate, unpretentious little house, which sits in the shadow of the old Colonial Hotel, is a block from the Spring Lake beach. Ashling is furnished with a mix of antiques and reproductions. Ocean breezes make air-conditioning unnecessary.

The atmosphere is easygoing, and innkeepers Goodi and Jack Stewart are experts at down-to-earth informality. "Jack's day gig is on the golf course," Goodi remarks. "Since he retired, he's become an expert at relaxation. We bought this place because I got jealous watching him on the couch reading the paper."

You can view the ocean and the lake as you breakfast or have tea in the solarium. The inn has an extensive collection of games and books for whiling away quiet hours.

Address: *106 Sussex Ave., Spring Lake, NJ 07762, tel. 908/449-3553.*
Accommodations: *8 double rooms with baths, 2 doubles share a bath.*
Amenities: *Cable TV with VCR in parlor; bicycles, beach tags, on-site parking, transportation from train.*
Rates: *$70–$135; full buffet breakfast. No credit cards.*
Restrictions: *No smoking indoors; 3-night minimum on weekends July–Aug., 2-night minimum other weekends, closed Jan.–Mar.*

BarnaGate Bed and Breakfast

If you can name the architectural style of this trim, pleasant 1896 Ocean City guest house, owners Frank and Lois Barna will be overjoyed. "We've had architects look it over and they can't figure it out," Lois says. "We call it seashore style." The exterior is vaguely Queen Anne, with a broad porch and bright burgundy awnings. Inside, a Second Empire oak dining room is the perfect setting to show off Lois's collections of spoons and bells. Frank collects John Wayne memorabilia, which he will show to interested guests.

Four blocks from the beach and convenient to Ocean City's busy downtown shopping area, the inn is reasonably priced by shore standards. Rooms have floral themes and

are dressed with country Victorian antiques and handmade quilts in pastel peach, rose, and mauve.

Leave the car at home: Frank will pick you up at the local bus terminal or the Atlantic City train station.

Address: *637 Wesley Ave., Ocean City, NJ 08226, tel. 609/391-9366.*
Accommodations: *1 double room with bath, 1 double with half-bath, 3 double rooms share 2 baths.*
Amenities: *Cable TV in parlor; beach tags.*
Rates: *$50–$70; Continental breakfast (Continental-plus in winter). MC, V.*
Restrictions: *No smoking indoors, no pets, 2-night minimum on holiday weekends.*

Bayberry Barque

This 19th-century house was built in 1888 for a member of the Philadelphia Orchestra. Now it's an easygoing inn where Pat and Glenn Miller (he works for the state and doesn't play an instrument) live year-round with their three children.

The rooms are decorated in deep colors authentic to the period of the house and are filled with a blend of antiques, reproductions, bric-a-brac, wicker, and country Victorian furnishings that makes visitors feel at home. The striking 4-foot-by-8-foot stained-glass window on the landing of the open staircase is part of the original structure.

The inn is within walking distance of restaurants, movies, a theater, night-clubs, and outdoor concerts, and it's just one short block from the beach.

Address: *117 Centre St., Beach Haven, NJ 08008, tel. 609/492-5216.*
Accommodations: *2 double rooms with baths, 7 doubles share 2 baths.*
Amenities: *Ceiling fans in bedrooms, cable TV in living room; beach tags, Saturday-night wine-and-cheese parties in summer.*
Rates: *$80–$120; Continental buffet breakfast. AE, MC, V accepted mid-June–mid-Sept.*
Restrictions: *No smoking indoors, no pets, 2-night minimum on weekends mid-June–mid-Sept., 3-night minimum on holiday weekends.*

Candlelight Inn

Paul DiFilippo and Diane Buscham, inspired by blissful stays in bed-and-breakfasts, sold their motel in order to transform this 1905 Queen Anne Victorian house into North Wildwood's first B&B, three blocks from the beach and boardwalk. "This is what we were meant to do," Diane says. "We enjoy everything about it. The people, the warmth—all of it." Original stained-glass windows and converted brass gaslight fixtures adorn the house, which is furnished with period antiques. There's an 1855 Empire sofa and an Eastlake piano in the parlor, and on the veranda, a swing and hammock.

The bedrooms have lace curtains and Oriental carpets; all are wallpapered. The Oak, Pine, and Walnut rooms are furnished and appropriately, as are Satin and Lace, Bay Window, and The Bride.

Address: *2310 Central Ave., North Wildwood, NJ 08260, tel. 609/522-6200.*
Accommodations: *7 double rooms with baths, 2 doubles share 1 bath with whirlpool tub.*
Amenities: *Air-conditioning in 3 bedrooms, cable TV in parlor, fireplaces in parlor and 2nd-floor foyer; off-street parking.*
Rates: *$85–$115; full breakfast, afternoon refreshments. AE, D, MC, V.*
Restrictions: *No smoking indoors, no pets, 3-night minimum on weekends July–Aug.*

The Carriage House

The Carriage House, a charming Victorian on a quiet residential street two blocks from the beach, has been a family-oriented bed-and-breakfast since 1980, and the tradition will be carried on by its new owners, Linda and Peter Foy. Suites, extra-large guest rooms, and an efficiency apartment in the carriage house are ideal for families and groups traveling together.

The Foys have maintained the mixture of antiques, reproductions, and modern furniture in pastel colors that gives the home a casual country feel. The living room provides a comfortable gathering place, as do the large dining room and shady front porch, where guests may enjoy their breakfast. In warmer weather, the grounds provide the added attraction of colorful flowers and 100-year-old trees. The Foys' planned changes include additional antiques as well as two more suites.

Address: *208 Jersey Ave., Spring Lake, NJ 07762, tel. 908/449–1332.*
Accommodations: *4 double rooms with baths, 2 doubles share 1 bath, 2 2-bedroom suites, efficiency apartment.*
Amenities: *Air-conditioning in bedrooms, cable TV in living room; tennis passes, off-street parking.*
Rates: *$75–$175; Continental breakfast. No credit cards.*
Restrictions: *No smoking, no pets, 3-night minimum on holiday weekends.*

Cashelmara Inn

Built in 1901 for the U.S. Postmaster General, this deceptively small-looking gabled house boasts a proud Greek Revival porch that faces Sylvan Lake. Cashelmara is on the block between Ocean Avenue and the beach, overlooking Sylvan Lake. Marty Mulligan, a professional Irishman and technical representative for Eastman Kodak, was smitten by the near-perfect location, so he bought the house in 1986 and named it the Gaelic word for "house by the sea." Overflowing with antiques, Oriental rugs, and period furnishings, all the rooms look out to either the ocean or the lake, right in front of the house. Cashelmara hosts occasional afternoon wine-and-cheese parties.

Address: *22 Lakeside Ave., Avon-By-the-Sea, NJ 07717, tel. 908/776–8727 or 800/821–2976.*
Accommodations: *13 double rooms with baths, 1 suite.*
Amenities: *Air-conditioning in 10 bedrooms, ceiling fans in all, fireplaces in dining room, parlor, and suite, minirefrigerator in suite, cable TV in parlor; beach towels, reduced-rate beach tags, off-street parking, transportation to and from bus and train station.*
Rates: *$90–$100; full breakfast. AE, D, MC, V.*
Restrictions: *Smoking on porch only, no pets, 3-night minimum on weekends (4-night minimum on holiday weekends) Memorial Day–Labor Day, 2-night minimum on other weekends.*

The Chateau

The Chateau is four blocks from the beach, convenient to the Spring Lake railroad station, and across from the municipal park and lake, where there are tennis courts and a children's playground. Owner Scott Smith says he considers the Chateau, with its rambling complex of rooms, to be in a niche between a bed-and-breakfast and a hotel.

The Victorian-cottage exterior contrasts drastically with the interior, which has plush wall-to-wall carpeting and contemporary and wicker furnishings. Rooms are named after some of the hotel's more famous guests, such as Buster Keaton, Basil Rathbone, and Arthur Treacher. Some rooms have private balconies overlooking the park. Twenty-two rooms and all the suites have wet bars, and many of the baths are marble.

Address: *5th and Warren Aves., Spring Lake, NJ 07762, tel. 908/974–2000, fax 908/974–2000, ext. 106.*
Accommodations: *40 double rooms with baths, 6 suites.*
Amenities: *Air-conditioning, VCRs, cable TV, radios, telephones, and refrigerators in bedrooms; wet bars and oversize tubs in some rooms; fireplace in most suites; beach tags, on- and off-site parking, bicycle rental.*
Rates: *$79–$150; Continental breakfast optional. AE, MC, V.*
Restrictions: *No pets, 3-night minimum on weekends June 21–Sept. 10.*

Conover's Bay Head Inn

Three porches adorn Ocean County's best-known bed-and-breakfast, a shingle-style cottage built in 1905 that had become a hotel. Beverly and Carl Conover bought it in 1970, and began their bed-and-breakfast, inadvertently becoming leaders in the movement. Beverly hosts B&B seminars and teaches at a local college. Carl spent four years restoring a 1936 Elco cruiser.

You can see the water from many of the inn's windows; six guest rooms have ocean views, and two have views of the bay. Interiors are furnished in a mix of antiques and reproductions in English country style, with lots of chintz, spriggy wallpapers, and ruffled linens. An enclosed English garden was added to the grounds in May 1990. Special brass and iron headboards were made for some of the beds, and one room, with oak furniture, has an ocean-view porch.

Address: *646 Main Ave., Bay Head, NJ 08742, tel. 908/892–4664.*
Accommodations: *12 double rooms with baths.*
Amenities: *Air-conditioning in bedrooms, turn-down service, fireplace in parlor; beach tags, beach towels, on-site parking, transportation to and from train station.*
Rates: *$110–$175; full breakfast, afternoon tea in cooler months. AE, MC, V.*
Restrictions: *No smoking indoors, no pets, 2-night minimum on weekends June–Sept., 3- and 4-night minimum on holiday weekends.*

Henry Ludlam Inn

Henry Ludlam has a small place in New Jersey's history books as the man who started the state's first public school. His 1740 house in the simple Federal style is now a bed-and-breakfast owned by Marty and Ann Thurlow. The house is decorated with country antiques and a variety of 18th- and 19th-century pieces in different woods. It sits on 55-acre Ludlam's Pond, which guests are encouraged to explore in the inn's canoe and inner tubes. Rods and reels are also available for anglers, and less active guests can admire the lake from the gazebo.

The ambience at the inn is reminiscent of the Chesapeake Bay area: Were it not for the traffic along Route 47, you'd think you were in a Maryland backwater. Stone Harbor is 20 minutes away, and antiques shops are nearby.

Address: *1336 Rte. 47, Dennisville (Cape May County), NJ 08270, tel. 609/861-5847.*
Accommodations: *4 double rooms with baths, 2 doubles share 1 bath.*
Amenities: *Air-conditioning in bedrooms, feather beds, fireplaces in 3 bedrooms, cable TV in parlor, fireside picnic baskets, beach tags, beach towels, inner tubes, canoe, fishing rods, off-street parking.*
Rates: *$75–$110; full breakfast, afternoon refreshments. AE, MC, V.*
Restrictions: *No smoking, no pets, 2-night minimum on weekends July–Aug.*

Hollycroft

On a bluff hidden by trees above South Belmar's Lake Como, Hollycroft was built in 1908. Its log beams and 16-foot ironstone inglenook fireplace suggest a Vermont log cabin or an Adirondack ski chalet. The lake can be seen from all but one of the guest rooms; one has a glassed-in porch.

Linda and Mark Fessler bought Hollycroft in 1985 and maintained its North Country mood throughout. The dining area has a minifridge that resembles an antique icebox, and the guest rooms are decorated with floral wallpaper, light woods, and brass and iron beds.

The inn is four blocks from the beach, and its proximity to Lake Como attracts anglers and birdwatchers. In the cooler months the Fessels host mystery weekends, and it is a most atmospheric place for a winter holiday.

Address: *506 North Blvd., South Belmar, NJ 07719, tel. 908/681-2254.*
Accommodations: *6 double rooms with baths.*
Amenities: *Air-conditioning in 4 bedrooms, 2 fireplaces in public areas; beach towels, off-street parking.*
Rates: *$85–$115; Continental breakfast. AE.*
Restrictions: *No smoking in bedrooms, no pets, 2-night minimum on weekends. Memorial Day–Sept., 3-night minimum on holiday weekends.*

Sea Crest by the Sea

This whimsical Queen Anne–style bed-and-breakfast seeks to be just a little bit different from the pack. The friendly owners, John and Carol Kirby, opened Sea Crest in 1990. Its colorful rooms are inspired by characters and themes from fairy tales, history, literature, and such exotic realms as Casablanca and New Orleans.

The three-story house is furnished with French and English Victorian antiques in beautiful condition. Favorite guest rooms are the Victorian Rose, which boasts a carved Victorian American-walnut bed, and the Sleigh Ride Room, where there's a brass sleigh on the mantel. Located next door to the Normandy Inn, Sea Crest is close enough to the beach for guests to hear the surf from its wraparound porch.

Address: *19 Tuttle Ave., Spring Lake, NJ 07762, tel. 908/449–9031.*
Accommodations: *12 double rooms with baths.*
Amenities: *Air-conditioning, cable TV in library, fireplaces in 2 bedrooms and 2 in parlor, turndown service, toiletries, player-piano recitals; croquet lawn, bicycles, beach towels, off-street parking, transportation to and from railroad station.*
Rates: *$84–$147; full breakfast, afternoon tea. MC, V.*
Restrictions: *Smoking on porch only, 2-night minimum mid-May–Sept., 3-night minimum on holiday weekends.*

The Seaflower

This Dutch-colonial house has a breezy mix of antiques and seashore bric-a-brac. It's about half a block from the beach and boardwalk, in a sleepy residential area away from the commercial district. Innkeeper Pat O'Keefe is a microbiologist, and her partner Knute Iwaszko is a salesman and a chemist. One bedroom has a painted and stenciled floor; the others are refinished pine. "I'm wild about wallpaper and flowers," says Pat, and the rooms reflect that love.

Although scientific types do visit, "Most people are less interested in work," Pat says, "and more interested in running." Knute is a serious runner who can plan courses of any length (the shortest is about 20 feet—just far enough to collapse on the porch). Runners of all levels, from slow joggers to such world-class competitors as Greta Waitz, stay at the Seaflower, run in the local races, and celebrate afterward with Pat and Knute.

Address: *110 9th Ave., Belmar, NJ 07719, tel. 908/681–6006.*
Accommodations: *5 double rooms with baths, 1 suite.*
Amenities: *Sinks in bedrooms, TV with VCR and games in parlor; beach tags, bicycles, off-street parking, transportation to and from railroad station.*
Rates: *$65–$95; full breakfast. AE.*
Restrictions: *No smoking indoors, no pets, 2-night minimum on weekends Memorial Day–Labor Day, 3-night minimum on holiday weekends.*

The Studio

The 1889 home of artist John F. Peto, the Studio is on the National Register of Historic Places and was restored with Victorian touches and many of Peto's paintings. It's in peaceful, historic Island Heights, on the Barnegat Bay, near Barnegat Peninsula beach resorts and Island Beach State Park. Visitors can walk to Bayshore beaches or sit in rocking chairs on the wraparound porch, looking out on Toms River.

Owner Joy Smiley, Peto's granddaughter, says guests just live in her enormous country kitchen, where breakfast is served. The bedrooms are carpeted with different colors— one with a river view has a beamed ceiling and a big double bed; another, with white-flowered spread and curtains, is big enough for three antique dressers and a desk. Joy says the quiet pace of the area makes it ideal for winter joggers, who can toast their toes on the specially designed "foot warmer" fireplace in the library. Artists and art historians are frequent guests.

Address: *102 Cedar Ave., Island Heights, NJ 08732, tel. 908/270–6058.*
Accommodations: *3 double rooms share 2 baths.*
Amenities: *Air-conditioning in 2 bedrooms, turn-down service, cable TV in parlor, fireplaces in studio and in library, baby-grand piano, small kitchen.*
Rates: *$50–$85; full breakfast. AE.*
Restrictions: *No pets.*

Victoria Guest House

Salvador Dalí was once a guest at this inn, which has grown to include a second 19th-century cedar-shake cottage in Beach Haven's historic district. Rooms here are informal, furnished with wicker, rag rugs, and a mix of antiques. A small heated outdoor pool was added for guests who don't want to walk one block to the beach.

Innkeepers Marilyn Miller, a former schoolteacher, and her husband, Leonard, a retired executive from United Technologies, are very sociable: They host bridge parties on Wednesday night and Saturday-evening wine-and-cheese gatherings, after which guests move to the porch to hear the outdoor concerts performed in the park across the street. Active in historic preservation, the Millers give guests free tickets to the Long Beach Island Historical Society Museum, which is across the park. The inn is close to the well-known Summer Stock theater, restaurants, cinema, and outdoor amusements.

Address: *126 Amber St., Beach Haven, NJ 08008, tel. 609/492–4154.*
Accommodations: *15 double rooms with baths.*
Amenities: *Complimentary Sun. New York Times; beach tags, beach chairs, bicycles, swimming pool.*
Rates: *$80–$130; Continental-plus breakfast, afternoon lemonade and iced tea. No credit cards.*
Restrictions: *No smoking indoors, no pets, 2-night minimum on weekends, closed Nov.–Apr.*

Along the Delaware

The Delaware River begins as a trickling brook in upstate New York and gathers momentum as it moves south, drawing the border between Pennsylvania and New Jersey. At the northwest corner of New Jersey it widens and forms the Delaware Water Gap, well known to canoeists, kayakers, and white-water enthusiasts. Just north of Trenton a historic park marks the spot where, in 1776, Washington surprised the British by crossing the river, which continues south through Philadelphia and empties into the broad basin of Delaware Bay.

The sites most interesting to tourists are concentrated along the 80 miles of river between the New York border and Washington's Crossing. Also of interest are Princeton, with its world-renowned university, and Lambertville, a small industrial village that is home to many of the artists, craftspeople, and restaurateurs of its neighbor across the river—New Hope, Pennsylvania. Lambertville is also where the Original Trenton Cracker Company turns out its famous walnut-size oyster crackers, found in seafood restaurants all along the East Coast. Lambertville, Stockton, and Frenchtown are good bases for antiquing and sightseeing in New Jersey and Pennsylvania. Flemington, about 10 miles east of Frenchtown, has a cluster of outlets, auctions, and antiques shops. Clinton, about 10 miles farther north, has a small historic area and is the site of a children's art festival. Still farther north are Hope and Fredon, nestled in a mountainous region that seems more a part of the Adirondacks than of New Jersey. Hot-air ballooning, water sports on the Delaware, spring and summer foliage-viewing, and skiing are highly recommended.

Places to Go, Sights to See

Ballooning. The still, windless mornings and tranquil twilight hours make
this area perfect for hot-air ballooning, which costs from $135 to $150 per
person for a 60-minute trip, transportation usually included. It's traditional to
open a bottle of champagne at the finish; ask if your carrier supplies one.
Sky Promotions (Pittstown, tel. 908/996–2195), near Clinton, operates year-
round.

Gliders. For those who would rather not travel by balloon, *Eagle Ridge
Soaring* (Blairstown, tel. 908/362–8311) offers trips in gliders.

Hiking and Biking. Though bicycles can be rented in the area, the steepness
of the hills along the Delaware can be formidable. The Princeton area isn't
quite so hilly, and the *Princeton University Cycle Club* (tel. 609/394–2221)
meets every Sunday at 8 AM, weather permitting, at Forrestal Village, on
Route 1. Hiking in state parks requires good boots, rugged clothing, sun
protection for your head, and, from July through September, plenty of insect
repellent.

McCarter Center of the Performing Arts (Princeton, tel. 609/683–8000).
Notorious as one of the ugliest buildings on the Princeton campus, this
theater presents memorable avant-garde and revival shows as well as
concerts and public lectures.

New Jersey State Museum (Trenton, tel. 609/292–6308). The dinosaur exhibit,
the geology displays, the Native American artifacts, and the changing fine-
arts exhibit at this museum make the drive into Trenton worthwhile.

Princeton University. *Orange Key Tours* (tel. 609/258–3603) employs
undergraduates to show visitors around campus. Free tours leave daily from
the Maclean House, next to Nassau Hall. *The Princeton Historical Society*
(tel. 609/921–6748) gives tours of the town every Sunday at 2, starting from
Bainbridge House (158 Nassau Street).

USGA Golf House Museum (Far Hills, tel. 908/234–2300). Housed in
a Georgian Colonial-style mansion built in 1919, this museum and library is
visited by golfers from all over the world. Two floors of exhibits lead you
through the history of golf. There are special exhibits throughout the year.

Waterloo Village (Stanhope, tel. 201/347–0900). In this beautifully restored
Revolutionary War–era canal town near Stanhope, you can watch resident
blacksmiths, potters, weavers, and candlemakers and buy samples of their
crafts. The village's Indian museum displays and sells Native American
crafts. The summer concert series, featuring a mix of jazz, classical, rock,
and country-western music, is a big draw.

Wineries. New Jersey's wineries offer daily tours that end with tastings for
those 21 and older. Don't expect first-class Bordeaux, but do expect to be
surprised at the reasonably good vintages produced at the *Four Sisters*

(Belvidere, tel. 908/475-3671), *Alba Vineyard* (Milford, tel. 908/995-7800), and *Amwell Valley* (Ringoes, tel. 908/788-5852). Ask your bed-and-breakfast hosts for other recommendations.

Restaurants

Scanticon-Princeton (tel. 609/452-7800), a somewhat modernistic conference-center hotel, serves the region's knockout Sunday brunch. In Lambertville **Hamilton's Grill** (tel. 609/397-4343) offers multinational Mediterranean cuisine enhanced by a view of the Delaware. The **Ship Inn** (tel. 908/995-7007), in Milford, has a menu of British fare and 15 British beers on tap. For German and Continental cuisine try the **Black Forest Inn** (tel. 201/347-3344), in Stanhope.

Tourist Information

Hunterdon County Chamber of Commerce (2200 Rte. 31, Box 15, Lebanon 08833, tel. 908/735-5955). **Mercer County Cultural & Heritage Office** (Box 8068, Trenton 08650, tel. 609/989-6701). **Princeton Area Convention and Visitors Bureau** (20 Nassau St., Princeton 08542, tel. 609/683-1760). **Sussex County Chamber of Commerce** (112 Hampton House Rd., Newton 07860, tel. 908/579-1811). **Warren County Dept. of Economic Development and Tourism** (Dumont Administration Bldg., Rte. 519, Belvidere 07823, tel. 908/475-8000, ext. 580).

Reservation Services

Bed & Breakfast of New Jersey (103 Godwin Ave., Suite 132, Midland Park 07432, tel. 908/444-7409). **Bed and Breakfast of Princeton** (Box 571, Princeton 08540, tel. 609/924-3189). **Northern New Jersey Bed & Breakfast/ Temporary Lodgings** (11 Sunset Trail, Denville 07834, tel. 908/625-5129).

Chimney Hill Farm

Moving about among the hot-air balloons that are launched on the grounds of Chimney Hill Farm is a surreal experience. The approach to the inn will take your breath away. As you climb the road, the Delaware River, which dominates the Lambertville–New Hope area, disappears from sight, and the house and its owner, Ken Turi, welcome you.

The original 1820 fieldstone building was enlarged in 1920 by Margaret Spencer, one of the first female architects to graduate from MIT. Spencer added three wings to the house and crowned them with Colonial Revival gables and dormers. There are also seven staircases—"If you're running away from somebody, you *can* get away," Ken quips.

Bright floral fabrics and Oriental carpets complement the reproduction 18th-century furnishings. The living room's Persian rug previously adorned the corporate boardroom of the Reading Railroad Company in Philadelphia.

Horticulturists can wander the inn's 8½ landscaped acres. The sloping, open fields contain a raspberry and exotic-fruit farm, whose harvests are used in Lambertville's Coryell Crossing preserves as well as in many Manhattan restaurants. In the inn's greenhouse Ken grows the plants that fill the guest rooms and the solarium, and visitors may lose themselves in the 50-year-old boxwood maze or in the sunken English garden.

Ken has restored 10 properties in this area in the past decade. "I'll probably move on, eventually," he says, "but you don't find them much better than this."

Address: *207 Goat Hill Rd., Lambertville, NJ 08530, tel. 609/397-1516.*
Accommodations: *7 double rooms with baths.*
Amenities: *Air-conditioning in bedrooms, fireplaces in 3 public areas; complimentary cookies, fruit, and snacks; on-site parking, balloon trips ($135 per person).*
Rates: *$105–$150; Continental breakfast. AE, MC, V.*
Restrictions: *No smoking indoors, 2-night minimum on weekends in season, 3-night minimum on holiday weekends.*

Inn at Millrace Pond

Nowadays, the paddlewheel doesn't turn inside the Inn at Millrace Pond, but you can pretend the millrace still flows into this 1769 stone gristmill, which supplied the flour to Washington's troops. Located on 23 acres of forested hills in Hope, a historic Moravian village, the inn is close to the scenic Delaware River Water Gap, Waterloo Village, wineries, ballooning, golf, and winter-sports facilities.

Now in its fifth year of operation, the inn complex has a restaurant, a tavern, two other Colonial buildings, the Millrace House and Wheelwright's House, and a small pond. When you enter the imposing four-story gristmill, you can look down a story and a half at the skeleton of the old wheel and walk downstairs between stone walls to the tavern, with its huge walk-in fireplace, cage bar, and old prints on the walls. The gristmill's architecture is stunning; on the top floor the cathedral ceilings of the bedrooms reveal the enormous timbers of the roof, and the building's beams and wide-board floors have been preserved throughout.

Innkeepers Gloria Carrigan, a former advertising executive, and Dick Gooding, a developer of historic restorations, are serious about the furnishings: The gristmill bedrooms have Shaker reproductions; elsewhere there are regional antiques—made in New York, Pennsylvania,

and New Jersey. The six-bedroom Millrace House, a frame building that was the miller's dwelling, has more formal furnishings and a parlor with a fireplace. Its bedrooms and the two in the stone Wheelwright's House have collections of Queen Anne, Chippendale, and Sheraton pieces. Each of the Wheelwright House bedrooms (one upstairs and one down) has its own entrance, and they are prized for romantic seclusion.

Active in the fight to preserve Hope's historic atmosphere, Gloria opens the inn to tours of the city's historic sites. In summer, guests often join one of the guided walking tours.

Address: *Rte. 519, Box 359, Hope, NJ 07844, tel. 908/459-4884.*
Accommodations: *17 double rooms with baths, 1 suite.*
Amenities: *Restaurant, tavern, air-conditioning, phones in bedrooms, cable TV in 9 bedrooms and parlor, fireplaces in parlor and tavern; tennis, off-street parking.*
Rates: *$85–$130; Continental breakfast. AE, MC, V.*
Restrictions: *No smoking in guest rooms, no pets, 2-night minimum with Sat. reservation.*

Stewart Inn

Six years ago attorney Brian McGarry had a midlife crisis that he thought he could cure with a grand purchase. "Some guys get blondes and Porsches," he explains. "I decided to do an inn."

His wife, Lynne, an antiques and needlework collector, approved, and the couple bought a 1770 fieldstone manor house originally built for the owner of Stewartsville's gristmill, which ground flour to feed George Washington's troops during the Revolutionary War.

Among the property's previous owners was Harry Bannister, a Broadway producer whose friends in the entertainment industry— among them Clark Gable—used the house as a retreat. Although the stars left nothing behind, the inn has retained a dramatic atmosphere that Brian describes as "privacy amid splendor."

About a 25-minute drive from the many fine restaurants of Lambertville, Stewart Inn has 16 acres of lawns; formal perennial gardens; a stocked trout stream; and a meandering pasture that leads to a working farm with ducks, sheep, goats, and peacocks. The eggs served at breakfast are provided by the farm's chickens.

The best times to visit the inn are summer, when the swimming pool offers a respite from the heat, and fall, when the maple and apple trees show off their bright colors. In the winter, the house is filled with plants brought in from the outside.

Inside, off-white walls bring out the richness of the dark cherry and mahogany furnishings and the bright tapestries and rugs. Many rooms have antique jam cupboards, and all have brass oil lamps on night tables beside the beds. Needlework is displayed throughout the house, and Lynne holds needlework seminars and workshops during sheep-shearing season. She also sells kits for those who are inspired.

Address: *Box 571, RD 1, Stewartsville, NJ 08886, tel. 908/479–6060, fax 908/459–5889.*
Accommodations: *6 double rooms with baths, 2 doubles share bath, 2 suites.*
Amenities: *Air-conditioning, color TV, and phones in bedrooms, 7 fireplaces in public areas; swimming pool, badminton court, trout stream, off-street parking.*
Rates: *$75–$95; full breakfast. MC, V.*
Restrictions: *No pets.*

Cabbage Rose Inn

Pam and Al Scott were tele-
phone-company executives
when they met in 1986. Two
years later they bought an 1890
Queen Anne house in Flemington,
and after working for three months
on the restoration they were married
in front of the house's hand-carved
mahogany fireplace. The Cabbage
Rose Inn opened to the public short-
ly thereafter.

Formerly the French restaurant La
Champagne, the inn is set on Flemington's busy Main Street and is
within the city's historic district. Inside, cabbage rose–motif wallpaper
and fixtures predominate. Many of
the antiques, which Pam describes
as "eclectic light Victorian," are family heirlooms.

Address: *162 Main St., Flemington,
NJ 08822, tel. 908/788–0247.*
Accommodations: *5 double rooms
with baths.*
Amenities: *Air-conditioning, complimentary chocolates in guest
rooms, cable TV in parlor, breakfast served in room on request,
baby grand piano and fireplace in
parlor; croquet area, on-site parking.*
Rates: *$80–$98; Continental-plus
breakfast (full breakfast on weekends), afternoon refreshments. AE,
MC, V.*
Restrictions: *Smoking on porch
only, no pets, 2-night minimum
with Sat. reservation May–Dec.*

Chestnut Hill

You can sit on the porch of
Chestnut Hill and admire the
wide river and the old metal
bridge that crosses it. If you're
lucky, one of the occasional trains
will slowly chug by. It's a five-
minute walk along the river if you
want to explore the cliffs where Indians used to live. Perched on the
bank of the Delaware River, Chestnut Hill is near bicycle-, canoe-, and
inner tube–rental shops, just 30 minutes from Lambertville and New
Hope. Innkeepers Linda and Rob Co-
stanza are still working on the 1860
frame house. They're aiming for
a balance of whimsy and Victorian
detailing—slowly returning the outside of the inn, as well as the cottage next door, to the original period
colors, while giving the guest rooms

a country Victorian look with flowers and tropical hues. A 9½-by-
13-foot black-walnut apothecary unit
and an 1872 pump organ dominate
the drawing room. The best views
are from the third-floor rooms.
There's a collection of 180 teddy
bears to keep you company.

Address: *63 Church St., Milford, NJ
08848, tel. 908/995–9761.*
Accommodations: *2 double rooms
with baths, 3 doubles share 1 bath,
2 suites (1 with full kitchen).*
Amenities: *Air-conditioning, cable
TV in 2 rooms, fireplace in parlor;
on-site parking, transportation
from Frenchtown bus stop.*
Rates: *$75–$160; Continental-plus
breakfast. No credit cards.*
Restrictions: *No smoking, no pets,
2-night minimum on weekends.*

Colligan's Stockton Inn

I n 1934 Richard Rodgers and Lorenz Hart escaped from Manhattan to this inn, where they wrote "There's a Small Hotel," which was used in the 1936 musical *On Your Toes*. The song made Colligan's Stockton Inn, which has been entertaining guests since 1796, the most famous in New Jersey, and the inn gets frequent calls from people who want to know if the wishing well is still there. It is.

The Colligan family, however, who gave the inn an eccentric air, are not. They sold the inn in 1983 to a corporation that renovated the rooms with Colonial-style reproductions. The historic touches remain—eight bedrooms and the five dining rooms have working fireplaces—but the mood is more that of a small hotel. There are terraced gardens with waterfalls and trout ponds and a good restaurant that serves American and Continental food.

Address: *Rte. 29, Stockton, NJ 08559, tel. 609/397-1250.*
Accommodations: *11 double rooms with baths.*
Amenities: *Restaurant, air-conditioning and TV in bedrooms, minirefrigerators in some rooms; outdoor dining in warm months, off-street parking.*
Rates: *$60–$145; Continental breakfast. AE, D, MC, V.*
Restrictions: *No pets, 2-night minimum on weekends.*

Jerica Hill

T he first bed-and-breakfast established in the small historic town of Flemington, Jerica Hill is a completely restored turn-of-the-century Victorian house set on a tree-lined street in the center of town. It's painted in shades of gray, with burgundy trim. Owner Judith Studer bought the property from her best friend's grandfather in 1984. She has chosen wicker, brass, oak, and mahogany furnishings to decorate what she calls her "Victorian country home." The large, first-floor bedroom is a favorite for its bay window, four-poster bed, and seating area.

Judith is an avid hot-air balloonist who will arrange balloon trips for guests. She has also designed a back-roads driving tour of the countryside and the wineries in the area.

Address: *96 Broad St., Flemington, NJ 08822, tel. 908/782-8234.*
Accommodations: *5 double rooms with baths.*
Amenities: *Air-conditioning in bedrooms, cable TV and fireplace in living room, free New York Times; off-street parking.*
Rates: *$75–$95; Continental-plus breakfast. AE, MC, V.*
Restrictions: *No smoking, no pets, 2-night minimum on weekends.*

Old Hunterdon House

This roomy 1864 Italianate Victorian mansion on Frenchtown's Main Street features high ceilings, a wraparound porch, and a belvedere with views of the Delaware (where guests congregate for late-afternoon refreshments). Guest rooms are dominated by huge, mixed-wood Victorian bedroom sets and are ornamented with period antiques. The inn is a short walk from the river and the crafts, antiques, and specialty shops that line Bridge Street. Lambertville and New Hope are a 12-mile drive; public transportation is nearby.

Clark and Karen Johnson bought the bed-and-breakfast in 1992 and with the help of historic preservationists have restored it inside and out. The third-floor garret suite has slanting ceilings and the Leonardo da Vinci–design circular window—the Old Hunterdon House trademark.

The highly rated Frenchtown Inn restaurant is across the street.

Address: *12 Bridge St., Frenchtown, NJ 08825, tel. 908/996-3632 or 800/382-0375.*
Accommodations: *7 double rooms with baths, 1 suite.*
Amenities: *Air-conditioning in bedrooms, fireplace in 1 bedroom and in parlor; on-site parking.*
Rates: *$110–$145; full breakfast. MC, V.*
Restrictions: *Smoking on porch only, no pets.*

Peacock Inn

In the center of Princeton, a two-minute walk from the university campus, the Peacock Inn has hosted visitors for more than a century. Built as a private home in 1770, the structure was moved in 1875 from its original site on the Princeton campus to its current Bayard Lane location. The Peacock Inn is the city's only full-time bed-and-breakfast, so guests should book far in advance for the fall and spring, when visiting educators fill its rooms. Albert Einstein, F. Scott Fitzgerald, and Bertrand Russell are listed among the inn's distinguished guests.

Although the rooms here vary in color scheme and decor, they all feature Victorian antiques and reproductions. The inn is one of only a few properties in the state that accept pets. Guests get a 50 percent discount on meals at Le Pelumet Royal, the inn's restaurant, where dinner for two, without discounts, averages $100.

Address: *20 Bayard La., Princeton, NJ 08540, tel. 609/924-1707.*
Accommodations: *9 double rooms with baths, 6 doubles share 4 baths, one triple with bath.*
Amenities: *Restaurant and bar with cable TV, air-conditioning in bedrooms, phones in 5 bedrooms, cable TV in lounge; on-site parking.*
Rates: *$80–$125; full breakfast. AE, MC, V.*

The Whistling Swan Inn

A 1904 late-Victorian-style house, with a marvelous Queen Anne octagonal tower room and unusual granite pillars supporting the veranda, the Whistling Swan is Paula Williams's and Joe Mulay's idea of where travelers should stay but rarely have the chance to. "Before doing this we worked for corporations and had to stay in Hiltons and Holiday Inns," Paula says. "When we traveled for ourselves we sought out bed-and-breakfasts and just had to have our own."

Located in a tiny village in New Jersey's highlands, the Whistling Swan is close to winter skiing and ice skating, summer water sports on the lakes, and cultural activities in Waterloo Village. The Delaware River is a 25-minute drive away.

Most of the inn's guest rooms contain country Victorian antiques and reproductions, but three have themes—Art Deco, 1940s, and Oriental.

Address: *110 Main St., Stanhope, NJ 07874, tel. 201/347–6369.*
Accommodations: *9 double rooms with baths, 1 suite.*
Amenities: *Air-conditioning in bedrooms, cable TV in guest parlor, fireplace in foyer and in dining room; off-street parking.*
Rates: *$75–$100; full breakfast. AE, D, MC, V.*
Restrictions: *Smoking on veranda only, no pets, 2-night minimum on holiday weekends.*

Cape May

Cape May, the southernmost resort town on the New Jersey shore, sits at the end of the Garden State Parkway, 40 minutes south of Atlantic City, at the tip of the Cape May County Peninsula. The town is known for its carefully researched and beautifully restored inns and small hotels, half of which, or about 35, are bed-and-breakfasts.

Believed to be the oldest ocean resort in New Jersey, Cape May was first sighted in 1620 by the Dutch explorer Captain Cornelius Mey, who modestly named the entire peninsula after himself. Early settlers were fishermen and whalers who came by boat from Philadelphia and from villages along Delaware Bay. Today the commercial fishing port is the third largest on the East Coast, providing Cape May's restaurants with fresh seafood.

As early as the 1760s, guest houses began to appear on the cape, and by the early 1800s they had expanded into huge hotels neighboring the summer mansions of people from Philadelphia, Wilmington, and Washington, DC. Fires and storms periodically ravaged the town, but an astonishing variety of structures managed to survive, including the gaudily appointed Italianate Victorian cottages, inns, and mansions of the city's 2-square-mile historic district.

In the 20th century Cape May lost most of its business to Atlantic City and, in the 1950s, to Wildwood, both more easily reached by car or train. A catastrophic 1962 storm forced the city fathers to take stock of what they had. They used America's first Urban Development Action Grant to create an outdoor pedestrian street, the Washington Mall, which inspired the renovation of the Victorian buildings.

At about the same time, Cape May attracted a group of restaurateurs, most of them from Philadelphia, who found the combination of fresh seafood, locally grown vegetables,

and low rents an incentive to try their luck in a town that
was still too far down the Garden State Parkway for most
tourists. When one succeeded, others followed. Now Cape
May has a large district of eclectic restaurants, all within
walking distance of one another.

The genteel, relaxing blend of architecture and cuisine in
a southern, small-town setting is Cape May's prime
attraction. Swimming, bicycling, fishing, and bird
watching in the nearby state park are also popular, and
the lighthouse is open to visitors. Most inns require a three-
or four-night minimum stay from June 15 to the end of
September. Victorian Week, usually at the beginning of
October, combines whimsy with serious lectures on
Victorian history and restoration. Most Cape May
restaurants and inns are closed in January, February, and
March.

The beach is adequate—a flat stretch of dark sand that is
not as dramatic as those farther north. The town has few
diversions for children, but the boardwalk amusement rides
of Wildwood are a 20-minute drive away.

Places to Go, Sights to See

Boat Rides. The *Schooner Yankee* offers sightseeing and sunset voyages in
summer, departing from the Ocean Highway Docks (tel. 609/884–1919). The
Cape May–Lewes Ferry (tel. 609/886–2718 or 302/645–6313) takes cars,
pedestrians, and bicycles to and from the small town of Lewes. The trip lasts
approximately 70 minutes, weather permitting.

Cape May Point State Park (tel. 609/884–2159). An eight-minute drive from
the historic district, this 300-acre wildlife preserve has nature trails; a small
museum; and a wild, rustic beach where swimming is discouraged because of
the rough tides. Call the *Cape May Bird Observatory* (tel. 609/884–2626) to
learn what migratory and water birds have been seen lately.

Cape May Point. A residential town founded as a Methodist retreat by
Philadelphia merchant John Wanamaker, Cape May Point is a pleasant
destination for an afternoon bicycle ride.

Carney's (Beach Dr. and Decatur St., tel. 609/884–4424). This restaurant is
also the closest thing Cape May has to a loud rock-and-roll bar.

The Old Shire (Washington Mall, tel. 609/884–4700). This is a genuine jazz-improv club, and the styles of music played vary widely.

Sunset Beach. At the end of Sunset Road, this pebbled Delaware Bay beach contrasts with the fine-grain ocean beaches less than a mile away. Ocean-polished lumps of quartz, called Cape May Diamonds, can be found along the tide line.

The Top of the Marq (tel. 609/884–3431). Here's the place for old-style dinner and dancing, in the Marquis De Lafayette Hotel.

Tours. The best way to see Cape May is to take a walking tour run by the Mid-Atlantic Center for the Arts (MAC, tel. 609/884–5404). *The Cape May Carriage Company* (tel. 609/884–4466) provides tours by horse and carriage.

Restaurants

Cape May is famous for its eccentric, informal, café-style restaurants, many of which do not have liquor licenses (no problem—you can usually bring your own). **The Mad Batter** (tel. 609/884–5970) started the trend, with a mixed Oriental, Continental, and American menu. Restaurants offering a similar cuisine include **Louisa's** (tel. 609/884–5882) and **Peaches Cafe** (tel. 609/884–0202). For slightly more traditional, Continental dining, try **Alexander's** (tel. 609/884–2555), which serves a five-course brunch that's the best in town, or **Maureen's** (tel. 609/884–3774). You'll find marvelous Cajun, Creole, and Caribbean-style dishes at **410 Bank Street** (tel. 609/884–2127). **Frescoes** (tel. 609/884–0366) serves nouvelle Italian. For seafood try the **Lobster House** (tel. 609/884–8296), on Fisherman's Wharf, a five-minute drive from the historic district; or **A & J's Blue Claw** (tel. 609/884–5878), on Ocean Drive, a five-minute drive from the causeway connecting Cape May to Wildwood Crest. Both get most of their entrées right off the fishing boats. One last, extraordinary feast is the traditional, southern-style Sunday supper, served in the late afternoon, at the **Chalfonte Hotel** (tel. 609/884–8409).

Tourist Information

Cape May Convention and Visitors Bureau (Box 403, Cape May 08204, tel. 800/528–7328). **Welcome Center** (405 Lafayette St., Cape May 08204, tel. 609/884–9562).

Reservation Service

Cape May Reservation Service (1400 Texas Ave., Cape May 08204, tel. 609/884–5329 or 800/729–7778) handles exclusively Cape May bed-and-breakfasts.

The Abbey

Built in 1869 as a summer home for Philadelphia coal baron John B. McCreary, the Abbey is one of Cape May architect Stephen Button's best works. With its impressive 65-foot tower and airy veranda, it is the finest example of Gothic Revival architecture in town.

There is nothing remotely religious about the property, which crowns the intersection of Columbia Avenue and Gurney Street. Calling it the Abbey was a bit of whimsy on the part of owners Jay and Marianne Schatz. "We always felt the Gothic Revival look had a religious quality to it," Jay says, "and because of my marketing degree I knew that anything that began with an *a* would be at the top of the list."

A lot more than its initial puts the Abbey at the top of many Cape May bed-and-breakfast lists: The quality of its restoration, the elegance of its appearance (the ruby-and-stenciled-glass windows are just one example), and the opulence of its period antiques all play a part. In addition there's the excellent location, one block from the beach and two blocks from the Washington Mall; and the humor of its owners, who can get just as excited over the 1875 secretary desk in the front parlor as over Jay's wacky hat collection hanging beside the mirror in the front hall (Marianne collects antique jewelry and clothing).

Jay and Marianne are most proud of their 1860 walnut-and-chestnut sideboard with its carved wolf's head and of the massive 11½-foot-tall matching bookcases in the back parlor. The couple were both chemists before their love of old houses and antiques brought them to Cape May, where they opened the Abbey in 1977.

In 1986 they bought and renovated the Second Empire house next door; McCreary had built it in 1873 for his son's family. Each house has two parlors, which are open to guests at all times. The rooms are named after cities and furnished appropriately (the San Francisco Room is the most opulent). Late-afternoon refreshments—wine, cheese, snacks, and tea—are served daily at 4:30.

Address: *Columbia Ave. and Gurney St., Cape May, NJ 08204, tel. 609/884–4506.*
Accommodations: *12 double rooms with baths, 2 suites.*
Amenities: *Air-conditioning in 8 bedrooms, minirefrigerators in 4 rooms; croquet, beach tags, towels, and beach chairs, some on-site parking.*
Rates: *$80–$175; Continental breakfast June 15–Sept. 15, full breakfast other times. AE, MC, V.*
Restrictions: *Smoking on veranda only, no pets, no T-shirts or bathing suits at breakfast, 2- 3-, or 4-night minimum on weekends, closed Dec. to Easter.*

The Chalfonte

A hotel like no other in Cape May—old, creaky, spartan, and proud of it—the Chalfonte is one of the city's most significant preserved structures. Built in 1876 by Colonel Henry Sawyer (on the northern side, he was captured and traded for Robert E. Lee's son), the hotel has dramatic wraparound porches on the ground and second floors, intricate gingerbread ornamentation, and a grand cupola from which the ocean can be glimpsed. It stands two blocks from the beach and four blocks from the Washington Mall. Although similar wood structures survive in the Spring Lake area of Monmouth County, the Chalfonte and its two cottages are a legend and an institution.

It is not, however, an up-to-date one. Some of the furnishings are simple to the point of being drab, and most guest rooms share bathrooms. The Chalfonte has no room service, no heat, and no air-conditioning (rooms do have louvered doors and ceiling fans, though). "First-timers wonder what they got themselves into," says manager Dan Walker. "But by the second day, they want to extend their stay."

Its faults and its lacks notwithstanding, the Chalfonte attracts well-to-do and blue-blooded visitors, many of them the children and grandchildren of families who have summered here in the past, who will stay nowhere else. The hotel caters to a growing contingent of college students and architecture buffs, who take over during spring and fall "work weekends," when, in exchange for eight hours of skilled or unskilled labor, they receive vastly discounted lodging and sumptuous meals.

The Chalfonte's food is renowned. The kitchen is supervised by the late Helen Dickerson's daughters. The menu may include spoon bread, fried chicken, fish, roast turkey, baked ham, sweet-potato pie, and other regional American specialties.

After such meals, guests struggle to stay awake for the free evening concerts, movie classics (shown with a vintage projector), poetry readings, plays, and comedy performances. The hotel holds many arts-and-crafts workshops and is unusually accommodating to families. Live entertainment, ranging from blues to bluegrass, is featured in the cozy King Edward Bar.

Address: *301 Howard St., Cape May, NJ 08204, tel. 609/884-8409.*
Accommodations: *11 double rooms with baths, 64 doubles and 2 singles share 11 baths.*
Amenities: *Dining room, bar, writing and reading room, cable TV in writing room, children's dining room, baby-sitting arranged.*
Rates: *$53–$151; MAP. MC, V.*
Restrictions: *No smoking in bedrooms, no pets, 2-night minimum on weekends, closed Nov.–Apr.*

The Mainstay Inn and Cottage

An 1870 men's social club formerly called Jackson's Clubhouse, the Mainstay vies with the Abbey as Cape May's best bed-and-breakfast. Many a gambler whiled away the hours under these 14-foot ceilings, and many a topic was discussed on the lofty veranda, which, more than 100 years later, is the city's most ostentatious spot for doing nothing.

The property was a deteriorating private house when, in 1976, it was purchased by Tom Carroll, who came to Cape May to serve at the nearby Coast Guard Training Academy, and his wife, Sue, an antiques and Victorian-costume collector. The Carrolls renovated the building with an astonishing attention to detail, and the Mainstay became a focal point in the move to revive Victorian Cape May as a resort town. Included in this magnificent restoration are the house's original chandeliers as well as most of the original furniture. Other antiques are of museum quality.

The Carrolls view their role as innkeepers as a beguiling performance. They socialize actively with guests, many of whom have been inspired to open B&Bs of their own.

"We try to inject a little informality into the formality of the surroundings," Tom says. "We like guests to feel as if they're not just staying with us, but that they're part of the Mainstay's atmosphere—that the inn is better because they're with us, even if all they're doing is sleeping here. If that has become the Cape May style, we're proud to have encouraged it."

In addition to being active in Cape May historic preservation and the city's Victorian Week festivities, the Carrolls are enthusiastic fans of Victorian culture and games, the more whimsical the better. (Check out the collection of bathing beauties in the small parlor.) Tom races sailboats, so you might see him on the ocean, from the cupola, which has a distant ocean view.

Address: *635 Columbia Ave., Cape May, NJ 08204, tel. 609/884-8690.*
Accommodations: *12 double rooms with baths.*
Amenities: *Gas fireplace in main-house drawing room, piano, games room; off-street parking for 3 rooms.*
Rates: *$80–$175; Continental breakfast June–Sept., full breakfast at other times. No credit cards.*
Restrictions: *Smoking on veranda only, no pets, 3-night minimum June–Sept. and on most weekends, closed mid-Dec.–mid-Mar.*

Barnard Good House

Near the edge of the historic district, on Perry Street, this lavender-trimmed Second Empire cottage is famous for serving Cape May's most filling, fanciful, and altogether outrageous within-an-inn breakfast. Don't even think about losing weight.

Before opening the Barnard Good House, Nan Hawkins was a marketing director for shopping centers and Tom was an engineer in the plastics business. The couple bought the inn in 1980 and totally restored it, adding baths and accommodations. They scrupulously chose antiques and Oriental rugs that match the Second Empire architecture. In the dining room they created a Victorian-style "Turkish corner," with tented draperies, an antique tufted and tasseled sofa and chairs, and a brass elephant table. The bedrooms have Victorian antique furniture, and one bathroom has a circa-1870 copper tub.

Address: *238 Perry St., Cape May, NJ 08204, tel. 609/884–5381.*
Accommodations: *3 double rooms with baths, 2 suites.*
Amenities: *Air-conditioning in bedrooms; beach tags, off-street parking.*
Rates: *$85–$113; full breakfast. AE, MC, V.*
Restrictions: *Smoking on porch only, no pets, 2-night minimum on weekends, 3-night minimum mid-June–mid-Sept., 4-night minimum on holiday weekends; closed Nov.–Mar.*

Captain Mey's Inn

Located in the center of town close to the Washington Mall and the beach, this 1890 house was built for a physician and named after Cape May's Dutch discoverer. It became an inn in 1979. It is furnished in European antiques with Dutch accents. A collection of delft blue china is scattered throughout the public areas, and three Tiffany-style stained-glass windows adorn the foyer.

Rooms are furnished with European antiques and Persian carpets, and guests can enjoy breakfast on the veranda or in the small courtyard with its tulip garden. Innkeepers Carin Feddermann and Millie LaCanfora started the city's April Tulip Festival and are active in promoting Victorian restoration.

Address: *202 Ocean St., Cape May, NJ 08204, tel. 609/884–7793.*
Accommodations: *6 double rooms with baths, 3 doubles share 1 bath.*
Amenities: *Fireplace in dining room; beach tags, towels, and chairs, off-street parking.*
Rates: *$90–$150; full breakfast, afternoon tea. MC, V.*
Restrictions: *Smoking on veranda only, no pets, 3-night minimum on weekends May–June and Sept.–Oct., 4-night minimum on weekends July–Aug., 2-night minimum on other weekends.*

The Carroll Villa

Those staying at this pleasantly restored Victorian hotel will enjoy breakfast at the Mad Batter Restaurant, one of Cape May's best dining establishments, which takes up most of the Carroll Villa's lower floor.

"Yankee fans may have to beg," jokes innkeeper Mark Kulkowitz, a baseball buff, who also manages the restaurant. "Phillies fans don't have a problem as long as the Phillies are not ahead of the Mets."

Guests have use of a separate living-room area, a garden terrace, and the cupola, from which the beach can be seen. The mostly 19th-century furnishings give the villa a less formal atmosphere than those inns that have museum-quality antiques. The hotel is a half block from the beach and a half block from the Washington Mall. Be warned that aromas coming from the Mad Batter kitchen can be fatal to diets.

Address: *19 Jackson St., Cape May, NJ 08204, tel. 609/884-9619.*
Accommodations: *21 double rooms with baths.*
Amenities: *Restaurant (closed Jan.), air-conditioning in 8 bedrooms, cable TV in lobby; beach tags.*
Rates: *$60–$115; full breakfast when restaurant is open, Continental breakfast other times. MC, V.*
Restrictions: *No pets, 2-night minimum on weekends May–Oct., 3-night minimum on holiday weekends, closed Jan.*

Colvmns by the Sea

Built by an eccentric doctor as his very eccentric summer retreat, Colvmns (eccentric spelling, too) is Cape May's get-away-from-it-all bed-and-breakfast, more than a mile from the historic district. It is named for the fluted Italianate columns that support the massive Colonial Revival second floor over its wraparound porch.

Guest rooms at Colvmns are enormous, and one has a superb Renaissance Revival mixed-wood bedroom set. The third floor commands wonderful views of the ocean. Although heavy seas have washed away much of the beach, at low tide there's plenty of shore to walk along. Swimming is prohibited here but allowed one block away.

The inn is a full-time home for innkeeper Barry Rein; his wife, Cathryn, works in Manhattan in the insurance industry and comes to the inn on weekends.

Address: *1513 Beach Dr., Cape May, NJ 08204, tel. 609/884-2228.*
Accommodations: *11 double rooms with baths.*
Amenities: *Cable TV in parlor, 2 fireplaces in public areas, hot tub on veranda; beach tags, bicycles, parking.*
Rates: *$110–$175; full breakfast, afternoon tea and snacks. No credit cards.*
Restrictions: *Smoking on veranda only, 2-night minimum Memorial Day–Sept., 3-night minimum on weekends, closed Jan.*

Holly House

This immaculate Jackson Street guest house is one of the Seven Sister properties, seven identical houses built in 1891 on the lot of a former hotel as summer rentals for well-to-do families. It is notable for its carefully detailed green-and-red exterior and the theatrical personality of its co-owner, Bruce Minnix, who directs television soap operas in New York. Corinne, his wife, runs the house and is often the person greeting visitors. "She's a lady," Bruce says, "casual, easygoing, friendly."

A former mayor of Cape May, Bruce fought for the preservation and restoration of the town and helped create its popular walking tours. Recently he produced and directed the video *Victorian Cape May.*

Rooms at Holly House all have three windows, high ceilings with ceiling fans, and natural-wood furniture. They're modern, decorated in earthtones, and free of clutter. There's a piano in the parlor and a three-story circular wooden banister along the stairs; each guest room offers an ocean "glimpse."

Address: *20 Jackson St., Cape May, NJ 08204, tel. 609/884-7365.*
Accommodations: *5 double rooms share 2 baths.*
Amenities: *Fireplace in parlor; porch swing with ocean view, beach tags, off-site parking.*
Rates: *$60–$65; no breakfast served. MC, V.*
Restrictions: *Smoking on porch only, no pets.*

The Manor House

Built in 1905 on a quiet treelined street, this bed-and-breakfast is amusing, thanks to host Tom Snyder's love of barbershop quartets, comedy, and jokes, the older the better. "Our rooms are named after significant numbers," quips the former marketing executive. Tom and his wife, Mary, prepare five- and six-course gourmet breakfasts, after which Tom recites his "reading of the day," an introduction to, and send-up of, the city's attractions and distractions. In mid-February the Snyders host a five-day cooking school, for which they gather chefs from all over the country to conduct cooking seminars—some at the Manor House and others at various restaurant kitchens in Cape May.

Rooms at the Manor House contain a harmonious mix of antiques and high-quality reproductions. Guests can snooze in the barber's chair in the den or serenade themselves on the player piano and guitar.

Address: *612 Hughes St., Cape May, NJ 08204, tel. 609/884-4710.*
Accommodations: *6 double rooms with baths, 2 doubles share a bath, 1 suite.*
Amenities: *Air-conditioning in 3 bedrooms, whirlpool bath in suite, bathrobes, hair dryers, fireplace in den; beach tags, beach towels, parking.*
Rates: *$60–$155; full breakfast, afternoon tea. MC, V.*
Restrictions: *Smoking on porch only, no pets, closed Jan.*

The Queen Victoria

This 1881 Second Empire–style villa and Stick-style adjacent cottage are living lectures in Victorian architecture. Dane and Joan Wells have transformed the property, in the center of the historic district, into an inn that feels immediately, genteelly private.

The furnishings in the Queen Victoria are nearly all carefully researched period pieces that create a dignified, privileged, country-Victorian atmosphere. The common rooms of the inn are decorated in the Arts and Crafts style. Dane did much of the work himself. Joan is active in the restoration and preservation of Victoriana nationwide.

Handmade quilts add color to the rooms, whose furnishings vary in style from white wicker to the dark woods of High Victorian.

Address: *102 Ocean St., Cape May, NJ 08204, tel. 609/884-8702.*
Accommodations: *16 double rooms with baths, 6 suites.*
Amenities: *Air-conditioning, whirlpools in suites and 6 bedrooms, cable TV in parlor and suites, phones in 2 suites, fireplaces in parlors and in cottage suite; bicycles, beach tags, beach towels, on- and off-site parking.*
Rates: *$80–$210; full breakfast, afternoon tea. MC, V.*
Restrictions: *No smoking, no pets, 2-night minimum on weekends.*

Springside

Like Holly House (*see above*), Springside is a Seven Sister property. It is decorated with bright modern art and 1930s mahogany furnishings. Innkeepers Bill and Meryl Nelson raised five children in the house. When the children grew up and moved away, Bill and Meryl felt a need for company.

"Bill and I really enjoy meeting and being with people who are doing interesting things," Meryl explains. Among their guests are college professors, theater people, and restoration experts.

Bill is the author of *Surfing: A Handbook* and is a boat builder. Meryl teaches computer science and desktop publishing. The couple share an interest in dollhouses and offbeat books. Their many books—"too many, we've only read about half of them," says Bill—are kept throughout the house and on bookcases in each guest room. The dollhouses can be admired in one of the common rooms.

Address: 18 Jackson St., Cape May, NJ 08204, tel. 609/884-2654.
Accommodations: *4 double rooms share 2 baths.*
Amenities: *Beach tags, off-site parking.*
Rates: *$50–$65; Continental breakfast. MC, V.*
Restrictions: *Smoking on porch only, no pets, 2-night minimum on weekends June–Sept.*

The Victorian Rose

Romance and roses go together, and this Gothic Revival house and adjacent cottage are almost engulfed by the aromatic flowers. The property is surrounded by 150 rose bushes, and rose patterns adorn dishes, wallpaper, and bed linens. Roses also show up in much of the Victorian detailing in the romantic guest rooms, which are furnished with antiques and some unobtrusive reproductions.

The bedrooms are carpeted, and all the curtains are patterned in roses; a first-floor suite has its own entrance, and the two rooms on the third floor are ideal for a family.

Innkeeper Bob Mullock, a former mayor of Cape May, leads town walking tours; he likes Mozart and big-band music. His wife, Linda, enjoys gardening and cooking breakfast.

Address: *715 Columbia Ave., Cape May, NJ 08204, tel. 609/884-2497.*
Accommodations: *5 double rooms with baths, 2 doubles share 1 bath, 2 housekeeping suites, adjacent cottage with bath sleeps 5.*
Amenities: *Air-conditioning in 4 bedrooms and cottage, cable TV in suites and cottage, gas fireplace in parlor; beach tags.*
Rates: *$75-$130; full breakfast, afternoon tea, wine, and cheese. No credit cards.*
Restrictions: *No pets, 3-night minimum on weekends June-Sept., 2-night minimum on other weekends, closed Dec.-Jan.*

The Virginia Hotel

The porches and balcony of this superbly restored, first-class small hotel are original, but in stepping through the door guests will find a completely modern interior in mild hues of taupe, peach, and green. The rooms' cherry and poplar furnishings are contemporary pieces with Victorian lines, designed by Tom McHugh, a popular furniture designer. Bathrooms have massage shower heads. One sitting area is furnished in 1870s wicker. The Virginia is highly recommended for those who want a full-service hotel on an intimate scale.

The conference room has all the latest equipment and makes this Cape May's best small property for executive retreats. The Ebbit Room Restaurant, on the premises, serves Cape May–eclectic cuisine of grilled seafood and meats, unusual sauces, and rich desserts (dinner is $50 for two). There's live music in the lobby piano bar.

Address: *25 Jackson St., Cape May, NJ 08204, tel. 609/884-5700 or 800/732-4236, fax 609/884-1236.*
Accommodations: *24 double rooms with baths.*
Amenities: *Restaurant, air-conditioning, cable TV, TVs with VCRs, bathrobes, room service, fireplace in lobby, videotape rentals, meeting room, word processor; beach tags, beach chairs, towels, valet parking.*
Rates: *$135-$220, Continental breakfast. AE, DC, MC, V.*
Restrictions: *No pets, 2-night minimum on weekends.*

Wilbraham Mansion and Inn

Perched on the southwestern edge of Cape May, this immense 1840 private house is the city's only bed-and-breakfast with a heated indoor swimming pool. Everything is larger than life at Wilbraham, from the 80-year-old stained-glass windows and 14-foot ceilings to the gilded mirrors and king-size beds.

Many of the original Victorian furnishings of the house remain: carpeting, wallpapers, carved headboards, and lace curtains, for example. Inspired guests can try their hand at playing the old-fashioned Packard pump organ or barbecuing out on the back porch behind the pool. Owner Susanne Moore advises guests that her mutt, Snoobs, can be "your pet away from home."

Address: *133 Myrtle Ave., Cape May, NJ 08204, tel. 609/884–2046.*
Accommodations: *6 double rooms with baths, 2 suites.*
Amenities: *Air-conditioning in bedrooms, turn-down service, cable TV in games room, fireplaces in 3 common rooms; swimming pool, beach tags, beach towels, bicycles, off-street parking.*
Rates: *$85–$145; full breakfast, afternoon tea, wine, and cheese. MC, V.*
Restrictions: *Smoking on porch and in pool area only, no pets, 2-night minimum on weekends Memorial Day–Dec., 3-night minimum on holiday weekends.*

The Wooden Rabbit

Children of all ages, and their parents, are welcome at this playful Hughes Street inn, where the storybook characters of Beatrix Potter dwell. Debbie Burow has been a Potter fan from the cradle, and rabbit figurines, dolls, and illustrations run rampant through her house.

"One of our guests counted 40 rabbits in the dining room and living room, and there are others about the house," Greg Burow says. "They tend to multiply."

The Federal house was built in 1838, and the furnishings are country-style: The rooms, in pastel colors and lace, have a cozy feeling, with wicker and oak, brass beds, and some light-wood antiques. Greg

stokes a breakfast fire on cool mornings. The Wooden Rabbit is home to Oscar the cat, who's known up and down the quiet tree-lined street and along the two blocks to the beach.

Address: *609 Hughes St., Cape May, NJ 08204, tel. 609/884–7293.*
Accommodations: *2 double rooms with baths, 1 suite.*
Amenities: *Air-conditioning and TV in bedrooms, fireplaces in dining room and living room; beach tags, beach chairs, off-street parking.*
Rates: *$90–$165; full breakfast, afternoon tea. MC, V.*
Restrictions: *No smoking, no pets, 2-night minimum on weekends, 3-night minimum July and Aug.*

Off the Beaten Track

Charlesworth Hotel

Although this tiny hotel lacks just about all the major amenities, its incomparable location and moderately priced seafood restaurant have kept it in business since 1924. The Charlesworth is located on the windswept Delaware Bay, in Fortescue, a tiny fishing village about 14 miles south of Bridgeton and a 20-minute drive from historic Greenwich.

The unadorned rooms have plain furniture, double beds, writing tables, chairs, and desk fans. There is no heat, no air-conditioning, and no parlor, games room, or television. The hotel closes when temperatures are cold enough to freeze the water in its pipes. It reopens when the ice melts.

Numerous sport-fishing charters and party boats leave from the town's docks from spring through early autumn. The Charlesworth is a fine base for exploring this least-traveled region of New Jersey.

Address: *New Jersey Ave., Fortescue, NJ 08321, tel. 609/447–4928.*
Accommodations: *1 double room with bath, 4 doubles share 1 bath.*
Amenities: *Restaurant open Fri.– Sun. for dinner (BYOB), fireplace in dining room; on-site parking.*
Rates: *$35–$50; breakfast not served. No credit cards.*
Restrictions: *No pets, closed Nov.– Apr.*

Jeremiah H. Yereance House

When developers threatened to tear down this 1841 farmhouse in suburban Lyndhurst, next-door neighbors Evelyn and Frank Pezzola bought the property and went to work restoring the former home of Passaic River shipbuilder Jeremiah Yereance. The Pezzolas used Laura Ashley fabrics and placed antiques, reproductions, and white wicker alongside furniture original to the house.

Located a half hour from the Big Apple but far from its hubbub, in a quiet residential neighborhood, Yereance House is 1 mile from Fairleigh Dickinson University. Guests can enjoy walking, biking, and playing tennis across the street in Bergen County Park, and the house is within walking distance of restaurants, a health club, a supermarket,

and commuter bus stops to New York City.

Address: *410 Riverside Ave., Lyndhurst, NJ 07071, tel. 201/438–9457, fax 201/939–5801.*
Accommodations: *2 double rooms and 1 single room share 1 bath, 1 suite.*
Amenities: *Air-conditioning in suite and 2 doubles, cable TV in parlor and in suite, guest phones in parlor, suite, and 1 double room, fireplace in parlor, kitchen and laundry privileges; off-street parking.*
Rates: *$50–$75; Continental buffet breakfast. AE.*
Restrictions: *No smoking indoors, no pets, closed Aug. 1–15.*

Delaware

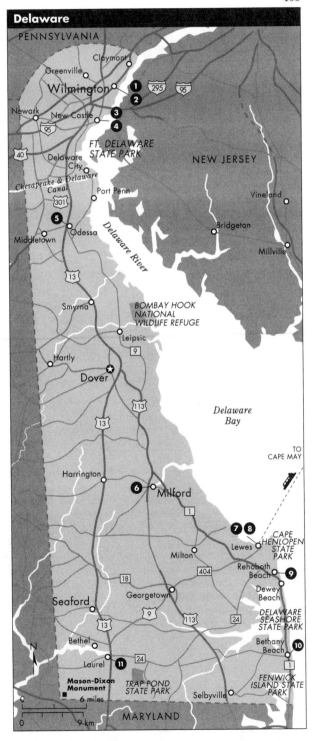

Delaware

PENNSYLVANIA

Claymont

Greenville

Wilmington

Newark

New Castle

FT. DELAWARE STATE PARK

NEW JERSEY

Delaware City

Chesapeake & Delaware Canal

Port Penn

Vineland

Middletown

Odessa

Delaware River

Bridgeton

Millville

Smyrna

BOMBAY HOOK NATIONAL WILDLIFE REFUGE

Leipsic

Hartly

Dover

Delaware Bay

Harrington

TO CAPE MAY

Milford

CAPE HENLOPEN STATE PARK

Milton

Lewes

Rehoboth Beach

Dewey Beach

Seaford

Georgetown

DELAWARE SEASHORE STATE PARK

Bethel

Bethany Beach

Laurel

Mason-Dixon Monument

TRAP POND STATE PARK

FENWICK ISLAND STATE PARK

Selbyville

6 miles

9 km

MARYLAND

Wilmington/Northern Delaware

Delaware is all of 96 miles long and 9 to 35 miles wide, but for such a small state, there's a great deal in it. Everyone knows about its long chain of Atlantic beaches, but Delaware's other points of interest are seldom touted on billboards. This is especially true in the industrialized northern section of the state where travelers zooming to Washington or New York on I-95 can easily bypass the sights worth seeing. Wilmington, the state's commercial hub, is trying hard to polish its cosmopolitan image by creating a downtown pedestrian mall and restoring some old buildings, such as the Victorian Grand Opera House, now home of the Delaware Symphony.

It's easy to track down the extraordinary legacy of Delaware's First Family; the name du Pont is plastered on smokestacks and street signs like tattoos on a sailor. The French du Ponts came to northern Delaware around 1800 and by 1920 were the wealthiest clan in the United States. They built estates such as Winterthur, in the rolling countryside north of Wilmington, where they could show off their gunpowder fortunes; today you'd have to travel to the Loire Valley to see such breathtaking châteaux.

To get a taste of Colonial America in the setting of a living village, head southeast from Wilmington to New Castle, on the Delaware River. The Swedes settled here around 1640; the Dutch came next, and in 1664 the British took possession. But the town's glory days came in the 18th century, when it attracted the Colonial world's rich and famous, including Washington and Lafayette. When the boundary between Delaware and Pennsylvania was surveyed, it was drawn as the arc of a circle whose center was the cupola of New Castle's courthouse. Today the cupolaed courthouse, narrow alleyways, hitching posts, mossy graveyards, and emerald town common remain much the same as they were then.

South of Wilmington are other villages redolent of the past; some, like Odessa and Delaware City, on the banks of the Chesapeake and Delaware Canal, are even quieter than New Castle. From Delaware City it's a 10-minute ferry ride aboard the Miss Kathy *to Pea Patch Island in the Delaware River, site of the 1823 Fort Delaware, the largest historic fort in the country, with massive ramparts from which nesting herons can be seen in the marshes below.*

Places to Go, Sights to See

Bombay Hook Wildlife Refuge (just north of Leipsic on Rte. 9, tel. 302/653–9345). On these 16,000 acres of tidal marsh and timberland, muskrats, otters, white-tailed deer, and opossums make their homes, and as many as 50,000 Canada geese visit in season.

Delaware Art Museum (tel. 302/571–9590). The English Pre-Raphaelite painters have their own gallery at this Wilmington museum, as does the illustrator Howard Pyle. In 1987 a new wing was added to accommodate sculpture, painting, ceramics, and photographs by American masters of the last 150 years.

Hagley Museum and Library (Greenville, tel. 302/658–2400). Here you can see how the du Ponts harnessed the waters of the Brandywine River to run a powder mill nearby. Eleutherian Mills, a modest, 12-room, white Georgian house where the first five generations of American du Ponts lived, is set on Hagley's manicured 200 acres.

Hotel du Pont (tel. 302/656–8121). At Wilmington's "company hotel," built in 1911, the du Ponts went to extremes to surround guests with the best: coffered ceilings, travertine marble walls, and a million-dollar collection of Andrew Wyeth canvasses in the Brandywine-Christina dining room.

Nemours Mansion and Gardens (Rockland Rd., off Rte. 141, tel. 302/651–6912). Alfred I. du Pont's 77-room "little Versailles" is a pink Louis XVI château groaning under the weight of its excesses. Along with gold-leaf ceilings, crystal chandeliers, and Aubusson carpets, Alfred loved gadgets, which explains the state-of-the-art 1910 bathrooms, steam cabinet, bowling alley, and spring-water-bottling generator.

Odessa. A Georgian architectural treasure trove stands on the banks of the swampily atmospheric Appoquinimink River. The Brick Hotel Gallery here (tel. 302/378–4069) houses rotating exhibits of American decorative arts and furniture. Guided tours of the Historic Houses of Odessa, under the auspices of Winterthur, are the perfect way to taste the daily domestic life of the 18th- and 19th-century families who inhabited them.

Wilmington and Western Railroad (tel. 302/998–1930). A steam-power iron horse leaves Greenbank Station (on Rte. 141, west of Wilmington) on Sunday, for trips into Delaware's Red Clay Valley.

Winterthur (Rte. 52 north of Wilmington, tel. 302/888–4600 or 800/448–3883). This 200-room estate in a lush 64-acre garden contains one of the world's prime collections of American decorative arts (1640–1840).

Restaurants

In New Castle, the **Cellar Gourmet** (tel. 302/323–0999) in the William Janvier House is an informal spot for soup and sandwiches. For more formal dining, try the **New Castle Inn** (tel. 302/328–1798) or **David Finney's** (tel. 302/322–6367 or 800/334–6640).

For a town with a population of 303, Odessa can still satisfy the palate. Seafood entrées at the **Brick House Restaurant** (tel. 302/378–2999) in Middletown, a 10-minute drive from Odessa, run $10–$18; crab cakes are especially recommended, and senior citizens can order from a small-portion menu. If you don't want to dress up or imbibe, try the **Market Place Restaurant** (tel. 302/378–0688) on South Du Pont Highway, where the waitress calls you "hon," the menus are laminated, "wing dings" are *de rigueur*, and faded gingham triumphs. You can get a colossal 8-ounce "gourmet burger" on a Kaiser bun with steak fries for $3.35 or duck-walk out with abdominal overhang from the all-you-can-eat Alaskan crab or shrimp, a once-a-week special at about $16.

In Milford, the **Banking House Restaurant** (tel. 302/422–5708) on Front Street serves a wide selection of beef, poultry, and seafood. The plain-faced **Geyer's** (tel. 302/422–5327) offers easy-on-the-wallet prices and a child-welcoming environment.

Wilmington has a four-star restaurant in the **Green Room** (tel. 302/594–3154) at the Hotel du Pont, but reserve at Pennsylvania Avenue's **Columbus Inn** (tel. 302/571–1492) for a special night out at half the price. If you hanker for al dente, the entrées at **Grigilia Toscana** (tel. 302/654–8001) range from $10 to $20.

Tourist Information

Delaware Tourism Office (99 Kings Hwy., Box 1401, Dover 19903, tel. 800/441–8846. **Greater Wilmington Convention and Visitors Bureau** (1300 Market St., Suite 504, Wilmington 19899, tel. 302/652–4088 or 800/422–1181).

Reservation Service

Bed & Breakfast of Delaware (Box 177, 3650 Silverside Rd., Wilmington 19810, tel. 302/479–9500).

The Janvier-Black House

Most people who stumble upon New Castle, Delaware, fall in love with the town. It's a place to take a brooding walk over the cobblestones of Packet Alley, romp across the town green, and feast gluttonously at the David Finney or at the New Castle Inn, a restaurant where the house specialty is a buttery seafood-and-chicken pie.

Unfortunately, most visitors to the town don't get the chance to stay at the Janvier-Black House, since it has only two suites. Those who do usually don't want just to visit New Castle: They want to settle in for the duration—preferably in a Federal double row house just like the Janvier-Black, on the Strand.

The house was built in 1825 as a gift from a doting papa, John Janvier, to his daughter, Ann, and features the finely carpentered door frames and moldings you'd expect in a vintage New Castle home. Its first floor holds a parlor and dining room, with detail work painted in airy blues and pinks and wallpaper that picks up colors and patterns from the Oriental carpets. In the rear there's a country kitchen, and a sun deck perched above the backyard boxwood garden offers views of Battery Park and the stone icebreakers in the Delaware River. The guest rooms have similar views of the river, as well as sitting rooms, commodious modern baths, fireplaces and country-classic decor. (The self-contained third-floor suite is the best.)

Annabelle and Hank Kressman are the innkeepers responsible for this gem among bed-and-breakfasts. The Kressmans leave a decanter of sherry and the makings for coffee and tea in the third-floor hall and have put together a collection of classic movies on videotape. Annabelle is a former executive director of the Girl Scouts who today spends her free time marketing women's clothing. Samples from her stock are stored in closets throughout the house, so if they like, guests can shop in the comfort of their own rooms. The Kressmans will also shower you with brochures on notable sights in old New Castle, such as the glorious George Read II House just down the block and the Old Dutch House Museum on the green. On the third Saturday in May the town celebrates A Day in New Castle, when many of the private homes are opened for touring. If you plan a trip then, book early.

Address: *17 The Strand, New Castle, DE 19720, tel. 302/328–1339.*
Accommodations: *2 suites.*
Amenities: *Air-conditioning, TV with VCR, fireplaces.*
Rates: *$95–$115; Continental breakfast. No credit cards.*
Restrictions: *No smoking, no pets, 2-day minimum weekends June–Oct.*

The Towers

Edgar Allan Poe's friend and fellow poet John Lofland lived at the Towers, which was once the Milford home of Lofland's stepfather, Dr. John Wallace. Lofland was an opium addict and Poe an alcoholic, but in their wildest hallucinations neither could have dreamed up a house like the Towers, a steamboat Gothic palace adorned with 10 varieties of gingerbread painted in 12 colors. Here flamboyant Victoriana radiates from the cherry, mahogany, and walnut finishings. Inside, the music room has a coffered sycamore ceiling and an 1899 Knabe grand piano. You're likely to find a record—perhaps Gene Autry's rendition of "Rudolph the Red-nosed Reindeer"—spinning on the Victrola. The parlor is decorated with French antiques, and the dining room provides views of the gazebo, pool deck, and rose garden in back.

The warm but unobtrusive custodians of this 200-year-old marvel (it's on the National Register of Historic Places) are Sharon and Daniel Bond, who bought it in January 1992 and now live on the premises in the old servants' quarters. They couldn't resist the ubiquitous stained glass, the carved garlands on the fireplaces, and the gold leaf peeking from behind the plywood walls. Sharon can tell you about the Italian architect commissioned in the 1890s to transform the structure into the Victorian extravaganza you see today; the owner is said to have spent between $30,000 and $40,000 on the renovation.

A favorite room is the Tower chamber, on the second floor, with a turret niche and lots of rosy stained glass. The third floor's two suites are a bit more modern in character but still whimsically wonderful. All four doubles have their own bathrooms, but guests occupying the second-floor rooms must walk through a common area to enter theirs, and the third-floor facilities have showers only.

Sharon fortifies her guests for a day of exploring or antiquing with a full breakfast—often her celebrated ricotta pancakes, served with fresh fruit or raspberry purée and ham. The inn is right across the street from one of Delaware's premier eating establishments, the Banking House, which is also an 18th-century-inspired bed-and-breakfast. Dinner at the Banking House and a stay at the Towers is a perfect combination.

Address: *101 N.W. Front St., Milford, DE 19963, tel. 302/422-3814, or, outside DE, 800/366-3814.*
Accommodations: *4 double rooms with baths.*
Amenities: *Air-conditioning, gas-log fireplaces in music room and dining room; pool.*
Rates: *$95-$125; full breakfast. MC, V.*
Restrictions: *No smoking, no pets.*

William Penn
Guest House

The historic marker stands on the streets of New Castle, a block from the banks of the Delaware River: "Near here October 27, 1682, William Penn first stepped on American soil. He proceeded to the fort and . . . we did deliver unto him 1 turf with a twig upon it, a porringer with river water and soil, in part of all." In the same year that Penn strode onto the shores of the New World, and on the same streets that he first trod, the William Penn Guest House appeared on the map, though perhaps not with quite the same historic significance. But Penn knew a good thing when he saw it; ask Irma Burwell, who runs the place now, she will tell you how the founder of Pennsylvania would bed down here.

Irma will also tell you what she and husband Dick charged when they started their bed-and-breakfast operation in 1956: $8 a night. Rates are still surprisingly reasonable, and they're not likely to rise in the near future, since the hosts like the sensibilities and spending habits of their longtime clientele (repeat visitors account for two-thirds of their business). The Burwells welcome an international set of diverse ages and tastes—senior ambassadors who snooze and dewy-cheeked naturalists who cycle—all of whom appreciate a quiet, civilized atmosphere that doesn't cost them an unearthly sum.

The William Penn is a handsomely restored, impressively maintained Colonial structure that is modest in its air and amenities. Soft, wide-board Delaware-pine floors, a claw-foot tub, and an 18th-century chandelier in the dining room take guests back to an earlier era. The bedrooms—two with twin beds and two with doubles—are carpeted blandly and furnished with pine antiques. If air-conditioning turns you off, there are ceiling fans to keep both second-floor units cool and ventilated in the summer.

You'll find the William Penn a perfect jumping-off point for touring Longwood Gardens, the Brandywine River Museum, Winterthur, the Hagley Museum, and Nemours Mansion. Cyclists in particular will delight in the area: The house borders Battery Park, which runs right along the river and has a 2-mile biking path and promenade, as well as benches, picnic tables, tennis courts, and play areas for children.

Address: *206 Delaware St., New Castle, DE 19720, tel. 302/328–7736.*
Accommodations: *4 double rooms share 2 baths.*
Amenities: *Air-conditioning, TV in 3 rooms.*
Rates: *$45–$65; Continental breakfast. No credit cards.*
Restrictions: *No smoking in bedrooms, no pets.*

The Boulevard Bed & Breakfast

It's only been a few years since Charles and Judy Powell said good-bye to suburbia and moved to fashionable Baynard Boulevard to realize their dream of opening a bed-and-breakfast. The attractive house they moved to is in the Triangle section of Wilmington. This B&B is a fancy, citified six-bedroom dwelling with a red-tile roof, neo-Georgian elements in the facade, and eccentric, fluted columns with Doric capitals. Inside, a graceful "good morning" staircase (couples descend via separate routes and meet for a kiss at the landing) greets you, as do Judy and Charles, who treat guests like family. Equally noteworthy are the elaborate Mueller tile surrounding the library fireplace, and Judy's mammoth industrial range, where she cooks breakfast.

The Powells attract a frequently returning business clientele, though families fare well here, too, because of the proximity of Brandywine Park and Children's Zoo, and the easy drive to the many Brandywine Valley attractions.

Address: *1909 Baynard Blvd., Wilmington, DE 19802, tel. 302/656-9700.*
Accommodations: *3 double rooms with baths; 1 double and 1 single share a bath, 1 suite with whirlpool.*
Amenities: *Air-conditioning, cable TV, fireplaces in library and parlor; off-street parking.*
Rates: *$55–$70; full breakfast. AE, MC, V.*
Restrictions: *No pets.*

Cantwell House

Odessa is a little-known historic village, a smaller, country version of New Castle. On the Appoquinimink River, surrounded by fertile fields, it fared well as a Colonial cosmopolitan center, but the railroad passed it by, and today it's charmingly frozen in time. The houses are lovingly maintained, and a branch of the Winterthur Museum has opened in town. The Corbit-Sharp House, built by a Quaker tanner in 1774; the Brick Hotel, displaying American crafts; and the Wilson-Warner House are just three of Odessa's architectural gems. The Cantwell House, a narrow, sea-green Victorian built about 1840, is the only bed-and-breakfast in town. Many faithful patrons of this small, immaculately kept establishment are parents of prep-school students at-

tending nearby St. Andrew's (where *Dead Poets Society* was filmed). Of the guest rooms, one has a canopy bed, another a fireplace. Proprietress Carole Coleman never serves any guest the same breakfast twice. Look to Carole also for local antiquing possibilities—she's an active auctioneer, and she knows her stuff.

Address: *107 High St., Odessa, DE 19730, tel. 302/378-4179.*
Accommodations: *2 double rooms share bath, 1 suite.*
Amenities: *Air-conditioning in suite and 2nd-floor canopy bedroom, TV in suite, fireplace in living room.*
Rates: *$50–$80; Continental breakfast. No credit cards.*
Restrictions: *No smoking, no pets.*

Guest Quarters Suite Hotel Wilmington

The Christina House isn't dead—
it has just changed its name.
One block away from Market
Square, Wilmington's shopping-and-
entertainment center, this recently
purchased and newly managed inn is
conveniently located for the Grand
Opera House and for business travelers. It can't claim to be historically
noteworthy, though it inhabits the
gutted shell of what was once
Braunstein's Department Store. The
King Street entrance leads to
a spacious atrium with a central fireplace, bar, bistro restaurant, and
glass-walled elevator. Upstairs, hallways snake through four connected
buildings, but once you orient yourself to the maze you'll be rewarded
with a comfortable guest room. The
rooms are all suites, with fold-out
sofas in the sitting rooms, fully

equipped wet bars, and luxurious
bathrooms. Room 306 is the largest
and has a skylight and gently sloping ceilings. The new management
oversaw the addition of 10 suites in
1992. A copy of *USA Today* comes
with breakfast.

Address: *707 King St., Wilmington,
DE 19801, tel. 302/656–9300 or
800/543–9106, fax 302/656–2459.*
Accommodations: *49 suites.*
Amenities: *Restaurant, air-
conditioning, 2 cable TVs and 3
phones in suites; 3 meeting facilities, computers, courier service,
nonsmoking floor.*
Rates: *$125, $75 weekends; Continental breakfast. AE, D, DC, MC,
V.*
Restrictions: *No pets.*

The Beaches

*As the first warm weekend in May heralds the arrival of
summer, the sun-starved citizens of Washington, Baltimore,
and Wilmington pack their beach umbrellas and head for
Delaware's Atlantic coast—a 25-mile strip of sand and surf
stretching from the hamlet of Lewes to the Maryland state
line. Here they find three splendid state parks, a handful
of beach towns, and opportunities aplenty for sailing,
fishing, clamming, and biking.*

*Rehoboth Beach is the undisputed nerve center of the
Delaware seashore. It sprang up as a Methodist camp-
meeting ground in the 1870s (Rehoboth means "one more
sinner") and was overrun by sun worshipers when the
railroad reached it 10 years later. Although some vintage
Victorian structures (such as the Anna Hazzard Museum
and the recently restored railroad station) remain, most of
Rehoboth's ocean-side motels, downtown shops, and cottages
date from the 20th century. The town is beloved above all by
families with children. The city's recreation department
schedules concerts in the bandstand; waterfront volleyball,
football, and softball games; children's arts-and-crafts
programs; and teen dance parties. It's all very wholesome:
This place is stuck in the early 1960s and is not about to
budge. For nightlife you'll have to head south to nearby
Dewey Beach, the seashore's hot spot for singles.*

*Who, besides modern-day Gidgets and Dobie Gillises,
gravitates to Rehoboth Beach? For an answer you need
only climb on a bike and investigate the neighborhoods
(such as Henlopen Acres) away from the boardwalk around
Lake Gerar and Silver Lake, where wealthy city families
have built handsome summer homes. With its variety of
upscale specialty shops and restaurants, downtown
Rehoboth caters to the older, moneyed crowd that has been
coming to the town for generations.*

If the bustle of Rehoboth and Dewey gets to be too much, you'll find other, more peaceable sandy kingdoms at the nearby Delaware Seashore, Cape Henlopen, and Fenwick Island state parks. There you can swim, try surf fishing, or go boating. Bethany Beach, a peaceful resort where well-kept summer homes far outnumber the few shops and restaurants, lies 10 miles south of Rehoboth. Increasingly, refugees from other, livelier Delaware beach towns are coming to Bethany. Watch for Saturday-night fried-chicken and oyster dinners at the town's fire hall. To the north is historic Lewes (pronounced Lewis*), a port community at Cape Henlopen, where charter fishing is a big draw.*

Places to Go, Sights to See

Bandstands. In summertime both Bethany and Rehoboth beaches hold starlit concerts at their beachside bandstands.

Bethel. On cloudy days it's worth leaving the seaside to visit this tiny inland village, a 19th-century shipbuilding center.

Cape May–Lewes Ferry (tel. 302/645–6313). This fleet of five vessels cruises across Delaware Bay in a 70-minute trip connecting Colonial Lewes and Victorian Cape May.

Carey's Camp Meeting Ground (tel. 302/856–7530.). It's on the National Register for Historic Landmarks by virtue of the fact that Methodists began coming here for sun and salvation back in 1888. They still follow Route 24 west of Millsboro to the meeting ground, with its open tabernacle and 47 frame tents.

Delaware's beach state parks. *Fenwick Island* (tel. 302/359–9060), at the south end of Route 1, is bordered by Little Assawoman Bay and the wide Atlantic; it's one of the few spots along the coast where surfing is permitted. *Delaware Seashore* (tel. 302/227–2800), on a largely undeveloped, 7-mile strip of sand between Dewey Beach and Bethany, has facilities for camping, boating, fishing, and swimming. Among the shifting sands of *Cape Henlopen* (tel. 302/645–8983) is the 80-foot Great Dune (thought to be the largest dune between Capes Cod and Hatteras). The 3,020 acres of shoreline at this park contain piping plover nests and cranberry bogs.

Fenwick Island Lighthouse (tel. 302/539–8129). Built in 1859, the 1,500-pound light still shines near the strait between Assawoman and Little Assawoman bays. To the south side of the light you'll find the first marker laid in the Mason-Dixon survey of 1751.

Laurel. The historic town of Laurel, which lies across Broad Creek from Bethel on the site of a Nanticoke Indian reservation, contains 800 buildings listed on the National Register. The free Woodland cable ferry carries hikers over the upper Nanticoke River.

Trap Pond State Park (tel. 302/875–5153). This 965-acre park, shaded by bald cypresses and loblolly pines, features wilderness canoe trails, fishing, and a swimming area that provides "wet wheelchairs" for the handicapped.

Zwaanendael Museum (tel. 302/645–9418). In 1631, 32 Dutch settlers began clearing land in Lewes, only to be massacred by the Leni-Lenape tribe. That sadly terminated colony, and Lewes's Dutch heritage, are remembered at this museum, a replica of a fantastically ornamented Dutch town hall found at the center of the town's historic district. Here you'll find a display on local shipwrecks, the Cannonball House Marine Museum, and the historic Fisher-Martin House, built about 1730.

Restaurants

In Lewes, **Kupchick's** (tel. 302/645–0420) is your best bet, but prices are stiff for this region (entrées $15–$20). The dark, warm, and clubby **Rose and Crown Restaurant and Pub** (tel. 302/645–2373) sells every known kind of beer. If you're a child of the '50s or '60s and you summered at any of the Delaware beach resorts, you know **Grotto's Grand Slam** (tel. 302/645–4900) like your mother knows Dr. Spock. It still holds the lead for pizza on the Atlantic seaboard.

Rehoboth is replete with fast-food franchises, boardwalk candy shops, and—on the more expensive end—the elegant **Garden Gourmet** (tel. 302/227–4747), **Victoria's** (tel. 302/227–0615), and the rooftop **Horizon Room** (tel. 302/227–2551). The quieter Bethany, boardwalk-barren and probably the better for it, touts the casual **Rusty Rudder** (tel. 302/227–3888) for crabs.

Tourist Information

Bethany-Fenwick Chamber of Commerce (Box 502, Bethany Beach 19930, tel. 302/539–2100 or 800/962–7873). **Delaware Tourism Office** (99 Kings Hwy., Box 1401, Dover 19903, tel. 800/441–8846). **Rehoboth Beach-Dewey Beach Chamber of Commerce** (73 Rehoboth Ave., Rehoboth Beach 19971, tel. 302/227–2233 or 800/441–1329). **Southern Delaware Development Office** (99 Kings Hwy., Box 1401, Dover 19903, tel. 302/739–4271 or 800/441–8846).

Reservation Services

Bed & Breakfast of Delaware (Box 177, 3650 Silverside Rd., Wilmington 19810, tel. 302/479–9500). **Maryland Reservation Center** (66 Maryland Ave., Annapolis 21401, tel. 410/263–9084).

The Inn at Canal Square

This decidely upscale inn is a relatively new addition to the lodging scene in Lewes, a small, historic town that serves as both a gateway to the Atlantic beaches and a peaceful retreat for travelers along the Atlantic seaboard. This inn is special because of its waterfront location and unusual accommodation choices. Aside from 19 conventional rooms in the main building, travelers here can also opt for *The Legend of Lewes*, a houseboat with modern galley, two bedrooms, and two baths that floats peacefully at dockside (this arrangement is not recommended for families with children under 14). The inn is conveniently situated in a meandering complex of shops and a restaurant. Design purists may protest the stylistic mélange; the exterior looks like a developer's reproduction of a Nantucket village, yet the decor in the apartment resembles the interior of a typical Malibu hideaway. You might find it a bit incongruous, but are ceiling fans, bushy potted plants, a canal-front sun deck, and a baby grand piano really so hard to bear?

In the three-story main building, the rooms are large and furnished with Federal reproductions. You'll pay slightly more for those with porch access and water views and considerably more for the honeymoon suite (Room 305), which has a cathedral ceiling, Palladian windows, and private balcony. It may not be terribly spacious, but it's cozy, enjoys the best view in the inn, and has a queen-size bed. King-size-bed advocates have their pick of three rooms on the top floor.

The simple Continental breakfast can be eaten downstairs or taken back to the bedrooms on trays. Innkeeper Laurie Sergovic recommends Kupchick's as the best restaurant in Lewes; and Gilligan's, the restaurant next door, is open daily in season, from 11AM to 1 AM.

Besides the Zwaanendael Museum and historic district, there are the beaches of Cape Henlopen State Park to keep you occupied; or you can try your hand at hooking a shark from a chartered fishing boat. In the summer, you can take your kids on the *Queen Anne's Railroad*, an old steam locomotive that now runs a 50-minute round trip from Lewes.

Address: *122 Market St., Lewes, DE 19958, tel. 302/645–8499 or 800/222–7902.*
Accommodations: *17 double rooms with baths, 1 suite, 1 houseboat.*
Amenities: *Air-conditioning, cable TV and phones in bedrooms; conference room.*
Rates: *$120–$150, houseboat $225 ($1,200 a week). AE, D, DC, MC, V.*
Restrictions: *No pets, 2-day minimum in houseboat on weekends, and in main building, weekends Memorial Day–Oct. and on some holiday weekends.*

The New Devon Inn

This hotel, with its striped awnings and lobby-level stores, opened in 1989 in the heart of Lewes's historic district and has fine views of St. Peter's Episcopal Church and historic cemetery. Built in 1926, the inn received a complete make-over at the hands of its new owner, Dale Jenkins. Little remains of its past except the lustrous heart-of-pine floors. Its lobby is reminiscent of a Bloomingdale's window, with curious elephant chairs and an old-fashioned cage elevator.

The guest rooms are furnished in feminine elegance, with antiques and beds swaddled in designer linens. Though they're relatively small, they are warmly appointed, immaculately clean, and extremely comfortable. The corner rooms (108, for example) are the ones most requested. Room 101, with a double bed, receives buckets of early-morning sunlight. And the inn offers special touches, such as turndown service, candy and cordials in the rooms, and morning coffee served in delicate antique cups. The inn has expanded its Continental breakfast and now offers an elegant presentation—on silver service, crystal, and china—of croissants, yogurt, sticky buns, cereal, and juice.

Of late the New Devon Inn has become known as a politician's hideout—Senators Simon and Biden have both stayed here to escape media frenzy—and business travelers can rely on a highly professional staff directed by manager Barbara Lloyd. Executive conference rooms, including the Thomas F. Bayard Room, which accommodates up to 100 people for formal receptions, and the smaller but still dignified Betsy Bonaparte Room are ample here and lend themselves ideally to the house specialty: seminars and meetings for groups of five to 75. Group rates attract corporate bookings and wedding celebrations. Provisions for the disabled are also available.

Lewes, unlike Rehoboth and Bethany, is a year-round destination, so you won't barrel into locked doors at restaurants and crafts shops in the dead of winter. April heralds the Great Delaware Kite Festival at Cape Henlopen State Park; July is the month for the town's annual antiques show and sale; and the Christmas House Tour, sponsored by the Lewes Historical Society, precedes the Christmas Parade and a tree-lighting celebration in December.

Address: *2nd and Market Sts. (Box 516), Lewes, DE 19958, tel. 302/645-6466 or 800/824-8754.*
Accommodations: *24 double rooms with baths, 2 suites.*
Amenities: *Air-conditioning, phones in bedrooms; 2 conference rooms.*
Rates: *$70–$140; Continental breakfast. AE, DC, MC, V.*
Restrictions: *No pets.*

Spring Garden Bed & Breakfast Inn

This inn reveals its character slowly and subtly. It's an abundantly lived-in place that is deeply appreciated by its owner, Gwen North. She was raised by her parents in this half-Colonial, half-Victorian farmhouse on the outskirts of Laurel before she flew the coop for New York. During that absence she came to realize that her heart lay back at home. Says Gwen, "When you stay in the same place all your life, you stop seeing what's there."

What's here is a red-shutter country house that stands beside a creek lined with daylilies in spring. As pleasant as its exterior is, the inside is even better. The Colonial section, built between 1760 and 1780 by a Captain Lewis of Bethel, remained in the Lewis family for 100 years. Its front parlor and back kitchen have wood-plank floors and the snug, slightly off-kilter feeling of a boat. Breakfast, highlighted by Scotch eggs and home-grown fruit, is served beside a wood-burning stove.

A steep, narrow staircase takes guests to the inn's two Colonial rooms; the one called Naomi (for Gwen's mother) has a fireplace, a lace-canopy double bed, and a walnut rocker. Three bedrooms in the Victorian section, added in the late 1800s, have views of the garden and are filled with a soothing collection of antique furnishings, including a Victorian spool bed and Belgian cathedral chairs.

The Atlantic beaches are about 20 miles from the inn, but Gwen is quick to point out the other diversions to be found in this landlocked region of Delaware, such as canoeing and fishing at Trap Pond State Park and exploring the historic districts of Bethel and Laurel. Gwen is the moving force behind the Southern Delaware Antiques and Arts Emporium in town and is an antiques dealer herself.

Tops among the activities here is bicycling, a pastime Gwen has encouraged by organizing the Biking Inn to Inn program, a series of four different Delmarva Peninsula trips, lasting three to five days, with lodgings at carefully selected inns. The routes take bikers along the flat back roads of the Eastern Shore and offer opportunities for crabbing, birdwatching, and impromptu swims.

Address: *Rte. 1, Box 283A, Delaware Ave. Extended, Laurel, DE 19956, tel. 302/875–7015.*
Accommodations: *2 double rooms with baths, 3 doubles share bath.*
Amenities: *Air-conditioning, TV in sitting room, 3 fireplaces.*
Rates: *$55–$75. No credit cards.*
Restrictions: *Smoking in designated areas, no pets.*

The Addy Sea

Like Rehoboth, delightful little low-profile Bethany Beach got its start as the site of religious camp meetings, and by the turn of the century a beachfront community had begun to develop here. The summer home built by John M. Addy, a plumber from Pittsburgh, had carbide lamps and indoor bathrooms, which in its day made it one of the most modern homes in Bethany. The front yard of this capacious Victorian encompasses a splendid stretch of Atlantic beach. The upper half of the house is covered with brown shingles, and the lower portion is painted white and decorated with lacelike gingerbread. Inside there are tin ceilings (made on a press in the basement), Oriental rugs, and round oak tables. All but one of the 14 rooms have ocean views, the best being from the two front corner chambers. The inn is occupied by group rentals in May, June, September, and October; in July and August anyone is welcome, but remember—no wet suits are allowed inside.

Address: *Atlantic Ave., Bethany Beach, DE 19930, tel. 302/539–3707.*
Accommodations: *2 double rooms with baths, 12 doubles share baths.*
Rates: *$80–$110; Continental breakfast. No credit cards.*
Restrictions: *No smoking in dining room, 2-day minimum stay, closed Nov.–Apr.*

The Pleasant Inn

In Rehoboth Beach, Peck Pleasanton's place is an anomaly, an inn with an adult air where you can imagine mature couples playing canasta on the porch until late and periodically ambling over to the wet bar to freshen their gin and tonics. Stylish, prettified, or even immaculately maintained it is not, though it does occupy one of central Rehoboth's most coveted properties: The big, foursquare Victorian with its widow's walk was built right on the boardwalk but was moved to its present location (a five-minute walk from the beach) following the Great Storm of 1918. There are 10 double rooms in the house plus a downstairs kitchen-apartment and studio. The guest rooms are furnished with well-worn items that may be old but are probably not antiques, and have private baths that appear to have been last decorated in the '50s. A carriage-house out back that sleeps four is rented by the week. Peck himself is a no-nonsense, slow-talking man who looks and acts as if he's seen it all. He doesn't provide breakfast for his guests, but he does make several bicycles available free of charge.

Address: *31 Olive Ave., Rehoboth Beach, DE 19971, tel. 302/227–7311.*
Accommodations: *10 double rooms with baths, 3 suites.*
Amenities: *Air-conditioning, TV on porch, wet bar, kitchenette in 2nd-floor hallway.*
Rates: *$65–$150; no breakfast. MC, V.*
Restrictions: *No pets, 3-day minimum mid-June–mid-Sept.*

Maryland

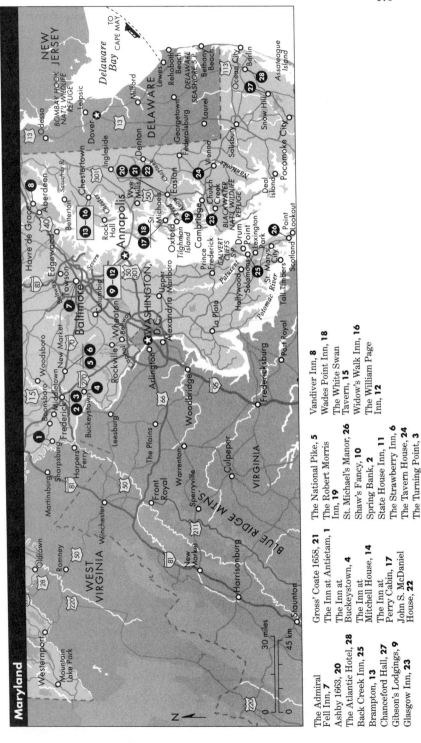

Maryland

The Admiral
Fell Inn, **7**
Ashby 1663, **20**
The Atlantic Hotel, **28**
Back Creek Inn, **25**
Brampton, **13**
Chanceford Hall, **27**
Gibson's Lodgings, **9**
Glasgow Inn, **23**

Gross' Coate 1658, **21**
The Inn at Antietam, **1**
The Inn at
Buckeystown, **4**
The Inn at
Mitchell House, **14**
The Inn at
Perry Cabin, **17**
John S. McDaniel
House, **22**

The National Pike, **5**
The Robert Morris
Inn, **19**
St. Michael's Manor, **26**
Shaw's Fancy, **10**
Spring Bank, **2**
State House Inn, **11**
The Strawberry Inn, **6**
The Tavern House, **24**
The Turning Point, **3**

Vandiver Inn, **8**
Wades Point Inn, **18**
The White Swan
Tavern, **15**
Widow's Walk Inn, **16**
The William Page
Inn, **12**

Oxford/Eastern Shore

In 1608 Captain John Smith called the Chesapeake "a faire bay encompassed . . . with fruitful and delightsome lande." This description was based on findings obtained while "gunkholing," Eastern Shore jargon for frittering away your time in a boat on the tidal rivers like the Miles, the Choptank, Tred Avon, Sassafras, and Nanticoke. Gunkholing is still a favorite pastime on Maryland's Eastern Shore, where every spring fleets of boats descend on sleepy little ports that haven't seen so much action since the War of 1812—or since last spring.

You could say that Baltimore is the reason Eastern Shore towns such as St. Michael's, Oxford, Cambridge, Chestertown, Rock Hall, and Vienna have retained their small-town charm. In the 18th century these were metropoli-in-the-making, growing fat off of trade with the British. But after the discovery of Baltimore City's enviable deep-water port, the parade passed them by, and for the last 200 years these waterfront Colonial towns have changed little. It fell to the reclusive rich of this century to rediscover the Eastern Shore. The du Ponts, Houghtons, and other wealthy families quietly bought property here and moved in to get away from it all. Since their digs are set discreetly off the roads, the best way to see them is by taking a cruise from St. Michael's up the Miles River.

Besides rubbernecking and gunkholing, there are plenty of other reasons to visit the Eastern Shore. Because the terrain is flat and traversed by a network of pleasant country roads, bicyclists flock to the area, inevitably heading toward shorefront seafood restaurants and marinas. Come November, tens of thousands of waterfowl fly through on their way south, followed by hunters and bird-watchers.

Each Eastern Shore town has a character of its own. Oxford is the quintessential retirement town. In landlocked Easton you'll find the Chesapeake Bay Yacht Club, numerous quaint shops, and the November Waterfowl Festival (now in its 20th year), which features an art show, decoy displays, retriever- and bird-calling, and an auction. St. Michael's, with its renowned Maritime Museum, is all about boats, as is Tilghman Island, one of the last domains of the Chesapeake Bay watermen.

Most visitors stick to these Talbot County haunts, but there are subtler pleasures and thinner crowds in neighboring Kent and Dorchester counties. Cambridge, across the broad Choptank River (the focus of James Michener's Chesapeake*), is the gateway to 700 square miles of government-protected wetlands. To the north lies Chestertown, a demure Colonial treasure whose brightest moment came in 1774, when a band of Revolutionary firebrands dumped a British brigantine's tea cargo into the Chester River—an event still celebrated every May with fife-and-drum corps, house tours, and crafts displays.*

Along Delaware and Maryland's Atlantic coast, the marlin, tuna, and piping plovers roam free, but the people flock to the beaches in rigid pecking order. Well-heeled Washingtonians head to Delaware's Bethany and Fenwick beaches, while blue-collar Baltimore goes to Ocean City, Maryland, where the long main drag and motel flats look forever frozen in 1958.

Places to Go, Sights to See

Betterton Beach. At the mouth of the Sassafras River, about 12 miles north of Chestertown, the bay's only jellyfish-free beach has a bathhouse, boardwalk, picnic pavilion, and boat ramp.

Blackwater National Wildlife Refuge (tel. 410/228–2677). Occupying 17,000-plus marshy acres 12 miles south of Cambridge, this preserve is a haven for endangered Delmarva fox squirrels, bald eagles, peregrine falcons, red-cockaded woodpeckers, and, in fall, hordes of Canada geese and ducks. For spectators there are a visitors center, a 5-mile wildlife drive, and myriad bike and walking trails.

Chesapeake Bay Maritime Museum (St. Michael's, tel. 410/745–2916). Here you'll see the bay's historic boats—including bugeyes, skipjacks, and log canoes—as well as the 100-year-old Hooper Strait Lighthouse, a working boat shop, and an assortment of other maritime displays.

Dixon's Auction Sale & Farmer's Market (Crumpton, tel. 410/928–3006). Auctioneer Norman Dixon starts the bidding here every Wednesday at 9 AM. Goods ranging from tractors to antiques are arranged in rows across six fields.

Oxford–Bellevue Ferry (tel. 410/745–9023). Highway 33 will get you to St. Michael's and Tilghman Island, but the ferry linking Oxford to Bellevue and carrying up to nine cars is a much more picturesque way to go. Begun in 1683, it's the oldest privately operated ferry in the United States.

The Patriot (tel. 410/745–3100). This 65-foot cruise boat berthed in St. Michael's takes 1½-hour excursions up the Miles River.

Trinity Church. In 1675 the Colonists built Trinity near the village of Church Creek in Dorchester County, which makes this brick building the country's oldest Episcopal church in continuous use. It's surrounded by a graveyard, where lie the remains of three Revolutionary War heroes.

Restaurants

Chestertown rolls up the sidewalks pretty early, but you'll notice clusters of cars in front of the **Ironstone Cafe** (tel. 410/778–0188) and the **Imperial Hotel** (tel. 410/778–5000). For a quick salad, sandwich, or fresh-baked dessert in the historic district, head for **Wilma's Kitchen** (tel. 410/778–5708) on Cross Street.

In the St. Michael's–Oxford–Easton triangle, first and foremost there's the **Crab Claw** (St. Michael's, tel. 410/745–2900), a crowded, high-spirited place with pitchers of beer and piles of crabs at very reasonable prices. **208 Talbot** (St. Michael's, tel. 410/745–3838) specializes in more formal dining at higher prices; the **Inn at Perry Cabin** (*see below*) is fine dining at its height, with expenses to match. Try the **Masthead** (Oxford, tel. 410/226–5303) for an upscale menu that doesn't break your pocketbook: The seafood isn't deep-fat-fried, and the $4.95 bar dinner is surprisingly good.

Cambridge isn't renowned for its dining, but it's so gloriously prepossessing and unpretentious that you should plant yourself here anyway. **Clayton's** (tel. 410/221–1665) and the **Blue Crab** (tel. 410/228–8877) are reliable and right on the water.

Tourist Information

Dorchester County Tourism (203 Sunburst Hwy., Cambridge 21613, tel. 410/228–1000).

Kent County Chamber of Commerce (Box 146, 118 N. Cross St., Chestertown 21620, tel. 410/778–0416). **Talbot County Chamber of Commerce** (Box 1366, 805 Goldsborough St., Easton 21601, tel. 410/822–4606).

Reservation Services

Amanda's Bed & Breakfast Reservation Service (1428 Park Ave., Baltimore 21217, tel. 410/225–0001). **Bed & Breakfast of Maryland/The Traveller in Maryland** (Box 2277, Annapolis 21401, tel. 410/269–6232). **Inns of the Eastern Shore** (1500 Hambrooks Blvd., Cambridge 21613, tel. 410/228–0575). **Maryland Reservation Center** (66 Maryland Ave., Annapolis 21401, tel. 410/263–9084).

Ashby 1663

T his is a manor house *magnifico*, or a Colonial estate with Italian dressing. The original foundation was laid in 1663 for a wealthy merchant family by the name of Goldsborough, who engaged the services of some 20-odd servants. The Italian influence entered the picture in the mid-19th century, when the villalike structure arose. Try to ignore the bumptious columned portico (rather as you would the dominating spouse who refuses to let the more reticent, more intelligent partner enter the conversation); it only obstructs the Italianate facade.

Jeanie Wagner and Cliff Meredith, both Eastern Shore natives, purchased Ashby in 1986 and transformed it from ramshackle to technologized high-gloss. Cliff, who once presided over his own contracting company, engineered all the wiring, heating, air-conditioning, and plumbing. Under his direction, small, divided spaces were demolished and opened up. No sign of the former kitchen exists, for Cliff created (from scratch) a wall-to-wall white custom-equipped design, which has since appeared on the cover of a popular builders' magazine.

The pièce de résistance, however, is the Goldsborough Suite on the second floor. If you've never seen a fireplace in a bathroom, now's your chance: The room is exceedingly large and sumptuous, with marble surfaces, brass railings, a bidet, a whirlpool-rigged bath, and a two-headed shower separate from the honeymooners' tub. The sleeping chamber is dominated by a four-poster canopy bed (king-size, of course) adorned with garden-print ruffles, but its best feature is its walls and walls of glass.

The list of perks here is endless. Warm, soft-spoken Jeanie will guide you through the downstairs fitness and tanning center, outdoors around the heated pool (with a river view) and lighted tennis courts, and back in to the screen porch. Some bed-and-breakfasts claim "full" morning meals and slap an egg on your plate. Not Jeanie. Request the California eggs with salsa and sour cream, or the Belgian waffles: Both presentation and quality are superior.

Address: *27448 Ashby Dr. (Box 45), Easton, MD 21601, tel. 410/822-4235.*
Accommodations: *9 double rooms with bath.*
Amenities: *Air-conditioning, TV and telephone in all manor house rooms, library, exercise room, tanning bed, pool table, kitchens in cottage and carriage house; swimming pool, boat dock, paddleboat, canoe, lighted tennis court.*
Rates: *$160–$575; full breakfast. AE, D, DC, MC, V.*
Restrictions: *No smoking indoors, no pets, 2-night minimum on summer weekends.*

Brampton

Brampton's charming character derives from both its house and its grounds. The inn is set in the fields south of Chestertown, framed by two towering, 120-year-old spruce trees at the end of a long drive. It's a three-story brick building with a white columned porch and 14 front windows, the perfect gentleman-farmer's country seat. The house is listed on the National Register of Historic Places, as are four of its surrounding 35 acres (the site of some famous experiments in crop rotation). Enter and pass through the airy foyer into a bookcase-lined living room, or climb the solid-walnut staircase. This front section of Brampton was built around 1860 by Henry Ward Carville, as a wedding present to his wife.

Upstairs in the six guest rooms the present owner's excellent taste becomes apparent. Michael Hanscom spent 10 years in San Francisco renovating old homes before moving here. His Swiss wife, Danielle, is responsible for the European atmosphere in the guest rooms. The bed linen and towels look and smell as if they'd been dried on a line in the Alps. Every room except the suite has a working fireplace or a wood-burning stove. The ceilings on the second floor are 11 feet high. The Yellow Room at the front of the house is a favorite, a sunny paradise with a Swiss cherry armoire and an antique lace canopy above the bed. The two third-floor rooms are tucked under the sloping eaves and are decorated in country style, with locally crafted chairs and trundle beds.

By September 1993 the Hanscoms will have been in operation for almost six years. Several additions and improvements have recently arrived: a mammoth Vulcan commercial stove that enables the hosts to offer guests a choice of breakfast entrées; a smoking and TV room downstairs; and the newly christened Rose Room, outfitted with a king-size bed and a large private bath (but reached by a staircase so narrow that Danielle advises no one over 6 feet to book this unit).

Danielle and Michael can suggest walks on the Brampton grounds to a pond or to the east fork of Langford Creek. There is something Old World about these unassuming hosts, both of whom are dedicated to perfecting every detail.

Address: *25227 Chestertown Rd., Chestertown, MD 21620, tel. 410/778–1860.*
Accommodations: *5 double rooms with baths, 1 suite.*
Amenities: *Air-conditioning, TV in suite.*
Rates: *$90–$110; full breakfast. MC, V.*
Restrictions: *Smoking downstairs only, no pets, 2-night minimum on weekends.*

Gross' Coate 1658

I f you respond to Walt Whitman's portrayal of Abraham Lincoln— "the sweetest, wisest soul," "head steady . . . with proud and resolute spirit"—then envision that image as a place reflective of the same passionate but dogged thoughtfulness and integrity, a structure resounding with the same magnificent, melancholy stateliness of spirit. Gross' Coate is like an architectural realization of that great spirit. Since the first brick was laid in 1760, the creators and keepers—including Jonathan and Molly Ginn, who bought the estate in 1983—have stubbornly minded every aspect of the surroundings (63 secluded waterfront acres of the flat coastal plain that characterizes the Delmarva peninsula). And they've remained sensitive through centuries of development to the importance of an integrated, dignified whole.

That sense of dignity begins on the steps of the large brick Georgian manor. The white wraparound porch is only slightly elevated—enough to offer a suggestion of ceremony—and distinguished by a unique double-columned arrangement topped by the graceful curves of a second-story balustrade. On the veranda is a soldiers' row of hunter-green rockers, which are there year-round.

Inside, the front foyer, sitting rooms, and upstairs chambers are large and light-filled, the appointments spare and discreet. Sixteen working fire-

places are distributed throughout the main house. Floor-to-ceiling windows downstairs shed floods of light over the dark black-walnut floorboards. Climb up the main staircase and walk out on the upstairs porch overlooking the water: The play of light over the Wye River at dusk is enough to produce mild heartache.

If such grandeur suggests an intimidating ambience, it shouldn't. The Ginns want their guests—from business travelers to honeymooners to young children—to have fun and, if they desire, to be assured of absolute privacy. They offer uncommon attentions (an open bar, gourmet breakfasts, dock and stable privileges) while demonstrating none of the museum-piece paranoia of other grand-home owners. Bring your boat, bring your dog, bring your horse, drink champagne in the treehouse: This is a gracious, friendly, happy environment.

Address: *11300 Gross' Coate Rd., Easton, MD 21601, tel. 410/819–0802, fax 410/819–0803.*
Accommodations: *4 suites.*
Amenities: *Fireplaces in suites, open bar; swimming pool, stable, practice golf range, dock, garden house, smokehouse.*
Rates: *$295 ($2,500 for the entire property); Continental breakfast or full-course gourmet brunch, afternoon tea. AE, MC, V.*
Restrictions: *Smoking in designated areas only.*

The Inn at Perry Cabin

The grand white frame house, much enlarged from the original farmhouse, sits serenely at the edge of the Miles River, as it has since 1810. Much of the decor of the Inn at Perry Cabin is pure Laura Ashley, which is only fitting, since this, the first Ashley Inn, is owned by Sir Bernard Ashley, husband of the late designer.

The reception rooms have been done à la English country-house hotel, and from time to time Sir Bernard and Lady Ashley swoop down on St. Michael's, bringing new furniture and decorations (not really new, of course, but brought from their house in the Bahamas or from the antiques emporiums of the world). Every object has been chosen with care, and most of them are antique—from the Colonial American chests of drawers, highboys, and bedside tables that came with the house to the mirrors, lamps, pictures, and the Oriental rugs spread everywhere you look. Many of the bedrooms are done in antiques, too, but others are completely Laura Ashley—fabrics, wallpapers, sprig-decorated tables, and beds with spiral posts.

The main dining room, a soaring chamber two stories high, has an ox-roasting fireplace at one end. The food is excellent, and the silent, unobtrusive service lives up to the British tone of the place. Boat owners would find it a welcome change from galley fare. The employees run the inn impeccably. The only conceivable drawback is the unfortunately situated residential development across the harbor, but that's hardly reason for second thoughts. Service, from the moment you enter the reception hall, is exemplary. Mineral water, ice, and a plate of fresh fruit await guests in their rooms, and the rate also includes a daily newspaper, full English breakfast, and afternoon tea. The addition of swimming and exercise facilities, a traditional English snooker room, and a conservatory has extended the house's pleasures, and nearby recreations are plentiful: The inn arranges outings for everything from golf, fishing, and sailing to helicopter tours and riding lessons. It's worth noting, for business travelers, that the management accommodates any and all conference and meeting requirements.

Address: *308 Watkins Lane, St. Michael's, MD 21663, tel. 410/745–2200 or 800/722–2949, fax 410/745–3348.*
Accommodations: *38 double rooms with baths, 3 suites.*
Amenities: *Restaurant, air-conditioning, cable TV and phones in rooms, indoor swimming pool, steam room, sauna, exercise room, snooker room, conservatory, library, room service; croquet, short-term docking facilities.*
Rates: *$205–$500; full breakfast, afternoon tea. AE, DC, MC, V.*
Restrictions: *No smoking in dining room, no pets.*

The Robert Morris Inn

Although the town of Oxford and its historic inn came vividly into the public eye around the time of the American Bicentennial, the Robert Morris has managed to avoid being spoiled by success. Built by Robert Morris, Sr., as a residence in 1710 and run as an inn since the 1940s, it was bought by Ken and Wendy Gibson in 1975 and is just what a country inn should be.

The 18th-century section of the inn is on Oxford's Morris Street, facing the ferry dock, where there's always a line of tourists waiting to board the tiny Tred Avon Ferry, which tools between Oxford and Bellevue. You might also find a line at the Robert Morris restaurant, which occupies most of the inn's first floor. Its Hitchcock chairs and murals (actually 140-year-old hand-printed wallpaper samples) make it an attractive place to eat; crab cakes and Oxford coolers head the rather predictable menu. The slate-floor tavern beyond the dining room has a working fireplace and is reputedly where James Michener wrote the outline for *Chesapeake.*

Staying at the Robert Morris may prove more difficult than simply supping there. The Gibsons begin taking reservations on January 10 of each year and won't book a room more than a year in advance. Historic-minded souls should be adamant about claiming rooms in the 1710 section, where there's a rare, en-closed Elizabethan staircase and white-pine floors fastened with hand-hewn pegs. Top choices among the four guest rooms here are 2 and 15, the latter with a step-up poster bed and hand-stenciled borders on the walls. You might also request the room once occupied by Robert Morris, Jr., a signer of the Declaration of Independence, or that of his father (who met a lamentable fate when he was hit by a cannon fired in his honor).

The Gibsons know that some people are willing to dispense with history altogether in favor of luxurious quietude. To that end they've restored a roomy 1875 Victorian home, surrounded by mimosa and weeping copper-beech trees, just steps from the main house. Almost all the rooms in Sandaway Lodge are suites featuring screen porches, pine paneling, and immense claw-foot tubs (ask for 203, which has a chandelier over the bath; for 303, with its own staircase; or for one of the romantic River Rooms overlooking the Tred Avon).

Address: *Box 70, on the Tred Avon, Oxford, MD 21654, tel. 410/226–5111, fax 410/226–5744.*
Accommodations: *33 double rooms with baths, 2 efficiencies.*
Amenities: *Restaurant, air-conditioning.*
Rates: *$70–$180; Continental breakfast Tues., breakfast extra other days. MC, V.*
Restrictions: *No smoking, no pets.*

Wades Point Inn

Aside from a chartered yacht, there's no better place from which to appreciate the blue sweep of the Chesapeake than the Wades Point Inn. Halfway between St. Michael's and Tilghman Island, this rambling bed-and-breakfast on 120 acres is surrounded on three sides by the bay.

The oldest section of the inn was built in 1820 by shipwright Thomas Kemp, whose sleek Baltimore clippers were credited with winning the War of 1812. On the land side, this glowing white Georgian house has porches on two floors and chimneys at either end; an observation nook attached to one chimney was Thomas Kemp's lookout and is reached through a trapdoor in one of three rooms in the old portion of the house.

In 1890, later Kemps built an addition to the house on the bay side and opened the place as an inn. The present owners, Betsy and John Feiler, call this addition the Bay Room and have put it to use as a common area; it's large enough to hold a cotillion and is lined with windows and furnished with white wicker. Above the Bay Room is the Summer Wing, which holds six small chambers. These aren't air-conditioned, but given their proximity to the water, porches, and plentiful windows, they don't need it. There are washbasins in some of the Summer Wing rooms, as well as pastel prints and dancing white curtains that catch the rejuvenating breeze. Maybe that's why Mildred Kemp, the last of the family to occupy Wades Point, looked so hearty at age 90, when Betsy Feiler met her. "If living at Wades Point made her look like that," Betsy says, "I wanted to buy the place."

Building additions seems to be something of a tradition with the owners of Wades Point. There's a four-room summer cottage, and in 1989 Betsy and John completed a 12-room guest house about 200 yards from the main inn. These modern rooms have water views and balconies, and the two double beds and kitchenette in Number 423 make it a good choice for families. If you're looking for bona fide old Chesapeake Bay atmosphere, however, opt for a room in the main house.

Address: *Box 7, St. Michael's, MD 21663, tel. 410/745-2500.*
Accommodations: *15 double rooms with baths, 9 doubles share 5 baths.*
Amenities: *Air-conditioning in new guest house, TV and fireplaces in common rooms; pond, private crabbing and fishing dock, walking and jogging trail, public boat ramp nearby.*
Rates: *$69–$165; Continental breakfast. MC, V.*
Restrictions: *Smoking on porches only, no pets, 2-day minimum with Sat. reservation, summer wing and summer cottage closed in winter.*

Glasgow Inn

The keepers of the Glasgow Inn are two retired teachers who went to college together and share a common interest in quilting and old homes. Louise Lee Roche is the people person, and quiet Martha Ann Raine the one who gets things done—such as breakfast, which, if you asked, can feature apple pancakes. Theirs is one of Dorchester County's most historic houses, a beautiful Georgian riverfront mansion with gable-end entry and Palladian windows, built by a refugee of the Stuart Rebellion. Glasgow's high-ceilinged, spacious rooms are decorated with Oriental rugs, 18th-century reproductions, and furniture from Martha Ann's family home in Ocean City. Beyond the Lombardy poplars on the long front lawn lies the Choptank River.

From Glasgow, it's an easy walk to the Brannock Maritime Museum, tennis courts, and the town dock, where the Cambridge skipjack fleet ties up. Ask Louise for directions to Blackwater Wildlife Refuge or to the Amish shop in East New Market. In January a week-long internship for innkeepers is held at the inn.

Address: *1500 Hambrooks Blvd., Cambridge, MD 21613, tel. 410/228-0575.*
Accommodations: *4 double rooms with baths, 4 doubles share 2 baths.*
Amenities: *Air-conditioning, TV in parlor.*
Rates: *$75–$100; full breakfast. MC, V.*
Restrictions: *No smoking, no pets, 3-day minimum during Waterfowl Festival.*

The Inn at Mitchell House

After an unsuccessful skirmish with the Americans near the village of Tolchester during the War of 1812, the British brought their wounded commander to Mitchell House. Sir Peter Parker didn't recover, but modern-day visitors to this country bed-and-breakfast, isolated on 10 corn-filled acres, will fare considerably better.

This three-story brick plantation house was built in 1743 and enlarged in 1825. Two of the five guest bedrooms have working fireplaces, and the top floor's Hermitage, with its low, slanting ceilings and dormer windows, is a great place to tuck in the children. The owners, Jim and Tracy Stone, welcome hunters in season and encourage their guests to stroll a half mile down the road to

Tolchester Marina, where from November 1 to March 15 they can learn how to dredge for oysters by chartering the classic wooden sailboat *Elsworth*.

Address: *8796 Maryland Pkwy., Chestertown, MD 21620, tel. 410/778-6500.*
Accommodations: *5 double rooms with baths.*
Amenities: *Air-conditioning, TV with VCR in living room.*
Rates: *$75–$95; full breakfast. D, MC, V.*
Restrictions: *Dogs allowed outside only, 2-night minimum on holiday weekends.*

John S. McDaniel House

This big, turreted Queen Anne in Easton has seven guest rooms, with the turret nook making the Prentiss Ingraham Room particularly desirable. The decor is a mixed bag of family-style collectibles: nothing fancy, but all neat as a pin. Host Rosemary Garrett took over here during the winter of 1992 after spending five years as an innkeeper in Baltimore. She'll be happy to fill you in on all the local action, including the inside scoop on the best places to eat—try Regal Spirits or Jin Jin, just a few blocks away.

Rosemary serves cider to newly arrived guests; it's just the right thing to sip while unwinding on the wide McDaniel House porch, where you'll find a swing, lots of white wicker furniture, and hanging plants. If you're headed to Easton for the November Waterfowl Festival, this is an excellent, homey place to stay.

Address: *14 N. Aurora St., Easton, MD 21601, tel. 410/822–3704 or 800/787–4667.*
Accommodations: *5 double rooms with baths, 2 doubles share bath.*
Amenities: *Air-conditioning.*
Rates: *$55–$80; Continental breakfast. AE, MC, V.*
Restrictions: *No smoking, no pets, 2-night minimum on holiday weekends.*

The Tavern House

Vienna, Maryland, is a genuine backwater on the Nanticoke River, and probably quieter now than during the Revolutionary War, when the British made a habit of raiding it. Recently a new bridge was built over the river, and now the view from the inn includes the bulwark of the old bridge and the splendid Nanticoke, bordered by marshes and cattails that shimmer in the breeze. The inn has been lovingly restored by Elise and Harvey Altergott. Ask Harvey to point out its wood-case door locks; a carving above the entryway featuring palm trees and coconuts; the gray, green, and blue wainscoting; and the gracefully curving stair. Upstairs is the River Room, the first choice because of its four-poster bed, working fireplace, Colonial wall sconces, and Nanticoke views. There are osprey nests in the marshes out front, an owl in the chimney, and peace. Bicyclists exult here, and stay-at-home partners can always curl up with something to read—Elise has a fine library of books and periodicals—in the most comfortable bedding offered anywhere on the peninsula. How long has it been since you've met anyone who irons the sheets?

Address: *111 Water St., Box 98, Vienna, MD 21869, tel. 410/376–3347.*
Accommodations: *4 double rooms share 2 baths.*
Amenities: *Air-conditioning.*
Rates: *$65–$70; full breakfast. MC, V.*
Restrictions: *No smoking in guest rooms, no pets.*

The White Swan Tavern

To Horace Havemeyer, Jr., old-house restoration was a science. He brought in a team of archaeologists when he bought the Colonial White Swan Tavern to help return it to its 18th-century appearance. A dig at the rear of the brick building unearthed clay pipes and mugs and a Pennsylvania-flagstone tavern yard. Today, the room that was the original kitchen, to the right of this patio area and shaded by a giant elm, is the inn's most requested guest room. Its rough ceiling beams, brick floor, and large fireplace attest to its antiquity and make it an eminently cozy place to sleep. The chambers in the tavern's main section are more formal, with stately wing chairs, canopy beds, and paneled walls. In the years since its renovation the White Swan has become a Kent County landmark, popular for its daily tea. Its enviable High Street location puts guests within walking distance of shops, an old-fashioned movie theater, the Confederate Monument on the green, a small park on the banks of the Chester River, and two good places to eat—the Ironstone Café and the fancy Hotel Imperial Restaurant.

Address: *231 High St., Chestertown, MD 21620, tel. 301/778-2300.*
Accommodations: *4 double rooms with baths, 2 suites.*
Amenities: *Tea room, air-conditioning, cable TV in sitting room.*
Rates: *$85–$135; Continental breakfast, no credit cards.*
Restrictions: *No pets, closed 2 weeks in Jan. and Feb.*

Widow's Walk Inn

A journalist once wrote of Chestertown: "Norman Rockwell would have plenty to paint, and Sinclair Lewis would be busy taking notes." Once a thriving port, Chestertown today claims the distinction of a population that has not increased since 1900.

Don and Joanne Toft's highly symmetrical Victorian (circa 1877) stands in the heart of the historic district. This large white clapboard residence, with red window shutters and lively eave detail, houses spacious spic-and-span rooms furnished with antiques, dried-flower arrangements, potted plants, ceiling fans, and family treasures. Pull back the drapes and bathe in the sun: The tightly clustered fenestration lets in abundant natural light.

Widow's Walk is a suitable situation for business travelers especially, because of its location: The historic district, the best restaurants, Washington College, and the Chester River are all in easy walking distance.

Address: *402 High St., Chestertown, MD 21620, tel. 410/778-6455 or 410/778-6864.*
Accommodations: *1 double room with bath, 2 doubles share bath, 2 suites.*
Amenities: *Refreshments on arrival.*
Rates: *$75–$105; Continental breakfast. No credit cards.*
Restrictions: *No smoking indoors, no pets, 2-night minimum on holiday weekends.*

Annapolis/Western Shore

*Bounded by 7,325 miles of coastline, the Chesapeake Bay is
not just the nation's largest estuary but Maryland's
defining feature. Its Eastern and Western shores were
joined in 1952 by the 4½-mile Chesapeake Bay Bridge.
Since then, sun worshipers from Baltimore, Philadelphia,
and Washington have had easy access to the Atlantic
beaches, making the bay a favorite with wealthy retirees,
recreational sailors, artists, and many others.*

*During their easterly migration along Route 50/301, the
sun-and-surf crowd was quick to rediscover Annapolis,
founded in 1647 near the mouth of the Severn River. John
D. Rockefeller passed it over in favor of Williamsburg while
looking for a Colonial capital to restore, but Annapolitans
don't care. Their city, the state capital, boasts more pre-
Revolutionary brick buildings than any other in America,
the oldest statehouse in continuous use, the U.S. Naval
Academy, a renowned harbor, a huge October boat show,
and a July feast during which 20,000 blue crabs are
devoured. The streets radiating from the heights around
Church and State circles are a walker's paradise, but
summer weekends can be crowded (and parking
a challenge), so it's a good idea to steal away to Annapolis
on weekdays or in the November-to-March off-season.*

*South of Annapolis on the Chesapeake's Western Shore lie
three Maryland counties that time forgot—Calvert, St.
Mary's, and Charles, where the broad Potomac and
Patuxent flow gently past tobacco fields, and the mood is
redolent of the Old South. Today, though Washington's
suburban sprawl is beginning to encroach from the north,
the three counties remain a fine frontier along which
travelers can investigate 18th-century churches; manor
houses such as Sotterley; the bustling marine center at
Solomons Island; lonely land's-end lighthouses; and St.*

Mary's City, which predates Annapolis as a capital of
Colonial Maryland.

Places to Go, Sights to See

Calvert Marine Museum (tel. 410/326–2042). This complex of buildings in the
town of Solomons includes the restored J. C. Lore and Sons Oyster House
and the Drum Point Lighthouse, built in 1883 to mark the entrance of the
Patuxent River, and one of the last cottage-type lights remaining on the bay.

City Dock. Here's where to find the Tourist Information Booth (tel. 410/268–
8687), a fleet of spiffy yachts, and sightseeing boats that cruise Annapolis
Harbor and call at Eastern Shore ports. The historic Victualling Warehouse,
Maritime Museum, Middleton Tavern, and seafood-laden Market House are
across the square from the dock.

Eastport. Just over the Spa Creek drawbridge is Eastport, a nautical hub full
of boat yards, marinas, and watering holes such as Marmaduke's (tel.
410/269–5420), a favorite with yacht crews.

Historic Homes of Annapolis. These debonair Georgian and Federal
buildings include the Hammond-Harwood, Chase-Lloyd, Brice, and William
Paca houses, the last a must-see for its grand Palladian design and formal
gardens. Maps pinpointing their locations (all within walking distance of one
another) are available at the Tourist Information Booth on City Dock, and
tours can be arranged through *Historic Annapolis, Inc.* (tel. 410/267–8149)
or *Three Centuries Tours* (tel. 410/263–5401).

Maryland State House (tel. 410/269–3400). The oldest American statehouse
in continuous legislative use, this Georgian brick building dates from 1772
and served as the nation's capital for nine months, in 1773 and 1774. In its
chambers, which are decorated with hand-carved tobacco-leaf borders,
General George Washington resigned his commission and the Treaty of Paris
was signed, ending the Revolutionary War.

Point Lookout State Park (tel. 301/872–5688). Point Lookout, at the tip of
the tri-counties peninsula, served as an appallingly overcrowded hospital
during the Civil War. Now its character is far more benign, offering
campsites as well as facilities for swimming, crabbing, and fishing.

St. Mary's City (tel. 301/862–0990). Approximately 60 miles south of
Annapolis, this restored village is the site of the fourth permanent
settlement in Colonial America. Points of interest include the Godiah Spray
Tobacco Plantation and a working reconstruction of *The Dove*, a square-rig
sailing vessel that brought settlers from England to St. Mary's in 1634. Some
800 acres here are devoted to a disarmingly vibrant re-creation of 17th-
century life, and recent archaeological finds—most prominently three 300-
year-old lead coffins—have made national headlines.

U.S. Naval Academy (tel. 410/267–3363). Every year 1,000 midshipmen are commissioned at the Academy, which was founded in 1845. The body of John Paul Jones rests beneath its chapel, and the wardroom is so big the entire student body (4,500 strong) can sit down to dine together. Guided tours of the 329-acre campus leave from the information center at Ricketts Hall.

Restaurants

Courtney's (tel. 301/872–4403), near Scotland, is the outstanding place for fresh fish (especially when Julie's cooking). On Solomons Island, **Dry Dock** (tel. 410/326–4817), a waterside, no-smoking space that changes its menu nightly, is dependable, judiciously priced, and exceedingly cordial. The larger, less intimate **Lighthouse Inn Restaurant** (tel. 410/326–2444) will run you $12–$22 for a full meal, excluding drinks, tax, and tip.

In Annapolis, **Griffins** (tel. 410/268–2576), on the city dock, is a solid choice for steaks and fresh seafood. **McGarvey's** (tel. 410/263–5700) is a celebrated saloon and oyster bar. **Treaty of Paris** (tel. 410/263–2641) and **Piccolo Italiano Ristorante** (tel. 410/280–0400) are fancier places. If you venture to Eastport, you can count on **O'Leary's** (tel. 410/263–0884) for the best seafood dinner in the area. Finally, sooner or later everybody goes to the honky-tonk **Buddy's Crabs & Ribs** (tel. 410/626–1100) on Main Street—bet you've never seen fish-shaped french fries.

Tourist Information

Calvert County Department of Economic Development (Calvert County Courthouse, Prince Frederick 20678, tel. 410/535–4583). **Charles County Tourism** (Charles County Government Building, Box B, La Plata 20646, tel. 301/934–9305). **St. Mary's County Chamber of Commerce** (6260 Waldorf Leonard Town Rd., Mechanicsville 20659, tel. 301/884–5555). **Tourism Council of Annapolis and Anne Arundel County** (6 Dock St., Annapolis 21401, tel. 410/280–0445).

Reservation Services

Amanda's Bed & Breakfast Reservation Service (1428 Park Ave., Baltimore 21217, tel. 410/225–0001). **Annapolis Association of Licensed Bed & Breakfast Owners** (Box 744, Annapolis 21404). **Bed & Breakfast of Maryland/The Traveller in Maryland** (Box 2277, Annapolis 21401, tel. 410/269–6232). **Maryland Reservation Center** (66 Maryland Ave., Annapolis 21401, tel. 410/263–9084).

State House Inn

When Paul Pearson came to Annapolis in 1966, the city was an eyesore, far from the Chesapeake jewel that it is today. Fortunately he turned his imagination loose, buying and restoring five antique properties in the next two decades—among them, the State House Inn. Unlike its sister property, the Maryland Inn, a landmark flatiron building that has served as a hostelry since 1776, the State House is a quiet, elegant respite from the bustle. Of Pearson's four-inn domain, known as Historic Inns of Annapolis, the State House is the best-kept secret. It's located on State Circle, a quiet street where there's an archaeological dig under way. Built in 1820 with dormer windows and a porch that is laden with rocking chairs today, it overlooks Maryland's distinguished capitol.

Though the inn doesn't have an elevator or common room, the nine guest chambers, all intriguingly varied in shape, easily make up for the lack. They are swathed in matching wallpapers and draperies and furnished with a mixture of antiques and reproductions; their plump beds are covered with ivory candlewick spreads in a traditional pattern. Lovers of luxury should note that three of the nine suites have whirlpool baths and that breakfast is served on a tray at your door, along with the morning newspaper every day but Sunday.

If you book a room at the State House Inn when the legislature is in session (January–March), you're likely to run into some of the harried politicians and lobbyists who favor the property. And in any of Pearson's inns, if you're lucky, some morning you might run into the cheerful, friendly mistress innkeeper, Peg Bednarsky (called "Mother" by the staff and the entire Maryland legislature), as she checks unoccupied rooms to make sure they're up to scratch.

Only 30 minutes from Baltimore on the relatively new Route 97, Annapolis is almost too easy to get to from the major Northwest metropolises. In 40 minutes, visitors arriving dockside from the nation's capital can step back 250 years. Once captivated by its history, you'll find the food and drink and shopping opportunities plentiful. Maryland Avenue provides a wealth of antiques and crafts boutiques.

Address: *16 Church Circle, Annapolis, MD 21401, tel. 410/263-2641, fax 410/263-3613.*
Accommodations: *6 double rooms with baths, 3 suites.*
Amenities: *Air-conditioning, cable TV and phones in rooms.*
Rates: *$90–$250; Continental breakfast. AE, DC, MC, V.*
Restrictions: *2-day minimum during Commissioning Week and Boat Show.*

The William Page Inn

If your travels take you to Annapolis for Commissioning Week at the Naval Academy, for the December Parade of Lights, or simply to nose around the city's walkable historic district, there's rest for the weary explorer at the William Page Inn. Built in 1908, this brown-shingle Victorian is a youngster by Annapolis standards, but one with an accommodating style. Its wraparound porch offers deep Adirondack chairs, and the boxwood in the William Paca House gardens perfumes the air. Somewhere over the high white wall at the end of Martin Street you might hear Naval Academy "middies" drilling, and four blocks away, at eateries around City Dock, crabs are being devoured, but on the William Page porch such distractions seem light-years away.

The genial innkeepers are Rob Zuchelli and Greg Page, a designer of theatrical lighting and a computer programmer. They took very early retirement to refurbish the inn, which had served as the First Ward Democratic Clubhouse for 50 years. They aired out the smoke-filled rooms; stripped 11 coats of paint from the massive staircase, to reveal oak, mahogany, and cherry wood; and filled the inn with Queen Anne and Chippendale reproductions. They also turned the third floor into one smashing suite, with a sleigh bed, skylight, window seats, and balloon shades that lift to reveal views of the Annapolis rooftops. Guests might take the presence of a whirlpool bath in the suite in stride, but they are likely to be surprised by the one attached to the little blue room on the second floor.

There's a wet bar stocked with setups, a working fireplace in the carpeted downstairs common room, and a discreet dog named Rascals who is always happy to accompany guests on walks. Breakfast, served from the sideboard in the common room, consists of freshly baked muffins and breads, fruit-and-cheese trays, and perhaps an egg casserole or crepes—depending on chef Rob's mood. Greg earns his keep by running a side business, Bed & Breakfast of Maryland/The Traveller in Maryland reservation service, and he can bend your ear describing other choice places to stay.

Address: *8 Martin St., Annapolis, MD 21401, tel. 410/626–1506.*
Accommodations: *2 double rooms with baths, 2 doubles share bath, 1 suite.*
Amenities: *Air-conditioning, cable TV in suite, wet bar, 2 whirlpool baths, robes for guests using shared bath; off-street parking.*
Rates: *$70–$120; Continental breakfast. AE, MC, V.*
Restrictions: *No smoking, no pets, 2-day minimum during special events, 5-day minimum during Boat Show and Commissioning Week.*

Back Creek Inn

Seascape painters and beachcombers would do well on Solomons Island, a finger of sand connected to the mainland by a bridge, bounded on the west by the Patuxent River and on the east by Back Creek Bay. They'd do well at Carol Szkotnicki and Lin Cochran's Back Creek Inn, too. Dating from the 1880s, the robin's-egg-blue waterman's house is unprepossessing from the front, but inside Carol has used her grandma's quilts and Lin her green thumb to brighten up the guest rooms. Lin's catering skills are evident in the homemade breakfast breads and muffins. The main house and an annex added in 1984 wrap around the heady-smelling herb garden, which in turn surrounds an outdoor whirlpool bath. From the garden and patio it's fun to watch the water traffic on Back Creek. Charter fishing, sailing, and exploring the Calvert Marine Museum are how most guests spend their salt-sprayed Solomons days.

Address: *Calvert and A Sts., Solomons, MD 20688, tel. 410/326-2022.*
Accommodations: *1 double room with bath, 3 doubles share 2 baths, 2 suites, 1 cottage.*
Amenities: *Air-conditioning, cable TV in common area and in cottage and suites; bikes, dock with 2 deepwater slips, access to nearby swimming pool.*
Rates: *$65–$125; full or Continental breakfast. No credit cards.*
Restrictions: *Smoking in Commons only, no pets, 2-day minimum holiday weekends, closed mid-Dec.–mid-Feb.*

Gibson's Lodgings

Two hundred years ago they called Annapolis Harbor's infamous dockside neighborhood Hell's Point. Well, yesterday's hell is a gentrified haven today, with narrow brick-paved streets, shade trees, and houses with landmark plaques. Two at the bottom of Prince George Street have been converted into a rambling inn by ex-Illinoisans Cary and Ayrol Ann Gibson. The Patterson dwelling, built between 1760 and 1786, is a brick Georgian town house with dormer windows. Next door, the red stucco Berman home dates from the last century. The Gibsons combed the towns along the Intracoastal Waterway for antiques, yet the decoration of these 18th- and 19th-century neighbors is extremely simple, a little like that of a small-town hotel. The annex built out back two years ago is too new to have much atmosphere, but it does have spacious conference rooms. These days Gibson's Lodgings is professionally managed, which gives it a businesslike air. The venerable houses are as close as can be to the Middleton Tavern's raw bar.

Address: *110–114 Prince George St., Annapolis, MD 20401, tel. 410/268-5555.*
Accommodations: *5 double rooms with baths, 13 doubles share 7 baths, 2 suites.*
Amenities: *Air-conditioning, TVs and phones in parlors and rooms with baths, conference room with kitchenette; free parking.*
Rates: *$68–$120; Continental breakfast. AE, MC, V.*
Restrictions: *No pets.*

St. Michael's Manor

Dusk is a good time to arrive at St. Michael's Manor, when there's a pale blanket of mist hanging over owner Joe Dick's vineyards and over the creek behind the house. Once inside, guests might find Nancy Dick playing her antique organ and Joe offering his homemade wine in front of the roaring fire in the parlor hearth. The four bedrooms at the manor are furnished with quilts and seem homey rather than grand. In the morning you'll awake to find yourself on an inlet of the Chesapeake Bay, at the southern tip of Western Shore Maryland. After breakfast, you can stroll the manor's 10 acres or try the tire swing out front, then perhaps go paddling in the canoe, visit nearby St. Mary's City, or cruise to Point Lookout State Park on a bike. At the state park there are boat excursions to isolated Smith Island and swimming (before jellyfish season starts in June). More than 3,300 Confederate soldiers died in prison at Point Lookout during the Civil War, which explains the monument across from the turn-off, and the vaguely haunted feeling of the place.

Address: *Scotland, MD 20687, tel. 301/872-4025.*
Accommodations: *4 double rooms share 2 baths.*
Amenities: *Air-conditioning, 2 fireplaces in parlor; swimming pool, tire swing, bikes, canoe, rowboat.*
Rates: *$50–$65; full breakfast. No credit cards.*
Restrictions: *Smoking downstairs only, no pets, 2-day minimum on holiday weekends.*

Shaw's Fancy

Shaw's Fancy is a perfect bed-and-breakfast for midshipmen's drags—that's Naval Academy slang for dates who are invited to the annual Ring Dance or homecoming game. This brown-shingle 1902 Victorian at the heart of Annapolis has a Greek Revival porch with a porch swing (perfect for long good-byes). Inside, proprietors Lilith Ren and Jack House, part-time federal workers, have sustained the romantic fantasy by filling the place with a splendid mixture of art-nouveau and new-age prints and furnishings, which harmonize better than you might expect with the Victorian tiger-oak woodwork and green-tile gas fireplace. The effect is eccentric, airy, and hedonistic, a little like Berkeley come to Annapolis. The three guest rooms feature Victorian brass beds, and if you book the Shaw's special Romance Package, you get satin sheets, candlelight, armloads of fresh flowers, and chilled champagne—Lilith says she picked up a lot of tips on such touches from the midshipmen themselves.

Address: *161 Green St., Annapolis, MD 21401, tel. 410/268-9750.*
Accommodations: *1 double room with bath, 1 double with shared bath, 1 suite.*
Amenities: *Air-conditioning, terry-cloth robes; hot tub in garden.*
Rates: *$75–$130; Continental breakfast. No credit cards.*
Restrictions: *No smoking, no pets, 2-day minimum on special Annapolis weekends.*

Frederick and Thereabouts

In Frederick, about an hour's drive west of Baltimore and Washington, DC, Interstates 270 and 70 meet, and although the character of these thoroughfares has changed dramatically in the last 200 years (I-270 has become such a jungle of office parks that it's known as the Technology Corridor), it is historically appropriate to think of the Frederick area as a transportation hub. America's oldest federal turnpike, the National Road, ran through the town, which was founded in 1745 by Daniel Dulaney. Frederick grew up as a way station on the route west. Some settlers—in particular those of German extraction—cut their journey short, unloaded their Conestoga wagons, and put down roots in town. To encourage settlement here, land speculators donated property for churches, resulting in a downtown of clustered spires, where there is a house of worship on almost every block. These, as well as the immaculately kept Federal and Victorian houses in Frederick's 34-block historic district, are well charted in a walking-tour brochure available at the visitors center, on Church Street.

The land around Frederick is dotted with farms and villages such as Woodsboro, New Market, Thurmont, and Emmitsburg (the site of a shrine to America's first native-born saint, Elizabeth Ann Seton). This area is ideal for biking and back-road exploring. Everywhere, historic markers tell tales of Civil War action along the Monocacy River, atop Sugarloaf and South mountains, and outside Sharpsburg, at Antietam.

Places to Go, Sights to See

Antietam (tel. 301/432–5124). Just outside Sharpsburg, in Washington County, is the Civil War battlefield where 87,000 Union soldiers under General George B. McClellan attacked General Robert E. Lee's 41,000-man army of Northern Virginia. Twenty-three thousand lives later the North had won the day, prompting President Lincoln to deliver the Emancipation

Proclamation. But Antietam is remembered not as a Union victory, but as the
scene of the ugliest carnage in the history of American warfare. The visitors
center shows an orientation film and provides maps.

Catoctin Mountain National Park and Cunningham Falls State Park (tel.
301/271–7574). Franklin Roosevelt established a presidential retreat here in
the Catoctin Mountains called Shangri-la, which later came to be known as
Camp David. Here you'll also find Cunningham Falls, a man-made lake, miles
of hiking trails, two campgrounds, and fly-fishing on Hunting Creek.

Frederick. Visitors to this pleasant town should not be deterred by the urban
sprawl that surrounds it. The city's charm lies downtown, where visitors
(April through November) will find the *Old City Hall*, built as a courthouse
in 1862; the *Barbara Frietchie House* (tel. 301/698–0360), a reproduction of
the Civil War heroine's home; the *Francis Scott Key Museum* (tel. 301/663–
8687), built in 1799; the *Frederick Historical Society Museum* (tel. 301/663–
1188), with displays of antique dolls, Native American artifacts, and Amelung
glass; the *Hessian Barracks*, on the grounds of the Maryland School for the
Deaf, constructed in 1777 as a prison for British prisoners of war; and the
Brunswick Rail Museum (tel. 301/834–7100).

Frederick County covered bridges. There are three, all in the Thurmont
area, all built in the mid-1800s: Loy's Bridge, on Route 77, which crosses
Owens Creek; the Roddy Road Bridge, also over Owens Creek, on Route 15;
and, on Utica Road a mile east of Route 15, the Utica Mills Bridge, which
once spanned the Monocacy River, before being swept downstream by the
Johnstown Flood of 1889.

Lilypons Water Gardens (tel. 301/874–5133; in DC, 202/428–0686). This
fascinating hatchery in Buckeystown, named for the opera star, is a prime
supplier of exotic fish and aquatic plants. Its landscaped ponds bloom with
lotuses and water lilies between Memorial Day and Labor Day. Lilypons
catalogues are available in the aquarium shop, and such special events as
jousting tournaments and lotus festivals are held regularly.

New Market. No one knows precisely why this immensely friendly village
cast its lot with the antiques trade, but today there are some 40 shops
peddling aged items, in a town that is only a few streets wide. *Mealey's
Restaurant* (tel. 301/865–5488), New Market's other attraction, occupies
a Georgian brick building on Main Street and serves Maryland cuisine.

Rose Hill Manor. This Colonial estate dating from the 1790s was home to
Maryland's first governor, Thomas Johnson, who nominated his close friend
George Washington as commander-in-chief of the Continental Army. Today
the estate's 43 acres encompass a county park and a children's museum (tel.
301/694–1648) where youngsters explore hands-on historic displays.

South Mountain and the Washington Monument. At the summit of South
Mountain, accessible by car along Alternate Route 40, lies the nation's first
monument to George Washington, constructed by the citizens of Boonsboro
in a single day. Nearby are the Dahlgren Chapel, built in 1882, and Old South

Mountain Inn. Now a restaurant (tel. 301/432–6155), the former stagecoach stop and hostelry was seized by John Brown just before he raided the Harper's Ferry arsenal.

Restaurants

Word has it George Will took regular lunches with Nancy Reagan at the **Yellow Brick Bank** (tel. 304/876–2208 or 304/876–2604), on a cozy corner of charming Shepherdstown, West Virginia, just a few miles southwest of Sharpsburg. The menu features inventive pasta and fish entrées. Other Antietam visitors can choose between the prime rib at the elegant, dress-up **Old South Mountain Inn** (tel. 301/371–5400) or the more casual, hearty fare of the Swiss-German **Café Berlin** (tel. 301/432–2443), both in Boonsboro. New Market proprietors will steer you to **Mealey's** (tel. 301/865–5488) for dinner and to the **Village Tea Room** (tel. 301/865–3450) for a generous, inexpensive lunch.

As for Frederick: The Continental **Brown Pelican** (tel. 301/695–5833) rates high marks for presentation, service, and cuisine (entrées $13–$19). The less formal **Province** (tel. 301/663–1441) specializes in "creative American" food and wonderful desserts. Pasta addicts opt for **Di Francesco's** (tel. 301/695–5499). In addition, dozens of pubs, coffee houses, tea rooms, and trendy hangouts line Market and Patrick streets in the historic district.

Tourist Information

Frederick Visitors Center (19 E. Church St., Frederick 21701, tel. 301/663–8687). Ask for the brochure "Inns of the Blue Ridge." **Maryland Office of Tourism Development** (217 E. Redwood St., Baltimore 21202, tel. 410/333–6611).

Reservation Services

Bed & Breakfast Accommodations of Frederick and Western Maryland (7945 Worman's Mill Rd., Frederick 21701, tel. 301/694–5926). **Bed & Breakfast of Maryland/The Traveller in Maryland** (Box 2277, Annapolis 21401, tel. 410/269–6232). **Maryland Reservation Center** (66 Maryland Ave., Annapolis 21401, tel. 410/263–9084).

The Inn at Antietam

Anyone who's ever visited a Civil War battlefield knows how haunting the site is, how the dawns seem to echo with the sound of bugles and gunfire, how at night the voices of soldiers rise like mist from the glades. Antietam, which surrounds the dusty little town of Sharpsburg, is surely one of the most stirring of such places, for it was here on a September day in 1862 that one of the worst battles of the Civil War claimed more than 23,000 lives in a single bloody day.

Just north of town there's a national cemetery, with a Daniel Chester French statue called "The Private Soldier" serving as headstone for 5,000 Union dead. Adjoining the graveyard on a hillock facing the hazy Blue Ridge is the Inn at Antietam, a 1908 Queen Anne cottage with a wraparound porch, shaded by a giant silver maple and set amid fields where horses graze. Owners Cal and Betty Fairbourn have restored the place in the style of the Civil War period, filling the parlor with Rococo Revival walnut furniture, the porch with white wicker, and guest rooms with Eastlake dressers and beds.

The Fairbourns, who'd restored another house in the area before moving into this one in 1987, enlisted the aid of a decorator here, which resulted in beautifully finished guest rooms. The converted smokehouse, at the rear, has a large brick fire-place, a sitting room lined with beaded paneling, and a loft bed. The master suite, another favorite, has an 1880s four-poster bed; matching spread, curtains, and wallpaper; and Battenberg lace.

After breakfast, served in the formal dining room on Royal Copenhagen china, Cal and Betty can offer tips on how best to see the battlefield—on foot, by bicycle, or even on cross-country skis. The surrounding area is also surprisingly rich in good restaurants, such as the Yellow Brick Bank, in nearby Shepherdstown, West Virginia, and Old South Mountain Inn and Café Berlin, both in Boonsboro. During the first weekend in December the Valley Craft Network runs an annual Holiday Studio Tour; pottery, quilts, furniture, and natural fiberwear make ideal Christmas offerings. Shutterbugs should ask Cal about local photo opportunities.

Address: *220 E. Main St., Box 119, Sharpsburg, MD 21782, tel. 301/432-6601.*
Accommodations: *4 suites.*
Amenities: *Air-conditioning, TV in smokehouse suite.*
Rates: *$95–$105; full breakfast. AE.*
Restrictions: *No smoking, no pets, 2-night minimum on weekends and holidays, closed Dec. 22–Jan. 3.*

Spring Bank

When you ask Beverly and Ray Compton why they bought their cavernous, 100-year-old farmhouse just north of Frederick in 1980, Beverly has a disarming answer: "We bought it to live and be happy in." And indeed it seems this warm couple is happy here, though the road to inhabiting the house was paved with hard work interspersed with joyful architectural surprises. While restoring the Italianate and Gothic Revival structure, the Comptons found details that seemed too good to be true: engraved designs in the glass of the front door, random-width hardwood floors, faux-marble mantels, antique William Morris wallpaper, and a wet-plaster fresco on the ceiling of the old billiard room—now a first-floor guest room. Some of these design points had been damaged over the years, but after a thorough cleaning, they stand as witnesses to another time and lifestyle. Ray is the son of a Chadd's Ford, Pennsylvania, antiques dealer, and perhaps his penchant for restoration is in his blood; in 1990 he received an award from the Historical Society of Frederick for the work he's done here. Beverly haunts local auctions and flea markets, and during the week she commutes to a federal job in Rockville.

The brick house is built in textbook-perfect telescoping style, with porches stretching across the front and along two stories on the side. The backyard gives way to farmland; the 20th century rarely intrudes at Spring Bank, despite its proximity to Highway 15. Choose your room upon arrival; the converted billiard parlor and the Sleigh Bedroom on the second floor are favorites, both sparely decorated with Eastlake-style antiques. In keeping with the 19th-century ethos the baths have not been extensively modernized—no whirlpool tubs or French magnifying mirrors here.

For breakfast, the Comptons serve homemade breads with local jams and plenty of information on nearby auctions, held almost every day. One note of advice: If you have fears about booking a room with a shared bath, you should put them to rest. No one has to wait in line here, and if you were to pass up Spring Bank for this reason, you'd be missing out on one of the handsomest, best-run establishments in western Maryland.

Address: *7945 Worman's Mill Rd., Frederick, MD 21701, tel. 301/694–0440.*
Accommodations: *1 double room with bath, 4 doubles share 2½ baths.*
Amenities: *Air-conditioning, cable TV in parlor.*
Rates: *$60–$90; Continental breakfast. AE, D, MC, V.*
Restrictions: *No smoking, no pets, 2-night minimum on holiday weekends and weekends Apr.–mid-June and mid-Sept.–mid-Nov.*

The Inn at Buckeystown

Buckeystown, on the Monocacy River, is a lovely collection of Federal and Victorian homes; the inn, built in 1897, is the grandest thing in town. It's a white frame building with three stories (one might say layers, since it looks like a wedding cake) on a 2½-acre lawn with azaleas. Owner Dan Pelz has created a true country inn crammed with eccentric memorabilia, including an American Indian collection, vintage postcards of Harper's Ferry, and Victorian furniture. Every day of the week an evening meal is served family style, with such dishes as consommé Madrilene, London broil in port sauce, and blueberry parfait. Plan to dress for it—this is a festive place. Dan, partner Chase Barnett, and general manager Rebecca Shipman-Smith keep busy all year, but they pull out all the stops for the Christmas season. For the traditional-inn feeling, we suggest the Winter Suite or the Love Room.

Address: *3521 Buckeystown Pike (General Delivery), Buckeystown, MD 21717, tel. 301/874-5755 or 800/272-1190.*
Accommodations: *3 double rooms with baths, 2 suites, 2 cottages.*
Amenities: *Air-conditioning, TV with VCR in cottages and Far West Suite; fireplace, kitchen, outdoor hot tub, piano in St. John's Cottage; fireplace in Winter Suite.*
Rates: *$167–$272; dinner and full breakfast. AE, MC, V.*
Restrictions: *No smoking in common rooms, no pets, 2-night minimum in Oct. and on holiday weekends.*

The National Pike

The National Pike lies just up Main Street in New Market from the Strawberry Inn, and right across from Mealey's Restaurant. Built in three sections between 1796 and 1804, this Federal-style brown-brick building was topped with a tower at the turn of the 20th century. Tom and Terry Rimel are the proprietors; he's a master at slate roofing, which sparked his interest in restoring old homes. The two have done a fine job on the National Pike, whose parlor has Williamsburg-blue paneling, a fireplace, and two armchairs for watching the action on the historic turnpike out front. There is also an organ, played by their son, who became organist for the local Episcopal church at the age of 10. The two snug guest rooms in the rear section have brass-and-oak beds and are decorated in a country style; they can also function as a suite. The long backyard has azalea gardens, a smokehouse, and carriage house from the 1830s. Terry is currently in the process of adding a new double room with private bath to the 1804 section of the house.

Address: *9–11 W. Main St., Box 299, New Market, MD 21774, tel. 301/865-5055.*
Accommodations: *3 double rooms with baths, 1 double suite.*
Amenities: *Air-conditioning.*
Rates: *$75–$125; full breakfast. MC, V.*
Restrictions: *No pets, 2-night minimum New Market Days (Sept.).*

The Strawberry Inn

New Market is the quintessential Maryland village, with a shady Main Street that was busier 200 years ago than it is today. Once, New Market busied itself outfitting wagonloads of settlers headed west on the National Pike. Today the town has taken a new lease on life, dealing in the past, with 40 antiques shops in the 12-block downtown area—making it the Antiques Capital of Maryland.

Ed and Jane Rossig bought their Victorianized 1850s farmhouse on Main Street as an investment, but when the mayor of the town persuaded them to open the house to overnight guests in 1973 the Strawberry Inn became one of the first bed-and-breakfasts on the eastern seaboard. Though the white frame house looks tiny, it holds five guest rooms and several shops' worth of Victorian antiques. Breakfast is served on the wide deck. The downstairs suite has a private porch, twin beds, and a pullout sofa; upstairs, the popular Strawberry Room has a brass bed and rose wallpaper. Out back is Ed's art gallery, in a log house transported from another part of New Market.

Address: *17 Main St., (Box 237), New Market, MD 21774, tel. 301/865-3318.*
Accommodations: *4 double rooms with baths, 1 suite.*
Amenities: *Air-conditioning.*
Rates: *$75–$95; full breakfast. No credit cards.*
Restrictions: *No pets, 2-night minimum on weekends.*

The Turning Point

The Turning Point, occupying a 1910 estate with a sweeping front lawn, is known locally for having one of the area's best restaurants. The hillside would be picture-perfect but for the mini shopping mall that's sprung up like a modern toadstool on its flank. Nonetheless, the grounds are lovely, with sundials, a barbecue, and lawn chairs scattered hither and you. You enter the inn by way of a white-columned porch and cross a carpeted foyer to reach the two dining rooms, the parlor, and the sun deck.

The restaurant's menu offers a sophisticated mix, including blackened swordfish, broiled Delmonico steak Espagnole, and sweetbreads Argentine style. Decorated with a harmonic blend of antiques and re-production furniture, the rooms are extremely comfortable. Owner-manager-hosts Suzanne and Charlie Seymour added a new cottage with a whirlpool tub, cable TV, wet bar, refrigerator, and coffee machine in 1992—a cozy haven for honeymooners, or a practical workplace and sanctuary for business travelers.

Address: *3406 Urbana Pike, Frederick, MD 21701, tel. 301/874-2421.*
Accommodations: *5 double rooms with baths, 1 cottage.*
Amenities: *Restaurant, air-conditioning, cable TV and whirlpool bath in cottage.*
Rates: *$75–$85 (cottage $125–$150); full breakfast. MC, V.*
Restrictions: *Smoking only in living room, no pets indoors, restaurant closed Mon.*

Off the Beaten Track

The Admiral Fell Inn

Funky chic is perhaps the best way to describe Fell's Point, a historic waterfront section of Baltimore where hulking warehouses cast long shadows on the narrow streets, tugs dock at the old City Pier, and the bars don't close until late. At the center of this Maryland Macao lies the Admiral Fell Inn, an assemblage of four buildings, constructed between 1770 and 1910, that once housed a vinegar-bottling plant. Rest assured that the place has since been fumigated; in fact it's been handsomely renovated and ingeniously converted into a 38-room inn with a restaurant and pub in the cellar. The rooms, which vary in shape, are decorated with Federal-style reproductions and antiques, and offer views of the erratic rooftops of Fell's Point. A suite and three of the rooms have whirlpool baths, and 15 have two double beds. Although there are other, more quietly graceful lodgings in town (such as the Shirley Madison Hotel), no place is more convenient to Baltimore's nightlife, and none better evokes this port city's past.

Address: *888 S. Broadway, Baltimore, MD 21231, tel. 410/522-7377 or 800/292-4667; fax 410/522-0707.*
Accommodations: *38 double rooms with baths (5 nonsmoking).*
Amenities: *Restaurant, air-conditioning, TV and phones in rooms, conference room, room service; parking, free van service in city 7 AM–10:30 PM.*
Rates: *$98–$165; Continental breakfast. AE, D, DC, MC, V.*

The Atlantic Hotel

The historic district in Berlin, Maryland, got a significant boost when a group of local investors renovated and opened the town's Victorian centerpiece, the Atlantic Hotel, built in 1895. This three-story, bracketed brick inn just 7 miles from Assateague National Seashore offers beachcombers a pleasant alternative to Ocean City's motels. The 16 guest rooms lining a wide central corridor are decorated with Oriental and floral-patterned rugs, tasseled draperies, Tiffany-style lamps, and antique double beds. Rooms 10 and 14, on the north and south ends, are notable for their spaciousness and Main Street views. Downstairs there's a companionable piano bar and a fancy restaurant whose menu features pricey delicacies such as roast duck Chambord. And you won't mind not having TV in your room when you discover the town's most recent addition: the restored, Spanish Mission-style Old Globe movie house, which shows classics exclusively.

Address: *2 N. Main St., Berlin, MD 21811, tel. 410/641-3589.*
Accommodations: *16 double rooms with baths.*
Amenities: *Restaurant, air-conditioning, phones in bedrooms.*
Rates: *$55–$125; Continental breakfast. MC, V.*
Restrictions: *No pets, 2-night minimum in summer.*

Chanceford Hall

What is a spruce little town like Snow Hill, Maryland, doing in among the chicken farms of the Delmarva Peninsula? For the answer, look to the narrow but deep Pocomoke River, which in the 17th and 18th centuries made Snow Hill a bustling port, frequented by tall-masted schooners sailing in from the Chesapeake. Today, if you like, you can stay at Chanceford Hall, a bed-and-breakfast inn that would have pleased any visiting Colonial dignitary. The mansion was constructed in three stages, beginning with the Georgian front section in 1759. Some 230 years later a pair of old-house restorers, Thelma and Michael Driscoll, moved in and turned Chanceford Hall into a showplace. The Federal-style mantels, painted in cool Williamsburg greens and blues,

match the moldings, and there are merino-wool mattress pads and down comforters on the lace-canopy beds. The house has seven working fireplaces and reproduction furniture crafted by Michael himself. Thelma welcomes guests with wine and hors d'oeuvres in the sitting room and will lend bikes or explain where to rent canoes for river exploring.

Address: *209 W. Federal St., Snow Hill, MD 21863, tel. 410/632–2231.*
Accommodations: *4 double rooms with baths, 1 suite.*
Amenities: *Air-conditioning, TV with VCR in sunroom, dinner on request; bicycles, lap pool.*
Rates: *$100–$125; full breakfast. No credit cards.*
Restrictions: *No pets.*

Vandiver Inn

Begin a trip to the Vandiver Inn by mastering the pronunciation of the town where it lies; it's Havre (rhymes with *cadaver*) de Grace, located where the Susquehanna River enters the Chesapeake Bay. The Marquis de Lafayette named Havre de Grace during the American Revolution; in the War of 1812 the British leveled the town, which explains its post-Colonial architecture. Indeed, on Union Avenue Victoriana prevails— and nowhere so flamboyantly as at the Vandiver Inn, a lime-green Queen Anne cottage built in 1886 by a Havre de Grace mayor. Inside you'll find a display of memorabilia (including his bride's high-button shoes) and large bedrooms. The Rodgers Room, which opens onto a porch, is a favorite. On Friday and Saturday evenings, innkeeper Mary

McKee, a graduate of the Culinary Institute of America, concocts lavish feasts for guests (the cost is extra). Although Havre de Grace is hardly cosmopolitan, it has its own eccentric diversions, including a Decoy Museum, a historic lighthouse, and a restored 1840 lock house, built to service the Susquehanna and Tidewater Canal.

Address: *301 S. Union Ave., Havre de Grace, MD 21078, tel. 410/939–5200.*
Accommodations: *6 double rooms with baths, 2 doubles share bath.*
Amenities: *Restaurant, air-conditioning.*
Rates: *$75–$95; full breakfast. AE, MC, V.*
Restrictions: *No pets.*

Virginia

Virginia

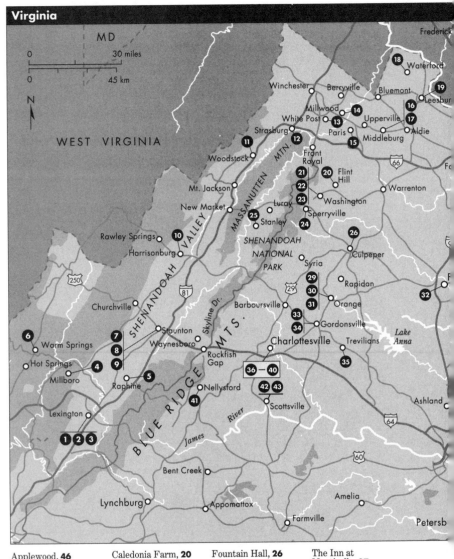

Liberty Rose, **48**
Miss Molly's, **57**
The Morrison
House, **28**
Newport House, **49**
The Norris House
Inn, **19**
North Bend
Plantation, **45**
Nottingham Ridge, **51**
Oak Spring Farm and
Vineyard, **5**

Pickett's Harbor, **52**
The Pink House, **18**
Prospect Hill, **35**
The Red Fox Inn, **16**
The Richard Johnston
Inn, **32**
Rocklands, **33**
Sea Gate, **53**
Seven Hills Inn, **2**
Sleepy Hollow
Farm, **34**

The Shadows, **30**
The Silver Thatch
Inn, **38**
Sycamore Hill, **23**
Thornrose House, **9**
Trillium House, **41**
200 South Street, **39**
War Hill Inn, **50**
The Watson House, **58**
Welbourne, **17**

Willow Grove
Plantation, **31**
Woodstock Hall, **40**
The Year of the
Horse, **59**

Northern Virginia

The verdant fields and rolling hills of northern Virginia have nurtured great numbers of American revolutionaries, and almost half the battles of the Civil War were waged in this countryside. Nowadays, though, it's refugees from Washington's bureaucratic wars who are claiming their rewards in northern Virginia. With the District's shiny office parks and shopping malls encroaching from the east, development is the area's only enemy, one being tenuously held at bay.

The fast track to this Eden west of DC is Route 66 (except on Friday and Sunday afternoon), but cognoscenti opt for Route 50, which in an easy hour of driving puts you in Middleburg, the capital of hunt-country. This discreet town breathes—and caters to—old money, with a collection of upscale galleries, antiques stores, and gun shops, with names like Dominion Saddlery, The Chronicle of the Horse, and Thoroughbreds. Hunt season in Loudoun, Fauquier, Clarke, and Rappahannock counties begins in late October with an opening meet, peaks around Thanksgiving, and continues into March, provided the ground doesn't freeze. Experienced riders can join in, but most content themselves with watching the colorful proceedings. A master of the hunt presides while tailgate picnickers slosh down coffee and Bloody Marys; then 20 or 30 hounds explode across the fields, followed by the handsomely outfitted riders.

Frankly, most hunt-country visitors prefer to spend their time window-shopping at Middleburg real-estate offices and driving Loudoun County's back roads. (Route 734 from Aldie to Bluemont is highly recommended, provided you're on the alert for careering Maseratis and BMWs.) These back roads lead to many country pleasures. Hamlets such as Hillsboro, Hamilton, Delaplane, Aldie, Purcellville, and Millwood offer plenty of opportunities for antiquing. All

*across the countryside, wineries—Naked Mountain,
Meredyth, Linden, Oasis—are flourishing. (For a map of
them, contact the Virginia Wine Marketing Program,
VDACS, Division of Marketing, Box 1163, Richmond 23209,
tel. 804/786-0481). Many farms have seasonal tours, pick-
your-own days, and choose-and-cut Christmas trees. (For
the "Farms of Loudoun Getaway Guide," contact the
Loudoun County Department of Economic Development,
Agricultural Development Office, 102 Heritage Way, NE,
Suite 303, Leesburg 22075, tel. 703/777-0426.)*

*Northeast of Middleburg lies Leesburg, founded about 1760,
which remained in Federal hands during the Civil War
and thus retains much of its Colonial architecture.
Leesburg's spruced-up storefronts and row houses are now
functioning as restaurants and shops.*

*South and west of Leesburg, a 30-mile corridor between the
hamlets of Flint Hill and Syria makes for peak auto
idling, too. Here the Blue Ridge asserts itself on the
horizon as the roads wind up into the foothills. Fauquier
County offers horseback riding in Shenandoah National
Park, with mounts to be claimed at the Marriott Ranch.*

*At the southern border of the area sits Fredericksburg,
boyhood stomping ground of George Washington, and hotly
contested site during the Civil War. Between 1862 and 1864
four major battles were fought—at Chancellorsville,
Wilderness, Spotsylvania Court House, and just south of
Fredericksburg itself—resulting in more than 17,000
casualties.*

*Established in 1749 by a group of Scottish merchants,
Alexandria—a mere 10-minute drive from Washington,
DC—has impeccable historical credentials. It was an
important Colonial port and a social and political center.
Tobacco was shipped from here to the smoky coffeehouses of
London, and dissident Scots rankling over the Act of
Union with England flocked here (which explains*

Alexandria's continuing fascination with things Scottish).
Alexandria is considered George Washington's hometown;
Light Horse Harry Lee and Robert E. Lee were both born
here. Old Town has more 18th- and 19th-century
architectural gems than any other city in the country.

A walk along Alexandria's shady lanes takes you by
handsome brick homes and offers peeks into mazelike
courtyards. Shoppers will find present-day Alexandria as
mercantile as ever. Ethnic variety makes dining both
outstanding and interesting; there are 80 restaurants
within walking distance of the visitors center.

The Saturday Morning Market at Market Square, by City
Hall, is the country's oldest operating farmers market
(George Washington sold produce from his farm here).
Vendors offer baked goods, fresh produce, plants, flowers,
and high-quality crafts. Come early; the market opens at
5 AM, and by 9:30 AM it's all packed up.

Places to Go, Sights to See

Alexandria Archaeology (tel. 703/838–4399). This research facility preserves the Colonial treasures hidden beneath the paving stones of Old Town.

Carlyle House (Alexandria, tel. 703/549–2997). Built in 1752 by Scottish merchant John Carlyle (and still the grandest house in town), it headquartered General Edward Braddock in 1755 when he summoned five Colonial governors to plot the strategy for the French and Indian War.

Christ Church (Alexandria, tel. 703/549–1450). Its parishioners included George Washington and Robert E. Lee.

Gadsby's Tavern Museum (Alexandria, tel. 703/838–4242). The rooms have been restored to their 18th-century appearance; of particular note is the hanging musicians gallery in the ballroom. George Washington socialized at **Gadsby's Tavern** next door (tel. 703/548–1288), which has dispensed spirits and victuals since 1795. Five U.S. presidents in all have signed the register there.

Gunston Hall (15 mi south of Alexandria, tel. 703/550–9220), the Georgian mansion of George Mason, author of the first Virginia constitution and Virginia Declaration of Rights, was built around 1755, with a Palladian parlor and Chinese-inspired dining room.

Historic Fredericksburg. Sights include the *Mary Washington House,* bought by a dutiful son for his retired mother, the *James Monroe Museum and Memorial Library,* the *Hugh Mercer Apothecary* shop, and *Rising Sun Tavern.*

Kenmore (tel. 703/373–3381). This Colonial mansion near Fredericksburg, famous for its decorative plaster moldings, was the home of George Washington's sister, Betty. Its drawing room has been called one of the 100 most beautiful rooms in America.

Manassas National Battlefield Park (tel. 703/361–1865). The scene of the First and Second Battles of Manassas, during which the Confederacy lost 11,456 men and the Union 17,170. This is where General Thomas J. Jackson's nickname was coined, when a soldier cried, "There stands Jackson like a stone wall! Rally behind the Virginians!"

Morven Park (tel. 703/777–2414) is a handsome Greek Revival mansion near Leesburg, built by a governor of Virginia, with a carriage museum and frequent special events, including steeplechase races.

Mount Vernon (tel. 703/780–2000). George Washington's estate lies 10 miles south of Alexandria. The museum holds Jean-Antoine Houdon's bust of Washington, as well as the first president's sunglasses and sword.

Oatlands (near Leesburg, tel. 703/777–3174), a Classical Revival mansion, was built in 1803 by George Carter, grandson of the Williamsburg planter, "King" Carter. Its terraced formal gardens are considered some of the most distinguished in the state.

Torpedo Factory (Alexandria, tel. 703/838–4565). It's just that: Naval torpedoes were produced here during World War II. The waterfront building is now a complex of workshops where artists produce and sell their works.

Trinity Church. West of Middleburg, in the hamlet of Upperville, this is one of the most beautiful Episcopal churches in America, the style being adapted from French country stone churches of the 12th and 13th centuries.

Waterford, a village north of Leesburg so reminiscent of rural England that it could tug at the heart of any Anglophile, is, from one end to the other, a National Historic Site.

White's Ferry. The historic ferry across the Potomac at the edge of Leesburg is now a six-car tugboat, the *General Jubal Early.* Dickerson, MD, tel. 301/349–5200, fare $4. Runs daily 5 AM–11 PM.

Restaurants

Many of northern Virginia's top inns offer outstanding meals. Not to be missed are the extraordinary dinners at the **Inn at Little Washington** (*see below*). At **Four and Twenty Blackbirds,** in Flint Hill (tel. 703/675–1111), all

the pastry is baked on the premises. Leesburg has a duo of fine restaurants:
Jordan's (tel. 703/777–1471), featuring contemporary American cuisine, and
Limelight (tel. 703/777–7492), for Continental fare. For local color,
reasonably priced sandwiches, and a fantastic selection of baked goodies, try
The Upper Crust (tel. 703/687–5666), across the street from Safeway in
Middleburg. In Alexandria, **Le Refuge** (tel. 703/548–4661) and **Le Gaulois**
(tel. 703/739–9494) are comfortable French bistros; **Landini Brothers** (tel.
703/836–8404) is the spot for fine Italian dining.

Tourist Information

Alexandria Convention and Visitors Bureau (221 King St., Alexandria
22314, tel. 703/838–4200). **Fairfax County Visitors Center** (7764 Armistead
Rd., Suite 160, Lorton 22079, tel. 800/724–7329). **Fredericksburg Visitors
Center** (706 Caroline St., Fredericksburg 22401, tel. 703/373–1776 or
800/678–4748). **Loudoun County Tourist Center** (108-D S. St., SE, Market
Station, Leesburg 22075, tel. 703/777–0518 or 800/752–6118). **Virginia
Division of Tourism** (1021 E. Cary St., Richmond 23219, tel. 804/786–4484).
Winchester and Frederick County Visitors Center (1360 S. Pleasant Valley
Rd., Winchester 22601, tel. 703/662–4135).

Reservation Services

Blue Ridge Bed & Breakfast Reservation Service (Rocks & Rills, Rte. 2,
Box 3895, Berryville 22611, tel. 703/955–1246). **Princely Bed & Breakfast
Reservation Service** (819 Prince St., Alexandria 22314, tel. 703/683–2159).
For a copy of **The Bed and Breakfast Association of Virginia's directory**,
describing more than 100 establishments, call the Virginia Division of
Tourism's B&B line (tel. 800/262–1293). The Division of Tourism's
Washington, DC, office also operates a **B&B and small-inn booking service**
(tel. 202/659–5523 inside the District, 800/934–9184 outside).

The Ashby Inn & Restaurant

West of Middleburg and Upperville along Route 50, the turnoff for minuscule Paris comes upon you suddenly; half the travelers looking for this hamlet in a hollow below the road probably miss it completely and end up crossing Ashby Gap or the Shenandoah River—not bad detours except that they delay your arrival at the Ashby Inn & Restaurant. Here you're treated to some of rural Virginia's most sophisticated food, prepared by chef Eric Stamer and masterminded by innkeepers Roma and John Sherman. The menu is changed nightly, though some Ashby favorites, like sautéed mixed mushrooms and duckling braised with turnips, routinely reappear. Dinner runs about $70 for two.

Perhaps the only danger in staying at the inn is that dinner will leave you too blissfully comatose to appreciate your room. The six rooms in the main building are furnished with a spareness that is a calming contrast to the rich food. Quilts, blanket chests, rag rugs, and the occasional cannonball bed set the country tone, though in every case, the views are the chief enhancement. As morning light shines through the windows, you'll spy the garden, the Blue Ridge foothills, lowing cows, and other pastoral delights. The coveted Fan Room has two skylights and a glorious fan window opening onto a private balcony.

There are four expansive rooms built into Paris's former one-room schoolhouse. Each has a private porch that opens onto those splendid countryside views. The Glascock Room has deep red walls, a four-poster bed, and an antique trunk with extra towels. Oriental rugs cover the hardwood floors, and there are two sinks in the large bathroom. Two wing chairs facing the fireplace and a window seat are inviting places to curl up with a book.

Roma, an avid horsewoman, and John are generally too busy during dinner to chat, but at breakfast—featuring fresh eggs cooked to order and succulent muffins—you might get to know your hosts. Roma left advertising for innkeeping, and John, once a House Ways and Means Committee staffer, still writes speeches for politicians and CEOs between stints as the Ashby Inn's maître d'.

Address: *Rte. 1, Box 2A, Paris, VA 22130, tel. 703/592–3900, fax 703/592–3781.*
Accommodations: *8 double rooms with baths, 2 doubles with sinks share a bath.*
Amenities: *Restaurant, air-conditioning; TVs, phones, and fireplaces in schoolhouse rooms.*
Rates: *$80–$175; full breakfast. MC, V.*
Restrictions: *No smoking in guest rooms; no pets, closed Jan. 1, July 4, Dec. 24–25.*

The Bailiwick

The Bailiwick's impeccable restoration befits its location in historic Fairfax. The early 19th-
century house sits on the old Ox
Road, one of the nation's first toll
roads. George Washington's will is
filed at the Court House across the
street; the first casualty of the Civil
War occurred on the Court House
lawn.

Thus it was only appropriate that
Anne and Ray Smith hire seven of
Washington's top decorators to fashion each room after a famous Virgin-
ian. The theme carries through from
favorite colors to portraits, accessories, and even biographies. Ray,
a prominent developer, and Anne like
to book guests in appropriate rooms;
thus, attorneys may find themselves
in the John Marshall.

All rooms have plump feather beds
and goose-down pillows, and no detail has been slighted. The window
treatment and red-and-gold scheme
in the Thomas Jefferson repeats the
decor of his bedroom in Monticello.
The James Monroe has fabric dupli-
cating material used for one of his
White House chairs (the 1816 order
was still on file). Lord Fairfax's coat
of arms determined the colors in his
room; its bath has a brocade shower
curtain. The current Lord Fairfax
was a recent guest here. The sumptuous third-floor bridal suite, the An-
tonia Ford (she was a Confederate
spy), has a pitched ceiling and dormer windows with pillowed seats.

Done up in tones of ivory, the suite
includes a Chippendale sitting room,
a king-size bed, and a bath with
whirlpool tub.

There are two elegant parlors for
lounging before the fire or taking
afternoon tea. One of them has full-
length portraits of Anne and Ray in
Colonial garb; Anne is holding the
keys to the Bailiwick.

The Smiths carry the Colonial authenticity into their dinners. Such
original recipes as Martha Washington's onion cream soup have been
adapted for modern tastes. The five-
course dinners cost $45; menus
change weekly, and there's a good
selection of Virginia wines. (The
Chippendale-designed garden recently yielded enough grapes for 36 bottles of Chateau Bailiwick.) From this
gem, guests can head west to the
countryside or hop the Metro into
the capital.

Address: *4023 Chain Bridge Rd.,
Fairfax, VA 22030, tel. 703/691-2266
or 800/366-7666, fax 703/934-2112.*
Accommodations: *13 double rooms
with baths, 1 suite.*
Amenities: *Restaurant, air-
conditioning, whirlpool tubs in 2
rooms, fireplaces in 4 rooms, 2
rooms wheelchair accessible, turndown service, robes.*
Rates: *$105–$225; full breakfast, afternoon tea. AE, MC, V.*
Restrictions: *No smoking indoors,
no pets.*

The Conyers House

If you want to climb Old Rag, make the scene at the meeting of the Rappahannock Hunt, have a group of companionable dogs lead you to a swimming hole (which a local church also uses for River Jordan-style baptisms), or go hilltopping on horseback, the Conyers House will suit you like a pair of jodhpurs. This 1790 Hessian soldier–built inn lies on a narrow country road southwest of Sperryville and shouldn't be attempted in the dark without directions. That's part of its charm—but only part.

The innkeepers, Norman and Sandra Cartwright-Brown, are responsible for the rest, for the Conyers House is a very comforting, personal place, stuffed with family mementos and curios the two have collected in their wanderings. In Uncle Sim's Suite, there's a stuffed zebra head and a Texas bed with—since everything's big in Texas—seven-foot posts. Jarring, you might wonder? Surprisingly not. One imagines that Sandra Cartwright-Brown could design a miniature golf course and still have it turn out tasteful.

She and Norman bought the house, which was a general store in 1810 and a hippie commune in the 1970s, as a summer retreat from their Chevy Chase, Maryland, home. The beige frame structure sits on the side of Walden Mountain. There are four porches and eight working fireplaces, seven of which are in the bedrooms. In addition to the six rooms in the main building, there's Springhouse Cottage and Hill House out back, where pets are allowed, not to mention a stall for your horse.

With prior arrangement, Sandra and Norman serve a seven-course dinner in the gigantic dining room with such entreés as local trout, tenderloin of pork braised in local cider, and breast of duck in orange sauce. The $67.50 price per person includes four wines, tax, and service.

The Conyers House has an air of unstuffy, slightly gone-to-seed elegance. It's the kind of place where you can appear for breakfast in jeans, disappear for the day canoeing on the Shenandoah, and return confident of being invited to sip a preprandial sherry.

Address: *Rte. 1 (Box 157), Slate Mills Rd., Sperryville, VA 22740, tel. 703/987-8025, fax 703/987-8907.*
Accommodations: *7 double rooms with baths, 1 suite.*
Amenities: *Air-conditioning, TV with VCR in common areas and suite, VCR in Springhouse and Hill House, double whirlpool bath in Hill House; riding arranged.*
Rates: *$100–$195; full breakfast, afternoon refreshments. No credit cards.*
Restrictions: *No smoking in bedrooms, 2-night minimum Oct.–mid-Nov. and on holiday weekends.*

The Inn at Little Washington

I n 1978 master chef Patrick O'Connell and his partner, Reinhardt Lynch, opened a restaurant that grew into a legend, in a village of 160 an hour and a half west of (Big) Washington, DC, in the eastern foothills of the Blue Ridge. From the outside the three-story white frame building looks like any quiet southern hotel; only the Chinese Chippendale balustrade on the second-floor porch suggests the decorative fantasy within. The sumptuous interior is the work of British designer Joyce Conwy-Evans, who has designed theatrical sets and rooms in English royal houses. The settees in the inn bear as many as 13 elegantly mismatched pillows each; the garden, with crab apple trees, fountain, and fish pond, cries out to be used as a backdrop in *The Importance of Being Earnest.* One bedroom has a bed with a bold plaid spread, shaded by a floral-print half-canopy— and, amazingly, the mélange works. And in the slate-floored dining room with Robert Morris wallpaper, a fabric-swathed ceiling makes guests feel like pashas romantically sequestered in a tent. (A room and a suite in the Guest House, across the street, are good for two couples traveling together, but the decor lacks the sumptuousness of the main building.)

Much has been written about Chef O'Connell's food, all of it giddily rhapsodic. The menu, which changes nightly, makes compelling reading it-self, and the five-course dinner costs $88 per person on Saturday, $78 Sunday and weekdays, not including wine and drinks. Some rare vintages rest in the 10,000-bottle cellar.

Breakfast, served overlooking the courtyard garden, is far above the usual Continental fare. Miniature pastries and muffins are tucked in a basket alongside tasty croissants; raspberries glisten in large goblets. Those not still sated from dinner can order, at extra cost, a full breakfast—a lobster omelet with rainbow salsa, a bourbon-pecan waffle.

Clearly the inn, with its staff of 40, is a place for indulgence, and anyone unwilling to succumb to it—both psychologically and financially— should opt for humbler digs. But judging from the waiting list, there are plenty of hedonists out there.

Address: *Middle and Main Sts., Washington, VA 22747, tel. 703/675–3800, fax 703/675–3100.*
Accommodations: *9 double rooms with baths, 3 suites.*
Amenities: *Restaurant, room service, air-conditioning and phones in rooms, robes, whirlpool baths and separate double showers in suites, turndown service, bicycles.*
Rates: *$230–$460 ($80 surcharge on Fri., Sat., holidays, and Oct.); Continental breakfast, tea and cookies at check-in. MC, V.*
Restrictions: *No pets, closed Tues. except in May, Oct., and late Dec.*

Bleu Rock Inn

Set on 80 acres of the Bleu Rock Farm, the Bleu Rock Inn enjoys a bucolic setting (if you disregard the front view to the highway). The Blue Ridge Mountains form the backdrop; a pond with ducks and geese, rolling pastures, and 7 acres of vineyards lie in the foreground. Guests can fish for bass and blue gill in the pond and pluck peaches and apples in the farm's orchards.

The guest rooms are pretty: simply, if unimaginatively, furnished in pastels, light woods, and lace curtains. Number 2 has a balcony with a mountain view, and its window overlooks the serene pond.

The food is the star here. (The inn has only five bedrooms but three dining rooms with fireplaces.) Owners Bernard and Jean Campagne operate the successful La Bergerie Restaurant in Alexandria. David Clawson wears a double hat as chef and third proprietor. His "modern cuisine" utilizes fresh local ingredients and emphasizes good health and nutrition.

Address: *U.S. 211 (Rte. 1, Box 555), Washington, VA 22747, tel. 703/987-3190, fax 703/987-3193.*
Accommodations: *5 double rooms with baths.*
Amenities: *Restaurant, air-conditioning, turndown service, disabled accessible.*
Rates: *$125 ($150 Fri., Sat., holidays, and Oct.); full breakfast. AE, MC, V.*
Restrictions: *No pets, closed Mon.*

Brookside

Even if Carol and Gary Konkel weren't such nice people, you would still like Brookside. This intimate bed-and-breakfast, right beside Spout Run and the historic Burwell Morgan Mill, was built in two stages in the 1780s by the grandson of Williamsburg's "King" Carter. It's a frame house with a bay added in the late 1800s, tucked into a picturesque hollow by a stream leading to the historic Burwell-Morgan Mill. The Konkels have an antiques shop and a gourmet take-out shop in the rear; they opened the B&B as a showplace for such treasures as a mid-1800s schoolmaster's desk, Staffordshire foxes, and everywhere horses—Carol's personal passion. The guest rooms have high feather beds, bed hangings, working fireplaces, and as a special bonus, Carol lays out antique nighties for ladies to wear. There's a housekeeping suite in the toll house that once taxed traffic over Spout Run. Antiquing and biking are occupations of choice here; Millwood's major industry is antiques, and Carol can attest that Jackie Onassis sometimes appears incognito to rummage through the village shops.

Address: *Millwood, VA 22646, tel. 703/837-1780.*
Accommodations: *3 double rooms with baths, 1 suite.*
Amenities: *Air-conditioning, fireplaces, turndown service.*
Rates: *$95-$140; full breakfast, afternoon tea. MC, V.*
Restrictions: *No smoking indoors, no pets, closed Mon.-Wed.*

Caledonia Farm

Before opening his Blue Ridge farmhouse to guests, Bill Irwin went to some 250 bed-and-breakfasts. An enthusiastic environmentalist, he has fought to keep a high-voltage cable out of the Fodderstack Valley. Caledonia Farm, built of local fieldstone in 1812, is now a landmark on the National Register and a Virginia Historic Landmark. On a clear day, you can see the Skyline Drive from it, and you can walk out the door and be atop The Peak (2,925 feet) in a little over two hours. There are two rooms on the second floor of the main house, and a suite occupies the old summer kitchen. Hessian soldiers who stayed after the Revolutionary War did much of the handsome carpentry. The historic and natural setting are the keynotes here—not luxury (the bathrooms, for instance, are simple, befitting a farmhouse). Bill is a host full of bonhomie and advice on exploring nearby caves and vineyards, hiking, cross-country skiing, and dining at the fine local restaurants. And he offers a menu of breakfast choices.

Address: *Rte. 1, (Box 2080), Flint Hill, VA 22627, tel. 703/675-3693.*
Accommodations: *2 double rooms share 1 bath, 1 suite.*
Amenities: *Air-conditioning, TV with VCR in common area, fireplaces in rooms, turndown service, wheelchair accessible, small conference room; bicycles, hayrides.*
Rates: *$80-$125 (50% surcharge Sat.); full breakfast. D, MC, V.*
Restrictions: *No smoking indoors, no pets, 2-night minimum in Oct.*

Fountain Hall

Fountain Hall, a baby-blue Colonial Revival mansion, is surrounded by boxwood bushes and reached by a long brick walkway. Steve Walker, the owner, opened it as a bed-and-breakfast out of sympathy for the business traveler; as night manager at a hotel in Niagara Falls he had listened to their tales of loneliness and displacement. So Steve and his wife, Kathi, their baby, and yellow lab, Oscar, provide business people temporarily stationed in Culpeper with a place to put down their briefcases and feel cared for. Fountain Hall is a bit cluttered, not plush—though a few of its bathrooms do have Jacuzzis—but it offers what many travelers deem essential: phones in every room, parlor TV and VCR, and comfortable corners for entertaining guests.

Downtown Culpeper is just a few blocks away, with the Davis Street Ordinary, its solitary hot spot, and the Amtrak station (where the Walkers will meet guests).

Address: *609 S. East St., Culpeper, VA 22701, tel. 703/825-8200.*
Accommodations: *5 double rooms with baths.*
Amenities: *Air-conditioning, phones in bedrooms, 1 room wheelchair accessible, bicycles.*
Rates: *$55-$105; Continental breakfast. AE, D, MC, V.*
Restrictions: *No smoking indoors, no pets, 2-night minimum on Oct. and holiday weekends.*

L'Auberge Provençale

L'Auberge Provençale is owned and operated by a fourth-generation chef from Avignon, who learned his art from his family. Behind the wide industrial stove in his jampacked kitchen, Alain Borel nightly concocts delicacies; he is renowned for his gourmet breakfasts, which have been known to include freshly baked croissants and lobster claws with tarragon maple syrup. The inn occupies a Victorianized 1750s stone house, but the feeling inside is all Provençale, with modern French prints, shelves of wine (only a few of the 200 varieties on the wine list), and carved Spanish carousel animals that are for sale. There are two additions to the main house. One has three *chambres* opening onto the herb garden and bright provincial prints and hand-painted tiles; number 9 features a canopied bed and a fireplace. In the main building, number 7 has a large upstairs deck. L'Auberge Provençale is a family-run inn, which, even more than the menu and decor, gives it its authentic French character.

Address: *Box 119, White Post, VA 22663, tel. 703/837–1375 or 800/638–1702, fax 703/837–2004.*
Accommodations: *9 doubles with baths, 1 suite.*
Amenities: *Restaurant, air-conditioning, fireplaces in 5 rooms, TV in suite.*
Rates: *$120–$175 ($25 surcharge Sat. and holidays); full breakfast. AE, DC, MC, V.*
Restrictions: *No pets, closed Mon., Tues., and Jan. 2–Feb. 10.*

The Morrison House

A Scottish flag snaps in the breeze above the white-pillared portico of the Morrison House, bespeaking the Scottish heritage of the owner, a Washington real-estate developer and world traveler. Robert E. Morrison built the five-story Federal-style building in 1985, under the eye of a curator from the Smithsonian. It's constructed of red brick laid in Flemish bond and has arched windows and a small fountained garden at the foot of the entryway. Little luxuries abound, including state-of-the-art marble bathrooms, triple-sheeting on the high mahogany beds, afternoon tea, and Mrs. Morrison's chocolate-chocolate-chip cookies in every room. All 45 guest rooms are different, decorated with camelback sofas, Chippendale-style chairs, swagged draperies, and a few fireplaces (which, alas, don't work). The Morrison House is a nine-block walk from a Metro station: Patrons can park their cars beneath the hotel and explore the District and Old Town Alexandria.

Address: *116 S. Alfred St., Alexandria, VA 22314, tel. 703/838–8000 or 800/367–0800 (800/533–1808 in VA), fax 703/684–6283.*
Accommodations: *42 double rooms with baths, 3 suites.*
Amenities: *Restaurant, room service, air-conditioning, TV with VCR with videotapes and in-house movies, turndown service, phones in rooms, robes, nonsmoking floor, wheelchair accessible.*
Rates: *$145–$250; breakfast extra. AE, DC, MC, V.*
Restrictions: *No pets.*

The Norris House Inn

Before leaving their marketing careers in California to become Virginia innkeepers, Pamela and Don McMurray spent four years looking at almost 200 B&Bs. In 1991 they finally settled on the Norris House, a handsome brick Federal-style home in the center of historic Leesburg. Once one of the finest properties in the area, the inn had been sadly neglected, and the Mc-Murrays have been busy with the restoration. Two celebrated early-19th-century builders, the Norris brothers, are responsible for the portico with turned spindles, the Adam-style mantel in the biscuit-toned Parlor, and the shiny wild-cherry bookcases in the Music Room. The Garden Room has a stenciled border along the walls and a four-poster bed with lace canopy. Across the gardens is the Stone House Tea Room, another McMurray business. Guests also have access to a full-service business center. The McMurrays are amateur genealogists, and they offer special packages to guests sharing their interest. But since 1991 there hasn't been much time for tracing ancestors.

Address: *108 Loudoun St. SW, Leesburg, VA 22075, tel. 703/777–1806, fax 703/771–8051.*
Accommodations: *6 double rooms share 3 baths.*
Amenities: *Air-conditioning, fireplaces in 2 rooms, turndown service, robes.*
Rates: *$85–$115; full breakfast, evening wine and cheese. MC, V.*
Restrictions: *No smoking indoors, no pets.*

The Pink House

The Pink House lies at a crossroads in the wee village of Waterford, founded in 1733 by Quakers. The town resisted embroilment in the Revolution but joined the Union during the Civil War, when Confederate troops laid to waste their rolling Loudoun County farms. Today the whole 1,400-acre town is a National Historic Landmark, special among such places because modern development hasn't touched its periphery. This Brigadoon is accessible by bike path from Alexandria or by car via Routes 7, 9, and 662. The Pink House is owned by Chuck and Marie Anderson, who love opera, books, theater, and long, cozy chats. The Opera Suite features 18th-century antiques, a whirlpool bath, TV with VCR, a baby grand piano, and a folk-arty mural depict-ing Waterford notables attending a gala at the Met. It also has a fireplace and a private entrance opening onto the Waterford fields, where walking is encouraged. Marie's breakfasts include Irish soda bread, but for lunch or dinner you'll have to drive to Leesburg (20 minutes away), as the village puts itself out for tourists only during the October Waterford Crafts Fair.

Address: *Waterford, VA 22190, tel. 703/882–3453.*
Accommodations: *1 suite.*
Amenities: *Air-conditioning, TV with VCR, whirlpool, fireplace, turndown service, phone, private outdoor sitting areas.*
Rates: *$90–$100; full English breakfast. No credit cards.*
Restrictions: *No pets.*

The Red Fox Inn

The Red Fox has always been at the center of things in Middleburg. In fact it predates the town, for the attractive yellow fieldstone structure was built by Joseph Chinn in 1728 at the halfway point on the road from Alexandria to Winchester. During the Civil War it served as the meeting place for General J.E.B. Stuart and Colonel John Mosby, and as a Confederate field hospital (the Tap Room's bar was an operating table). Today the Red Fox is still an inn, albeit a rather impersonal one, whose busy restaurant packs crowds into five dining rooms on the first and second floors. Given the tourist traffic, we suggest overnighters opt for rooms 18 or 19 on the top floor, or rooms in annexes called the Stray Fox Inn and McConnell House, which lie about a half block off Route 50. In the Stray Fox, ask for the palatial Belmont Suite, big enough to include a grand piano, or the snugger but equally attractive Hulbert Room, which has a fireplace. All the rooms are individually done in 18th-century antiques, and a *Washington Post* is delivered to your door with breakfast.

Address: *Rte. 50 (Box 385), Middleburg, VA 22117, tel. 703/687-6301 or 800/223-1728 (in DC, 202/478-1808), fax 703/687-3338.*
Accommodations: *12 double rooms with baths, 7 suites.*
Amenities: *Restaurant, TV and phones in rooms, fireplaces in 4 rooms, wheelchair accessible.*
Rates: *$125-$225; Continental breakfast. AE, D, DC, MC, V.*
Restrictions: *No pets.*

The Richard Johnston Inn

For such a sweet old town so tied up in history, Fredericksburg isn't exactly blessed in the inn department, but of all its choices the Richard Johnston is the best, owing to its prime Caroline Street location, just across from the visitors center. It's a diminutive-looking 18th-century brick rowhouse with a dormer on the third floor and a pleasant patio adjoining the parking lot in the rear, shaded by magnolia trees. Inside, restoration work has been top-drawer, and new owner Susan Thrush has lavished loving care on the immaculate inn. In the common rooms downstairs board floors are polished to a rich luster and covered with Oriental rugs. The furnishings are Chippendale- and Empire-style antiques. Still, the guest rooms above the kitchen are recommended; Room 8 holds a fireplace, rag rug, and brass double bed. Two commodious suites, with living rooms, wet bars, and wall-to-wall carpeting, open onto the patio.

Address: *711 Caroline St., Fredericksburg, VA 22401, tel. 703/899-7606.*
Accommodations: *7 double rooms with baths, 2 suites.*
Amenities: *Air-conditioning, TV in 3 rooms.*
Rates: *$85-$130; Continental-plus breakfast. AE, MC, V.*
Restrictions: *No smoking, no pets, closed Dec. 24-25.*

Sycamore Hill

Get out your cameras, please, for the serious photo opportunities at Sycamore Hill, a ranch-style house seemingly dropped from the sky onto the crest of Menefee Mountain. As you wind up the mile approach from town, you begin to doubt there could possibly be a lodging at the end of the road. Fear not. Eventually the forest gives way to Kerri Wagner's extensive gardens, and finally you arrive at the Virginia fieldstone house wrapped by a 65-foot veranda. The view from this spot is the raison d'être of Sycamore Hill—there's Old Rag to the right, Tiger Valley, and Red Oak Mountain. And the 52-acre lot is a certified wildlife sanctuary. With its views and gardens, this is a spot for the nature lover. The best view is from the 6-foot picture window in the Master Bedroom, which has a queen-size four-poster bed. Kerri Wagner is an energetic hostess who treats her guests like friends, aided by a shaggy white mop of a dog named Molly Bean, and her husband, Steve, an artist whose fascinating magazine covers line the walls.

Address: *Rte. 1 (Box 978), Washington, VA 22747, tel. 703/675–3046.*
Accommodations: *3 double rooms with baths.*
Amenities: *Air-conditioning, TV in living room.*
Rates: *$95–$120; full breakfast. MC, V.*
Restrictions: *No smoking indoors, no pets, 2-night minimum on holiday weekends and Oct.*

Welbourne

There are so many stories attached to this 1775 mansion that it makes your head spin. Thomas Wolfe visited and later wrote to his host, "Your America is not my America and for that reason I loved it even more." F. Scott Fitzgerald came often and set his short story "The Last Case" here. During the Civil War a Dulany of Welbourne served J.E.B. Stuart breakfast on horseback outside the front door. Beyond the stories, Welbourne is the genuine, blueblooded hunt-country article, a sweeping, yellow stately home fronted by six columns and surrounded by 550 acres. It's been in the same family for seven generations, though as owner Sherry Morison says, "We have the acreage, but not the bank account." Welbourne definitely isn't for everyone. Recognizing that the old homestead isn't in peak condition, Mrs. Morison downplays it. "Look at these bathrooms. They're awful," she says. But for lovers of history, they're not *so* awful—and perhaps the working Louis XIV table clock and 1790s French porcelain downstairs will compensate. Meanwhile, don't ask where she got the antiques; they've been in the family for years.

Address: *Middleburg, VA 22117, tel. 703/687–3201.*
Accommodations: *5 double rooms with baths, 3 cottages.*
Amenities: *Air-conditioning in bedrooms, fireplaces in 4 rooms and 2 cottages, TV in living room.*
Rates: *$85–$96 (plus $10 a day for firewood); full Southern-style breakfast. No credit cards.*

The Eastern Shore

*Most people think of the long peninsula east of the
Chesapeake Bay as territory claimed by the states of
Maryland and Delaware. Indeed, the most developed and
touristy parts of Delmarva are; but if you look closely at
a map you'll see a boundary line with the word* Virginia
*printed beneath. The border lies about 75 miles north of the
peninsula's tip, and in between is Virginia's very own
toehold on the Eastern Shore, encompassing two counties—
Northampton and Accomack—with a combined population
close to that of Charlottesville. The area was settled in the
1600s, by English Colonists; visited by vacationers (who
made the trip by ferryboat) in the 19th century; and
surveyed by the railroad, which reached the peninsular
terminus, at Cape Charles, in about 1885. Several decades
ago the peninsula was bisected by a highway, Route 13,
which brought some—but not many—1950s-style motels and
drive-in restaurants. Off Route 13, however, the Eastern
Shore lives and looks the way it did around the turn of the
century—no quaint restored villages or tony resorts. True
back-roaders will like it immensely—providing they
understand in advance a few basic facts.*

*Above all, Virginia's Eastern Shore is not a beach haven,
except for the stellar sandy stretches at its northeast corner
lying within the Chincoteague National Wildlife Refuge.
On the bay side, tidal creeks and marshes predominate.
Seaside, a string of barrier islands has kept beaches from
forming at the shoreline. The islands themselves are either
privately owned, or, like the islands of Cobb, Smith, and
Hog, are provinces of the Nature Conservancy's Virginia
Coast Reserve. To reach them you'll need to charter a boat
or sign up for one of the VCR's infrequent island trips.
There are spring and fall boat tours and three-day
photography weekends (tel. 804/442-3049) led by trained
naturalists.*

Nor are there any cities of note on Virginia's Eastern Shore, with the possible exceptions of Chincoteague, whose meager population swells in peak summer months but otherwise figures at about 3,500, and Cape Charles, which thrived during ferry and railroad days but now has only a cranking cement factory to keep it from becoming comatose. County maps show many other towns (with colorful names such as Temperanceville, Birds Nest, and Oyster), but these are really only crossroads with, if you're lucky, a general store. East of Route 13, skinny local arteries such as Routes 679 and 600 reach these villages and the architectural contradictions that surround them. The Virginia peninsula has its own unique building style, followed for hundreds of years: "chain" houses made of frame, consisting, when the pattern holds, of big house, little house, colonnade, and kitchen linked in a row. You can glimpse a good example, the privately owned Holly Brook Plantation, on the west side of Route 13, some 8 miles south of Nassawadox.

The town of Chincoteague lies on 8-mile-long Chincoteague Island (not to be confused with the island holding the wildlife refuge, Assateague Island, to which it provides access via a bridge) and exists almost wholly to cater to tourists, with motels, restaurants, and shops. It is atmospherically similar to other Atlantic beach resorts in Maryland and Delaware, but its low-lying, marshy location brings septic and mosquito problems. Nonetheless, it has one attraction that will probably never cease drawing crowds: the legendary Pony Penning event, held in late July. The miniature horses swim the channel between Assateague and Chincoteague and are then corraled and auctioned off, usually for about $400 each. This roundup began in 1924, though it was made nationally famous by Marguerite Henry's Misty of Chincoteague *in 1947. Misty herself was a real pony; her descendants can be seen, along with miniature horses, at the Misty Pony Farm in Chincoteague (tel. 804/336-3066).*

Places to Go, Sights to See

Accomac. A particularly pretty town and the seat of Accomack County, this is one of two villages on the Eastern Shore (the other is Eastville) with an 18th-century debtors' prison. The Victorian clerk's office on the west side of the courthouse green holds records dating to 1663.

Accomack Vineyards (tel. 804/442–2110). This peninsula winery near the town of Painter completed its first pressing in 1986. Wines produced and sold here include chardonnay, riesling, merlot, and cabernet sauvignon. Tours are available by arrangement.

Cape Charles, a place decidedly in the slow lane, was by 1953 abandoned by the passenger railroad and ferry service that made the town boom briefly around the turn of the century, then—to hammer the nails into its coffin— was bypassed by Route 13. Today most of its 136 acres are a historic district, though an unusual one because the houses date from the first quarter of the century. A walking tour takes you past two Sears-catalog homes built in the mid-1920s, the pleasant bayside boardwalk, and a wonderful art-deco moviehouse. Some will feel that industrial works to the south mar the townscape, though at these you can watch freight trains being loaded onto barges that take them across the mouth of the bay to Norfolk. In all, it's a funky, beyond-the-pale sort of place that attracts more and more refugees from northern metropolises, who are finding that they can still buy property in Cape Charles for a song.

Chesapeake Bay Bridge-Tunnel. This 17.6-mile engineering marvel links the peninsula with Norfolk and Virginia Beach. Completed in 1964, after costing taxpayers $400 million in concrete and steel, it has brought the Eastern Shore into the Virginia fold only to a degree, largely due to the hefty $10 toll each way—which, as some peninsula dwellers see it, keeps the Navy riffraff out. To support its mammoth span, islands were built, where there are scenic stopping places, a fishing area, and a snack bar; and to accommodate Chesapeake Bay ship traffic, the two-lane bridge gives way to two tunnels, one more than a mile long. The trip is either awesome, unsettling, or soporific, depending on the soundness of your stomach and nerves.

Chincoteague National Wildlife Refuge (tel. 804/336–6577). Despite the surfboarders and sun worshipers headed toward its long stretch of Atlantic beach, the refuge exists first and foremost for the benefit of birds, snakes, ponies, rare Delmarva gray squirrels, and Sika deer. Many of the species preserved in this veritable Noah's Ark are visible from a 6-mile loop drive that winds through forests and marshes. There are, as well, a visitors center, lighthouse (built 1866), crabbing ridge, and fishing area—but no restaurants, camping, or bonfires. In season the refuge sponsors fishing expeditions, evening cruises, and a wildlife safari (tel. 804/336–5593), which takes nature lovers along back roads where they can observe the intimate habits of the famed Chincoteague feral ponies.

Custis Tombs. The Custises were Eastern Shore gentry who married into the Lee and Washington clans. At this walled gravesite 6 miles north of the Bay Bridge-Tunnel on Route 644 you'll find the grave of John Custis, known chiefly for his legendarily chilly marriage to Frances.

Eyre Hall. The peninsula's handsomest and most historic plantation was built in 1733, on land granted to the owners in 1662. The brick and frame house near the Bay is open only during Historic Garden Week in April, but its grounds, with ancient plantings, flowering shrubs, and venerable trees, can be visited year-round. Turn left 3 miles above the Cheriton stoplight, onto the private lane opposite Route 636.

Hopkins & Bro. General Store (tel. 804/787–8220). This 1842 country store-cum-restaurant at Onancock's town dock is a Virginia Historic Landmark, with a companionable bar and a menu featuring shore inevitables such as crab cakes and seafood salad.

Kerr Place (tel. 804/787–8012). The distinguished brick mansion on the outskirts of Onancock was built in 1799. Housed within are the collections of the Eastern Shore of Virginia Historical Society, including costumes, portraits, and furnishings.

NASA Goddard Flight Center and Wallops Flight Facility Visitor Center (tel. 804/824–2298). The first rocket at this 6,000-acre NASA enclave (encompassing Wallops Island and areas surrounding Chincoteague) was launched in 1945. The visitor center, which is the only part of the complex open to visitors, displays space suits, moon rocks, and scale models of satellites and space probes. On the first Saturday of every month NASA conducts model-rocket launches on the grounds.

Pear Valley. Constructed in 1672, this is the peninsula's oldest house. This one-room cottage with a chimney and loft is owned by the Association for the Preservation of Virginia Antiquities, though currently it is unrestored. It can be seen from Route 689, near Johnsontown.

Refuge Waterfowl and Oyster Museums (tel. 804/336–5800 and 804/336–6117 respectively). These two tiny museums are neighbors on Piney Island (barely an island really, as it's only tenuously separated from Chincoteague, by skinny Eel Creek). The Waterfowl Museum has a collection of handcrafted decoys, and the Oyster Museum tells the life story of the bivalve and how generations of watermen have pursued it.

Tangier Island. To reach this tiny island, stuck like a buoy in the middle of Chesapeake Bay, catch the *Captain Eulice*, at Onancock harbor (tel. 804/787–8220), sailing June–September at 10 and returning at 3.
A livestock-grazing range before the Revolution, Tangier is now home to approximately 900 souls—most of them named Crockett, Parks, Thomas, and Pruitt—whose speech is Elizabethan cockney, barely changed since the first settlers moved in. It's an insular place, devoted to seafood harvesting and Methodism, with one main street, too narrow for cars, and the **Chesapeake House** (tel. 804/891–2331), whose reputation for family-style shellfish feasts

has spread far and wide. Slightly less renowned is **Double-Six** (tel. 804/891–2410), a local haunt once featured in *National Geographic* because it serves hot oyster sandwiches.

Wachapreague. This sleepy village on the Atlantic side of the peninsula once held a 30-room hotel and attracted vacationers from as far away as New York City. But the hotel burned down, leaving only the 340-odd permanent residents, along with a carnival ground that still lights up in late July. It remains a fishing mecca, with charter boats tied up to its dock; flounder is the prized catch.

Restaurants

There are two culinary stars on Virginia's Eastern Shore. At the **Channel Bass Inn** (Chincoteague, tel. 804/336–6148), Jim Hanretta serves Spanish, Basque, and Continental cuisine to 20 guests each night. At **The Garden and the Sea** (New Church, tel. 804/824–0672), Victoria Olian creates a French-flavored menu that changes every two weeks. Both are bed-and-breakfast establishments.

Naturally, seafood is on most menus in the area. For casual dining, try **Ray's Shanty** (Wattsville, tel. 804/824–3429), **AJ's on the Creek** (Chincoteague, tel. 804/336–9770), or the **Beachway** (Chincoteague, tel. 804/336–5590). **Armando's** (Onancock, tel. 804/787–8044), with its bistro atmosphere, and tiny, intimate **Nonnie's** (Chincoteague, tel. 804/336–5822; not recommended for children) both feature Italian fare. **Hopkins & Bro.** (Onancock, tel. 804/787–4478) is a pleasant setting for lunch. The very casual **Formy's Pit Barbecue** (Painter, tel. 804/442–2426) is the Shore's only barbecue restaurant.

Tourist Information

Chincoteague Chamber of Commerce (Box 258, Chincoteague 23336, tel. 804/336–6161). **Virginia Division of Tourism** (1021 E. Cary St., Richmond 23219, tel. 804/786–4484). **Virginia's Eastern Shore Tourism Commission** (Drawer R, Melfa 23410, tel. 804/787–2460).

Reservation Services

Amanda's Bed & Breakfast Reservation Service (1428 Park Ave., Baltimore, MD 21217, tel. 301/225–0001). **Bed & Breakfast of Tidewater Virginia Reservation Service** (Box 6226, Norfolk 23508, tel. 804/627–1983). **Inns of the Eastern Shore** (1500 Hambrooks Blvd., Cambridge, MD 21613, tel. 301/228–0575). For a copy of **The Bed and Breakfast Association of Virginia's directory,** describing more than 100 establishments, call the Virginia Division of Tourism's B&B line (tel. 800/262–1293). The Division of Tourism's Washington, DC, office also operates a **B&B and small inn booking service** (tel. 202/659–5523 or 800/934–9184).

The Channel Bass Inn

The Channel Bass occupies a pale-lemon building constructed in the 1880s—making it one of Chincoteague's oldest—and added onto in the 1920s, resulting in an untroubled asymmetry and a kind of appealing architectural buxomness. But the inn's design style, history, even its proximity to Chincoteague National Seashore, are all eclipsed by another feature—its restaurant.

Jim Hanretta, who is both innkeeper and chef, opened the Channel Bass in 1972, and since then its culinary reputation has spread. The restaurant is known for its unusual recipes, invented on the premises by Jim, who learned his craft in Barcelona. Here you'll find local seafood brightened with Spanish and Basque sauces, as well as French cuisine. Jim cooks every dish all alone in his compact kitchen, which is why only 20 people can be served each night; dining here is a little like hiring yourself a private chef. The dining room is intimate, with windows providing views of the romantically lit garden in back. Wedgwood china, silver, and linen table napkins are de rigueur. Of course, you pay dearly for the Channel Bass dining experience, with the average dinner for two running $110–$140, depending on the wines. (The private reserve list is topped off with an $800 bottle of 1966 Château Lafîte Rothschild). Breakfasts are on the pricey side, too—$15 for Continental, $15–$18 for one of Jim's breakfast soufflés.

The nine guest rooms, on the second and third floors, are luxurious, with original art on the walls, plump picture books on the coffee tables, triple-sheeted beds, down pillows, and Egyptian-cotton towels. But they don't have the unique personality the restaurant does; rather, they are immensely comfortable, very private neutral zones. (A romantic dinner can be arranged in the two suites.)

Off season, Jim holds special three-day cooking vacations, which include dinners and rooms as well as hands-on lessons in the kitchen, during which some of the Channel Bass's secrets are revealed.

Address: *100 Church St., Chincoteague, VA 23336, tel. 804/336–6148.*
Accommodations: *7 double rooms with baths, 2 suites.*
Amenities: *Restaurant, air-conditioning, TV in suites.*
Rates: *$140–$175; breakfast extra. AE, D, DC, MC, V.*
Restrictions: *No pets, 3-night minimum during Pony Penning, 2-night minimum on weekends, closed Dec. 20–Jan. 20 and holidays.*

The Garden and the Sea Inn

When Victoria Olian and her husband, Jack Betz, traveled to southern France in 1986, they hardly imagined that their enchantment with the area would lead to new careers as innkeepers in tiny New Church, just 1½ miles south of the Maryland border.

For 25 years they had lived in Washington, DC, where Jack was an attorney and Victoria an interior designer (her talent is evident at the inn). After the year in France on sabbatical from city life, they bought a country Victorian—the 1802 Bloxom's Tavern and its 1901 addition— which they remodeled and opened as the Garden and the Sea in 1989.

The quietly sophisticated, light and airy Garden and the Sea brings the feel of a small French inn to the Eastern Shore. The decor mixes antique furnishings, ballooning fabrics, Victorian moldings and detail, and bay windows. From the multicolored gingerbread trim on the wide front porch to the sunny, rose-hued dining room, it's exceptionally inviting. Guest rooms are spacious. In the main house, the Chantilly room, with a wicker sleigh bed and painted dresser, and the Garden Room, with floral prints and dark green lacquered wrought-iron furniture, both have large baths with double sinks and bidets.

A while back, Jack and Victoria moved New Church's oldest house onto the property. It's now the newly remodeled Garden House, with a music room and library, the honeymoon suite, and two other rooms, all three with whirlpool baths.

Victoria, who had worked with a chef in Provence, enrolled in culinary school and now creates the marvelous French meals of fresh ingredients from local farms and waters in menus that change every other week. Jack serves as the amiable maître d'. There are two fixed-price menus, as well as à la carte choices (entrées run about $15–$20). Specialties include bouillabaisse, grilled duck breast with cassis berries, and scallops with sautéed cabbage and parsley. There are quarterly chamber-music dinner concerts and occasional art shows.

The inn stands on Route 710, off Route 13, 15 minutes west of Chincoteague.

Address: *Box 275, New Church, VA 23415, tel. 804/824-0672.*
Accommodations: *5 double rooms with baths.*
Amenities: *Restaurant, air-conditioning, ceiling fans, whirlpools in 3 rooms, robes.*
Rates: *$84–$135; hearty Continental breakfast, afternoon tea. AE, D, MC, V.*
Restrictions: *No smoking in guest rooms, no pets, 2-night minimum on summer weekends, closed Nov.–Mar.*

The Burton House and Hart's Harbor House

The business of little Wacha-preague, on the Atlantic side of the peninsula, is fishing. It's always been that way, although a hundred years ago it attracted many more sports enthusiasts than it does today. The pretty village sits alone, though in late July its amusement park lights up for the Fireman's Carnival. The Burton House, just across the street from the carnival grounds, is a pale green, surprisingly ungingerbready Victorian built in 1883. In back there's a gazebo and deck, and to the side a rack of bikes, which guests may borrow.

Next door is the tan 1870 Hart's Harbor House. Friendly, down-to-earth Pat and Tom Hart have remodeled it into a three-bedroom B&B with fireplaces in the parlor, den, and kitchen. Both establishments are simply adorned and comfy. The Harts can arrange guided pontoon boat trips to the barrier islands.

Address: *9 and 11 Brooklyn St. (Box 182), Wachapreague, 23480, tel. 804/787-4560.*
Accommodations: *3 double rooms with baths, 6 doubles with half-baths share 2 baths.*
Amenities: *Air-conditioning, TV in parlors, bikes.*
Rates: *$65-$75; full breakfast, afternoon tea. MC, V.*
Restrictions: *No smoking, no pets, 2-night minimum on summer weekends, closed Dec. 24-25.*

Colonial Manor Inn

This exceptionally homey, neat, and reasonably priced inn has been owned and operated by the same family for more than 50 years. It lies on the road to Onancock, a bayside harbor town that's recently caught the attention of Chesapeake boat people, though it was founded 300 years ago. The white frame house has three stories and 20 rooms, 14 of which are guest chambers. For families traveling with children, hoping to spend something less than a fortune on lodgings, it's a godsend. Its huge, third-floor dormer room has a double bed and two singles and according to owner June Evans is intended to remind you of Grandmother's attic. Other guest rooms are small but adequately equipped, with sinks; here you'll find no frills—you will be served coffee but no breakfast. For that you'll have to head into town to the Corner Bakery or the Market Street Inn. Onancock harbor is the place to catch the cruise boat to Tangier Island. The town itself, with a number of 18th-century buildings and well-maintained frame houses overlooking the creek, is worth at least a brief nose around.

Address: *84 Market St., Onancock, VA 23417, tel. 804/787-3521.*
Accommodations: *4 double rooms with baths, 10 doubles share 3 baths.*
Amenities: *Air-conditioning, cable TV; parking for recreational vehicles and boats.*
Rates: *$40-$60; no breakfast. No credit cards.*
Restrictions: *No pets.*

Miss Molly's

Effusive hostess Barbara Wiedenheft immediately makes her guests at home in this 1886 Victorian on Chincoteague's Main Street. Miss Molly, daughter of the builder J.T. Rowley, lived in the house until she was 84. The sunny corner room named after her—it has roses on the walls, bedspread, and linens—is where Marguerite Henry stayed while she was writing *Misty of Chincoteague.*

Barbara and her husband, David, are expatriates from Washington, DC. (Barbara used to work for the British embassy and is fluent in three languages.) In good weather she serves what she laughingly calls her "world-famous" breakfasts and her "world-famous" tea (with homemade scones) on the screen porch, facing the channel and its fishing activity. There's some commercial areas nearby, but not enough to detract from the charms of this cozy spot.

Address: *4141 Main St., Chincoteague, VA 23336, tel. 804/336-6686.* **Accommodations:** *5 double rooms with baths, 2 doubles share 1 bath.* **Amenities:** *Air-conditioning, TV with VCR in parlor, beach towels.* **Rates:** *$89–$115; full breakfast, afternoon tea. No credit cards.* **Restrictions:** *No smoking, no pets, 2-night minimum on weekends, closed Jan.–early Feb.*

Nottingham Ridge

Bonnie Nottingham's sister-in-law, Sara Goffigan (of Pickett's Harbor just up the lane), convinced her that she should open her brick Williamsburg-style house, built in 1975, to guests. And so she did. Two miles off the main road, it shares a long stretch of private beach with Pickett's Harbor, as well as the smashing Chesapeake Bay sunsets and visitations by herons and egrets. Situated on the Eastern Flyway, this is a bird-watcher's paradise. Inside, it's a cheerful, slightly homier, less composed place than Pickett's Harbor, with two fireplaces in common rooms, a back porch, and three guest rooms.

Bonnie is a warm, lovable host. Be sure to sample her sweet-potato biscuits, scrapple, and homemade jam at breakfast. She can help you locate a charter boat for trips to Atlantic-side barrier beach islands, direct you to a nearby pond, and map out canoe trips on peaceful tidal creeks. Exact directions to both Nottingham's Ridge and Pickett's Harbor (neither has signs) are given with reservation confirmation.

Address: *Box 97–B, Cape Charles, VA 23310, tel. 804/331-1010 (at night).* **Accommodations:** *3 double rooms with baths.* **Amenities:** *Air-conditioning, TV in den; beach.* **Rates:** *$75; full breakfast, afternoon refreshments. No credit cards.* **Restrictions:** *No smoking, no pets, 2-night minimum on weekends Apr.–Oct.*

Pickett's Harbor

Sara and Cooke Goffigan's beige frame-and-brick house sits off an isolated road 4 miles north of the Chesapeake Bay-Bridge Tunnel and 2 miles west of Route 13. (You'll get more precise directions when your reservation is confirmed.) The front yard is a vast stretch of private beach frequented by deer and horseshoe crabs.

The house itself boasts high-ceilinged rooms furnished with antiques and family items. The floors were built of rafters from a 200-year-old barn on the James River. The one downstairs bedroom has a four-poster bed, easy chairs, and an exceptional water view. The upstairs rooms, separated by a narrow hallway, are pretty, too.

Sara serves a breakfast that routinely features sweet-potato biscuits, Virginia ham, and popovers. Before she heads off to teach school, you may be able to get her to talk about her family, a clan that came to the Eastern Shore in the 1600s, not long after Captain John Smith explored the peninsula.

Address: *Box 97–AA, Cape Charles, VA 23310, tel. 804/331-2212.*
Accommodations: *2 double rooms with baths, 4 doubles share 2 baths.*
Amenities: *Air-conditioning, TV in common areas.*
Rates: *$85–$100; full breakfast. No credit cards.*
Restrictions: *Smoking on porch only, no pets, 2-night minimum on holiday weekends, closed Christmas.*

Sea Gate

Jim Wells and Chris Bannon, both formerly of New York City (as are so many recent arrivals to the town), have laughingly taken to calling Cape Charles "the Cape." The Sea Gate was built in 1912; it's a rotund pink frame house a block from the water, on one of the town's prettiest residential streets. There's a wide porch out front, a grand piano in the entryway, and fireplace in the living room. The furnishings are comfortable but hardly rare; rather, it's the relaxed tone of the place, and the interesting shapes of some of the guest rooms, that are winning. Generally guests sit up late talking in the living room—about 1930s musicals, Tahitian islands, real estate, anything. The next morning at breakfast (perhaps French toast made from homemade cinnamon

bread) the conversation picks up as if it had never ended. Then it's off to explore Cape Charles, followed by a visit to the beach, afternoon tea, and phenomenal sunset-watching. For dinner in town, there's Rebecca's or the Cape Charles Pizzeria.

Address: *9 Tazewell Ave., Cape Charles, VA 23310, tel. 804/331-2206.*
Accommodations: *1 double room with bath, 2 doubles with half-baths and 1 double with sink share 1 hall bath.*
Amenities: *Air-conditioning, TV and clock radio in rooms; bicycles.*
Rates: *$60–$75; full breakfast, afternoon tea. No credit cards.*
Restrictions: *Smoking in public areas only, no pets, 2-night minimum on holiday weekends.*

The Watson House

With freshly painted gingerbread trim, hanging planters, pots of flowers, and wicker rockers, the Watson House porch is a charmer. The innkeepers—David and JoAnne Snead, their daughter Jacque Derrickson, and Jacque's husband, Tom—had no experience in the field, but, inspired by a workshop in Cape May, they restored an 1873 Victorian "disaster" to perfection in less than a year.

Chincoteague's newest bed-and-breakfast opened for business in the spring of 1992. The deluxe rooms have sitting porches. The inn blends the new shine of a fine restoration with the traditional B&B touches: It's an immaculate mix of antiques, wicker, lace curtains, floral wallpaper, and needlework.

Address: *4240 Main St. (Box 905), Chincoteague, VA 23336, tel. 804/336-1564.*
Accommodations: *6 double rooms with baths.*
Amenities: *Air-conditioning, clock radios and ceiling fans in rooms, TV in library; bicycles, beach chairs, outdoor shower.*
Rates: *$69–$99; full breakfast, afternoon tea. MC, V.*
Restrictions: *No smoking indoors, no pets, 2-night minimum on weekends, 3-night minimum on holidays, closed Dec.–Feb.*

The Year of the Horse

Every year one man comes to the Year of the Horse just to crab, spending his days on the 50-foot dock overlooking Chincoteague Sound. For those similarly inclined, the Year of the Horse is an excellent casual, almost funky retreat, occupying a summer house built in the 1920s, whose garage once stabled Misty's colt, Cloudy. Carl Bond has surrounded it with Florida-style lawn ornaments—pink flamingos and the like—and filled its sitting rooms with a weird assortment of collectibles, including a rocking camel, fedora-decked hat rack, Buddha, and Victorian fainting couch. Three guest rooms looking out on the bay have private decks. Room number 1 offers white wicker furnishings and a private balcony with a channel view, but the rest of the rooms have motel-style decor. There's also a two-bedroom, one-bath apartment. Carl is a tall, lanky man, soft-spoken and just plain nice; when guests don't finish the cinnamon rolls, he takes the leftovers out to the school-bus stop and distributes them to the kids.

Address: *600 S. Main St., Chincoteague, VA 23336, tel. 804/336-3221.*
Accommodations: *2 double rooms with baths, 1 efficiency with kitchenette and bath, 1 apartment with kitchen.*
Amenities: *Air-conditioning, kitchen in 1 double, cable TV; dock.*
Rates: *$75–$95; Continental breakfast (except apartment). D, MC, V.*
Restrictions: *No pets, 2-night minimum on weekends, 3-night minimum on holidays, closed Dec.–Feb.*

Williamsburg and the Peninsula

*"Down in Virginia there is a little old-fashioned city called
Williamsburg. It stands on the ridge of the peninsula that
separates the James and York Rivers." This is how* The City
of Once Upon a Time, *a children's book written by Gilchrist
Waring in 1946, opens. That book and* The Official Guide to
Colonial Williamsburg *are two of the best introductions to
the legendary city, which is visited by a million people
every year.*

*As both books explain, Williamsburg was the capital of
Virginia between 1699 and 1780, when the colony was
immense, extending west to the Mississippi River.
A planned city like Annapolis, Maryland, and a thriving
business center serving the farms and tobacco plantations
between the rivers, it was a beautiful place and still is. In
1926 the rector at Williamsburg's Bruton Parish Church
persuaded John D. Rockefeller to restore the town, and the
continuing project has resulted in a living-history museum
of 173 acres, a mile long and half a mile wide, holding 88
restored and 50 major reconstructed buildings and
surrounded by a 3,000-acre "greenbelt." The restoration has
become a pattern for similar endeavors nationwide.
Outlying malls and commercial strips woo travelers with
shopping opportunities at bargain emporiums like the
Williamsburg Pottery Factory and Berkeley Commons. The
charming Merchant's Square, adjoining the historic
district, houses a movie theater, restaurants, and 34 shops.*

*Once you've located Colonial Williamsburg proper, you can
simply wander in and soak up the atmosphere, perhaps
slaking your thirst on a cup of cider, peddled streetside, or
you can stop at the visitor center (tel. 804/220–7645 daily
8:30–5), which lies off the Colonial Parkway (the National
Park artery that connects Jamestown, Williamsburg, and
Yorktown), to view a 35-minute film and buy passes that*

entitle you to enter the buildings and ride the fleet of shuttle buses that link the top sights.

Williamsburg is not the oldest English settlement in the United States. That title is held by nearby Jamestown, where a sea-weary party of 104 men and boys aboard the Sarah Constant, Godspeed, *and* Discovery *landed in 1607 and hung on, despite hostile Indians, disease bred in nearby swamps, and chaos engendered by the fear that they'd been forgotten by suppliers across the Atlantic. Today Jamestown Island, the site of a national park, is a much more rustic place than civil Williamsburg.*

It is entirely understandable that visitors to the area should feel overwhelmed. Besides Jamestown and Williamsburg there's nearby Yorktown to explore (the scene of the last battle of the Revolution and the surrender of General Cornwallis) and scores of plantations along the James that should not be missed. Charles City County, which hugs the river between Richmond and Williamsburg, is truly a place apart. The same handful of families have owned and farmed its plantations since the 17th century and have stoically kept development out. So a drive along Route 5, which offers access to all the historic homes, makes a scenic trip indeed.

Finally, the thing to keep in mind about Williamsburg's bed-and-breakfasts is that none of them lies within the historic district; indeed, none of them occupies a historic home, though a number of them are exceedingly fine places to stay. Those intent on booking accommodations in a bona fide Colonial structure with a historic pedigree should contact the Williamsburg Inn (tel. 804/229–1000 or 800/447– 8679). It manages 85 rooms in taverns and houses in the restored district.

Places to Go, Sights to See

Abby Aldrich Rockefeller Folk Art Center (tel. 804/2200–7670). Some 3,000 pieces—furniture, paintings, carvings, textiles, and decorative useful wares— make this the nation's leading American folk-art center. Mrs. Rockefeller's 424-work collection forms the core.

Busch Gardens/The Old Country (off Rte. 60, tel. 804/253–3350). This theme park re-creates things German, French, Italian, and English and offers rides on such curiosities as the Loch Ness Monster, Roman Rapids, Drachen Fire Roller Coaster, and Big Bad Wolf.

Carter's Grove (tel. 804/220–7452). An 18th-century plantation 8 miles east of the historic district, Carter's Grove was built in 1750 by a grandson of the Colonial tobacco tycoon Robert "King" Carter and renovated and enlarged in 1928. It's now part of the Colonial Williamsburg Foundation, and a lovely one-way country road wends its way back to the historic district. The Winthrop Rockefeller Archaeological Museum explores the discovery of the Wolstenholme Towne site here. This village had fewer than 50 inhabitants; all were massacred by Indians in 1622.

The College of William and Mary. The second oldest college in the United States was founded in 1693 by charter from King William and Queen Mary of England. Its centerpiece, the Wren Building, begun in 1695, is the oldest academic building still in use in the country.

Colonial Williamsburg (tel. 800/447–8679). In the restored district, some of the most interesting historic buildings are the *Capitol*, where Patrick Henry delivered his famous speech, *Bruton Parish Church*, and the handsome *Governor's Palace*, with its stable, kitchen, exquisite gardens, and working wheelwright's shop. The *Courthouse* in *Market Square*, fronted by pillories and stocks, offers reenactments of 18th-century court trials. Along Duke of Gloucester Street are the *Printing Office, Shoemaker's Shop*, the *James Anderson Blacksmith Shop*, and *Golden Ball Silversmith*. Crafts shops in the historic district include *Prentis Store*, for pottery, baskets, soaps, and pipes; the *Post Office*, for books, prints, maps, stationery, and sealing wax; and *Raleigh Tavern Bake Shop*, for gingercakes and cider.

DeWitt Wallace Decorative Arts Gallery (tel. 804/220–7724). This modern museum behind the Public Hospital in Williamsburg contains 10,000 examples of English and American furniture, ceramics, textiles, and costumes primarily from the 17th and 18th centuries.

Historic Air Tours (Williamsburg Airport, tel. 804/253–8185 or 800/822–9247). Narrated flights over Colonial Williamsburg, Yorktown, Jamestown, the James River Plantations, and Hampton Roads—an intriguing perspective on the area's history and growth.

The James River Plantations. On state Route 5, where descendants of Virginia's earliest families still live, work, and preserve a way of life spanning three centuries, these estates are open for tours. **Berkeley** (tel. 804/829–6018) is a perfect Georgian. Built in 1726 and later inhabited by Benjamin Harrison, a signer of the Declaration of Independence, and two U.S. presidents, William Henry Harrison and Benjamin Harrison, it is surrounded by 10 acres of formal boxwood gardens. You can dine in its Coach House Taverns. **Evelynton** (tel. 804/829–5075 or 800/473–5075) was the site of several fierce Civil War skirmishes. Today the 2,500-acre farm is still family-owned and -occupied, the house filled with photographs and portraits. **Sherwood Forest** (tel. 804/829–5377) was purchased in 1842 by John Tyler, the 10th president of the United States, who moved here when he left the White House. The current occupants are the third generation of Tylers to live here. At 321 feet, this is the longest frame house in the country. **Shirley Plantation** (tel. 804/829–5121 or 800/232–1613), a Georgian house surmounted by a hand-carved pineapple finial, has been owned by 10 generations of Hills and Carters (Anne Carter was the mother of Robert E. Lee). Shirley was founded six years after the settlers arrived in Jamestown; the house went up in 1723. Especially noteworthy are its three-story "flying" staircase, which appears completely unsupported, and the Queen Anne forecourt. **Westover** (tel. 804/829–2882), seat of the Byrd family, is one of the finest Georgian plantations in the United States. Its spectacular grounds are open daily, though the house can be seen only in late April, during Virginia's Historic Garden Week.

Jamestown Colonial National Historical Park (tel. 804/229–1733). The site is an island, which is why the colonists selected it as a settlement site in 1607. It was to prove a bad choice; in one year alone nine-tenths of the settlers died of starvation, violence, or disease, and the capitol there burned four times before it was relocated to Williamsburg. You'll find a visitor center, museum, paths leading through the ruins of "James Cittie," a scenic loop drive, and Glasshouse, where craftspeople demonstrate one of Virginia's first industries, glassblowing.

Jamestown Settlement (adjacent to the National Historic Site, tel. 804/229–1607). Run by the state of Virginia, this outdoor re-creation of Jamestown village offers reproductions of James Fort, a Powhatan Indian village, and full-scale replicas of the three ships that brought the original settlers.

The Mariner's Museum (Newport News, tel. 804/595–0368). Here maritime history is documented, from the Indian dug-out canoe and Chesapeake workboats to modern shipbuilding at Newport News.

Virginia Air & Space Center (tel. 804/727–0800 or 800/296–0800). The center depicts Hampton Roads' importance to aviation and serves as the official visitor center for the NASA Langley Research Center, where the first Mercury astronauts trained in the 1960s. It includes an IMAX theater, full-size aircraft and spacecraft, and a seven-story observation deck.

Williamsburg Winery (tel. 804/229–0999). Tours and tastings. Especially noteworthy are the chardonnay and the Governor's White.

Yorktown and **Yorktown Battlefield Colonial National Historic Park** (tel. 804/896–3400). Here Washington laid siege to Cornwallis's army, and in 1781 the British surrendered in the (restored) Moore House. English, French, and American breastworks still line the battlefield, and it's a good idea to stop first at the visitors center to view the dioramas and rent a taped tour.

Yorktown Victory Center (tel. 804/887–1776), a multimedia museum, offers a film about the Siege of Yorktown, a timeline walkway, and a re-created Continental Army camp with costumed interpreters.

Restaurants

When hunger overtakes you, you'll find Colonial taverns are scattered around Williamsburg's historic district, among them the **King's Arms, Shields,** and **Chownings** (tel. 804/229–2141). These serve such traditional fare as prime rib, game pie, Sally Lunn (slightly sweet raised bread), and peanut soup. For expensive formal dining there's the award-winning **Regency Room,** at the Williamsburg Inn (tel. 804/229–2141). The **Trellis** (tel. 804/229–8610), in Merchant's Square, features a seasonally changing menu of regional food and decadent desserts. The **Old Chickahominy House** (Jamestown Rd., tel. 804/229–4689) is noted for its Brunswick stew; **Pierce's** (tel. 804/565–2955), just off I–64, has good barbecue; and at **Indian Fields** (Rte. 5, tel. 804/829–5004) the menu includes such Tidewater delicacies as Virginia ham in pineapple-raisin sauce, and scallops in puff pastry.

Tourist Information

Colonial National Historical Park (Jamestown–Yorktown) (Superintendent, Yorktown 23690, tel. 804/898–3400). **Colonial Williamsburg Foundation** (Williamsburg 23187, tel. 804/229–1000 or 800/447–8679). **Jamestown-Yorktown Foundation** (Box JF, Williamsburg 23187, tel. 804/253–4838). **Virginia Division of Tourism** (1021 E. Cary St., Richmond 23219, tel. 804/786–4484). **Virginia Peninsula Tourism** (8 San Jose Dr., Suite 3B, Newport News 23606, tel. 804/873–0092 or 800/333–7787). **Virginia Plantation Country** (Box 1382, Hopewell 23860, tel. 804/541–2206). **Williamsburg Area Convention & Visitors Bureau** (Box GB, Williamsburg 23187, tel. 804/253–0192 or 800/368–6511).

Reservation Services

Bensonhouse (2036 Monument Ave., Richmond 23220, tel. 804/648–7560). For a copy of **The Bed and Breakfast Association of Virginia's directory,** describing more than 100 establishments, call the Virginia Division of Tourism's B&B line (tel. 800/262–1293). The Division of Tourism's Washington, DC, office also operates a **B&B and small-inn booking service** (tel. 202/659–5523 or 800/934–9184).

Edgewood

Says frothy innkeeper Dot Boulware in her liquid southern accent, "I have to tell you, I am a romantic." And so is Edgewood—three marriage proposals were made in one week here. But before she and her husband, Julian, bought Edgewood Plantation, on scenic Route 5 approximately half an hour from Colonial Williamsburg, in 1978, she didn't care a bit for Victoriana. Fortunately tastes change, and when she became the mistress of an 1850s Carpenter Gothic house she began collecting Victorian antiques like a woman possessed.

Dot's eight-bedroom house, visible from Route 5, looks on the inside like Miss Havisham's dining room, minus the cobwebs. It is full to bursting with old dolls, antique corsets and lingerie, lace curtains and pillows, love seats, baby carriages, stuffed steamer trunks, mighty canopied beds, highboys, Confederate caps . . . the list goes on and on. At Christmastime she personally decorates 20 trees and festoons the banister of the graceful three-story staircase with bows. Clearly, more is more at Dot Boulware's Edgewood.

In her hands, Victoriana is thoroughly feminine, even though in one chamber, the Civil War Room, she's tried to cater to the opposite sex, decorating with intimate details of men's 19th-century apparel. Large people of either sex will have a hard time moving freely in this wildly crowded bed-and-breakfast. Lizzie's Room, the favorite, has a king-size pencil-post canopy bed and a private bath. The room enshrines the memory of a teenager who, Dot says, died of a broken heart when her beau failed to return from the Civil War. Prissy's Quarters, upstairs in the carriage house, has a kitchen area.

Breakfast is served in the dining room by candlelight. The brick-walled, beamed-ceilinged basement is a cozy sitting area with a fireplace, backgammon board, TV, and popcorn machine. Outside there's an unrestored mill house dating from 1725, an antiques shop, gazebo, a swimming pool, and a formal 18th-century garden (which makes a delightful wedding setting). Edgewood is centrally located for touring the James River plantations and is down the road from the area's best restaurant, Indian Fields.

Address: *4800 John Tyler Memorial Hwy., Charles City, VA 23030, tel. 804/829–2962 or 800/296–3343.*
Accommodations: *3 double rooms with baths; 4 doubles share 2 baths; 1 suite.*
Amenities: *Air-conditioning, turndown service, phones on request; swimming pool, bicycles.*
Rates: *$90–$155; full breakfast, afternoon refreshments. MC, V.*
Restrictions: *No pets, no smoking in rooms, 3-night minimum on holiday weekends.*

Liberty Rose

Bed-and-breakfast keepers in Williamsburg are in something of a bind. Because all the historic buildings in town are owned by either the Williamsburg Foundation or the College of William and Mary, they can't offer travelers authentic Colonial accommodations. Some have Colonial-style decoration anyway, but others, like Sandy and Brad Hirz, owners of the Liberty Rose, have come up with different, imaginative solutions to the dilemma.

Understand first that Sandy and Brad are a tremendously romantic story. They were just friends when Sandy decided to leave the West Coast to open a B&B in Williamsburg. Brad was helping Sandy house-hunt when they looked at a 1920s white clapboard and brick home a mile west of the restored district (on the road to Jamestown), and Sandy bought it in five minutes. Then Brad started seriously courting her, but it was Sandy, and not the B&B, who inspired him. Now they're a devoted married couple who run Williamsburg's most romantic B&B, decorated à la nouvelle Victorian with turn-of-the-century touches.

Sandy, a former interior designer, has a special talent for fabrics and is responsible for the handsome tie-back curtains, many-layered bed coverings, and plush canopies. The patterns are 19th-century reproductions. Brad has held up his end of the business by managing remodeling details. The bathrooms are particularly attractive: One has a floor taken from a plantation in Gloucester, a comfortable claw-foot tub, and an amazing free-standing, glass-sided shower. The sumptuous Suite Williamsburg has an elaborate carved-ball-and-claw four-poster bed and a fireplace. All rooms have a TV with VCR with a collection of films and an amenities basket bulging with everything the traveler might need, from bandages to needle and thread. The furnishings are a copacetic mix of 18th- and 19th-century reproductions and antiques. Antique handmade Santas, black folk art, Russian dolls, and Noah's Ark carvings are tucked away in corners and sold in the tiny gift shop.

Liberty Rose sits on a densely wooded hilltop, and the lake on the William and Mary campus is a pretty walk away. Romance, above all, is the tone pursued and achieved at Liberty Rose.

Address: *1022 Jamestown Rd., Williamsburg, VA 23185, tel. 804/253–1260.*
Accommodations: *2 double rooms with baths, 2 suites.*
Amenities: *Air-conditioning, TV with VCR, turndown service.*
Rates: *$95–$165; full breakfast. MC, V.*
Restrictions: *No smoking indoors, no pets.*

North Bend Plantation

Routinely, a stay at this Charles City County plantation begins with a tour of the house and grounds conducted by Ridgely Copland, a farmer's wife and a nurse (several years ago named Virginia nurse of the year). Along the way Ridgely points out Union breastworks from 1864, wild asparagus, herds of deer, a swamp, and the wide James River. Only one other Virginia bed-and-breakfast—Welbourne, near Middleburg—is so strikingly authentic, but North Bend differs from that slightly gone-to-seed mansion in that it's a well-maintained working farm. The Coplands are salt-of-the-earth people striving to keep their 850 acres intact in the face of modern agricultural dilemmas.

North Bend, on the National Register and also a Virginia Historic Landmark, was built for the sister of William Henry Harrison, the ninth president. It's a fine example of the Academic Greek Revival style, a wide white frame structure with a red roof and a slender chimney at each corner. Built in 1819 with a classic two-over-two layout, large center hall, and Federal mantels and stair carvings, it was remodeled in 1853 along Asher Benjamin designs. But beyond its architectural distinctions, North Bend is drenched in history. Its premier guest bedroom represents both sides of the Civil War. It contains a walnut desk used by the Union general Philip Sheri-

dan, complete with his labels on the pigeon-holes. His map was found in one of its drawers, and a copy is framed on the wall of the billiard room. The room's bed belonged to Edmund Ruffin, the ardent Confederate who fired the first shot of the war at Fort Sumter. The headboard is a reproduction; the Yankees shot out the original one in 1864.

Above all, though, at North Bend history means family. George Copland is the great-great-nephew of William Henry Harrison and the great-great-grandson of Edmund Ruffin. Family heirlooms are everywhere, as is the amazing collection of Civil War first editions, which make fascinating bedtime reading. There's an inviting upstairs wicker-furnished sun porch, and the cozy children's area has vintage toys.

Address: *12200 Weyanoke Rd., Charles City, VA 23030, tel. 804/829–5176 or 800/841–1479 (after 5:30).*
Accommodations: *4 double rooms with baths, 1 suite.*
Amenities: *Air-conditioning, TV, robes, turndown service; tandem bicycles, croquet, horseshoes, swimming pool.*
Rates: *$95–$110; full breakfast. No credit cards.*
Restrictions: *Smoking on porches only, no pets. Closed Dec. 25.*

Applewood

Applewood, so named because its owner collects things with an apple theme, is a spotlessly tidy bed-and-breakfast on Richmond Road, about four blocks from the historic district. It contains ceramic apples, apple prints, and even a copy of John Cheever's *The World of Apples*. Like other houses in the area, it was built in the late 1920s by a Colonial Williamsburg restorer, who added many of the kinds of details he'd been working on in the historic area: The house has a Flemish-bond brick exterior, a handsome 18th century-style portal, and detail crown moldings in the interior—and the trim is painted in those milky blues and greens that are so common in Williamsburg. Applewood has four bedrooms for travelers; one suite has a canopy bed,

fireplace, private breakfast area and entrance, and a convertible sofa bed—a fine choice for families with children. And the Golden Pippin Room sleeps four, one in a trundle bed. Innkeeper Fred Strout serves afternoon tea and a deluxe Continental breakfast, including, of course, apple muffins.

Address: *605 Richmond Rd., Williamsburg, VA 23185, tel. 804/229–0205 or 800/899–2753.*
Accommodations: *3 double rooms with baths, 1 suite.*
Amenities: *Air-conditioning, TV in parlor, portable phones; bicycles.*
Rates: *$70–$100; Continental breakfast, afternoon tea. MC, V.*
Restrictions: *No smoking indoors, no pets, 2-night minimum on holiday and special-events weekends.*

Colonial Capital

The Colonial Capital, a frame three-story house painted spring-mist green, is within walking distance of the historic district, Merchant's Square, and the College of William and Mary. The exceedingly nice innkeepers, Phil and Barbara Craig, are a retired stockbroker and a university administrator who moved to Williamsburg after 25 years in North Carolina. The Colonial's five rooms are named after Tidewater-area rivers. The York has an enclosed, canopied high rope bed. Prettiest, though, is Pamlico, with dormer windows on three sides and a white-canopied bed. The third floor can be made into a two-bedroom suite, a plus for families. Downstairs, there's a large living room with a wood-burning fireplace and access to a sun porch, where the

Craigs keep games, books, and puzzles. And, perhaps best of all, the Colonial Capital has parking in the rear for guests, which could otherwise prove a serious problem in teeming Williamsburg.

Address: *501 Richmond Rd., Williamsburg, VA 23185, tel. 804/229–0233 or 800/776–0570.*
Accommodations: *4 double rooms with baths, 1 suite.*
Amenities: *Air-conditioning, cable TV with VCR in guest parlor, turndown service, phones on each floor with jacks in rooms; bicycles, parking.*
Rates: *$90–$125; full breakfast, welcome drink. MC, V.*
Restrictions: *Smoking only in guest parlor, no pets, 2-night minimum on weekends and holidays.*

Newport House

The Newport House takes the prize as the most unusual bed-and-breakfast in Williamsburg, if not all of Tidewater Virginia. The house is a meticulous reproduction of one that once stood in Newport, Rhode Island, designed by the Colonial architect Peter Harrison. The house is totally furnished in period style, with English and American antiques and reproductions. Both guest rooms have canopy beds. The three-story, dormered house, painted creamy yellow, stands just across the street from the William and Mary Law School on a small lot that contains an herb garden. The owners, Cathy and John Millar, are practicing Colonial country dancers; they hold country-dancing evenings in the ballroom on Tuesday and, occasionally, Scottish country dances on Thurs-

day. (They also rent costumes.) Breakfast, from Colonial recipes, is accompanied by a historical lecture from the fascinating host and a visit from this offbeat B&B's pet—a house-trained rabbit named Sassafras, who is let out of its kitchen hutch for morning floor shows.

Address: *710 S. Henry St., Williamsburg, VA 23185, tel. 804/229–1775.*
Accommodations: *2 double rooms with baths.*
Amenities: *Air-conditioning, TV with VCR available, fireplace, ballroom.*
Rates: *$105; full breakfast. No credit cards.*
Restrictions: *No smoking indoors, no pets, 2-night minimum on weekends and holidays.*

War Hill Inn

The War Hill Inn is three miles north of town; this is a drawback or an attraction, depending on whether you prefer to stay overnight in the thick of Colonial things, or put some space between your lodging and the crowds. The War Hill's feeling of remoteness is stressed by the fact that it's surrounded by pastures where owner Bill Lee's prize-winning Black Angus cows munch on the grass—though a condo development has risen up on one of the property's flanks. Bill is a retired veterinarian who built the house in 1968 to raise a family. It's a copy of the Anderson House in Colonial Williamsburg, and a fine one at that. Inside are architectural features that came from other places—the heart-of-pine floors from a schoolhouse and a staircase from

a Lutheran church. The decor in the guest rooms is a mélange of Colonial reproductions and family things; the downstairs chamber is notable for its size and privacy. A good choice for families—thanks to its fenced-in grounds, a small orchard of peaches and plums, and a cottage—two of its rooms sleep four.

Address: *4560 Long Hill Rd., Williamsburg, VA 23185, tel. 804/565–0248.*
Accommodations: *5 double rooms with baths.*
Amenities: *Air-conditioning; cable TV in bedrooms, whirlpool tub in cottage.*
Rates: *$65–$95; full breakfast. AE, MC, V.*
Restrictions: *No smoking, no pets, 2-night minimum on weekends.*

Around Charlottesville

Few cities in this country are so deeply devoted to—one might say, so in love with—a single man as is Virginia's Piedmont capital, Charlottesville. On a farm east of town (in the present-day hamlet of Shadwell) Thomas Jefferson, the third president of the United States, was born; and on a mountaintop overlooking a countryside Jefferson himself considered Edenic, he built his home. We have all seen Monticello, for it appears on one side of the nickel, though its minted image hardly does it justice. The breathtakingly beautiful edifice, constructed on architectural principles that would change the face of America, is a house that reveals volumes about the man who built it and lived there.

For instance, in the terraced vegetable gardens (restored according to Jefferson's Garden Book*) he introduced the tomato to North America and raised 19 types of English peas, his favorite food. (Mr. Jefferson, as he is called around here, attributed his long life—he lived to be 83—to his vegetarian eating habits.) Here he built a glass-enclosed pavilion, where he came to read, write, and watch his garden grow. Most of the 20,000 letters he wrote were penned in his study in a reclining chair with revolving desk (he had rheumatism and worked from a semi-recumbent position). Jefferson was also a collector; the walls of the formal parlor are lined with portraits of friends, like Washington and Monroe, and the east entrance hall displays mastodon bones and a buffalo head brought back from the West by Lewis and Clark.*

"Architecture," wrote Jefferson, "is my delight and putting up and pulling down one of my favorite pastimes." Originally he built Monticello in 1779 as an American Palladian villa, but after seeing the work of Boullée and Ledoux in France, he returned to Monticello with a head full of new ideas, above all, about its dome, and an aversion to grand staircases, which he believed took up too

much room. Today the full effect is best seen from the flower gardens on the west side.

Another reason for Charlottesville's love affair with Jefferson lies at the western end of town—the University of Virginia. If Monticello is a taste of Jeffersonian style, the school's rotunda and colonnade provide the banquet. Jefferson began designing the university buildings at the age of 74; in 1976 the American Institute of Architects voted them the most outstanding achievement in American architecture. The rotunda was inspired by the Pantheon, in Rome, but the dual colonnade that extends from it, intended as both dwelling place and study center for students and faculty, is all Jefferson's own. Students still inhabit the Colonnade rooms, amid fireplaces, porches, and rocking chairs.

Downtown Charlottesville has been converted into a pedestrian mall where shoppers find intriguing stores, such as Paula Lewis for quilts, antique trunks, and pueblo pottery; the Signet Gallery for extraordinary crafts; and Tastings, a café and wine shop with a vast array of vintages.

Charlottesville lies in the Piedmont, the Blue Ridge foothills, and the driving here is fun and scenic. Highway 20, called the Constitution Route, takes travelers past Montpelier (James Madison's home) in Orange, 25 miles north of Charlottesville, and south past Ash Lawn— Highland (where James Monroe lived) and through Scottsville. This village on the James River, once the seat of Albemarle County, is rich in Revolutionary and Civil War history. It's a favorite spot for canoe and inner-tube trips. Twenty miles to the west the Blue Ridge rises, with access to the Skyline Drive or Parkway at Rockfish Gap.

Places to Go, Sights to See

Ash Lawn—Highland (tel. 804/293–9539). Just down the road from
Monticello, this is the restored home of James Monroe; its mountaintop site
(selected by Jefferson) offers views of Monticello's dome. It burned in 1840
and was rebuilt in Victorian-farmhouse style 30 years later. Today it's still
a working 550-acre farm where sheep and peacocks roam. Summertime
brings a Festival of the Arts and Plantation Day.

Barboursville Vineyards (north of Charlottesville, tel. 703/832–3824). The
output here includes pinot noir blanc, chardonnay, merlot, and cabernet
sauvignon wines, among others. Here you can also explore the ruins of
Governor James Barbour's plantation home. Other area vineyards include
Oakencroft and **Montdomaine.** (For a map of Virginia wineries, contact the
Virginia Wine Marketing Program, VDACS, Division of Marketing, Box 1163,
Richmond 23209, tel. 804/786–0481).

Court Square, in downtown Charlottesville, is the locus of Albermarle
County government, with a courthouse built between 1803 and 1867. The
square also holds an impressive equestrian statue of Stonewall Jackson.

Michie Tavern (tel. 804/977–1234). This tavern, dating from 1765, was moved
to its present location on the road to Monticello in 1920. With its ceaseless
crowds, recorded tours, and general store, it's very commercial. The
cafeteria-style restaurant serves historic fast food—fried chicken, black-eyed
peas, stewed tomatoes, and the like. The Virginia Wine Museum is adjacent.

Monticello (tel. 804/295–8181). Jefferson's home lies about 2 miles southeast
of the intersection of Routes 64 and 20. The tour, which ascends Mr.
Jefferson's "little mountain" by shuttle bus, lasts about half an hour and is
extremely rewarding. Afterward visitors are free to roam the gardens, view
the hidden dependencies, and make a pilgrimage to the great man's grave.
The museum shop is worth a stop, if only for its extensive collection of books
by and about Jefferson. Note that Monticello is best taken in before the tour
buses arrive around 11 AM.

Montpelier (south of Orange, tel. 703/672–2728). James Madison, Jr., served
as president after Jefferson and before Monroe. Known as the Father of the
Constitution, he saw America through the War of 1812. He and his wife,
Dolley, lived here from 1817 to 1836, followed by William du Pont, Sr., who
bought it in 1901. The guided tour of the estate leads visitors over the 2,700-
acre grounds, through the 55-room house, and past Madison's grave. The
Montpelier Hunt Race takes place here on the first weekend in November.

Rapidan. This village about 5 miles northeast of Orange is bisected by the
Rapidan River and holds the Waddell Memorial Presbyterian Church, an
architectural hymn in Carpenter Gothic. Nearby you'll also find Marmont
Orchards (tel. 703/672–2730) or 800/572–2262), where, in season, you can pick
your own apples, peaches, plums, and nectarines.

Scottsville sits on the James River and is where Lafayette made a successful stand against General Cornwallis in 1781. The village holds 32 Federal-style buildings and the locks of the James River Kanawha Canal, which were a target for 10,000 bluecoats under General Sheridan during the Civil War. Nearby you'll find the James River Runners (tel. 804/286–2338), where you can rent tubes, rafts, and canoes.

1740 House (tel. 804/977–1740). This antiques store located near Ivy, west of Charlottesville on Route 250, is known for its museum-quality 18th- and 19th-century furniture.

University of Virginia (tel. 804/924–7969). Tours leave the rotunda several times daily (except during holidays and exams). It's just as enjoyable to wander the grounds on your own, though. Inside the rotunda stands Alexander Galt's statue of Jefferson, which students saved from the fire of 1895.

Restaurants

Charlottesville's restaurant scene is surprisingly cosmopolitan. **Duner's** (tel. 804/293–8352) and **Metropolitan** (tel. 804/977–1043) are favored for French and nouvelle American cuisine. **Memory & Company** (tel. 804/296–3539) offers $25 prix fixe dinners and a terrific wine list. **C & O** (tel. 804/971–7044) has a friendly bistro downstairs and formal French dining upstairs. For casual dining, there's the **Blue Ridge Brewing Company** (tel. 804/977–0017), which makes its own beers; **Court Square Tavern** (tel. 804/296–6111), with a pub atmosphere and more than 120 imported beers; **Southern Culture** (tel. 804/979–1990), a reasonably priced mix of Caribbean and Cajun; and in Scottsville, **Pig 'N Steak** (tel. 804/286–4114), a real country café.

Tourist Information

Charlottesville/Albemarle Convention & Visitors Bureau (Box 161, Charlottesville 22902, tel. 804/293–6789). **Orange County Visitors Bureau** (Box 133, Orange 22960, tel. 703/672–1653). **Virginia Division of Tourism** (1021 E. Cary St., Richmond 23219, tel. 804/786–4484).

Reservation Services

Guesthouses Bed & Breakfast, Inc. (Box 5737, Charlottesville 22905, tel. 804/979–7264) is a reservation service run by Mary Hill Caperton, which can arrange entrée to private houses otherwise closed to the public. For a copy of **The Bed and Breakfast Association of Virginia's directory,** describing more than 100 establishments, call the Virginia Division of Tourism's B&B line (tel. 800/262–1293). The Division of Tourism's Washington, DC, office also operates a **B&B and small inn booking service** (tel. 202/659–5523 or 800/934–9184).

Clifton

rom the cozy paneled library and the comforter-covered beds to the sunny terrace, the wood chairs on the lawn, and the languid lake, there are reasons aplenty to settle in here at one of the state's top inns.

Clifton stands in the quiet Shadwell, near Jefferson's birthplace. No wonder it's a National Historic Landmark—the handsome white-frame, six-columned manse was once home to Thomas Mann Randolph, governor of Virginia, member of Congress, and husband of Jefferson's daughter, Martha. It's now owned by a Washington attorney but ably administered by innkeepers Craig and Donna Hartman. As chef, Craig also oversees Clifton's wonderful meals (applewood-smoked loin of veal with Vidalia-onion marmalade, anyone?). Saturday-night dinners ($45) are served to period music.

There are guest rooms in the manor house, the carriage house, the livery, and Randolph's law office. All have wood-burning fireplaces, antique or canopy beds, and large baths and may also feature French windows, lake views, and antique bedcoverings. Rooms in the dependencies have a fresh, cottage feel: whitewashed walls, bright floral prints, lots of windows. Suites in the carriage house boast shutters, windows, and other artifacts from the home of the explorer Meriwether Lewis.

The grounds spread through 48 acres of woods. The 20-acre lake offers good fishing (the inn has fishing rods and tackle boxes) and lazy floats on inner tubes. There are also a Har-tu tennis court, croquet pitch, horseshoes, and badminton. The extensively renovated gardens are carefully tended: The estate grows its own flowers, lettuce, and herbs. In the fall the gardener hangs the last of the flowers to dry for winter arrangements.

Clifton offers a magical combination of elegance and hominess. A corner of the big butcher-block island in the kitchen is for guests. There's always a jar of cookies there, and sodas, wine and beer in the refrigerator, and guests often sit and chat with Craig as he cooks.

Address: *Rte. 729, Shadwell, VA (Rte. 13, Box 26, Charlottesville, VA 22901), tel. 804/971–1800, fax 804/971–7098.*
Accommodations: *3 double rooms with baths, 11 suites.*
Amenities: *Restaurant, air-conditioning, fireplaces in guest rooms and common areas, wheelchair accessible; pool, tennis court, lake.*
Rates: *$143–$193; full breakfast, afternoon tea. AE, MC, V.*
Restrictions: *No smoking, no pets, 2-night minimum on weekends.*

High Meadows and Mountain Sunset

igh Meadows, which stands on 50 acres in Scottsville, is above all a bed-and-breakfast inn done by hand. The hands in question are those of Peter Shushka, a retired submariner, and his wife, Mary Jae Abbitt, a financial analyst. In this unique B&B, Federal and late-Victorian architecture exist side by side, happily joined by a longitudinal hall. It wasn't always so. The Italianate front section was built in 1882 by Peter White, who intended to level the older house several paces behind it. But bearing in mind her growing family, his wife refused to give up the old place, built in 1830, and for a time a plank between the two was the tenuous connector that kept the marriage intact. Today High Meadows is on the National Register.

Peter and Mary Jae have decorated the place with great originality, keeping intact the stylistic integrity of each section. They've also used fabrics imaginatively on the bed hangings and windows. Fairview, in the 1880s portion, is the quintessential bride's room, with a fireplace, flowing bed drapery, a three-window alcove, and claw-foot tub. The Virginia suite, upstairs in the Federal section, has stenciled walls lined with antique stuffed animals, a fireplace, and rafters across the ceiling. A two-person whirlpool sits in the middle of the Music Room. The Carriage House is a contemporary building of cedar,

glass, and slate on the site of the original; this two-room suite has a kitchen and a deck. The property also includes the Mountain Sunset (named for its view), a Queen Anne manor house with two suites, two rooms, and plenty of privacy.

Breakfast consists of Shushka specialties like cranberry-almond muffins and ham-and-egg cups laced with tomatoes and Gruyère cheese. The dining room is open for dinner on the weekends; Saturday, the meal's a six-course affair with wine for $35. And to cap all this off, there are 50 acres of vineyards, which produce pinot noir grapes for the inn's own private-label wine.

Address: *Rte. 4, Box 6, Scottsville, VA 24590, tel. 804/286-2218.*
Accommodations: *7 double rooms with baths, 5 suites.*
Amenities: *Restaurant, air-conditioning in 5 rooms, fireplaces in 3 rooms and 2 common areas, TV with VCR in 1 suite, whirlpools in 2 rooms, some rooms wheelchair accessible.*
Rates: *$85–$145; full breakfast, evening hors d'oeuvres. MC, V.*
Restrictions: *No smoking, pets permitted in ground-level rooms by arrangement. 2-night minimum in spring and fall and on holiday weekends, closed Dec. 24.*

Prospect Hill

For elegance and luxury, Prospect Hill is one of Virginia's finest inns. Added to its architecturally noteworthy setting, that makes staying here something worth filling your piggy bank for. Prospect Hill lies east of Charlottesville, in the 14-square-mile Greensprings National Historic District. It's the oldest continuously occupied frame manor house in Virginia. But except for the obligatory dependencies and impressive boxwood hedges, Prospect Hill doesn't look like a plantation, because it was rebuilt in the Victorian era, when a columned facade and decorative cornices were added. The innkeepers have painted it lemony yellow.

There are four nicely furnished rooms in the main house, but the big treat is the six refurbished dependencies. Sanco Pansy's cottage, 100 feet from the manor, has a sitting room and whirlpool tub for two. The Carriage House, lit by four Palladian windows, offers views of ponies in the meadow nibbling the green Virginia turf. Surrounded by such *luxe, calme, et volupté*, it's strange to consider that in the last century the dependencies were filled with hams, ice blocks, and livestock.

Dinner at the inn is a marvelous production, not so much because of the cuisine (French-inspired and well above average) as the ceremony. You begin with complimentary wine and cider a half hour before supper—outdoors in good weather. When the dinner bell rings, in you file to hear the menu recited by innkeeper Bill Sheehan or his son, Michael. (Michael looks like a college halfback, but thanks to his delightful mama, Mireille, his French is impeccable.) Then comes an earnest grace and five excellent courses.

A hot breakfast is brought to your dependency on a tray. You can take it in the dining room, but why spoil the fun? In your dependency, you can eat in a whirlpool tub. This really splendid inn is a class act that hasn't become too smoothly professional. You're bound to meet the gregarious innkeepers and appreciate the way they've put their stamp on Prospect Hill.

Address: *Rte. 3, Box 430, Trevilians, VA 23093, tel. 703/967-0844 or 800/277-0844, fax 703/967-0102.*
Accommodations: *5 double rooms with baths in main house, 5 doubles with baths and 3 suites in dependencies.*
Amenities: *Restaurant, air-conditioning, fireplaces in 12 guest rooms, Jacuzzis in 7 rooms; pool, meeting room.*
Rates: *$195–$290; MAP, afternoon tea. MC, V.*
Restrictions: *No pets, 2-night minimum with Sat. stay, closed Dec. 24–25.*

Chester

A number of years ago, Gordon Anderson, a legal administrator, and Dick Shaffer, an investment banker, retired from the New York rat race and bought an 1847 Greek Revival mansion in Scottsville. They brought their antiques along, their sophisticatedly urban lifestyle, their Russian wolfhounds, VCR tapes of Leontyne Price's farewell appearance at the Met, and details we saw nowhere else in Virginia—like cigarettes laid out in dishes on coffee tables. The two of them are relaxed hosts who run their bed-and-breakfast like a Noel Coward house party. Take dinner, which they serve by arrangement, cook themselves, and eat along with guests: It's a four-course affair for $24 per person, including California wine, with Gordon and Dick chatting until the wee hours of the night about movies, art, and the Chester's brush with the Civil War. They also know interesting facts about the area—for instance, where the richest man in America lives. There are five bedrooms, eight fireplaces, and a laundry room, which guests are free to use.

Address: *Rte. 4, Box 57, Scottsville, VA 24590, tel. 804/286-3960.*
Accommodations: *1 double room with bath, 4 doubles share 2 baths.*
Amenities: *Air-conditioning, robes, fireplaces in 4 bedrooms; bicycles, kennel.*
Rates: *$65-$100; full breakfast, complimentary beverages. AE.*
Restrictions: *2-night minimum some weekends.*

The Holladay House

T he Holladay House, in the center of Orange, makes a good stop for anyone visiting Montpelier or driving the pretty country roads in between. Pete Holladay, a former school administrator in the Shenandoah Valley, welcomes guests in the 1899 Federal-style home where his grandfather raised Pete's father. Pete says that despite his extensive renovations, much of the house looks just as it did then. His great-grandmother's crazy quilt hangs on one wall; most of the furniture is family pieces.

The simply furnished guest rooms have modern black-and-white tiled baths. Pete's most recent project is the "decadent" (his word) bathroom in the suite: a vast whirlpool tub, a double-head shower, and heated towel racks. Downstairs, Room 7, with a kitchen, TV, and phones, is ideal for business travelers.

Pete brings breakfast to his guests' rooms—often accompanied by Zachary Taylor, his cat.

Address: *155 W. Main St., Orange, VA 22960, tel. 703/672-4893.*
Accommodations: *4 double rooms with baths, 1 suite.*
Amenities: *Air-conditioning, TV in 1 room, whirlpool in suite.*
Rates: *$75-$185; full breakfast. MC, V.*
Restrictions: *No smoking in rooms, no pets, 2-night minimum on weekends in Oct.*

The Inn at Monticello

Carol and Larry Engel forsook the plains of the upper Midwest because they were enchanted with Virginia. The Inn at Monticello, which they found and renovated, is an 1850s farmhouse with a two-story front gallery and a brook trickling over the long front lawn. The prospect from the back—condos on a hill—is not as bucolic, but curtains block the view from guest rooms. Downstairs there's a parlor, a twin-bedded room, and a nicely furnished honeymoon room. Of the three upstairs bedrooms, we liked the Yellow Room best because of its white cotton balloon shades and plump rope bed. The Engels take special care with the bed linen, which is downy soft and complemented by European coverlets.

Mornings begin with gourmet breakfasts (for instance, orange yogurt pancakes topped with fresh berries). The rest of the day can be spent visiting nearby Monticello or snoozing in a rocker on the wide front porch.

Address: *Rte. 20 S, RR 19, Box 112, Charlottesville, VA 22901, tel. 804/979-3593 fax 804/296-1344.*
Accommodations: *5 double rooms with baths.*
Amenities: *Air-conditioning, turndown service, fireplaces in 2 guest rooms; lake for swimming.*
Rates: *$95–$135; full breakfast, afternoon refreshments. MC, V.*
Restrictions: *No smoking, no pets, 2-night minimum on some weekends.*

Rocklands

Standing stately on a hill above Route 231, one of Orange County's prettiest byways, Rocklands nestles among 1,800 secluded acres adjoining Montpelier. The brick Classic Revival mansion was built in 1905 and extensively modified in 1933. Ask innkeeper Maggie Neale to tell you how it was lifted to get rid of the basement and how a rear guest wing was removed. Recent renovation, including new walls and ceilings, has put the mansion into impeccable shape—no fading paint, no peeling paper here.

The main house is vast. Bedrooms are spacious, well separated, simply furnished; there are several smaller ones in separate structures. Six Ionic columns flank the front porch, and there's an airy loggia on the north side that, with its commanding view, is a favorite place for breakfast. On hot summer days, the spring-fed pool beckons from its shady glade. Guests can laze in a hammock or hike the extensive trails.

Address: *17439 Rocklands Dr., Gordonsville 22942, tel. 703/832-7176, fax 703/832-7044.*
Accommodations: *6 double rooms with baths, 5 doubles share 3 baths.*
Amenities: *Air-conditioning, TV with VCR in library, fireplaces in 4 rooms, phones in rooms, robes, turndown service; swimming pool.*
Rates: *$125; full breakfast. MC, V.*
Restrictions: *No smoking, no pets, 2-night minimum on some weekends.*

The Shadows

You won't find a home (or guests) more lovingly tended than at the Shadows. Pat and Barbara Loffredo have filled their 1913 stone farmhouse, serenely set in a grove of old cedars just up the road from Montpelier, with a cheerful collection of country Victorian antiques. Prize pieces include an intricately carved Civil War–era board, an old pump organ, numerous claw-foot tubs, and Maxfield Parrish prints wherever the eye rests. The house is what Barbara calls Gustav Stickley Craftsman style, a modified bungalow built of wood and local fieldstone. It has lustrous oak floors and windowsills around which lace curtains flutter. The four spotless guest rooms upstairs all have standard Victorian trappings. All the tangibles here are pleasant enough, but Pat and Barbara put the Shadows over the mark. They're refugees from New York, where Pat was a policeman, and their joy in their newfound home is infectious. The two of them delight in coddling guests, overwhelming them at breakfast, laying open their library, and sending them on their way with a hug.

Address: *14291 Constitution Hwy., Orange, VA 22960, tel. 703/672-5057.*
Accommodations: *4 double rooms with baths, 2 cottage suites.*
Amenities: *Air-conditioning, turn-down service, fireplace in 1 cottage.*
Rates: *$80–$125; full breakfast. MC, V.*
Restrictions: *No smoking, no pets, 2-night minimum some weekends.*

The Silver Thatch Inn

The Silver Thatch, north of Charlottesville off Route 29, was formerly called the Hollymead. The oldest part of its semicircle of connected buildings is log, built by Hessian prisoners during the Revolution. New owners Vince and Rita Scoffone became innkeepers because they wanted to spend more time together. (He was a workaholic banker.) The inn is decorated in a comfortable country-Colonial style with richly colored walls and trim. The guest rooms all have quilts, down comforters, and antiques; some have fireplaces. The four cottage rooms surpass those in the main house because of their sparkling new bathrooms.

The menu, which changes every six to eight weeks, has flair: Rock Cornish hen rubbed with mustard and Caribbean jerk spices, shrimp and Moroccan sausage with currant and couscous salad. The wine list has received an award of excellence from the *Wine Spectator.* Silver Thatch guests may use a pool and tennis courts nearby.

Address: *3001 Hollymead Dr., Charlottesville, VA 22901, tel. 804/978-4686, fax 804/973-6156.*
Accommodations: *7 double rooms with baths.*
Amenities: *Restaurant, air-conditioning, cable TV in bar.*
Rates: *$105–$125; Continental-plus breakfast. MC, V.*
Restrictions: *No smoking, no pets, closed Dec. 23–26, first 2 weeks in Jan. and Aug., 2-night minimum on weekends Apr.–June, Sept.–Nov.*

Sleepy Hollow Farm

North of Charlottesville, as you roller-coaster past horse farms and vineyards on Route 231, you'll also pass the bright red roof of the barn at Sleepy Hollow Farm. This two-story brick house, begun in the 18th century (though 20th-century renovations keep it from looking historic), is surrounded by fields grazed by Black Angus and Tarentais cattle. It's eminently suited to families with children: There's a play set on the grounds, bunnies in the hedgerows, and a spring-fed pond for swimming. The main house has four rooms, and there are two suites in the chestnut-wood cottage. Sleepy Hollow's owner, Beverley Allison, came to the house as a bride, raised a family, produced the ABC News, served as an Episcopal missionary in Central America, then returned to open her bed-and-breakfast. Thus, she has stories to tell, if you can persuade her; ask for the one about a ghost who frequented one of the guest rooms.

Address: *16280 Blue Ridge Turnpike, Gordonsville, VA 22942, tel. 703/832-5555.*
Accommodations: *4 double rooms with baths, 2 suites.*
Amenities: *Air-conditioning, TV in 2 rooms, TV/VCR in sitting room, 3 fireplaces and 2 stoves in common rooms and suites; kennel, riding arranged.*
Rates: *$60–$95; full breakfast, afternoon refreshments. MC, V with surcharge.*
Restrictions: *No smoking in dining room, 2-night minimum on some weekends.*

200 South Street

This popular small hotel in downtown Charlottesville is across the street from and next door to two trendy eateries, Memory and Company and South Street. The complex consists of two Victorian homes built between 1850 and 1900, painted yellow, which cheers up South Street considerably. They're brimming with English and Belgian antiques, including capacious armoires and lace-canopied four-posters. The walls are lined with changing displays of local artwork and an interesting collection of historic Holsinger photographs. We preferred the 10 rooms and suite in No. 200 to those in the neighboring cottage, because there's a parlor there, and train tracks in back make a front room desirable. But all the rooms are inviting and immaculately renovated, and some of them contain such luxuries as whirlpool baths and fireplaces. Youthful innkeeper Brendan Clancy fixes breakfast, and in the afternoon, tea and wine are served in the sitting room.

Address: *200 South St., Charlottesville, VA 22901, tel. 804/979-0200 or 800/974-7008, fax 804/979-4403.*
Accommodations: *17 double rooms with baths, 3 suites.*
Amenities: *Air-conditioning, TV in 3rd-floor lounge, phones in rooms, turndown service, whirlpools in 6 rooms, fireplaces in 9 rooms, wheelchair accessible.*
Rates: *$90–$170; Continental-plus breakfast, afternoon tea and wine. AE, MC, V.*
Restrictions: *No pets, 2-night minimum on weekends Apr.–May and Sept.–Oct.*

Willow Grove Plantation

Angela Mulloy, who runs Willow Grove, is friendly but no-nonsense. She adamantly insists that Willow Grove is not one of those country inns where they force camaraderie with social hours and hors d'oeuvres. Instead, she offers good food and plenty of it, rooms that are clean and antiques laden, but perhaps a tad ragged around the edges. Convivial surroundings and comfort (triple sheeting, down pillows and comforters) take precedence over pristine conditions. Angela is also extremely proud of Willow Grove's architectural distinctiveness. This grand plantation house with a Greek Revival facade was built in numerous stages beginning in the 1770s and lived in by just a handful of families who didn't remodel during its long history.

Dinners are served in the dining rooms and the tavern; guest rooms occupy the second and third floors. Continental breakfasts are delivered to your room, accompanied by the morning newspaper, and a full breakfast is served downstairs.

Address: *14079 Plantation Way, Orange, VA 22960, tel. 703/672–5982 or 800/949–1778.*
Accommodations: *3 double rooms with baths, 2 suites.*
Amenities: *Restaurant, air-conditioning, fireplaces in 3 rooms.*
Rates: *$195–$255 first night (includes $100 credit in dining room or tavern), $95–$155 thereafter; full breakfast. MC, V.*

Woodstock Hall

This Colonial way station has two distinctions. It's one of the least altered historic structures in the area, and owners Clarence and Mary Ann Elder also own the 1740 House antiques shop in Ivy. This explains the fine period furnishings and the careful renovation. The Woodstock stands on a hill near Charlottesville, a prim, mustard yellow beacon in excellent biking country. Inside you'll find a case full of artifacts unearthed during the restoration, fireplaces in all rooms, burnished wood floors, case locks on the doors, much of the original window glass, and a copy of Poe's *The Tale of the Ragged Mountains*—because the poet's stay here inspired him to write it. In the main house, one snug and particularly pleasant room is called the Duc Liancourt Room, and

a suite in the old detached kitchen contains two fireplaces and a rather short antique canopy bed. The inn lacks warmth, though. On a blustery, rainy November evening, not even a log was laid in the fireplaces. But it's still a good choice for those who want to visit Charlottesville, but stay in the country.

Address: *RR 637, Ivy (Rte. 10, Box 297, Charlottesville, VA 22903), tel. 804/293–8977.*
Accommodations: *3 double rooms with baths, 1 suite.*
Amenities: *Air-conditioning, TV in rooms.*
Rates: *$95–$130; full breakfast, afternoon tea. No credit cards.*
Restrictions: *No smoking, no pets, 3-night minimum on graduation and parents' weekends.*

The Blue Ridge/
Shenandoah Valley

The standard way to see the Blue Ridge Mountains is to pile into a car on a weekend in October and drive south from Front Royal along the Skyline Drive. If you do this, bumper-to-bumper traffic could keep you from covering the full 105-mile course, and you probably won't get past Rockfish Gap (just east of Waynesboro), where the drive becomes the equally (some would claim more) splendid Blue Ridge Parkway. Above all, you'll have only the foggiest idea of the landscape at Virginia's western border, markedly different from the rest of the state.

In geographical terms the Blue Ridge is the eastern wall of the wide Shenandoah Valley, which is retained at the other side by the Allegheny Mountains. Down the middle of the valley, bisecting it for some 50 miles, rises an other mini-mountain range called Massanutten Mountain, even though it holds a pretty valley of its own. The Shenandoah River, which runs through the valley, divides north of Massanutten—to further confuse the issue—into a North and South Fork.

Once you've got the geography down you can plot a more informed assault by crossing the ridge along such strategic and scenic routes as Highways 211, 33, and especially 56, an untrammeled two-laner that's a favorite even of view-jaded locals. These paths lead into the central and southern sections of the Shenandoah Valley.

Shenandoah National Park holds the heights of the Blue Ridge in a 100-mile strip from Front Royal to Waynesboro and provides nonpareil views of the Virginia Piedmont to the east and the splendid Shenandoah Valley to the west. To the park come fishermen to catch the crafty brook trout, and hikers who find meanders aplenty. Even a short stroll from a trailhead on the Skyline Drive brings visitors

*within viewing range of the park's abundant and varied
wildlife. Spring and fall are peak seasons for nature
lovers. In May the green of new foliage moves up the ridge
at a rate of 100 feet a day, with clouds of wild pink azaleas
providing contrast. Fall colors are at their most vivid
between October 10 and 25, when migrating hawks join the
human leaf-gazers to take in the display.*

*Once over the ridge and in the valley there are better ways
to take in the countryside than by zooming along I–81.
Route 11 parallels the superhighway in a delightfully
labyrinthine fashion, providing access to big-name sights
such as the New Market Battlefield and Luray Caverns,
and running through small towns, including Woodstock,
Edinburg, Mt. Jackson, and Steele's Tavern, where produce
stands, flea markets, and local-history museums further
delay your progress.*

*Among Shenandoah's gems, the town of Staunton, as hilly
as Rome, was Woodrow Wilson's home, and it also boasts
the pretty campus of the Mary Baldwin College and the
Museum of American Frontier Culture. Lexington lives
and breathes for Stonewall Jackson and Robert E. Lee, who
was named president of Washington and Lee University
after the Civil War ended. Nearby stands the Virginia
Military Institute, where Jackson taught natural
philosophy before bedeviling Union armies as
a Confederate general.*

*West along winding country roads from Staunton and
Lexington lies a countryside often neglected by valley
visitors. Routes 33, 250, and 39 lead to the Appalachian
plateau and West Virginia, bordered by the thick foliage of
the George Washington National Forest. The roads
frequently cross rocky waterways—such as that lovely trio
of rivers, the Bullpasture, Cowpasture, and Calfpasture—
providing excellent spots for wading and picnicking. Most
of the towns in this area are no more than crossroads, with
the exception of Hot Springs, site of The Homestead,*

a 15,000-acre resort that's a Virginia institution. The town at the gates of The Homestead has a pleasant collection of arts-and-crafts shops, gourmet delis, and restaurants.

Places to Go, Sights to See

Belle Grove (1 mi south of Middletown, tel. 703/869–2028). The mansion, built of local limestone in 1794, shows the architectural influence of Thomas Jefferson. It suffered greatly in 1864, when Confederate forces launched an attack on a Union Army headquartered at the mansion.

Blue Ridge Parkway (tel. 704/627–3419). One of the country's most breathtaking drives begins at the southern end of the Skyline Drive and follows the mountain crest south to Tennessee.

George C. Marshall Museum and Library (Lexington, tel. 703/463–7103). The famous general was a graduate of Virginia Military Institute. He is the only professional soldier awarded the Nobel Peace Prize (on display here), which he received for his plan to rebuild Europe's economy after World War II.

Luray Caverns (tel. 703/743–6551). They're famed for the "stalacpipe organ," which gets played on cave tours. The valley's underground world can also be surveyed at Grand, Shenandoah, Endless, Skyline, and Dixie caverns.

Massanutten (tel. 703/289–9441). Downhill skiing on 11 slopes, as well as golf, tennis, and indoor swimming.

Museum of American Frontier Culture (Staunton, tel. 703/332–7850). In four farmsteads reminiscent of those the early settlers left behind in Europe, costumed workers demonstrate how farm families planted, harvested, and tended to domestic chores.

Natural Bridge (Natural Bridge, tel. 703/291–2121 or 800/533–1410). Thomas Jefferson was so impressed by this 215-foot-high, 90-foot-long rock span that he bought it, in 1774. In recent decades it's been degraded by commercialism and is now the focus of a hokey light show and the site of a wax museum.

New Market Battlefield (tel. 703/740–3101). Of all Civil War memorials, this is one of the most affecting, for in 1864, 247 cadets from the Virginia Military Institute were sent here to a "baptism of fire." Though some in the battalion were just 15, the VMI soldiers became heroes that day.

The Shenandoah National Park (Luray, tel. 703/999–2266). Extending 80 miles along the Blue Ridge, the park was created to restore the scenic terrain to the condition in which the earliest settlers found it. A movie shown at the Byrd Visitors Center at Big Meadows tells the story of the park's regeneration. Information on trails, overlooks, facilities, and activities is available here and at the Dickey Ridge Visitors Center just south of Luray.

Shenandoah River Floating. The lazily meandering river offers opportunities for mostly gentle canoe and raft rides, with a little fishing, swimming, and inner-tubing thrown in. Good outfitters include the *Downriver Canoe Company* (Bentonville, tel. 703/635–5526) and *Shenandoah River Outfitters* (Luray, tel. 703/743–4159).

Skyline Drive. The spectacular 105-mile route that meanders through Shenandoah National Park passes scenic overlooks, hiking trails, restaurants, and visitor centers along the way.

Statler Brothers Complex (tel. 703/885–7297). Staunton loves the Statlers, because the four country musicians are local boys who defied Nashville by cutting their records in their hometown. A converted elementary school showcases artifacts from their career.

Stonewall Jackson House (Lexington, tel. 703/463–2552). This trim, brick two-story is where Thomas Jonathan Jackson, a natural philosophy professor at VMI, lived with his second wife before he rode away to lead the men in gray. General Jackson died at the Battle of Chancellorsville at the age of 39.

Theater at Lime Kiln (Lexington, tel. 703/463–3074). Set in an abandoned lime quarry, this stage for a professional company of actors has been called the most unusual theater setting in the United States. The Memorial Day–Labor Day schedule includes concerts and plays.

Virginia Horse Center (Lexington, tel. 703/463–7060). A huge equestrian complex, with 577 stalls, a 1,000-seat grandstand, regulation dressage areas, horse trails, cross-country courses, and a full calendar of shows and events.

Virginia Military Institute (Lexington, tel. 703/464–7207) was founded in 1839 as the nation's first state-supported military school. Uniformed cadets conduct tours of the campus (an austere and blocky Gothic Revival fortress) and parade most Fridays at 4 PM.

Washington and Lee University (Lexington, tel. 703/463–8460) was founded in 1749, subsidized by George Washington when the institution was near bankruptcy in 1796, and presided over by Robert E. Lee in the late 1860s. An extraordinary front Colonnade and the Lee Chapel and Museum, beneath which the general is buried, are its most noteworthy sights.

Wintergreen (tel. 804/325–2200). This 11,000-acre resort lies on the eastern flanks of the Blue Ridge. It has golf, skiing, horseback riding, swimming pools, restaurants, and an acclaimed nature program.

Woodrow Wilson Birthplace and Museum (tel. 703/885–0897). The imposing white Greek Revival home in the prettiest residential section of Staunton, offers lots of Wilson memorabilia, including his spiffy Pierce Arrow limousine.

Restaurants

There's sophisticated dining in Staunton at **23 Beverly** (tel. 703/885–5053), which features locally grown ingredients; across the street, the casual, family-run **Beverly** (tel. 703/886–4317). **McSylvies** (Middletown, tel. 703/869–1911) has a well-rounded menu, and **The Springhouse** (Woodstock, tel. 703/459–4755) serves up reasonably priced food in a comfortable setting. In Lexington, **The Willson-Walker House** (tel. 703/463–3020) offers fine American cuisine in a Colonial setting; when a burger sounds best, try **The Palms** (tel. 703/463–7000).

Tourist Information

Front Royal Chamber of Commerce (Box 568, Front Royal 22630, tel. 703/635–3185). **Harrisonburg–Rockingham Convention and Visitors Bureau** (800 Country Club Rd., Box 1, Harrisonburg 22801, tel. 703/434–2319). **Lexington Visitors Center** (102 E. Washington St., Lexington 24450, tel. 703/463–3777). **Shenandoah Valley Travel Association** (Box 1040, New Market 22844, tel. 703/740–3132). **Staunton Tourism** (Box 58, Staunton 24402, tel. 703/332–3972). **Virginia Division of Tourism** (1021 E. Cary St., Richmond 23219, tel. 804/786–4484).

Information and Reservation Services

Bed & Breakfasts of the Historic Shenandoah Valley (402 N. Main St., Woodstock 22664, tel. 703/459–4828). **Blue Ridge Bed & Breakfast Reservation Service** (Rock & Rills, Rte. 2, Box 3895, Berryville 22611, tel. 703/955–1246). **Historic Country Inns of Lexington** (11 N. Main St., tel. 703/463–2044). **Virginia Inns of the Shenandoah Valley** (Box 1387, Staunton 24401). For a copy of **The Bed and Breakfast Association of Virginia's directory,** describing more than 100 establishments, call the Virginia Division of Tourism's B&B line (tel. 800/262–1293). The Division of Tourism's Washington, DC, office also operates a **B&B and small-inn booking service** (tel. 202/659–5523 or 800/934–9184).

Jordan Hollow Farm

As anyone who's traveled much in rural America knows, farms aren't always the idyllic-looking places city folk fantasize about. However, Jordan Hollow, a working horse farm set in its own little valley beneath Hawksbill Mountain (on the western side of the Blue Ridge), comes as close to the ideal as possible. It's surrounded by 150 acres of fields and meadows where the horses graze, one can only assume in deep contentment. The passel of cats who have the run of the place also have it good—they sleep on the porch on top of an electric blanket!

Marly and Jetze (pronounced Yetsuh) Beers are the proprietors, and they're a handsome, outdoorsy couple; Marly's blond, and Jetze strikingly tall and dramatically bearded. They met in Liberia, where she was working for AID and he represented a Dutch marine engineering firm. They opened Jordan Hollow as an inn in 1981. Half the guests come for the riding, half to savor the tranquillity. Every day, several equestrian groups (including beginners) leave the farm to wander over the foothills; youngsters go on pony rides. And when Marly gets a break from her cooking duties, she might be prevailed upon to hitch up the carriage. Jetze's forte is keeping things jovial at the Watering Trough, a lounge and game room several paces from the barn. Guests can play volleyball, croquet, and boccie ball, hike along 6 miles of trails, or swim at the public pool across the street.

The main section of the inn is in a white clapboard farmhouse fronted by a galleried porch. Portions of this structure were built of log around 1790, and in two dining rooms the rough wood and chinking is still visible. Breakfast and dinner are served here and in two other dining rooms. Box lunches are available, too.

Guests can choose from the low-ceilinged Farmhouse Room in the main house, 16 more in the Arbor View Lodge, and four upscale rooms in the Mare Meadow Lodge, which is built of hand-hewn logs. The latter are carpeted and have fireplaces, quilts and matching curtains, cedar furniture, and Jacuzzi tubs.

Address: *Rte. 626 (RR 2, Box 375), Stanley, VA 22851, tel. 703/778-2209 or 703/778-2285, fax 703/778-1759.*
Accommodations: *21 double rooms with baths, 1 suite.*
Amenities: *Restaurant, air-conditioning, TV in 5 rooms and lounge, fireplace in lounge, phones in rooms; horseback riding.*
Rates: *$140–$180; MAP. D, DC, MC, V.*
Restrictions: *No pets.*

Trillium House

You've got to hand it to Ed and Betty Dinwiddie. To them, building a bed-and-breakfast on the grounds of Wintergreen resort may have seemed the most natural thing in the world; after all, their family had vacationed there for years. But to skiers, refugees from the Blue Ridge Parkway, wildflower enthusiasts, and all-round mountain devotees, the idea was a stroke of genius. The simple fact that Trillium House lies across the road from the gargantuan sports complex, with its indoor pool, tennis courts, ski slopes, hiking trails, golf course, and stables, should give you a clue as to the kinds of activities available.

From Wintergreen's gate, a rollercoasterish road brings you 3½ miles to the doorstep of Trillium House. The beige frame building fronted by a porch and a Palladian window, surrounded by trees and stylish condominiums owned by Wintergreen residents, was built in 1983. You enter the Great Room, which is two stories high, near a staircase at the side leading to a loft library. The front sitting area has a woodburning stove, above which hang several organ pipes; by the front door, a canister holds a collection of walking sticks. Breakfast is served in the dining rooms, with views of birdfeeders and the backyard gazebo, and on Friday and Saturday dinners are cooked by chef Ellen, who formerly worked in one of Wintergreen's restaurants. The 12 guest rooms at Trillium House lie in two wings off the Great Room. Their architectural tone is slightly motelish, but decorative touches add some personality—here a quilt or a framed picture that could only have been created by one of the Dinwiddie brood, there a writing desk from The Homestead or a bed with a lace canopy.

The odds are that you'll spend most of your stay here pursuing varieties of R&R on the resort or ensconced in the Great Room, chatting with other guests or Ed and Betty, who manage to seem amazingly relaxed despite their demanding housekeeping duties. The single disappointment is that Trillium House doesn't have mountain views; if that's what you're after, you'll have to grab a stick and walk.

Address: *Box 280, Nellysford, VA 22958, tel. 804/325-9126 or (reservations only) 800/325-9126, fax 804/325-1099.*
Accommodations: *10 double rooms with baths, 2 suites.*
Amenities: *Dinner served Fri. and Sat. by reservation, air-conditioning turndown service, wheelchair accessible, TV/VCR in sitting room with videotape-movie collection; stables.*
Rates: *$80–$140; full buffet breakfast. MC, V.*
Restrictions: *No smoking in dining room, no pets. 2-night minimum on weekends.*

Ashton Country House

S heila Kennedy, a teacher, says she turned this 1860 Greek Revival home on the outskirts of Staunton into a B&B because she likes meeting new people and loves to cook, entertain, and spend money. And she does know the extras that please guests: four plump pillows on each bed, good mattresses, cozy flannel sheets in the winter, reading lights, oversize showers, two bath towels per person, bathroom vanities with lots of counter space, big armoires with padded hangers. The large Master Suite features a high four-poster Charleston Rice bed. The Cottage Room has a Victorian bedroom suite with faux woodgrain finish and its own second-floor porch. Stanley Polanski, Sheila's husband, works with computers by day; by night and during breakfast he's the inn's accomplished jazz pianist. The resident goats often accompany guests on their walks over the surrounding 20 acres of pastures.

Address: *1205 Middlebrook Rd., Staunton, VA 24401, tel. 703/885–7819 or 800/296–7819.*
Accommodations: *4 double rooms with baths.*
Amenities: *Ceiling fans in rooms, fireplace in dining room.*
Rates: *$70–$85; full breakfast, afternoon tea. No credit cards.*
Restrictions: *No smoking inside, no pets, 2-night minimum on holiday weekends and during fall-foliage season. Open daily June–Aug., weekends and holidays Sept.–May.*

Belle Grae Inn

T he Belle Grae is a classic small-town hotel occupying an old Victorian house and several surrounding buildings close to Staunton's downtown. On your arrival you'll be met by Bellboy, a sanguine boxer, who, according to owner Michael Organ, works for biscuits. The Old Inn, built circa 1870, has a wide porch offering views of Bessie Belle and Mary Grae, two of the town's many hillocks. Its eight bedrooms have high ceilings and are decorated with amiable Victorian antiques, and downstairs there are two restaurants—one fancy, in Staunton terms, the other a bistro bar lined with windows. The suites in the Townhouse, adjoining the bistro, are Belle Grae's top-of-the-line, for their upscale decor and such amenities as fireplaces, phones, and cable TV. Varied accommodations are also available in Jefferson House, in a bungalow near the hotel's terrace garden, and in the Bishop's Study. But best of all is the earnest tone at the Belle Grae, a place that's trying hard to be the best Staunton has to offer, and succeeding, if quirkily.

Address: *515 W. Frederick St., Staunton, VA 24401, tel. 703/886–5151, fax 703/886–6641.*
Accommodations: *10 double rooms with baths, 4 suites, 1 apartment.*
Amenities: *Restaurant, bistro, fireplaces in 12 rooms and 3 common areas, air-conditioning, cable TV and phones in 12 rooms.*
Rates: *$75–$125; full breakfast. AE, D, MC, V.*
Restrictions: *Some nonsmoking rooms, no pets.*

Fassifern

Think of it. There are 96,000 horses in Virginia. If you want to buy or show one of them, the place to do it is the Virginia Horse Center, just north of Lexington. And if you make the trip, you'll be glad to know there's one of the Shenandoah Valley's prettiest bed-and-breakfasts just a trot down the road. The place is called Fassifern, after the Scottish ancestral home of its builder, who erected this three-story, smoky lavender brick farmhouse circa 1867. It's owned by Francis Whitsel Smith and managed by her animated daughter, Ann Carol Perry, who keeps two Welsh ponies and a horse in the pasture. There's no particular history connected to Fassifern; it's just a lovely country place with a pond, towering maple trees, and an old icehouse that's been converted into two extra guest rooms. We liked the Colonel's Quarters best because of its wide plank floors and pasture views. In the main house, three more guest rooms are furnished with Victorian armoires, Oriental rugs, and crystal chandeliers. Ann Carol is energetic, fun, and helpful.

Address: *Rte. 39 W. (RR 5, Box 87), Lexington, VA 24450, tel. 703/463–1013.*
Accommodations: *5 double rooms with baths.*
Amenities: *Air-conditioning, fireplace in living room.*
Rates: *$79–$88; Continental breakfast. MC, V.*
Restrictions: *No smoking, no pets, closed Thanksgiving, Dec. 24–25, Dec. 31.*

Hotel Strasburg

This white frame landmark (a former private hospital) at the northern end of the Shenandoah Valley is a showcase for the most baroque Victoriana—a statue of a nymph riding a stallion; a mock-heroic painting of Daniel in the lion's den; antique lace curtains; dark, clunky beds with soft mattresses; mirrors so elaborately ornamented that they seem ready to grab you if you admire yourself too long. Some people dote on this kind of thing; others despise it. The furnishings are supplied by the Strasburg Emporium, a vast antiques market, and every piece and every picture in the hotel is for sale. The hotel has a restaurant, which draws mixed reviews, and a convivial Depot Lounge. Among the hotel's annexes is the recently added neighboring Taylor House, which is perhaps the best choice, since it's somewhat secluded and has four suites with whirlpool tubs.

Address: *201 Holliday St., Strasburg, VA 22657, tel. 703/465–9191 or 800/348–8327, fax 703/465–4788.*
Accommodations: *17 double rooms with baths, 10 suites.*
Amenities: *Restaurant, air-conditioning, cable TV and phones in rooms, whirlpools in some suites.*
Rates: *$69–$149; Continental breakfast Mon.–Fri., breakfast extra on weekend. AE, DC, MC, V.*
Restrictions: *Five nonsmoking rooms, no pets.*

The Inn at Narrow Passage

Pack your inner tubes, gang, and your swimming togs and fishing rods; they'll all prove useful at the Inn at Narrow Passage, which sits right above the North Fork of the Shenandoah River. Ed Markel, owner of the Inn, will kindly put you in about a mile south, and from there it's a 3½ hour float to reach home. The oldest section of the inn was built as a way station on the Great Wagon Road (now Route 11) around 1740, and the Markels meticulously restored it, but guests still claim that you can see daylight through the chinks. There are three guest rooms on the second floor of this section, and nine more in wings built in 1985. The most inviting rooms are the older ones with handmade hinges, tongue-and-groove pine walls, and pegs instead of clos-

ets. When the valley is blanketed in snow, the inn is a cozy place—especially the living room with its blue plaid couches and big limestone fireplace (one of 10 here).

Address: *Rte. 11 S, Woodstock, VA 22664, tel. 703/459-8000, fax 703/459-8001.*
Accommodations: *10 double rooms with baths, 2 doubles share a bath.*
Amenities: *Air-conditioning, TV with VCR in sitting room, fireplaces in 7 guest rooms.*
Rates: *$55-$90; full breakfast, afternoon refreshments. MC, V.*
Restrictions: *No smoking in guest rooms, no pets, 2-night minimum fall and holiday weekends, closed Dec. 25.*

Joshua Wilton House

In Harrisonburg's neighborhood of well-kept, handsome old homes, the Joshua Wilton House strikes the highest note—it's a lovingly renovated and luxuriously equipped mauve, lavender, and pink Queen Anne cottage with triple-decker bays and a turret. Throughout, owners Roberta and Craig Moore have provided a sense of polished professionalism, a put-together look of coordinated decor. You enter by way of a front door surrounded by leaded glass and through a foyer with gleaming parquet floor, a chandelier, and bushy potted plants. Throughout the four downstairs dining rooms you'll find painted mantels and pictures displayed by the Shenandoah Valley Watercolor Association. The guest chambers are really lovely, particularly Room 5, with its four-

poster bed and white wing chairs, and Room 4, which has a three-window alcove in the turret. Fancy dinners and breakfasts, perhaps with crab-and-cheese omelettes, are available.

Address: *412 S. Main St., Harrisonburg, VA 22801, tel. 703/434-4464.*
Accommodations: *5 double rooms with baths.*
Amenities: *Restaurant, bar, air-conditioning, phones in rooms, fireplace in 1 room; bicycles.*
Rates: *$85-$100; full breakfast. AE, MC, V.*
Restrictions: *Smoking in bar only, no pets, 2-night minimum some weekends, closed Dec. 24-25.*

Lavender Hill Farm

Four miles west of Lexington, in a hollow across the road from a river, stands Lavender Hill, a working 20-acre farm with pet goats, sheep, dogs, cats, and rabbits. The central section of the main building is a 200-year-old log cabin. (One guest stayed here because his research revealed that it was his grandfather's birthplace.) Don't be deceived by the rather ramshackle outbuildings. Cindy Smith, a former investment banker in Europe, and her jovial husband, Colin, a retired British military officer, designed Lavender Hill to impart the feel of an English B&B—not antiques-filled, not laden down with quaintness. In keeping with the farm setting, rooms are simply furnished (lace curtains and, say, fresh blue and white stripes). Colin is the chef, providing sophisticated four-course meals for $20; his homegrown herbs are his culinary trademark. Cindy spins wool from the farm's sheep. Guests can fish in the river, bird-watch, or—the usual favorite—lounge on the porch with a cool drink. Special horseback-riding packages are available.

Address: *Rte. 631 (RR 1, Box 515), Lexington, VA 24450, tel. 703/464–5877 or 703/261–1910.*
Accommodations: *3 double rooms with baths.*
Amenities: *Dinner (by reservation), ceiling fans, TV with VCR in living room.*
Rates: *$55–$70; full breakfast. MC, V.*
Restrictions: *No smoking indoors, no pets.*

Oak Spring Farm and Vineyard

Oak Spring is a two-story plantation house whose sections were built in 1826 and 1840. During its recent restoration, owners Jim and Pat Tichenor discovered walls in the ell made of oak planks stacked up like pancakes—an architectural point that should make Oak Spring a shoo-in for the National Register of Historic Places. The restoration was impeccable; you won't find any cracked plaster or peeling paper here. The three guest rooms are on the second floor, and are filled with fine antiques; we liked the Regency Room best, because a window by its claw-foot tub provides pastoral views while you soak. Jim's great-grandmother's quilt lies spread upon a bed in the Victorian room. The farm is surrounded by 40 acres planted in hay and alfalfa, a meadow where burrow, donkeys, miniature horses, and an occasional llama or two graze, and 5 acres of grapes. Oak Spring Farm is a good out-of-town headquarters for exploring nearby Lexington and Staunton, and an excellent spot in which to lay over during trips on the Blue Ridge Parkway.

Address: *RR 1, Box 356, Raphine, VA 24472, tel. 703/377–2398.*
Accommodations: *3 double rooms with baths.*
Amenities: *Air-conditioning, turn-down service, fireplace in guest living room.*
Rates: *$63–$73; Continental-plus breakfast. MC, V.*
Restrictions: *No smoking, no pets, 2-night minimum on parents' and graduation weekends.*

Seven Hills Inn

Seven Hills Inn, a classic brick white-columned southern Colonial dwelling in the heart of Lexington's historic Main Street district, was built in 1928 as a fraternity house for nearby Washington and Lee University. Hence the expansive living room, dining room, and casual downstairs chapter room with its fireplace, TV with VCR, and games. It's doubtful, though, that the house had such an impeccably fresh and inviting appearance when the college crowd was occupying it. Ben Grigsby, a W&L alumnus, bought the place and restored it, removing walls between the small fraternity bedrooms to create large guest rooms. When Ben's work sent him out of the country, he asked his parents, Jane and Vern Daniel, to operate the B&B.

The pale yellow third-floor Holly Hill room, with a sloping ceiling, has a bath that's bigger than the bedroom. Fruit Hill has a Jacuzzi tub and a four-poster bed, and it can be opened into a suite with a parlor.

Address: *408 S. Main St., Lexington, VA 24450, tel. 703/463-4715, fax 703/463-6526.*
Accommodations: *5 double rooms with baths, 2 bedrooms in family suite share 1 bath.*
Amenities: *Air-conditioning, whirlpool in 1 room, TV with VCR in chapter room.*
Rates: *$75–$140; Continental-plus breakfast. MC, V.*
Restrictions: *No smoking in guest rooms, no pets, 2-night minimum some weekends.*

Thornrose House

Nine years ago, Susie and Otis Huston spent the night at their first B&B. Someday, they said, *we'll* do this, and they started a portfolio of properties and ideas. After a lengthy search they bought Thornrose and moved down from Buffalo, New York, where Otis had been in management with DuPont and Susie taught school. They immediately got to work redoing every single surface: painting, papering, refinishing the hardwood floors. With changes on the order of replacing velvet draperies with lace curtains, Thornrose now has a lighter, fresher appearance. Windsor (all the guest rooms carry English names) has antique twin beds pushed together to form a queen with a white quilted spread and white lace-trimmed pillows, and an

antique armoire and dresser. The blue-and-rose Canterbury Room overlooks bucolic Gypsy Hill Park, where there are a swimming pool, tennis courts, a golf course, and the July Fourth Statler Brothers concerts.

Address: *531 Thornrose Ave., Staunton, VA 24401, tel. 703/885-7026.*
Accommodations: *5 double rooms with baths.*
Amenities: *Air-conditioning, cable TV in guest sitting room; bicycles.*
Rates: *$55–$70; full breakfast, afternoon tea. No credit cards.*
Restrictions: *No smoking, no pets, 2- and 3-night minimum Oct., July 4th, and graduation weekends.*

Off the Beaten Track

Fort Lewis Lodge

On a 3,200-acre farm in the Allegheny foothills, John and Caryl Cowden raise Angus cattle, soybeans, and corn. The beautiful Cowpasture River deepens into a swimming hole nearby, and Shenandoah Mountain looms above, traversed by paths and logging roads. Below the manor house there's a dining hall in an old mill, and a lodge. The common rooms contain bears, raccoons, and red fox—all Allegheny Highland species. The lodge rooms are exceptionally comfortable, with locally handcrafted furniture. There's a laundry room, and a stone hearth in the gathering room. The rooms in the converted silo are round.

Surrounded by fields, rivers, mountains, and forests and standing 10 miles off the main road, Fort Lewis Lodge is blissfully outdoorsy: There's an old-fashioned swimming hole, tubing down the river, fishing, hiking, biking, and terrific birdwatching. It's great for kids. Camping can be arranged, and guide services are available during the spring and summer hunting season. And at the end of the day you return to Cowden hospitality—starring Carol's homemade dinners in the dining hall.

Address: *HCR3, Box 21A, Millboro, VA 24460, tel. 703/925-2314.*
Accommodations: *8 double rooms with baths, 3 suites.*
Amenities: *TV with VCR in game room; bicycles, hot tub.*
Rates: *$120–$135; MAP. MC, V.*
Restrictions: *No smoking in guest rooms, no pets, closed mid-Oct.–mid-Apr.*

The Inn at Gristmill Square

Bath County in western Virginia covers 540 bumpy square miles inhabited by just 5,000 souls, and it hasn't got a single stoplight. Warm Springs, the county seat, boasts a post office, courthouse, and inn—and that's about all. Still, the Inn at Gristmill Square, occupying several 19th-century buildings—a blacksmith's barn, restored mill, miller's house, and hardware store—is reason enough to visit this quintessentially peaceful spot. Its Waterwheel Restaurant is one of the area's best places to sup, with a chef trained at the Culinary Institute of America and a cool subterranean wine cellar. The Steel House, across the lane, has a small swimming pool, sauna, and tennis courts. The Silo has a round living room, and the large, rustic Board Room, our favorite, is paneled with barn siding and features a claw-foot tub. Janice McWilliams and her son, Bruce, are the able proprietors, former owners of an inn in Vermont. They serve a simple breakfast and the *Richmond Times Dispatch* in a picnic basket at your door.

Address: *Box 359, Warm Springs, VA 24484, tel. 703/839-2231.*
Accommodations: *14 double rooms with baths, 2 apartments.*
Amenities: *Restaurant, air-conditioning in 10 rooms, fireplaces in 8 guest rooms, cable TV, phones, and minifridges in rooms; swimming pool, sauna, 3 tennis courts, store.*
Rates: *$80–$95; MAP available; Continental breakfast. MC, V.*
Restrictions: *No pets.*

West Virginia

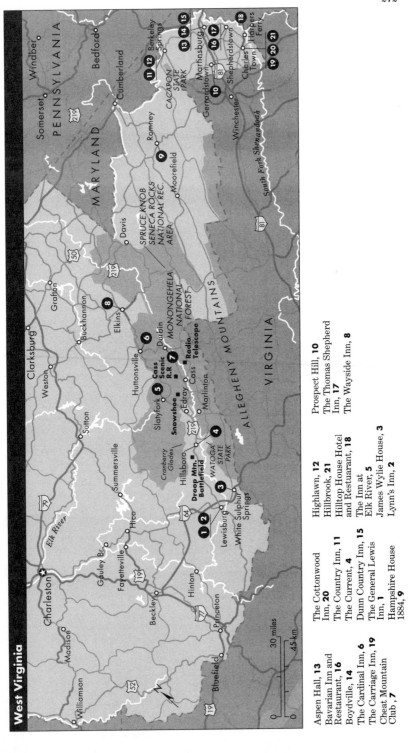

Aspen Hall, **13**
Bavarian Inn and
Restaurant, **16**
Boydville, **14**
The Cardinal Inn, **6**
The Carriage Inn, **19**
Cheat Mountain
Club, **7**

The Cottonwood
Inn, **20**
The Country Inn, **11**
The Current, **4**
Dunn Country Inn, **15**
The General Lewis
Inn, **1**
Hampshire House
1884, **9**

Highlawn, **12**
Hillbrook, **21**
Hilltop House Hotel
and Restaurant, **18**
The Inn at
Elk River, **5**
James Wylie House, **3**
Lynn's Inn, **2**

Prospect Hill, **10**
The Thomas Shepherd
Inn, **17**
The Wayside Inn, **8**

The Eastern Panhandle

*Like so much of West Virginia, the three eastern counties
that make up the panhandle region are mountainous,
reaching elevations of 2,300 feet. Long a wild,
uninhabitable part of the west, it was not until George
Washington surveyed the area in the mid-1700s that
a number of villages sprang up along the Potomac River,
among them Shepherdstown, Harpers Ferry, Charles Town,
and Martinsburg.*

*Today, the state is still relatively untamed and is
a wonderland for explorers, who can drive for miles along
surprisingly well maintained highways without tripping
over condo developments or fast-food restaurants. In the
last few decades the state government, based in Charleston,
has turned its attention to nurturing the wildest portions
of the Allegheny Front and Plateau, once devastated by
lumbering and strip mining, by creating a first-rate
network of parks. Six-thousand-acre Cacapon State Park—
with its hiking trails and Robert Trent Jones golf course—
is among these, as is Berkeley Springs State Park, a funky
spot equipped with tiled Roman baths, steam cabinets, and
some of the best spring water in the world (beloved by
George Washington, in fact).*

*One of West Virginia's most popular tourist attractions
lies in the Eastern Panhandle—Harpers Ferry National
Park. Thomas Jefferson described it best, writing: "On your
right comes up the Shenandoah, having ranged along the
foot of the mountains a hundred miles to seek a vent. On
your left approaches the Potomac, in quest of a passage
also. In the moment of their junction they rush together
against the mountain, rend it asunder, and pass off to the
sea . . . This scene is worth a voyage across the Atlantic."
The spot where these rivers converge so dramatically is also
where, on October 16, 1859, the abolitionist zealot John
Brown led his 21-man assault on the Harpers Ferry*

*arsenal. Today, strips of Harpers Ferry national parklands
line the rivers like a glove, and historic markers tell the
story of John Brown's raid and of the town's tumultuous
involvement in the Civil War.*

*Shepherdstown, sitting high above the Potomac across from
Sharpsburg, Maryland, was founded in 1762 and is the
oldest town in West Virginia. Visitors can browse the
pleasant collection of shops along the main drag here and,
since all the Panhandle's main towns are close together,
can make a short trip to the Charles Town track to take in
the horse races before heading back to one of the area's
many fine inns.*

*Potomac and Shenandoah river rafting abounds, and there
are numerous bicycling routes (among them Route 230
between Harpers Ferry and Shepherdstown and the
Tuscarora Pike near Martinsburg) and a great variety of
outlet stores in Martinsburg where you can snap up name-
brand clothing and other products for a fraction of the
department-store price. If you have more time to explore,
head west to Berkeley Springs and Cacapon State Park,
where you'll discover the real West Virginia—that of
logging trucks, black bear, wild turkey, and mountains that
don't let up until the Ohio River.*

Places to Go, Sights to See

Berkeley Springs State Park (tel. 304/258–2711 or 800/225–5982). Located
within the city limits of the town of Bath, this state park has a museum and
a pool. In the bathhouse you can sample the therapeutic waters, which rush
out of the springs at an unvarying temperature of 74.3°F and a volume of
2,000 gallons a minute. The bathhouse itself has seen better days; still,
where else but here can you have a massage and get wrinkled in a Roman
tub for a slim $27? The water's the same at other places, where the
surroundings are tonier and the price tag higher. In fact, the water's the
same everywhere in funny little Berkeley Springs (a.k.a. Bath); it comes out
of every tap.

Cacapon State Park (tel. 304/258–1022 or 800/225–5982). Cacapon lies 10
miles south of Berkeley Springs, off Route 522, and encompasses a narrow
strip of mountains that reaches almost to the Maryland and Virginia borders.

A paved road leads to the summit of Cacapon Mountain, and the park has 27 miles of hiking trails, as well as a lodge, golf course (for which reservations are encouraged), and a man-made lake with a sandy beach.

Charles Town Races (tel. 304/725–7001). The thoroughbreds pound the turf from January to December (nightly, as well as Wednesday and Sunday afternoon) at this track just outside Charles Town (about 5 miles southwest of Harpers Ferry).

Harpers Ferry National Historic Park (tel. 304/535–6223 or 304/535–6298). This is the site of the arsenal that John Brown held for two days before it was stormed by marines under Robert E. Lee. A network of hiking routes pass through Harpers Ferry, including the Appalachian Trail.

O'Hurley's General Store (tel. 304/876–6907). This Shepherdstown emporium is crammed with "the most extensive variety of time-tested products available in this modern age," including boxes, barrels, baskets, anvils, harnesses, coffins, guns, books, and dinner bells.

Panorama Point. Follow Route 9 for 4 miles west of Berkeley Springs to the shoulder of Prospect Peak for a view of the Great Cacapon Valley, where three states—Maryland, West Virginia, and Pennsylvania—converge.

Restaurants

For German cooking and wild-game dishes, try the **Bavarian Inn** (Shepherdstown, tel. 304/876–2551), overlooking the Potomac River. The **Yellow Brick Bank** (Shepherdstown, tel. 304/876–2208) is a favorite of Washingtonians, and the Continental menu reflects those urban tastes; the food at **The Country Inn** (Berkeley Springs, tel. 304/258–2210 or 800/822–6630) is plain but good.

Tourist Information

Jefferson County Convention and Visitors Bureau (Box A, Harpers Ferry, 25425, tel. 304/535–2627 or 800/848–8687.) **Travel Berkeley Springs** (304 Fairfax St., Berkeley Springs 25411, tel. 304/258–3738). **West Virginia Department of Commerce** (2101 Washington St. E, Charleston 24305, tel. 800/225–5982).

Reservation Service

Blue Ridge B&B Reservation Service (Rocks & Rills, Rte. 2, Box 3895, Berryville 22611, tel. 703/955–1246).

Boydville

The story always told about Boydville, Martinsburg's grandest house, concerns its near destruction by Union troops during the Civil War. One often hears how some pretty southern belle pleaded with roughshod Federals to spare her family manse, but in the case of Boydville, the tale is documented. Mary Faulkner, of the clan that has resided in Boydville for 150 years, wired Abraham Lincoln, whose decision to let Boydville stand arrived just before northerners lit the torch.

A later Faulkner served as U.S. senator, commuting to the nation's capital by train (just as present owner LaRue Frye does today). When the six o'clock train from the District hooted over nearby Bull's Eye Bridge, the Boydville servants began crushing ice for the senator's mint julep. And when he arrived on the wide front porch and reclined in a green rocker (the very one there today), his drink was waiting.

Boydville, a limestone manor house covered with white stucco, was completed in 1812 by General Elisha Boyd, a hero of the War of 1812 and a friend of Martinsburg's founder, Adam Stephen. Obviously it's a historic place, and perhaps the northernmost outcropping of the old South. The mansion, with its ivy-covered walled patio, is surrounded by 10 parklike acres of lawn and garden. The new owner has given Boydville a new roof and repaired

the water damage that had marred this historic gem. Guests are shown the case locks stamped with the imprimatur of the locksmith to King George IV, the English molding in the downstairs parlors, and English hand-painted wallpaper dating to 1812 in the foyer. The rooms are enormous, the most desirable being the Adam Stephen Room; it has hand-painted mural wallpaper imported from France in the early 1800s and the first tiled bathroom in Martinsburg.

Confederate general Stonewall Jackson retreated to Boydville for physical and emotional renewal many times during the Civil War. Thanks to LaRue and the other three working professionals who lovingly tend Boydville, the mansion still has that power to soothe.

Address: *601 S. Queen St., Martinsburg, WV 25401, tel. 304/263–1448 or 202/626–2896.*
Accommodations: *6 double rooms with baths.*
Amenities: *Air-conditioning in bedrooms, fireplace and cable TV in common area, fireplaces in 2 bedrooms.*
Rates: *$100–$140; Continental-plus breakfast. MC, V.*
Restrictions: *No smoking, no pets, 2-night minimum Memorial Day weekend and on Oct. weekends.*

Hillbrook

Would Hillbrook, hidden along a country lane outside Charles Town, be such a special place without its innkeeper, Gretchen Carroll? One tends to think not, although the house itself is spectacularly eccentric, splayed in six stages along a hill, never more than one room wide or one room deep. The house has 13 sharply peaked gables, half-timbered white-stucco walls, and mullioned windows—the one in the living room has 360 panes. Ann Hathaway would feel right at home. Gretchen calls the style "Norman Tudor" and explains that during World War I a civil engineer by the name of Bamford fell in love with an inn in Normandy and determined to re-create it in the wilds of West Virginia. Erratically, he chose to start with two ancient log cabins. The logs and mortises of one of these are still apparent in the dining porch.

Gretchen was a foreign-service brat who grew up in the far corners of the world, including Turkey, Thailand, and the Ivory Coast; and Hillbrook is full of exotic curios and objets d'art. The living room holds pottery and a Senegalese fertility statue; in bedrooms you'll find Oriental rugs, an antique Vuitton steamer trunk, and a Thai spirit house. Richly patterned wallpaper, upholstery, and pillows; randomly angled ceilings; potted plants; and architectural cubbyholes complete the Hillbrook picture. The Cottage guest room, with its private entry overlooking an ancient springhouse (from which Hillbrook gets its water), has paisley-pattern wallpaper and a wood-burning stove backed with Italian tile. Locke's Nest overlooks the 20-foot-high living room and has brass double and single beds and a lavender bathtub.

The inn's seven-course dinners have been known to include grilled swordfish with jasmine rice; feta-cheese-and-pomegranate salad; and chocolate fudge cake. Gretchen's breakfast specialty is French toast Tatiana, dripping in cranberry-orange syrup and sour cream.

Bullskin Run Creek trickles away at the bottom of the Hillbrook lawn, the haunt of ducks, swans, inn guests and a cat named Smudge. There are, of course, attractions to visit in the surrounding area, but nothing that would keep one away from idyllic Hillbrook for long.

Address: *Rte. 2 (Box 152), Charles Town, WV 24514, tel. 304/725-4223.*
Accommodations: *11 double rooms with baths.*
Amenities: *Dinner Thurs.–Sun. ($68 per person, including wine), air-conditioning in bedrooms, fireplaces in 7 rooms, tavern, high tea on Sun.*
Rates: *$165; full breakfast ($190 MAP). D, MC, V.*
Restrictions: *No pets, closed Mon.–Wed.*

Aspen Hall

Aspen Hall, in Martinsburg, is a native-limestone Georgian manor house with a very long history. It was begun sometime around 1754 as the fortified residence of a settler named John Mendenhall and by 1761 was a grand enough place for a wedding, which was attended by George Washington. As you turn onto Boyd Avenue you may be put off by several ill-kept rental properties, but the scene quickly changes to nicely tended homes. Aspen Hall is at the end, in a hollow alongside Tuscarora Creek, shaded by giant locusts that were probably saplings in Washington's time. A walk bounded by a rock wall and border of plants leads to a gazebo by the creek, where tea is often served. Inside a picket fence there's a small herb garden.

Inside, Aspen Hall's blond-floor foyer is a space suitable for presidential entrances. Its twin parlors have 12-foot ceilings, 19th-century antique furniture, and swag draperies. In those parlors retired antiques dealers Gordon and LouAnne Claucherty serve tea to the overnight guests. The nicest of the five guest bedrooms is the front one, with fireplace, a four-poster canopy bed, and a claw-foot tub.

Address: *405 Boyd Ave., Martinsburg, WV 25401, tel. 304/263-4385.* **Accommodations:** *5 double rooms with baths.* **Amenities:** *TV in common room.* **Rates:** *$110; full breakfast. MC, V.* **Restrictions:** *No smoking, no pets, closed Dec. 24–Feb. 10.*

Bavarian Inn and Restaurant

Because of its setting high above the Potomac River in a town with one traffic light, the Bavarian Inn is "country," but it's also the last word in luxury. That won't appeal to everyone, because it means the coat and tie go into the suitcase along with the jeans. Munich-born Erwin Asam, a former Washington restaurateur, and his British wife, Carol, have turned the 1930s mansion into a slice of Erwin's homeland, with alpine chalets overlooking the river, dining rooms with the feel of an elegant mountain lodge, and an extensive menu loaded with German specialties. Everything's here for a pampered stay, right down to the mints on the pillow. Despite big-hotel amenities, the Asams try to preserve a relaxed, personal atmosphere. Not up to the coat and tie? Slip downstairs to the wood-beamed, informal Rathskeller for dinner from the same menu, plus entertainment.

Address: *Shepherd Grade Rd., Rte. 480 (Rte. 1, Box 30), Shepherdstown, WV 25443, tel. 304/876-2551, fax 304/876-9355.* **Accommodations:** *42 double rooms with baths.* **Amenities:** *TV and phones in rooms, fireplaces, whirlpool tubs, private balconies; restaurant, 3 conference rooms; tennis courts, swimming pool.* **Rates:** *$65–$135; breakfast extra. AE, DC, MC, V.* **Restrictions:** *No smoking in some areas and rooms, no pets, 2-night minimum on holiday weekends.*

The Carriage Inn

When generals Ulysses S. Grant and Philip Sheridan met at what is now the Carriage Inn to map out the Union Army's Shenandoah Valley campaign, there was a picket fence around the house and a Greek Revival portico. Otherwise, things haven't changed much at the old Rutherford place in Charles Town—anyway, guests don't mind the addition of a broad front porch and modern plumbing. The owner of this shady gray Colonial-style house is Robert Kaetzel, who helped restore Shepherdstown's Thomas Shepherd Inn before deciding to fix up a bed-and-breakfast of his own. He not only made every canopy bed at the Carriage Inn, he cut down the wood to make them. And he has a strong aversion to the ubiquitous "Continental" breakfast. "Either it's breakfast or it's not," he says. Besides hearty morning meals, the Carriage Inn offers big bedrooms (four with fireplaces), two sitting rooms, polished floors, solid brick walls, and a bookful of Civil War stories to tell—like the one about Stonewall Jackson's flag, which was buried behind the house when the Federals came.

Address: *417 E. Washington St., Charles Town, WV 25414, tel. 304/728-8003.*
Accommodations: *5 double rooms with baths.*
Amenities: *Air-conditioning.*
Rates: *$65–$95; full breakfast. MC, V.*
Restrictions: *No smoking in bedrooms, no pets.*

The Cottonwood Inn

About 5 miles south of Charles Town along Kabletown Road, a trio of silos rises, marking the winding road to the Cottonwood Inn. This yellow frame farmhouse has occupied a hollow alongside Bullskin Run Creek for almost 200 years—as its uneven pine floors and big brick dining-room hearth attest. Colin and Eleanor Simpson and their nine children arrived in 1976. After the kids left this lovely nest, Colin and Eleanor began taking in bed-and-breakfast guests. Days at the Cottonwood are spent communing with cows amid farmy scents, fishing for trout in the creek, pitching horseshoes, or snoozing in a hammock out back. And when night falls the guest rooms are exceptionally cozy places to rest: in particular, the fireplace suite and four-postered double room in the rear. Several years ago the Simpsons added a wing to the farmhouse with two guest rooms that are spacious and handsomely decorated, though not as atmospheric as the rooms in the old section. The Cottonwood is close to the Blue Ridge, which beckons on the horizon; and to the north lie the Charles Town Race Track and Harpers Ferry.

Address: *Rte. 2 (Box 61–S), Charles Town, WV 25414, tel. 304/725-3371.*
Accommodations: *7 double rooms with baths, 1 suite with fireplace.*
Amenities: *Air-conditioning, TV in rooms.*
Rates: *$85–$105; full breakfast. AE, MC, V.*
Restrictions: *No smoking in dining room, no pets, closed Dec. 23–29.*

The Country Inn

From the outside, the Country Inn in Berkeley Springs looks a little grander than the image the name summons up; it's a four-story brick building, with a columned front porch, that was built in 1932. Then came a set of wings in 1937, and then, after Jack and Adele Barker bought the place in the early 1970s (because Jack, a former teacher, disliked retirement), a conference center, motel annex, and spa out back. The additions haven't damaged the integrity of the old inn much, for its rooms are still old-timey, with mismatched quasi-antiques; a long, carpeted central corridor; and a country store downstairs. The inn is next door to Berkeley Springs State Park, but the spa facilities at the inn come with a view of the town and the ridge.

The inn has two dining rooms, one a garden affair with a dance floor, where there's live music on weekends.

Address: *Berkeley Springs, WV 25411, tel. 304/258–2210 or 800/822–6630, fax 304/258–3986.*
Accommodations: *58 double rooms with baths, 12 doubles share 4 baths, 1 suite.*
Amenities: *Restaurant, pub, room service, air-conditioning, cable TV in rooms, phones in hall and in annex rooms, spa, 2 conference rooms.*
Rates: *$35–$145; breakfast extra. AE, D, DC, MC, V.*
Restrictions: *No smoking in suite, no pets, 2-night minimum on weekends May–Oct. and major holiday weekends.*

Dunn Country Inn

The busy kitchen at the Dunn Country Inn, with its easy chairs and stone hearth, is the nerve center for activities at this homey bed-and-breakfast. This is as it should be, since the building, begun in 1805, is a cozy farmhouse. Around 1870 the resident farmer felt able to expand, adding a grand front addition (like the back, of native limestone), with Romanesque windows, elaborate molding, and 12-foot ceilings. Dianna Dunn is responsible for the inn's decoration, which includes folk-arty stenciling and teddy bears, wreaths, and a pleasant assortment of country antiques—all of which make the place very much like one of the painter Carl Larsen's Scandinavian interiors. That, too, is as it should be, because Dianna is half Norwegian. Her husband,

Prince, grew up in Martinsburg and these days commutes to the Pentagon, where he's a consultant. Other family members include the Dunns' 3½-year-old son, Colin, and a pair of exuberantly friendly stray dogs named Jessica and Rose. Dianna's breakfasts, always hearty, often include her grandmother's *pankakas*—Norwegian crepes.

Address: *Rte. 3 (Box 33J), Martinsburg, WV 25401, tel. 304/263–8646.*
Accommodations: *2 double rooms with hall baths.*
Amenities: *Air-conditioning, picnic lunches prepared.*
Rates: *$100; full breakfast. No credit cards.*
Restrictions: *No smoking, no pets, 2-night minimum late Sept.–early Nov. and holiday weekends.*

Highlawn

The house Algernon R. Unger built for his bride, Chaffie Ziler, is just the sort of place for an Algie and Chaffie to summer in: a white Queen Anne cottage with 21 rooms, a wide front porch, and a tin roof that vibrates musically when it rains. The present owner, Sandra Kauffman, takes a Roman bath at the state park about once a week and cheerfully reminds guests that every tap in her house dispenses the miracle cure. The private suite has its own tin-roofed porch and hand-painted Victorian furniture. All the bedrooms have lace-curtained windows, plump pillows, and turn-of-the-century furnishings like brass beds and rockers. On Saturday (May–October and holidays) Sandra serves a gourmet silver-service dinner at Highlawn. During her murder-mystery weekends, dinner is served at Berkeley Castle, a half-scale copy of the English original that overlooks the town. Her breakfasts include such delicacies as lemon bread with lemon butter and chocolate-chip coffee cake. Sandra and partner Tim Miller have recently opened Aunt Pearl's, an adjacent Victorian with four luxury rooms.

Address: *304 Market St., Berkeley Springs, WV 25411, tel. 304/258–5700.*
Accommodations: *9 double rooms with baths, 1 suite.*
Amenities: *Air-conditioning, TV in bedrooms.*
Rates: *$70–$105; full breakfast, dinner extra. AE, MC, V.*
Restrictions: *No pets, 2-night minimum most weekends.*

Hilltop House Hotel and Restaurant

You simply haven't seen Harpers Ferry unless you make the pilgrimage to Hilltop House, which opened in the 1880s and has hosted the likes of Mark Twain, Woodrow Wilson, and Pearl Buck. Unless you stay overnight you may miss the sunrise show: Dawn pulls the curtain, and the rivers make their entrance, thinly veiled in mist. The view is everything it can be; the inn is not—not yet, that is. A million-dollar renovation by its Washington-based owners has put a lot of the disrepair right, and the work continues at the rate of about five rooms a year. The rooms not yet redone are still clean and comfortable, if you can overlook the occasional broken tile or patched wall and the poor taste of earlier decorators. The top-floor rooms are huge (one has a whirlpool tub), and the view is the best in the house. The food doesn't pretend to be fancy, but it's good. Dining areas have more view than atmosphere, but the oak bar, with its live entertainment on Saturday nights, is a winner.

Address: *Ridge St. (Box 930), Harpers Ferry, WV 25425, tel. 304/535–2132 or 800/338–8319; fax 304/535–6322.*
Accommodations: *62 double rooms with baths, 4 suites.*
Amenities: *Restaurant, air-conditioning, TV in some bedrooms, phones in rooms, 6 conference rooms, special packages.*
Rates: *$59–$95; breakfast extra. AE, DC, MC, V.*
Restrictions: *No pets, 2-night minimum with Sat. reservation.*

Prospect Hill

This handsome Georgian house, built of brick in 1804, is surrounded by a 225-acre farm that stretches to the top of North Mountain and lies along what was once the Pack Horse Trail, a main road to the West. Its old dependencies—including Flemish-bond brick slave quarters, now converted into an apartment—are in particularly good condition, with a stream wandering beside them. Owners Charles and Hazel Hudock restored the place and are proud of its unusual details, like the several working Franklin fireplaces dating from the 1790s and a mural depicting Prospect Hill and scenes from American life. Charles is an inveterate collector who indulged his interest during his years as a Navy meteorologist. In the spring, you may see deer grazing with their fawns on the grounds. Two ponds yield fine bass in the summer and freeze for skating in the winter. The Hudocks are also gardeners, and the fruits of their labors—homemade grape juice, fresh raspberries, and peaches—often appear on the breakfast table.

Address: *Box 135, Gerrardstown, WV 25420, tel. 304/229-3346.*
Accommodations: *2 double rooms with baths, 1 apartment.*
Amenities: *Air-conditioning in bedrooms, TV in apartment and living room, phones and fireplaces in rooms.*
Rates: *$85–$95; full breakfast. MC, V.*
Restrictions: *Smoking in living room only, no pets, 2-night minimum on Oct. weekends.*

The Thomas Shepherd Inn

Shepherdstown is easily the prettiest village in Panhandle West Virginia, built in the mid-1800s, and thus a showplace for late-Federal architecture. Its shop-lined business district lies along German Street, where up a ways you'll find the Thomas Shepherd Inn, named for the town's founder, whose grist mill still stands, with a huge cast-iron wheel. The inn was built in 1868 as a Lutheran parsonage and expanded in 1937. It's a gracious place that would look at home in Colonial Williamsburg, with green molding, inset shutters, and a spacious courtyard garden in the rear. Though it's been an inn since 1981, Margaret Perry, a former homemaker who loves to sew and cook, took over in 1989. Her breakfasts can be elaborate, featuring eggs Benedict with caviar and French toast made from brioches. All guest rooms have polished floors, Oriental rugs, and handsomely coordinated upholstery and spreads, but the favorite is Room 6 because of its garden view, claw-foot tub, and four-poster bed. The inn has become a prime way station for bike-trippers on back roads and for people heading for Maryland's Antietam Battlefield, 5 miles north.

Address: *Box 1162, Shepherdstown, WV 25443, tel. 304/876-3715.*
Accommodations: *6 double rooms with baths.*
Amenities: *Air-conditioning, TV in library.*
Rates: *$85–$95; full breakfast. AE, D, MC, V.*
Restrictions: *No smoking, no pets.*

The Mountains

*The Allegheny Mountains of West Virginia are
a substantial range, reaching from around Davis in the
north to the Greenbrier Valley in the south. They are wide,
too—it takes a hard day of driving to cross them east to
west—and it's easy to sympathize with the early pioneers,
who struggled over the same hills without the convenience
of automobiles. Not all of the settlers made it to the West,
though: some, particularly Scotch-Irish immigrants, gave
up before reaching the fertile Ohio Valley and settled in
this high, wild territory that would become West Virginia.
They fought with the Shawnee Indians in the late 1700s, but
they managed to hang on to the land that would later
prove a valuable, if limited, source of timber and coal.*

*Long overlooked by the rest of the country, West Virginia
has recently been rediscovered. Tourism, especially skiing,
has begun to replace mining and lumbering as an
Allegheny Mountain cash crop. The region's ski resorts—
Canaan Valley State Park, Timberline Four Seasons
Resort, and Snowshoe and Silver Creek on Cheat
Mountain—have one of the longest skiing seasons in the
East. Hikers, naturalists, hunters, anglers, and cyclists will
also find a paradise in the Allegheny Mountains, 900,000
acres of which are part of the Monongahela National
Forest. There are plenty of state parks, too, including
Watoga, Cranberry Glades, and the remote Dolly Sods
Wilderness. The Seneca Rocks–Spruce Knob Recreation
Area is at the top of the mountain chain, with Spruce
Knob, at 4,860 feet, officially the highest point in the state.*

*As you journey south, the mountains relax into hills,
sloping down to the idyllic Greenbrier Valley and the
historic town of Lewisburg. This former frontier fort was
the site of battles in both the Revolutionary and Civil wars.
Today it's a peaceful town of fine Federal and Victorian
homes. To the east, the famed Greenbrier resort, where the*

Vanderbilts and Astors took the waters in the early part of the century, is still as grand as ever.

Visitors who want to see America in all its variety and eccentricity couldn't do better than to drive into the mountains of West Virginia, where they can attend ramp festivals (ramps are a potent mountain onion that make the eater a social outcast for a week); go rafting on whitewater rivers rated among the wildest in the nation; bike the 75-mile Greenbrier River Trail on an inn-to-inn odyssey; or hike the strange tundralike plateau of the Dolly Sods Wilderness Area and ponder how anyone could ever have forgotten about West Virginia.

Places to Go, Sights to See

Canaan Valley State Park (tel. 800/225–5982). Long known for downhill skiing, this 21-trail park is particularly good for families because of its low prices and great variety of activities.

Cass Scenic Railroad (tel. 304/456–4300 or 800/225–5982). Near the intersection of routes 250 and 28, Cass is the base for the logging line that once carried lumberjacks up Bald Knob Mountain and now carries sightseers on a four-hour trip to the Allegheny plateau. Pack a lunch and warm clothes; you'll reach an altitude of almost 5,000 feet.

Dolly Sods Wilderness (tel. 304/257–4488 or 304/567–2827). Near the town of Davis and the Canaan Valley, this remote refuge is overrun with sphagnum bogs, wind-blown spruce, heath barrens, and patches of wild onions.

Droop Mountain Battlefield State Park (tel. 304/653–4254 or 800/225–5982). This restored Civil War battlefield offers a small museum, observation tower, and hiking trails.

National Radio Astronomy Observatory (Green Bank, tel. 304/456–2011). If there is intelligent life out there, the people manning the wires at this federal installation are likely to be the first to know. The observatory has a 300-foot movable radio telescope, the largest of its kind in the world.

New River Bridge. The world's biggest single-arch span (3,000 feet long) is situated on Route 19 between Hico and Fayetteville. On Bridge Day, the third Saturday in October, hang gliders, bungee jumpers, and assorted other daredevils are permitted to throw themselves off the bridge.

New River Gorge National River (tel. 304/465–0508). Rangers conduct guided tours of this 52-mile-long "Grand Canyon of the East." For information about river running and outfitters, tel. 800/225–5982.

Pearl Buck Home (tel. 304/653–4430 or 800/225–5982). The Pulitzer- and Nobel Prize–winning author of *The Good Earth* came from Hillsboro, West Virginia, and her home is now preserved as a museum.

Seneca Rocks (tel. 800/225–5982). These twin Tuscarora-sandstone promontories rise 1,000 feet above the North Fork River; the visitors center provides telescopes for watching the precarious progress of rock climbers. Should you be tempted by the heights, contact the *Seneca Rocks Climbing School* (tel. 304/567–2600) or *Blackwater Outdoor Center* in Davis (tel. 304/259–5117 or 800/328–4798).

Snowshoe/Silver Creek Mountain Resort (Snowshoe Ski Area, tel. 304/572–1000; Silver Creek Ski Area, tel. 304/572–4000). With the acquisition of Silver Creek, Snowshoe has become the largest ski area in the Mid-Atlantic region. Snowshoe has 33 trails and full snowmaking; Silver Creek has 17 trails. One lift ticket serves both areas. Snowshoe's Gary Player–designed golf course opened in 1993 as the latest improvement to the year-round resort.

Watoga State Park (tel. 800/225–5982 or 304/799–4087). Seventeen miles south of Marlinton, this is West Virginia's first and largest state park, bordered by the beautiful Greenbrier River. Recreational facilities, including a pool, cabins, commissary, and lake, are open in the summertime.

Restaurants

The **Red Fox** (tel. 304/572–1111), slopeside at Snowshoe Mountain Resort, has haute cuisine with a country touch. Almost all ingredients are from local sources, and the food, atmosphere, and service are outstanding. The restaurant at **Blackwater Falls State Park** (tel. 304/259–5216), perched on the Blackwater Canyon rim near Davis, has a limited but tasty menu. **Bright Morning B&B** (tel. 304/259–5119) in Davis serves good breakfast and dinner buffets. You can join the mountain bikers for local trout and other hearty, healthy fare next to the fireplace at the **Inn at Elk River** (tel. 304/572–3771; *see below*).

Tourist Information

Lewisburg Convention and Visitors Bureau (105 Church St., Lewisburg 24901, tel. 304/645–1000). **Pocahontas County Tourism** (Box 275, Marlinton 24954, tel. 304/799–4636 or 800/336–7009). **Potomac Highlands Convention and Visitors Bureau** (Box 2758, Elkins 26241, tel. 304/636–8400 or 800/347–1453). **West Virginia Department of Commerce** (2101 Washington St., E, Charleston 24305, tel. 800/225–5982).

Cheat Mountain Club

Standing 3,800 feet above sea level, on the shoulder of the colossal Cheat Mountain and surrounded by nine of West Virginia's 10 highest precipices and the 70,000-acre Monongahela National Forest, the Cheat Mountain Club has a setting that will always be enough to make it special among inns. Lovers of the outdoors are sure to appreciate the changing seasons here, whether the lodge is buried in snow, blanketed with wild rhododendrons, or enveloped in a fog so thick that no one bothers to step outside the front door. The grounds include 180 acres, across which the trout-rich Shavers Fork River flows. From it a tracery of old logging roads spirals away into the mountains—one route leading 18 miles south to Bald Knob. Five miles of trails within the club's boundaries, along which shy black bears are often spied, are groomed for hiking, mountain biking, and cross-country skiing.

Until 1988 this Elysium was privately owned, used as a retreat for the executives of a logging company. Later it was sold to a group of five West Virginia families, who brought in resident managers Deb and Norm Strouse and opened it to the public. Norm is a graduate of the Forestry School of West Virginia, a latter-day mountain man who knows everything there is to know about the area. Deb is a trained hotelier who cooks and serves the three excellent meals included in the club's daily rate.

The pine-paneled guest rooms on the lodge's second floor are functionally decorated and immaculately kept. Only one has a private bath, but the large, multiple shared bathrooms (one for women, another for men) are extremely comfortable and outfitted with tubs, showers, and piles of fresh linen; there's also a sink in each guest room. The third floor holds a dormitory-style room that can sleep extra kids. Downstairs is a gigantic gathering hall, and there is almost always a crackling fire in the stone hearth. The room is full of topographical maps, magazines, and books and is a meeting place where guests enjoy predinner drinks.

Address: *Box 28, Durbin, WV 26264, tel. 304/456-4627.*
Accommodations: *1 double room with bath; 7 doubles, 1 single, and dormitory (sleeps 6) share 2 multiple baths.*
Amenities: *Box lunches available; fishing, mountain biking, cross-country skiing, canoeing, horseshoes, 2 meeting rooms.*
Rates: *$69–$99 per person; full breakfast, lunch, and dinner and use of recreational gear. No credit cards.*
Restrictions: *No smoking in bedrooms, no pets in lodge, 2-night minimum on weekends, closed Christmas Day.*

The General
Lewis Inn

This is a country hostel of perfect proportions (just 26 rooms), run by the Hock family since 1928. It lies in a shady residential section of Lewisburg, a National Register town with a historic academy, stone church, and Confederate cemetery. Down the street from the inn are pleasant shops selling West Virginia quilts, ladies' dresses, and antiques. You can see everything Lewisburg has to offer in an easy afternoon, leaving you lots of time to sit on the veranda at the General Lewis. Out front there's a restored carriage, which used to rumble over the James River and Kanawha Turnpike (now Route 60), and in the back garden is owner Mary Hock Morgan's large old dollhouse.

Mary's parents started the General Lewis in the original house, built in the early 1800s; the architect who designed the West Virginia governor's mansion in Charleston later supervised a 1920s addition to the building, which blends flawlessly with the older section. The Hocks were great antiques collectors, and the inn is full of their prizes, including farming implements and a nickelodeon that still plays "The Man in the Moon Has His Eyes on You." The front desk came from the Sweet Chalybeate Springs Hotel and was reputedly leaned on by Patrick Henry and Thomas Jefferson. In fact, the only nonantiques you'll come across are the chairs in the dining room.

Though the inn is ably managed by young Rodney Fisher, Mary Hock Morgan is usually around to show children where to find the checkers. She lived in the General Lewis until the age of 15 and is dedicated to keeping it retrogressive. Rodney has talked her into some newfangled touches, such as central heat and air-conditioning with individual room controls. But Mary won't let him refinish the furniture; she wants guests to see where generations of hands have rubbed and polished the cannonball beds.

All the rooms on the first and second floors are different, and when unoccupied, the doors are left open so that guests can nose around. Because the same rate can apply to rooms of radically varying size, guests might want to ask for the largest in any given category. But even if you wind up in a cozy chamber, you won't be disappointed.

Address: *301 E. Washington St., Lewisburg, WV 24901, tel. 304/645–2600 or 800/628–4454.*
Accommodations: *24 double rooms with baths, 2 suites.*
Amenities: *Restaurant, room service during restaurant hours, air-conditioning, cable TV, phones in rooms.*
Rates: *$50–$95; breakfast extra. AE, MC, V.*
Restrictions: *$10 charge for pets, no smoking in dining room and some guest rooms.*

James Wylie House

The James Wylie House may not be the biggest or poshest lodging in White Sulphur Springs, but it's the only true bed-and-breakfast in this resort town. It's also one of the oldest buildings in Greenbrier County, predating the town of White Sulphur Springs and the Federal Fish Hatchery (still open), which were once part of the original 107-acre Wylie estate. Listed on the National Register, this historic house was built in 1819 by a local surveyor whose 1794 log cabin still stands out back. The main house was Victorianized at a later date, giving it its single-gable brick facade and broad, white front porch, and completely renovated in 1989. The lawn stretches down to Route 60, just south of the business district. On the second floor are three high-ceilinged bedrooms decorated in country style by owners Cheryl and Joe Griffith. There's a large porch perfect for reading or snoozing, a croquet setup on the lawn, and bikes for those who wish to explore White Sulphur Springs. When the sun goes down, guests gather in two parlors for board games, piano playing, or the more conventional television and VCR.

The log cabin, one of the oldest structures in Greenbrier County, still has musket holes in its walls. Renovated and opened in 1992, it's ideal for guests seeking privacy. There's a stone fireplace and small kitchenette on the first floor, and a double bedroom and private bath with the original claw-foot bathtub on the second. The cabin is charmingly decorated in country red and blue and hung with prints.

The Wylie House is a convenient headquarters for excursions into the mountains to the north or to the wet and wild New River, about an hour's drive west. Just down the street is the famous Greenbrier Resort, offering golf, tennis, swimming, riding, and elegant dining. There are local festivals, museums, battlefields, and shopping; and you can trust the Griffiths to have the latest information on nearby hiking, fishing, canoeing, rafting, caving, golfing, and skiing.

Address: *208 E. Main St., White Sulphur Springs, WV 24986, tel. 304/536-9444.*
Accommodations: *3 double rooms with baths, cabin with double bedroom and convertible sofa.*
Amenities: *Air-conditioning, TV in rooms.*
Rates: *$65 (cabin $100–$120); full breakfast. AE, MC, V.*
Restrictions: *No smoking, no pets.*

The Cardinal Inn

Eunice Kwasniewski has single-handedly worked miracles at this inn, a yellow-brick Queen Anne Victorian overlooking the Tygart River Valley. She restored this cavernous place all by herself (it took a full year and 438 gallons of stripper to remove the paint from the oak woodwork) and runs it solo as well, cooking lunches and dinners for groups by arrangement, tending an herb garden, and cleaning the nine guest rooms. As if that weren't enough, she's restoring a 19th-century log cabin out back; after a two-year search, her son has found a suitable replacement for a rotten log that's a threat to the cabin's structural integrity, and now Eunice is digging in to her new project. The turreted main house was built by Elihu Hutton in 1901 and is surrounded by a big white wrap-around porch, providing views of the valley and the Cheat Mountain range beyond. Two of the most desirable guest rooms are the five-window Paisley Room and the rather eerie third-floor Turret Room, complete with a mounted deer head. The inn is 25 miles north of Snowshoe, making it perfect for those who love to ski but don't care for the resort's condo-style accommodations.

Address: *Rte. 219 (Rte. 1, Box 1), Huttonsville, WV 26273, tel. 304/335-6149.*
Accommodations: *9 double rooms share 3 baths.*
Amenities: *TV with VCR in sitting room, phones on each floor.*
Rates: *$50; full breakfast. MC, V.*
Restrictions: *No smoking, no pets.*

The Current

The Current, a 1904 white frame farmhouse with only a modest touch of gingerbread, stands along a winding country lane outside the town of Hillsboro, once the home of writer Pearl Buck. It's also the site of a fine eatery called the Rosewood Café and the General Store, which sells everything from red Union suits and antiques to handmade butter and cheese carved from huge rolls. To reach the house you'll have to pass fields inhabited by buffalo, peacocks, and llamas (part of a rich weekend farmer's private zoo), the huge Denmar State Hospital, and a one-room Presbyterian Church. The bed-and-breakfast is owned by Leslee McCarty, who came to this part of her home state to work in rural community development and married a farmer while she was here. Her house is full of oak woodwork, quilts, Victorian clothing, and airy white curtains. Leslee has bought the old Presbyterian Church and is converting it to additional lodging to accommodate the demands of the cycling crowd. In fact, most of her guests arrive on foot or bike from the nearby Greenbrier River Trail and are thrilled with a soak in the hot tub and a quiet afternoon snooze on the porch.

Address: *Denmar Rd. (Box 135), Hillsboro, WV 24946, tel. 304/653-4722.*
Accommodations: *4 double rooms share 3½ baths.*
Amenities: *TV in sitting room, hot tub; kennel.*
Rates: *$50; full breakfast. MC, V.*
Restrictions: *No smoking.*

Hampshire House 1884

Route 50, the main route across the state in the north, passes through the town of Romney at the South Branch of the Potomac River. Here you'll find Hampshire House, a perfectly kept redbrick Victorian, on a street behind the courthouse. The house and its garden are owned by Scott Simmons and his wife, Jane, who manage the property with the help of three local women. Though the dining room is only occasionally open to guests, breakfast is always included in the room rate—and a substantial breakfast it is, including steak and eggs.

Scott is a collector of antique lamps, which occupy tables all over the inn. The five guest rooms are lovely, decorated almost exclusively with Victorian antiques, including Eastlake beds, Rococo Revival chairs and settees, and quilts. In addition to the formal parlor downstairs, you'll also find a kitchenette, laundry facilities, and a big music room with a wide-screen TV and piano.

Address: *165 N. Grafton St., Romney, WV 26757, tel. 304/822–7171.*
Accommodations: *5 double rooms with baths.*
Amenities: *Fireplaces in 2 rooms, air-conditioning, TV in all rooms, TV with VCR in music room.*
Rates: *$60–$75; full breakfast. AE, D, DC, MC, V.*
Restrictions: *No smoking, no pets.*

The Inn at Elk River

Also known as the Willis Farm, this lodging complex on the banks of the Elk River is an outdoor recreation center, too. Owner Gil Willis came to the area in 1977 for the downhill skiing; today he outfits Nordic skiing expeditions on a 50-kilometer trail system, conducts mountain-biking clinics, and organizes several multiday bike trips. The 100-year-old sheep farm now offers five guest rooms in the old farmhouse, a two-bedroom cottage, and a new lodge holding five more guest rooms, an equipment shop, and a restaurant (where diners feast on local trout and game, homemade biscuits, and other stick-to-the-ribs mountain-biker fare at tables comfortably clustered around a fireplace). The lodge is best for couples, since all its rooms have private baths. But the old farmhouse, with its many-bedded rooms, common space with wood-burning stove, and hot tub, is perfect for families and groups. You wouldn't call any of the accommodations luxurious, but at Elk River no one spends much time indoors.

Address: *Elk River Touring Center, Slatyfork, WV 26291, tel. 304/572–3771.*
Accommodations: *5 double rooms with baths, 5 suites share 3 baths, 2-bedroom cottage.*
Amenities: *Restaurant, hot tub; swimming hole, Nordic ski trails.*
Rates: *$35–$115; full breakfast. MC, V.*
Restrictions: *No smoking in farmhouse, no pets, 2-night minimum on weekends in ski season.*

Lynn's Inn

This white-columned farmhouse, built in 1935 on 16 acres just north of the Lewisburg town line, has a long history as an inn. Owner Richard McLaughlin is no stranger to innkeeping either; his parents ran McLaughlin's Tourist Home in this house for many years while he was growing up. There are four guest rooms on the first and second floors, upstairs and downstairs sitting rooms, and a peaceful front porch from which you can see the McLaughlins' Hereford and Angus cows and watch Lynn McLaughlin gathering eggs. The guest rooms feature many pleasant touches, including locally handmade quilts, Fenton glass lamps, white wicker and golden oak furniture, walnut bedsteads that have been in the family for years, and rocking chairs, which Lynn feels are important to have in every room. Her breakfasts include those fresh eggs, homemade jellies and jams, and country ham. Often she'll whip up something special, like a hash-brown casserole or a quiche, and there's always freshly ground gourmet coffee. In the evening Lynn serves homemade refreshments in the sitting rooms.

Address: *Rte. 4, Box 40, Lewisburg, WV 24901, tel. 304/645-2003.*
Accommodations: *4 double rooms with baths.*
Amenities: *Ceiling fans in rooms, cable TV and phones in the two sitting rooms.*
Rates: *$45–$60; full breakfast. MC, V.*
Restrictions: *No smoking, no pets.*

The Wayside Inn

For five weeks every July and August the town of Elkins hosts the popular Augusta Festival, at which visitors can sign up for courses in blacksmithing, Appalachian literature, autoharp playing, weaving, herb gardening, and log-house construction, among other topics. For accommodations while visiting the festival there's no better place than the Wayside Inn, which sits close to the grounds of the local college, where the festival takes place. The white Queen Anne cottage was built in 1886 and is operated by Brooke Rodgers and her two girls. The house wears its years reasonably well, with the help of glowing stained glass, an intricately detailed terra-cotta fireplace, and a grand old front porch. It features a sun porch, two parlors, a library, and a formal dining room. The house is undergoing a painstaking face-lift inside and out, most of it at the hands of Mrs. Rodgers.

Across the street there's an inviting park with a playground and picnic tables. The college has tennis courts, and downtown the Starr Café and Augusta Books are good idling spots. October is a prime leaf-viewing time. Spring draws rafters to the nearby rivers, and hikers to the Monongahela National Forest.

Address: *318 Buffalo St., Elkins, WV 26241, tel. 304/636-1618.*
Accommodations: *2 double rooms with baths, 2 doubles share a bath.*
Rates: *$45; full breakfast. AE, MC, V.*
Restrictions: *No smoking, no pets.*

Directory 1:
Alphabetical

Directory 2:
Geographical

Delaware

Bethany Beach
The Addy Sea *173*
Laurel
Spring Garden Bed &
Breakfast Inn *172*
Lewes
The Inn at Canal
Square *170*
The New Devon Inn
171
Milford
The Towers *163*
New Castle
The Janvier-Black
House *162*
William Penn Guest
House *164*
Odessa
Cantwell House *165*
Rehoboth Beach
The Pleasant Inn *173*
Wilmington
The Boulevard Bed &
Breakfast *165*
Guest Quarters Suite
Hotel Wilmington
166

Maryland

Annapolis
Gibson's Lodgings *195*
Shaw's Fancy *196*
State House Inn *193*
The William Page Inn
194
Baltimore
The Admiral Fell Inn
204
Berlin
The Atlantic Hotel *204*
Buckeystown
The Inn at
Buckeystown *202*

Cambridge
Glasgow Inn *187*
Chestertown
Brampton *182*
The Inn at Mitchell
House *187*
The White Swan
Tavern *189*
Widow's Walk Inn *189*
Easton
Ashby 1663 *181*
Gross' Coate 1658 *183*
John S. McDaniel
House *188*
Frederick
Spring Bank *201*
The Turning Point *203*
Havre de Grace
Vandiver Inn *205*
New Market
The National Pike *202*
The Strawberry Inn
203
Oxford
The Robert Morris Inn
185
St. Michael's
The Inn at Perry
Cabin *184*
Wades Point Inn *186*
Scotland
St. Michael's Manor
196
Sharpsburg
The Inn at Antietam
200
Snow Hill
Chanceford Hall *205*
Solomons
Back Creek Inn *195*
Vienna
The Tavern House *188*

New Jersey

Avon-by-the-Sea
Cashelmara Inn *129*

Bay Head
Conover's Bay Head
Inn *130*
Beach Haven
Bayberry Barque *128*
Pierrot by the Sea *126*
Victoria Guest House
133
Belmar
The Seaflower *132*
Cape May
The Abbey *147*
Barnard Good House
150
Captain Mey's Inn *150*
The Carroll Villa *151*
The Chalfonte *148*
Colvmns by the Sea
151
Holly House *152*
The Mainstay Inn and
Cottage *149*
The Manor House *152*
The Queen Victoria
153
Springside *153*
The Victorian Rose
154
The Virginia Hotel *154*
Wilbraham Mansion
and Inn *155*
The Wooden Rabbit
155
Dennisville
Henry Ludlam Inn *131*
Flemington
Cabbage Rose Inn *140*
Jerica Hill *141*
Fortescue
Charlesworth Hotel
156
Frenchtown
Old Hunterdon House
142
Hope
Inn at Millrace Pond
138

Island Heights
The Studio *133*
Lambertville
Chimney Hill Farm
137
Lyndhurst
Jeremiah H. Yereance
House *156*
Milford
Chestnut Hill *140*
North Wildwood
Candlelight Inn *128*
Ocean City
BarnaGate Bed and
Breakfast *127*
Princeton
Peacock Inn *142*
South Belmar
Hollycroft *131*
Spring Lake
Ashling Cottage *127*
The Carriage House
129
The Chateau *130*
Normandy Inn *125*
Sea Crest by the Sea
132
Stanhope
The Whistling Swan
Inn *143*
Stewartsville
Stewart Inn *139*
Stockton
Colligan's Stockton
Inn *141*

New York

Albany
Mansion Hill Inn *24*
Amenia
Troutbeck *44*
Averill Park
The Gregory House *22*
Berlin
The Sedgwick Inn *21*

Bolton Landing
Hilltop Cottage Bed
and Breakfast *12*
Cambridge
Maple Ridge Inn *20*
Canaan
The Inn at Shaker Mill
41
Chestertown
The Balsam House *7*
The Chester Inn *10*
The Friends Lake Inn
12
Cold Spring
Hudson House, A
Country Inn *45*
Pig Hill Inn *46*
Plumbush Inn *47*
Craryville
The Martindale Bed
and Breakfast Inn
46
East Hampton
Bassett House Inn *56*
Hedges' Inn *56*
The Huntting Inn *52*
The Maidstone Arms
57
Mill House Inn *58*
The 1770 House *54*
East Windham
Point Lookout
Mountain Inn *36*
Elka Park
The Redcoat's Return
32
Forestburg
Inn at Lake Joseph *35*
Garrison
The Bird and Bottle
Inn *45*
Goshen
Anthony Dobbins
Stagecoach Inn *40*
Greenville
Greenville Arms *34*

Hadley
Saratoga Rose *14*
High Falls
Captain
Schoonmaker's Bed-
and-Breakfast *31*
Hillsdale
The Swiss Hutte *47*
Hopewell Junction
Le Chambord *42*
Hunter
Scribner Hollow Motor
Lodge *36*
Lake Luzerne
The Lamplight Inn *9*
Lew Beach
Beaverkill Valley Inn
30
Livingston Manor
Lanza's *35*
Millerton
Simmons Way Village
Inn *43*
Queensbury
Crislip's Bed and
Breakfast *11*
Sanford's Ridge Bed
& Breakfast *13*
Rhinebeck
The Village Victorian
Inn *48*
Rock City Falls
The Mansion *19*
Saratoga Springs
The Adelphi Hotel *18*
Chestnut Tree Inn *22*
The Inn at Saratoga
23
Saratoga Bed and
Breakfast *25*
The Six Sisters *25*
The Westchester
House *26*
Schuylerville
The Inn on Bacon Hill
23

West Virginia

Berkeley Springs
The Country Inn *280*
Highlawn *281*
Charles Town
The Carriage Inn *279*
The Cottonwood Inn
  279
Hillbrook *277*
Durbin
Cheat Mountain Club
  286
Elkins
The Wayside Inn *291*
Gerrardstown
Prospect Hill *282*

Harpers Ferry
Hilltop House Hotel
  and Restaurant *281*
Hillsboro
The Current *289*
Huttonsville
The Cardinal Inn *289*
Lewisburg
The General Lewis Inn
  287
Lynn's Inn *291*
Martinsburg
Aspen Hall *278*
Boydville *276*
Dunn Country Inn *280*

Romney
Hampshire House
  1884 *290*
Shepherdstown
Bavarian Inn and
  Restaurant *278*
The Thomas Shepherd
  Inn *282*
Slatyfork
The Inn at Elk River
  290
**White Sulphur
  Springs**
James Wylie House
  288